Command of the Sea

William Pakenham and the Russo-Japanese Naval War, 1904-1905

Quintin Barry

Helion & Company Limited

Helion & Company Limited
Unit 8 Amherst Business Centre
Budbrooke Road
Warwick
CV34 5WE
England
Tel. 01926 499 619
Fax 0121 711 4075
Email: info@helion.co.uk
Website: www.helion.co.uk
Twitter: @helionbooks
Visit our blog http://blog.helion.co.uk/

Published by Helion & Company 2019
Designed and typeset by Mary Woolley (www.battlefield-design.co.uk)
Cover designed by Paul Hewitt, Battlefield Design (www.battlefield-design.co.uk)
Printed by IBI, Dulles VA, USA

ISBN 978-1-912390-66-3

British Library Cataloguing-in-Publication Data.
A catalogue record for this book is available from the British Library.

For details of other military history titles published by Helion & Company Limited contact the above address or visit our website: http://www.helion.co.uk.

We always welcome receiving book proposals from prospective authors.

Contents

List of Illustrations

In plate section

List of Maps and Sketches

Map 1: Yellow Sea

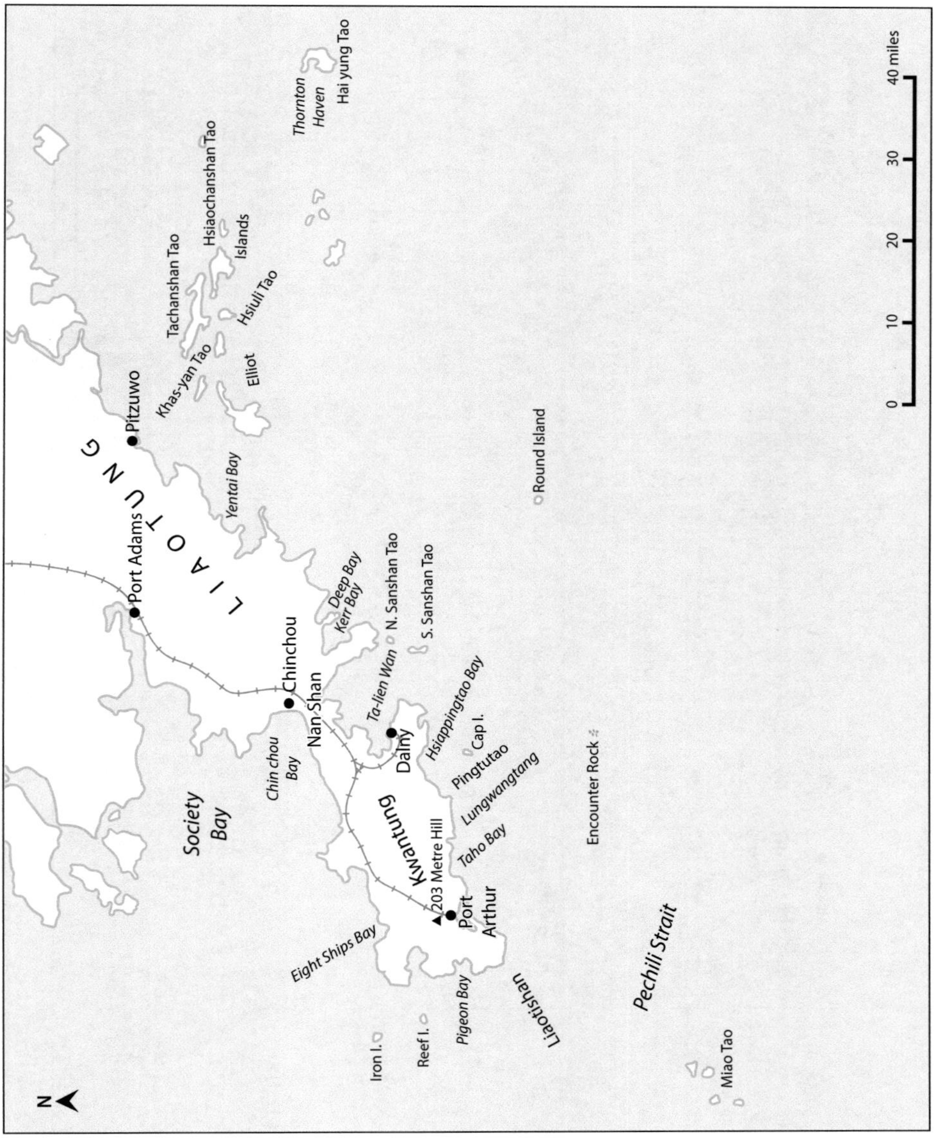

Map 2: Kwantung Peninsula

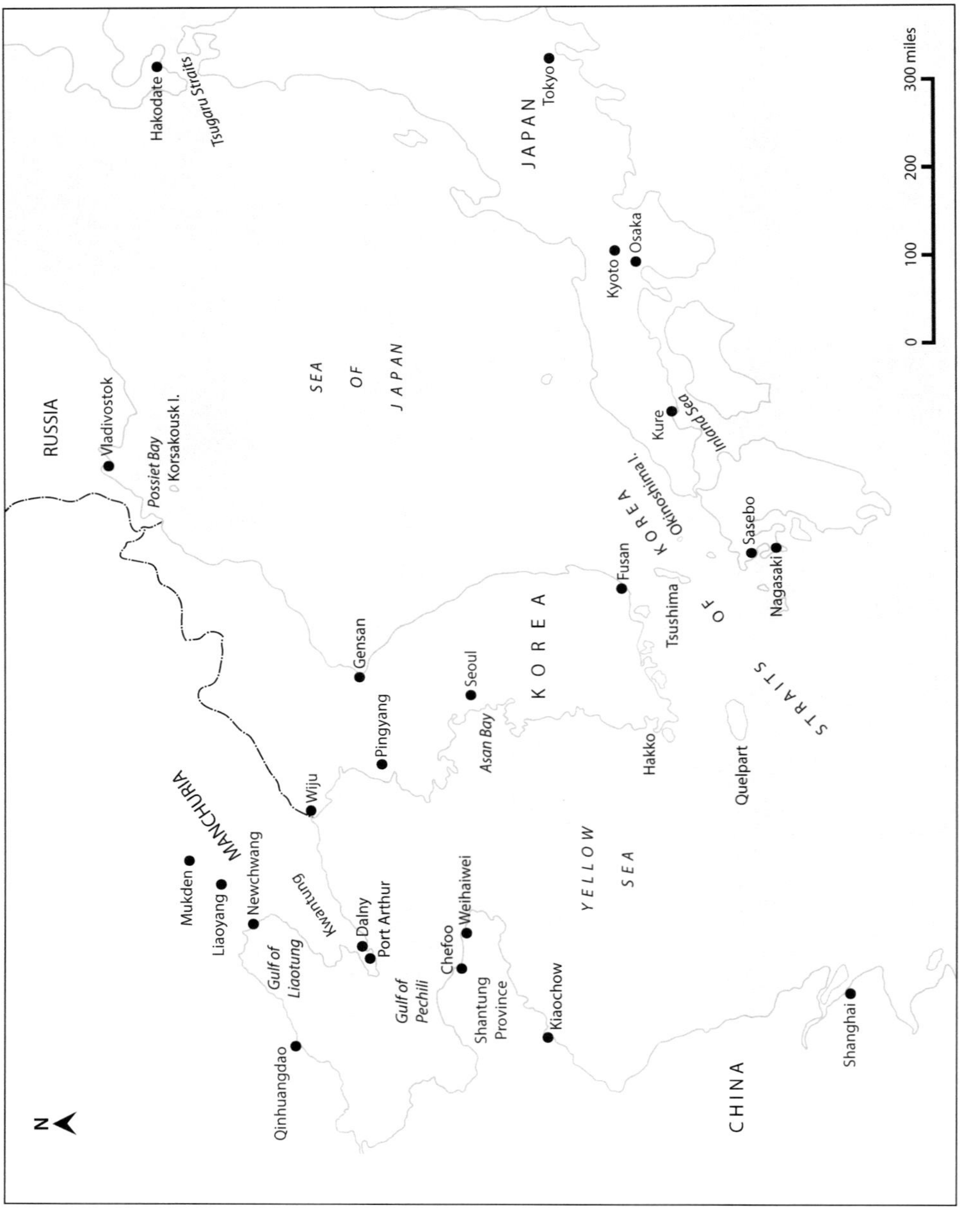

Map 3: General Map

Acknowledgements

This book is largely based on the reports which Captain William Pakenham, as British Naval Attaché, sent back to the Admiralty during the course of the Russo-Japanese War, and on Julian Corbett's masterly history of the war, and I should begin by acknowledging my debt to them. In addition, it is always a great pleasure to be able to record my appreciation of those that have helped to produce the book. Duncan Rogers, my publisher, has as usual supported me throughout, particularly with regard to the illustrations; Laurence Townsend also assisted in the preparation of these. My thanks go also to George Anderson, who produced the maps with his invariable efficiency; to Tim Readman, who read the book in draft and made several valuable suggestions; and to Jean Hawkes and Katie Proctor, who assisted with the typing of the book. Finally, I should like to record my thanks to the staff of the Caird Library at the National Maritime Museum, where research is always a pleasant and fulfilling experience.

Preface

The outbreak of the Russo-Japanese War of 1904-1905 gave the Great Powers an excellent opportunity to evaluate the effect of recent developments on the conduct of modern warfare. Their military and naval attachés, together with other observers, provided detailed reports on the course of the fighting. The British attachés were afforded special facilities denied to other attachés, thanks to the recently concluded Anglo-Japanese alliance. Captain William Pakenham, as Naval Attaché in Tokyo, was a particular beneficiary of this, being allowed to serve almost continuously with the Japanese fleet. His comprehensive reports to the Admiralty were of the greatest importance at a time of technological and tactical change. Throughout this book his voice is to be heard on a wide range of issues with which at this time his profession was particularly concerned.

The reports of the military and naval attachés provided much of the raw material for the British Official History of the war produced by the Committee of Imperial Defence, which was published in three volumes, the first of which appeared in 1910, the second in 1912 and the third not until after the end of the First World War in 1920. Its authors also had the opportunity to consult the many official histories produced by other Great Powers, including those published by Japan and Russia.

The Admiralty, however, was doubtful that the CID history would entirely serve its purpose; it was feared that this would lay greater emphasis on the military aspects of the war. Accordingly, the Naval Intelligence Department embarked on the preparation of a confidential study of the naval war. The first to take up the task of writing this was Captain Thomas Jackson, in 1906; he had been assistant Naval Attaché in Tokyo during the war. In 1908 Commander John Luce took it over. Captain Edmund Slade, the new Director of Naval Intelligence, showed the draft to Julian S Corbett, who has been described by John B Hattendorf and Donald M Schurman as 'one of the greatest naval historians in the early years of the twentieth century.[1]

Corbett dismissed the draft as useless, and convinced Slade that the work needed a better author. In due course the job was offered to Corbett himself, who wrote in his diary that this was 'the summit of ambition.' All was not, however, plain sailing; the

1 Julian S. Corbett, *Maritime Operations in the Russo-Japanese War, 1904-1905* I (Annapolis, Maryland, 1994), p. 14.

cost of the project became an issue between the Treasury, the Committee for Imperial Defence and the Admiralty, while there were those who felt that it should only be written by a serving naval officer.

Finally, however, the Secretary of the Admiralty, Graham Greene, who did not believe this to be the case, asked Corbett for his views on the CID history. He replied that it was 'hopelessly flawed' by its adoption of the German approach to military history, which produced a very detailed narrative of events followed only by a narrow conclusion. Corbett proposed instead a broader narrative of the war as a whole, showing how events on land and sea were related to each other and how they led to the ultimate outcome.

In due course, Corbett was commissioned to write his history of *Maritime Operations in the Russo-Japanese War 1904-1905*. The first volume was finally produced in 1914, but the Admiralty printed only six copies; the second volume, of which 400 copies were printed, appeared in the following year.

As his biographer Donald M Schurman has pointed out, in this work Corbett 'declined to discuss the war as if the result was a foregone conclusion.' It was his aim to show 'that sea warfare had rules which conferred special advantages in the present as it had in the past.'[2]

The outbreak of the First World War meant the book did not receive the readership that was intended, though the First Sea Lord in 1914, Prince Louis of Battenberg, did read it; but the timing of its publication was unfortunate: 'It lay on the shelves of the Admiralty Library unheeded and forgotten by any but Slade, Corbett, Prince Louis and perhaps a few others through two world wars.'[3]

It remains, however, a remarkably clear and perceptive work of history, from which many valuable conclusions might have been drawn. Andrew Lambert, the editor of a recently published collection of Corbett's essays, calls his maritime history of the Russo-Japanese War his 'unpublished masterpiece,' as indeed it was.[4] Corbett had entirely achieved his objective, which was to show the practical application of the fundamental lessons of naval history. This was so much the case that his name ought really appear alongside that of Pakenham in the subtitle to this book, which draws heavily on his penetrating analysis of the naval war. Corbett's history provides an invaluable background to Pakenham's eyewitness accounts and the conclusions which he reached in the immediate aftermath of the events of the war.

2 Donald M Schurman, *Julian S Corbett, 1854-1922* (London, 1981), p. 150.
3 Ibid., p. 144.
4 Andrew Lambert (ed.), *21st Century Corbett* (Annapolis, Maryland 2017), p. 147.

1

Britain & Japan

Following the establishment of the Meiji empire in 1868, it was immediately apparent to the new government of Japan that the nation's military weakness when compared to the industrial West required action to be taken to develop the empire's armed forces. In its early years the Japanese navy's role was confined to that of coast defence. It possessed few warships, and neither the leadership nor training of its personnel were adequate. It has, however, been pointed out that the opening of Japan to trade with the Western world came at a fortunate moment for the country, since it coincided with a time of rapid technological advance. As a result, 'the development of new materials for ship construction, improvements in both ordnance and armour, and the invention of new propulsion systems' were as readily available to the Japanese navy as they were to the navies of the industrialised world.[1] In addition, the Japanese navy was free from the inhibitions of history and tradition. For its leaders, therefore, the fact that they were effectively starting from scratch brought considerable advantages.

It was, of course, immediately necessary to obtain professional naval instruction from abroad, and in 1870 an imperial decree selected the Royal Navy as the model to be adopted. In 1873 a British naval mission, led by Lieutenant Commander Archibald Douglas, arrived, and for the next six years it was responsible for the development of the Japanese navy. As a result, British naval traditions had a lasting effect on the personality of the new navy. In 1879 the British Lieutenant Commander LP Willan was appointed instructor at the naval academy, where he taught many of those who were themselves in due course to become influential in the development of Japanese naval thought. In 1887 Captain John Ingles followed his compatriot and became an instructor at the newly established Naval Staff College, as well as an adviser to the Navy Ministry in the modernisation programme which it was undertaking.

His influence was considerable. He persuaded Navy Minister Saigo Tsugumichi that warships equipped for sails should be replaced by steam driven ships of the latest

1 David C Evans and Mark R Peattie, *Kaigun: Strategy, Tactics and Technology in the Imperial* Japanese *Navy 1887-1941* (Annapolis, Maryland 1997) p. 10

design. He was also responsible for ensuring that 'advanced training of line officers should include a thorough grounding in the practical applications of modern science particularly mathematics and physics.' In addition to this, it has been said that 'his greatest contribution to the development of the Japanese navy was his series of lectures on modern naval tactics delivered to the second, third and fourth classes of the Naval Staff College from September 1889 to September 1892.'[2]

This British influence was naturally felt in the choice of foreign shipyards to build the new ships which were required. Although steps were being taken to develop an indigenous warship building capability, for the moment Japanese yards were not yet able to build modern warships, and it was to British yards that the Navy Ministry turned. A number of vessels, excellent for their time, were delivered to the Japanese navy. In spite of this, however, in the late 1880s an important order was placed for the construction in France of three cruisers, a decision taken as a reflection of the influential theories of the *Jeune École*, which promoted the concept of a fleet composed of smaller, faster warships. These cruisers, the 'Sankeikan' class, were of 4,277 tons, mounting one 12.6 inch gun. The design was influenced by the large warships of German design recently acquired by the Chinese navy. Although the concept of one large gun was found in practice to be flawed, the possession of a large secondary armament of quick firing guns proved to be invaluable in combat.

In 1892 the Navy Ministry purchased the Elswick built cruiser *Yoshino*; with a speed of 23 knots she was said to be the fastest cruiser in the world. Meanwhile a lot of attention had been paid to the potential of torpedo boats, and a number of officers were sent to Britain for training in their employment, returning to set up a Torpedo Training Centre at Yokosuka.

By now there had come to the fore in the Japanese navy a man of whom it has been written that 'it is no exaggeration to write that the navy of late Meiji Japan was in purpose, composition, and armament, the navy of Yamamoto Gombei.'[3] In 1891, at the age of forty, Yamamoto was appointed director of the secretariat of the Navy Ministry, with a wide brief to achieve reform, and with responsibility for personnel. In this position he presided over a thorough reorganisation of the navy, enabling the rise of a generation of younger officers who determined the strategic, tactical and technological development of the navy, particularly after the ending of the Sino-Japanese War of 1894.

By the time that war broke out, the navy had already reached a considerable level of efficiency. Admiral Ballard, in his account of the influence of the sea on the history of Japan, wrote:

> In the first place, it was a single organisation under the control of a central authority and administered as such. Secondly, the administration was honest and

2 Ibid., p. 13
3 Ibid, p. 21.

> important appointments went by merit, with the result that the discipline was second to none in the world, and all ranks and ratings were animated by a high professional spirit. Training was thorough, great care and attention was devoted to the upkeep of the vessels and their armaments, and all stocks and reserves of war munitions were maintained at proper levels.[4]

The qualities thus described owed a good deal to the influence of the Royal Navy on the development of the Japanese navy since 1868. Another historian of the period was able to write that 'Japan had indeed become the Britain of the East.'[5] The contrast with the Chinese fleet was striking; the quality and training of the latter's personnel left a great deal to be desired:

> The officers were brutal tyrants, and the rank and file were little better than cattle. Corruption was in every department and although China had big ships and great guns, they were not properly manned or equipped. Japan had no doubt when she entered upon this war as to what would be the final results.[6]

During the years before the war, Yamamoto had been strenuously working to create an independent naval staff; hitherto the navy had been effectively subordinated to the Army General Staff, and it was not until 1893 that a Navy General Staff was established with the right of direct access to the Emperor. The Chief of the Staff was, however, responsible only for coast defence, and the Army Chief of Staff retained overall control of all military and naval operations. Yamamoto drew particular encouragement in his campaign for the independence of the navy from the works of contemporary Western writers on naval affairs, including in particular Captain Alfred Mahan in the United States, and the Colomb brothers and John Laughton in Britain. For him and his supporters the doctrine of the command of the sea was central to his assessment of Japan's strategic situation. Yamamoto fiercely maintained the importance of the navy in all aspects of war planning; Evans and Peattie have pointed out, however, that the way in which the staff systems of the army and navy evolved meant that, 'in its status as an independent organ of the state, the navy was extremely reluctant to accept any compromise that appeared to infringe on its authority.' This, and the internal bureaucratic squabbles that developed, would ultimately damage the effectiveness of the Japanese navy.[7]

In 1894, that lay far into the future. For the moment, the navy had a war to fight, which it expected to win, and which, in spite of a cautious approach to the tactics to

4 Vice Admiral G.A. Ballard, *The Influence of the Sea on the Political History of Japan* (New York, 1921) pp. 137-138

5 Rear Admiral Francis J Higginson, *Naval Battles of the Century* (London, 1906) p. 206.

6 Ibid.

7 Evans and Peattie, p. 31.

be employed, it duly won. This was in spite of the theoretical advantage of the Chinese fleet which possessed two armoured vessels which were, ship for ship, superior to anything in the Japanese fleet. It was apparent to the navy that to ensure command of the sea against any opponent, Japan must have modern, heavily armed and heavily armoured battleships. Yamamoto is said to have demanded of the Cabinet that never again should the navy 'go naked into battle, sword in hand against an enemy shielded by heavy armour.'[8]

Although, by the terms of the peace treaty that had ended the war with China, in 1895 Japan had gained Port Arthur and the Liaotung Peninsula, she was forced by a combination of Russia, Germany and France to return these to Chinese control. This humiliating reverse was deepened when three years later Russia was able to secure a twenty-five year lease of these territories. Thereafter, there was little doubt about the next adversary that Japan might have to face in war, and the need to create a battle fleet capable of standing up to Russia was abundantly clear. Moreover, Japan must also find diplomatic support for its position in Asia and the world. It was to Britain that she now turned to achieve both these ends.

The Sino-Japanese War, and its unsatisfactory aftermath, had large consequences which were not confined to the Far East. The other Great Powers took notice of Russia's advance. For Britain, an important new dimension had been added to the question of its relationships:

> Japan's victory over China and her rapid development as a naval power had an immediate effect on British naval policy. It opened the Far Eastern question. It was clear to all in 1895 that the recent developments must lead to keen and active maritime competition in the Far East… Whatever hope the English may have entertained of a rapprochement with Russia was blasted by Russia's encroaching policy in the Far East.[9]

The Japanese navy already had two modern battleships, the *Fuji* and *Yashima*, under construction in Britain. Yamamoto, who was still Chief of the Naval Affairs Bureau, drew up a proposal to strengthen the fleet by ordering four further battleships. In addition, there would be four armoured cruisers and four protected cruisers in the construction programme, together with twenty-three destroyers and sixty three torpedo boats. This vast programme was approved by the Cabinet in late 1895, to be completed in two stages; the first would begin in the following year for completion in 1902, and the second would begin in 1897 and be completed in 1905. Yamamoto justified his plan with a detailed review of the possible combinations that Japan might have to face, although naturally identifying Russia as the most probable opponent.

8 Ibid., p. 49.
9 Arthur J Marder, *The Anatomy of British Sea Power* (London, 1972) p. 238.

Yamamoto's intentions went beyond the immediate naval arithmetic; his aim was to create a fleet that would be immune to changes in public opinion or political crises.[10]

Yamamoto also intended that his fleet should consist of vessels which were pre-eminent in their class. The *Fuji* and the *Yashima*, which had been ordered prior to the Sino- Japanese War, were a development of the British *Royal Sovereign* class. The four additional battleships, *Shikishima*, *Hatsuse*, *Asahi* and *Mikasa*, represented a considerable further advance in fighting value. Their basic specifications were similar to the British *Majestic* class but, taking advantage of developments in armour plate, they were superior to the originals.

While Japan was thus taking effective steps to acquire the modern battle fleet that her strategic situation demanded, the British Admiralty was becoming more than a little anxious about Russian intentions in the Far East. It appeared to be the case that there was a plan to form a fleet, based on Port Arthur, which would consist of six or eight battleships, eight cruisers, and twenty destroyers. There was some uncertainty about the timescale involved but it seemed definite that the Russians proposed to lay down four battleships during 1898. In July 1898 the government brought forward to the House of Commons a supplementary Naval Estimate which called for the construction of four additional battleships, four cruisers and twelve destroyers, these being the number of vessels in each category in excess of what had previously been assumed was the Russian programme. The supplementary estimate was approved, while press and public opinion appeared to be generally favourable. Not for the first or last time, however, the threat from abroad had been somewhat overstated, as Fred T Jane pointed out in *Brassey's Naval Annual, 1899*: 'Nearly all those ships that the Navy League have shouted themselves hoarse about have no present existence [1899] nor are there even vacant slips in Russians dockyards where they could be built.' He went on to explain that the near panic arose from a misunderstanding of Russian methods, which contemplated the building of further ships in an entirely tentative manner based on the success of the first of a class.[11]

As time passed, however, and issues continued to arise between Great Britain and Russia in Asia, the Russians did steadily build up their naval forces at Port Arthur, which was becoming a strong naval base. In April 1898, before the scare that had led to the supplementary estimate of that year, Russia had had only two battleships based in the Far East; by April 1901 she had five modern battleships based there, and the indications were that this force would be further strengthened by vessels under construction that were approaching completion. The demands made on British fleets nearer home by reason of the naval programmes of France and Germany, and also of the United States, made it impossible to spare enough major warships to do more than maintain a marginal superiority over the Russian fleet in the Far East. In April

10 Evans and Peattie, pp. 57-59.
11 Marder, *Anatomy*, p. 316 n.

1901, in terms of comparative tonnage in warships based in the Far East, Britain had 170,000 tons; Russia 120,000 tons; France 80,000 tons; and Japan 200,000 tons.[12]

One man who had particular responsibility for keeping under review the balance of naval power in the Far East was Vice Admiral Sir Edward Seymour, the Commander in Chief of the China station. On March 24 1901 he wrote to Lord Selborne, who had been in post for three months as First Lord, to set out his views on the situation:

> I want to say a few words about our national position out here. It sometimes seems to me as if in England the notion of Russia in the 'Far East' is not appreciated. Her aims are in my opinion boundless out here and Asia generally... Japan has the sense I believe to know that Russia is her great enemy and rival for Continental territory; and therefore Japan would declare war against Russia the moment Russia was embroiled with another power; and Russia knows this; which would make her pause before she entered on a war, specially with us. There are of course other reasons regarding home policy. Japan would I believe now begin war with Russia if she thought we or Germany or America, would stand by her, so strong is her feeling. I look on Germany as resolved to keep the peace at present, and for reasons you know better than I do, I believe it her best policy. Germany fears Russia, and surely hates her too; she would not fight her, but probably look on till Russia was getting the worst of it. Out here we and Japan should be a match for Russia and France, but of course Japan is no use to us in Europe.[13]

Given the naval situation in the Far East, there began in 1900 to be heard calls in the British press for consideration to be given to negotiating an alliance with Japan, if no comprehensive understanding with Russia could be reached. By the middle of 1901 informal discussions between the governments of Great Britain and Japan had taken place, in which the possibility of an alliance was seriously explored. These did not immediately lead anywhere, possibly because there had been negotiations between Russia and China that might have a marked effect on the diplomatic situation. These negotiations came to an end, however, with the death of the Chinese leader Li Hung Chang, while anxiety in Whitehall about Russian intentions continued to deepen, particularly with regard to Persia. An agreement between Russia and Great Britain would of course bring these concerns to an end, but when it seemed that this could not be achieved, discussions were resumed with Japan. A draft treaty was handed to Hayashi, the Japanese minister in London, on November 6, and although there was a momentary hesitation on the part of the Japanese government because of the apparent possibility of some kind of deal with Russia, this did not materialise, and the Japanese put forward some amendments to the draft on December 12.

12 Ibid., pp. 428-429

13 D. George Boyce, ed, *The Crisis of British Power* (London, 1990) p. 112.

The British Cabinet considered these on December 19. There were some reservations about the scope of the proposed treaty, particularly as it seemed that what Japan was seeking was a free hand in Korea, which would inevitably lead to friction with Russia. Lansdowne, the Foreign Secretary, sought to take a firm line with Hayashi:

> It seemed… scarcely reasonable that, while we were to face the possibility of war with two great European Powers in consequence of a dispute between Japan and Russia in regard to Korea, we were not to have any assistance from Japan should we find ourselves involved with the same two Powers in regard to a dispute as to India.[14]

The Japanese were not disposed to widen the scope of the treaty in this way, while continuing to demand freedom of action in Korea. A convoluted process of amendments back and forth ensued, 'until a wording could be found which gave Japan what she wanted, while at the same time making the concession so unnoticeable that it would not arouse strong opposition in the English parliament.'[15]

In the end, 'the all-important Article 1 was a masterpiece of careful wording'; it acknowledged the independence of China and Korea, renounced any aggressive tendencies in either country and noted the special interests of Great Britain in China and of Japan in Korea. It went on, however, to recognise that either party might safeguard those interests if it became necessary to do so. If either party had become involved with a third power in defence of those interests, the other party would remain neutral. If any other power or powers should join in a war against the ally, the other contracting party would make war in common with its ally. The treaty was to last in the first instance for five years. On the face of it, Japan had got much the best of the deal.

The treaty was signed on January 3, 1902 and was laid before Parliament on February 11. Although there had been calls for such an alliance in some quarters, it came generally as a surprise to the press and public; it had been hoped that an agreement might be reached with Russia, but this treaty created an alliance that was clearly directed against Russia. There were voices raised in Parliament opposing the alliance. Sir Henry Norman, an expert on Far Eastern affairs, pointed out that it might bring about war with France and Russia at a moment of Japan's choosing. 'Our only interest in Korea is that it is of very great importance to Japan, whose welfare is always a matter of consideration to us.' He argued that Korea was a 'worthless country,' and that it would be 'horrible' to go to war over it, adding that it was useless to deny that the alliance was aimed at Russia. For the government Lord Cranborne

14 William L Langer, *The Diplomacy of Imperialism 1896-1902* (New York, 1935), II pp. 776-777

15 Ibid. II, p. 777.

maintained that the real origin of the treaty was Britain's anxiety to maintain the status quo in China.[16]

In the end, the treaty, once it had passed through Parliament, was generally seen as acceptable. Predictably, it was well received in Japan, while the German government saw no objection to it. In France and Russia, however, the news of the alliance came as a distinct and extremely disagreeable surprise; after prolonged negotiations between them, the two governments on March 20, 1902 reserved the right to take counsel as to the means to be used to safeguard their interests.' William L Langer has noted that this gesture was not in fact an extension of the Franco-Russian alliance to the Far East, but 'was probably meant only as a demonstration; but it illustrated the deep suspicions that pervaded the international scene.' Even between the new allies there continued to exist some uncertainty as to how far the treaty could be depended on.

It was a concern with naval affairs that had prompted the British government's willingness to enter into the treaty. On the face of it, the alliance would have in Chinese waters a distinct superiority over the combined squadrons of France, Russia and Germany, and it was assumed by many navalists 'that the whole meaning and purport of the alliance was to free Britain's hands in China waters and enable her to utilise part of the Far Eastern squadron in home waters.'[17]

This was not, however, the case. Although the British Admiralty was reluctant to accept 'any stipulation which might fetter their discretion in disposing of the distribution of their fleets,' there was an exchange of secret notes whereby the two Powers were committed to maintaining a fleet in the Far East equal to that of any third power. The Admiralty did, however, succeed in qualifying the obligation by adding the words that it would do so 'as far as may be possible' and defining such a fleet as one that was 'available for concentration in the waters of the Extreme East.'

In this, their Lordships were behaving in a very slippery manner, as was apparent in their reply to an enquiry from the Foreign Office as to whether the government could show that the obligations in the secret notes had been compiled with. Admiral Sir Walter Kerr, the First Sea Lord, complained that this was a question that was 'unnecessarily direct and that it was undesirable that the Admiralty should be driven into a corner in this way.' The formal response to the Foreign Office was, therefore, extremely shifty:

> Looking to the importance of preserving a proper balance of strength in the Western group, which if not maintained would assuredly react to the detriment of the Alliance in the Eastern group, My Lords conceive that the obligation imposed on HM Government by the notes exchanged between Great Britain

16 Ibid. II, pp. 779-780.
17 Marder, *Anatomy*, p. 429.

> and Japan on 30 January 1902, has been complied with, in the words of the passage quoted in your letter under reply, 'so far as possible.'[18]

The effect of the alliance was seen in the Admiralty as solely related to the possibility of war with Russia. The terms of the treaty were, it was considered, such that a war between Japan and Russia would not involve Great Britain, while the alliance would always be prepared to face the Franco-Russian alliance. The Japanese would, it was supposed, always accept that Britain must always keep in view the 'tremendous factor' of France becoming hostile, which practically affected Britain alone given the distribution of the French navy.

Naval opinion favoured the Japanese alliance, as Admiral Sir Cyprian Bridge, now commander of the China Station, made clear in a letter to Lord Selborne, the First Lord, on April 22. 1902:

> As regards the strategic conditions concerning which you have been pleased to write to me, I would say that the Anglo Japanese Agreement has profoundly modified them as regards the Far East. Japan was certain to join with some occidental state and it would have been deplorable if we had sat still and seen her combine with those who would be against us instead of getting her to combine with us. The bellicose character of the governing class in Japan is not to be denied; and, no doubt, there are many valiant warriors in the Japanese Army and Navy who are spoiling for a fight. Nevertheless, I think that this need not make us very apprehensive of being dragged into unnecessary quarrels.[19]

The conclusion of the alliance naturally strengthened the cooperation between the two navies. In October 1902 at the suggestion of the British Admiralty, the Japanese Naval Attaché in London was permitted to go aboard a vessel taking part in the annual manoeuvres in home waters. Reciprocally, the same privilege was extended to the British Naval Attaché in Tokyo, Captain Ernest Troubridge, who had taken up his posting there in September 1901. Sir John Fisher, at the time Commander in Chief in the Mediterranean, considered that 'it would be of great benefit if the two Far Eastern fleets manoeuvred together once a year and carried out battle exercises such as practised off Lagos by the Channel-Mediterranean fleets in 1901.'[20]

Nothing appears to have come of this idea, but the existence of the alliance gave a formal underpinning to what had become a traditional feeling of mutual respect between the Royal Navy and the Imperial Japanese Navy. The possibility that they might find themselves at war together against Russia concentrated the minds of the leaders of each fleet when they came to assess the other. The comments of Bridge in

18 Quoted Ibid., p. 432.
19 Boyce, p. 143.
20 Marder, *Anatomy*, p. 431.

a letter to Selborne written soon after the outbreak of war in 1904 may be taken as typical of the views of other senior officers who had been in close contact with the Japanese navy. He observed of the Japanese reaction to the crisis which had developed in the Far East that 'their patient, self restrained, and dignified demeanour was a pattern to the world,' and reminded the First Lord of his favourable opinion which he had reported of 'the general grasp of the principles of naval strategy by the senior Japanese officers.' He was also profoundly impressed with Japanese professional efficiency:

> The Japanese have nothing to learn from anyone on the matter of dockyard organisation. I am convinced, and not till after close observation, that in that matter we ourselves have a great deal to learn from them. To see the Japanese dock a ship would be a revelation at Portsmouth or Devonport; and their superior organisation does not end there... The average intelligence of the Japanese is very high. Their cleverness is almost demonic... It may be permissible to dwell at length on one particular in which the Japanese navy has no superior or – if it be not too much say – has no equal. That is its spirit. Every officer and man in it wants to get at the Russians and would rather take death on doing this than gain life in keeping away.[21]

21 Boyce, p. 169.

2

Sea Power at the Turn of the Century

It has often been observed that Francis Drake would not have felt much out of place on the quarterdeck of Nelson's *Victory*, so little had technology changed over the course of two centuries. Even aboard the ironclad *Warrior* in 1859, he would have broadly understood her design and purpose. It was with the arrival of the *Devastation* in 1873 that the hypothetical Drake would have found himself totally at a loss to comprehend a modern warship, which would have represented to him nothing but a 'hopelessly confusing mass of machinery.' Vice Admiral Sir Spencer Robinson, the Controller of the navy, summarised the point that had been reached:

> We have come, therefore, of necessity to ships of low freeboard, thick shot resisting armour, guns few in number but of the heaviest known power, revolving in turrets, with an uncompromised all-around fire, twin screws, double engines, and vast stores of coal.[1]

The *Devastation* was designed by Edward Reed, the British Admiralty's Chief Constructor, and it has been described as his masterpiece. The rapid process of development of warship design, weapons, turrets and engines came together to produce the first seagoing, mastless battleship; the general outlines of her design determined to a great extent the shape of warships to come. However, at the time of her construction there was a great deal of public and professional suspicion about her design. Oscar Parkes wrote that 'no ship had ever left harbour under such a cloud of pessimism and general forebodings as the *Devastation*.' He went on, however, to point out that when she and her sister the *Thunderer* were extensively refitted in 1891, a different view prevailed: 'By this time public opinion had veered round to an opposite

1 Quoted Stanley Sandler, *The Emergence of the Modern Capital Ship* (Newark, Delaware 1979), p. 241.

extreme and had adopted the two ships as symbolic of British sea power, more by virtue of their names and appearance than anything else.'[2]

The ten years that followed the completion of the *Devastation* have been described as the 'dark ages' of the Victorian navy. The most distinguished British admiral of the period was pungent in his criticisms both of the government and of the Admiralty's ship building policy. Sir Geoffrey Phipps Hornby, who rose to be an Admiral of the Fleet, described the state of the navy at this time in a farewell speech on November 27 1885:

> We have ships without speed, guns without range and boilers with only a few months' life in them. This is called economy, but it is really only not spending money, closing the purse strings, and keeping our fleet in such a state of inefficiency and unpreparedness as to render it comparatively useless should we at any time become involved in war with a Maritime Power.

He went on to say that it was as if he were to let his barns go to ruin to avoid spending money to repair and replace them. He was sure that naval officers would not be held irresponsible should disaster occur; it was incumbent on them to speak out when they had the opportunity.[3]

During this period ships were still being commissioned with a full sailing rig; the *Inflexible*, completed in 1881, was the last battleship so fitted. Perpetually concerned about making large investments in ships that might become rapidly obsolete, it was the Admiralty's policy to order one, or sometimes two, battleships at a time, so that there was never any chance of developing a homogeneous fleet. The failure of the early British breech loading guns meant that a quarter of a century passed before muzzle loaders became a thing of the past, and with the benefit of hindsight it can be seen that the Royal Navy of the time was strikingly ill equipped, not least because the Conservative administration under Disraeli appeared to be indifferent to its needs. This was in spite of the considerable advance to be seen in the French navy; between 1874 and 1880 France had laid down 22 ships of 164, 451 tons compared to Britain's 13 ships of 107,220 tons.

Designing new warships in an era of rapidly changing technology was not at all straightforward, and as the years passed naval architects did not have much in the way of actual battle experience on which to base their designs. Such actions that had taken place were carefully studied for the lessons which might be learned from them, particularly with regard to the effectiveness of gunfire against armour plate. The first opportunity to assess this came with the American Civil War, especially with the battle of Hampton Roads between the USS *Monitor* and the CSS *Virginia* (formerly

2 Oscar Parkes, *British Battleships* (London, 1970), p. 202.

3 Mrs Fred Egerton, *Admiral of the Fleet Sir Geoffrey Phipps Hornby* (Edinburgh, 1896), p. 359; Parkes, p 230

Merrimac). The engagement was inclusive; the armour of both ships stood up to a considerable pounding, and neither was seriously damaged. Other actions during the Civil War confirmed that an ironclad could survive a considerable number of hits. All the evidence from the naval war pointed to the effective end of the wooden warship although even then some more traditional opinion found this hard to accept.

In 1855, during the Austro-Prussian War, the success of the Austrian fleet at the battle of Lissa was very largely due to the tactic of ramming, and this led designers down a cul-de-sac. The distinguished British naval writer Admiral Colomb, at the time a captain, wrote:

> The power of the new weapon was conclusively proved, and it is henceforth impossible to doubt its practical value. The rise of the ram in foreign estimation is one of the most remarkable features of the age… France has pushed her old system of evolutions into the background, in the firm belief that the ram and the ram only, need be feared at sea.[4]

Only a few vessels expressly designed to employ the ram as their principal weapon were ordered by the British Admiralty. On the other hand, practically all battleships thereafter were designed with a ram bow which, although not successfully employed in battle, caused a number of disastrous accidents.

One action that did attract some attention was that involving the unarmoured British cruiser *Shah*, which with the corvette *Amethyst* engaged the Peruvian ironclad *Huascar* on May 29, 1877. The *Huascar*, a small, slow, turret ship carrying two 10-inch muzzle loaders, was in the hands of insurgents in revolt against the Peruvian government and was being operated in such a way as to threaten British merchant shipping in the area. In an action which lasted a little under three hours, the *Huascar* was hit by 60-70 shells; only one 9-inch common shell pierced her 3½ inch plating, and another dented her armoured turret. The conclusion to be drawn from this was that the *Shah*'s 9.2-inch guns, firing what was supposed to be armour piecing shell, had been ineffective, a serious warning to British designers that the guns with which British battleships were equipped might not do their job.

During the bombardment of Alexandria by the British Mediterranean Fleet on July 11, 1882, several battleships were hit by the guns of the Egyptian forts. Oscar Parkes noted that 'in all cases the resistance of armour proved to be better in action than estimated from proving ground results, and none was penetrated at ranges varying from 1,500 yards to 4,000 yards.[5] The evidence, such as it was, suggested that the balance between guns and armour had tipped in favour of the latter.

The Admiralty had at last felt confident enough in the general design principles of the current vessels to begin ordering larger classes of battleships, the 'Admiral'

4 Quoted Parkes, p. 176.
5 Parkes, p. 315.

class of four ships completed 1888-1889 being followed by the *Sans Pareil* and the ill-fated *Victoria*, then by two ships of the *Nile* class and, crucially, the eight ships of the *Royal Sovereign* class. These entered service between 1892 and 1894. They have been described as 'the first group of fighting ships afloat which sat the water with majesty and distinction.'[6] They were the first British battleships to carry their main armament on the weather deck, to have their secondary armament in casemates, and to have sheet armour. They were also substantially larger than their precursors, displacing 14,150 tons, being 380 feet long with a beam of 75 feet. Their 13.5-inch guns were mounted in barbettes, except for the *Hood*, the eighth ship of the class; her guns were mounted in turrets. Three smaller battleships followed before the arrival of the 14,900-ton *Majestic* class of nine ships. These carried 12-inch guns, a weapon that was to be the basic main armament for most pre-dreadnoughts thereafter. They came into service between 1895 and 1898 and gave the British navy a really decisive preponderance in first class battleships for the first time since the days of the wooden walls.

Throughout this period of the evolution of the modern battleship, designers had to balance a number of conflicting considerations. Against the rapidly developing power of the latest naval ordnance must be set the need to ensure adequate protection. Maximising the speed of new vessels required larger and more powerful machinery, which in turn required steady increases in size and, inevitably in cost. This meant that the plans put forward by the leaders of every navy for new warships were constantly the subject of political scrutiny frequently leading to bitter controversy. In Britain, the Admiralty had had to face, in 1887-1888, the unpalatable fact that its shipbuilding policy over the previous two decades had left it with a large number of vessels that were, or would shortly become, obsolete. This was highlighted by a report from William White, the new Director of Naval Construction, and it led to the passing of the Naval Defence Act of 1889. This produced the addition to the British fleet of no less than seventy new warships at a cost ot £21.5m, a huge upscaling of naval construction, of which the centre piece was the *Royal Sovereign* class.

Before its arrival, the British navy could count 22 first class battleships, of varying effectiveness, compared with the 14 of France and the 7 of Russia. From time to time, international tension had led to some panic buying by the Admiralty of ships being built in Britain for foreign powers. It was France and Russia, together or separately, that were seen as the likely adversaries, and it was the combined strength of their fleets which was the principal concern of the British Admiralty in deciding what its shipbuilding policy should be. It possessed one significant advantage; the speed of construction in Britain was much greater than in France or Russia. The *Royal Sovereign* herself was completed in two years eight months, far more quickly than any French or Russia battleship of the same period.

6 Ibid., p. 356.

However, there were real anxieties about aspects of British warship design. During the 1880s, British battleships were designed with unarmoured ends, concentrating the protection on the central citadel. The outspoken Edward Reed denounced them as merely 'ships armoured in places.' Lord Charles Beresford in the House of Commons sought to introduce a motion that one of these vessels should be tested by perforating its ends and putting it into a simulated battle situation. A member of the Cabinet asked him not to press the matter, saying: 'Suppose that your theory is correct, do you think it would be to the advantage of England to show other nations that 13 out of her 22 first class battleships are inferior to those of France and that they can be made dangerous from small gun fire?'[7] By 1893 William White considered that the ships of the 'Admiral' class were becoming obsolete because of their unarmoured ends and their lack of larger quick firing guns.

There was also considerable debate about the efficiency of the main armament of the British battleships. Up to the mid 1880s, their guns were described as 'short dumpy things like soda water bottles, muzzle loaders, rifled and with studded projectiles, which frequently broke up in the gun, or else turned end over end and went in any direction but the right one; but the guns made plenty of smoke.'[8] During this period British warships were still equipped with muzzle loaders, after the failure of the first generation of breech loaders, but by 1887 the development of new forms of gunpowder had so far advanced that, if advantage was to be taken of improvements in initial velocity and penetrative power of shells which they enabled, larger powder charges in larger chambers were necessary; 'the new conditions called for a new type of gun that was much longer, with powder chambers of a larger diameter than that of the bore, and these requirements could only be provided if the gun was loaded at the breech.'[9] By the end of the 1880s the smokeless powder that was then in use was cordite, which was slow burning and efficient, and permitted longer gun barrels and increased muzzle velocity.

One effect of the changed climate in Whitehall after the passing of the Naval Defence Act was a steep rise in the cost of building a battleship of the size now considered necessary. Completed in 1883, the *Ajax*, a vessel of 8,100 tons, cost £548,393; the *Anson* of 10,600 tons in 1888, cost £662,582; but in 1892 the final cost of the *Royal Sovereign* of 14,150 tons was £913,986. The cost of such ships prompted a debate as to whether they represented value for money; it was argued that a greater number of smaller vessels would be a better use of the huge expenditures involved. William White wrote a memorandum for the Admiralty in December 1892 reviewing the arguments put forward:

7 Quoted Marder, *Anatomy*, p. 138.
8 Admiral Penrose Fitzgerald, quoted in Marder, *Anatomy*, p. 138.
9 Warren Berry, *The Pre-Dreadnought Revolution* (Stroud, 2013) p. 110.

> The capital expenditure on a few large battleships carrying heavy guns in strongly armoured positions, and a great weight of armour on certain portions of their hulls, can be made to produce a considerably greater number of smaller ships, each of which, it is considered, is as efficient against underwater attacks as larger ships. The united action of these smaller ships against the less number of vessels of larger type would, according to the advocates of the former, almost certainly secure their victory ... For many services besides fleet actions – such as covering a stretch of coastline or sweeping an area of sea – the increase in numbers would be of immense value. With larger numbers in a fleet small squadrons could be detached from the main body without seriously crippling the force.[10]

However, he went on to point out serious objections to such a policy. Larger, better protected vessels were less likely to be put out of action by a single blow and could carry heavier weapons with a consequently greater concentration of gunpower. Tactically, he accepted the arguments of those who regarded the hypothetical concerted attack by several smaller vessels on a larger ship as impossible in practice; in fleet actions the risks of the smaller vessels ramming or injuring each other would be even greater.

The huge cost of building battleships meant that the arguments in favour of a greater number of smaller vessels did not go away One distinguished adherent to this point of view was Alfred Mahan, who contended that gunpower was more important than speed, and numbers rather than size. His fear was that too large ships would mean fewer ships and advocated an upper limit on size: 'While I deplore the present tendency, in size as in speed, I admit that no one nation can wholly resist it ... it does not therefore follow, however, that no modification of a tendency, no brake, is possible.'[11]

The outbreak of the Sino-Japanese War in 1894 was an opportunity for naval architects to review the actual experience of more or less modern armoured ships in a combat situation. Both sides included a number of foreign built warships. There were divided opinions as to the balance of advantage. Admiral Sir Edmund Fremantle, fot instance, at that time the commander of the British China Station, held a high opinion of the Chinese fleet, observing that 'certainly they are not a *quantité negligible* at all events', adding that he did not doubt Japanese pluck, but their navy was very inferior in power to that of the Chinese.[12]

The principal vessels in the Chinese fleet, which was commanded by Admiral Ting, were two German-built battleships, *Ting Yuen* and *Chen Yuen*, completed some ten years earlier. Displacing 7,144 tons, they carried four 12-inch breech loaders in two barbettes, located en echelon forward of the machinery spaces, and two 5.9-inch guns in single turrets, one at the bow and one at the stern. They attained trial speeds of

10 Parkes, pp. 378-379.
11 William E Livezey, *Mahan on Sea Power* (Norman, Oklahoma 1947), p. 255.
12 Marder, *Anatomy*, p. 231.

15.4 knots. The armour of the central citadel was fourteen inches thick, and that of the barbettes twelve inches. A 3-inch armoured deck covered their whole length; otherwise their ends were unprotected. There was to have been a third ship of the class, but its place was taken by a protected cruiser, *Tsi Yuen*, of 2,330 tons. Her twin 8.2-inch guns were mounted in a barbette with 10-inch armour; she had a 3-inch armoured deck.[13]

Ting's fleet also consisted of a number of other cruisers, some built at Foochow, some German built and two Elswick built cruisers which were the fastest vessels in his fleet. The Japanese fleet, commended by Admiral Ito, was organised around the three French built cruisers of the 'Sankeikan' class, described in Chapter 1. One of these, the *Matsushima*, flew Ito's flag. The key naval battle of the war, fought off the mouth of the River Yalu on September 17 1894, resulted in a convincing victory for the Japanese fleet. Ito had approached his enemy in line ahead; Ting, on the other hand, advanced in line abreast, with his two battleships in the centre. In the confused battle that followed, the opening salvo from the Chinese was fired at 6,000 yards, to no effect, and thereafter the Japanese closed to 3.000 yards before opening fire. The Japanese had much the best of things, sinking four Chinese cruisers and a sloop. The *Ting Yuen* and *Chen Yuen* were hit scores of times; in spite of this, they inflicted not inconsiderable damage before Ito withdrew his fleet, leaving the Chinese to struggle back to safety in Port Arthur.

The survival of the *Ting Yuen* and *Chen Yuen*, in spite of their unarmoured ends, seemed to vindicate the design of the British battleships built on the same lines. Apart from this, which was scarcely definitive of the issue, there were a number of other conclusions that could be drawn. The advantage of higher speeds and the ability to act offensively were tactical lessons that were unsurprising. The effectiveness of quick firing guns, which inflicted a lot of damage on the Chinese cruisers, and the uselessness of thin shields around them, was especially noteworthy, as was the need to take all possible precautions against fire by the removal of woodwork. Taken overall, however, the battle did not have any significant effect on battleship design, either in Britain or elsewhere. The French built 'Sankeikan' cruisers were not, however, regarded as having performed satisfactorily, and the Japanese Admiralty placed no further orders in French shipyards.

In 1895 William White's services were recognised by the award of a knighthood by Lord Rosebery, who had succeeded Gladstone as Prime Minister. Reviewing the situation in the Far East that resulted from the Sino-Japanese War, White noted that Japan had ordered two first class battleships in England. The balance of sea power in the Far East had, he thought, changed:

> Should the Japanese succeed, as seems probable, in refitting the captured Chinese ships, including the battleships, their fleet will receive in the next two

13 Richard N.J. Wright, *The Chinese Steam Navy 1862-1945* (London, 2000) pp. 50-53.

> or three years a very great accession of strength, which obviously must have a direct bearing in the types and numbers of ships of the Royal Navy required for the defence of our interests in Eastern seas.[14]

The Admiralty's thinking about the next class of ships to follow the *Majestics* had been much affected by the wave of anxiety that had swept over the British press and public from 1893, when the situation of the navy, particularly in the Mediterranean, was exposed as being extremely vulnerable. As usual, it was the relative strength of the British fleet compared with those of France and Russia that had stimulated the furore, which had begun with an article in *The Times* of October 31, 1893 by W Laird Clowes. So serious was the position in the Mediterranean that he concluded by saying: 'For the moment we are at Malta, at Cyprus, in Egypt and at Gibraltar on sufferance… It would be wiser either to throw up the comedy or to keep in the Mediterranean a fleet amply strong enough for any task which the future may place upon it.'[15]

When this particular scare had burst upon the country in 1893, Gladstone was still Prime Minister, and he dismissed the uproar, telling the House of Commons that neither it nor the country 'need entertain the smallest apprehension as to the maintenance of the distinct naval supremacy of Great Britain.' He was perfectly satisfied, he said, with the capacity of the navy to do all that was required of it. In this complacent view he was entirely at odds with Rosebery who was strongly in favour of strengthening the navy. *The Times* shared this view, accusing Gladstone and Sir William Harcourt of 'financial purism' and of being insensitive to the 'larger responsibilities of a world-wide Empire.' The First Lord, Lord Spencer, had the difficult task of selling to the Cabinet the Admiralty proposals that went well beyond what the Prime Minister wanted to hear:

> He occupied the position of a buffer, holding the balance between his naval advisers and the politicians. The admirals stated the requirements of the country in naval defence and brushed aside financial considerations. To the politicians, on the other hand, financial considerations were always paramount. That Spencer succeeded in piloting the amended minimum programme through torpedo-infested waters, without causing the Sea Lords to resign or the Cabinet to break up, speaks volumes for his skill and energy.[16]

The rising cost of battleships meant that the task of a First Lord was still more difficult. The most expensive of the *Majestic* class cost just short of £1m, though the *Canopus* class which followed averaged somewhat less, at a little under £950,000.

14 Quoted Parkes, p. 391.
15 Quoted Marder, *Anatomy*, p. 181.
16 Ibid., p. 193.

Gladstone was adamant in his view of the need to curtail naval expenditure, but by February 1894 even Harcourt was against him, and he finally stepped down, being replaced by Rosebery on March 3. For Spencer, it was now plain sailing, and seven battleships were approved for construction in the coming years, with the promise of more if France and Russia increased their building programme before the end of 1899. Spencer was able to write to Fremantle, in the Far East:

> There are no signs of coming storms. The French are quieting down, the Russians are not warlike and certainly the Emperor is disposed to peace: even if the war party became master of the situation Russia would not choose this year or even next to go to war. They will be better prepared in two years or thereabouts. Still, there is plenty of inflammable material about, and a spark may set it on fire.[17]

The perceived weakness of the British fleet seriously inhibited the conduct of British foreign policy; in March 1895 what Marder calls 'the climax of scuttlerism' was reached in an article by Clowes in the *Nineteenth Century* when he advocated immediate evacuation and sealing up of the Mediterranean, arguing that to be obliged to do so in an emergency would be 'precarious and disgraceful:'

> It is absurd to suggest that our interests in the Mediterranean are paramount to those of France, of Italy, or of Spain. It is ridiculous to assert that our occupation of the Mediterranean brings us any corresponding benefit of a substantial kind. But it is true that our attempt to hold the Mediterranean as we do is terribly perilous and may even be fatal. Let us then in the future be merely visitors there, like the Americans or the Danes.[18]

Predictably, this brought forth a howl of protest. Among others, Sir George Clarke condemned Clowes's policy, arguing that 'national honour, splendid traditions and the eternal principles of naval strategy' required Britain to maintain her position in the Mediterranean. This was the mainstream position; apart from the 'scuttlers' like Clowes, there was also a view that rather than attempt to match the French in the Mediterranean, to which they would only respond by strengthening their fleet, it would be better to strengthen the Channel Fleet, which it was calculated could be at Gibraltar within four days. Spencer wrote in April to Seymour, the Commander in Chief of the British Mediterranean Fleet to reassure him that Clowes's policy 'would not prevail.'

The plan to concentrate the Mediterranean and Channel Fleets at Gibraltar only applied, he wrote, to the outset of war. 'I can never admit that if the policy is adopted, it is the abandonment of the Mediterranean. It is only the first step in the policy of

17 Ibid., p. 209 n.
18 Ibid., p. 211.

meeting the French in the Mediterranean, and of crushing their Fleet if it comes out from Toulon.'[19]

At this time, however, the French navy was still driven by a violent dispute which went to the heart of its fundamental strategy, and which as a consequence had a powerful effect on the country's shipbuilding policy. Admiral Theophile Aube held office as Minister of Marine for only a short time, between January 1886 and May 1887. This was not unusual in France; between 1871 and 1902 there were no less than thirty-one ministers in post. However, Aube exerted an enormous influence over the development of the French navy during the period, promoting the doctrines of the *Jeune École.* These were based on the conviction that the torpedo had become the decisive naval weapon. It was argued that this changed completely the fundamental principles of naval strategy, based hitherto on winning the command of the sea by the employment of a powerful battle fleet. The *Jeune École* contended that in a future war the weaker fleet would remain in its bases, avoiding combat; the stronger would be obliged to do the same for fear of the torpedo; and that the only real activity would be ruthlessly conducted commerce raiding.[20] The application of this policy meant that resources should be concentrated on the building of cruisers and torpedo boats. Aube accordingly postponed the completion of the four battleships then building in order to make funds available for the construction of vessels which he saw as more effective and less expensive.

In Britain arguments about the future pattern of naval warfare took a different form. The Naval Defence Act of 1889 had sanctified the principle of the two-power standard, requiring the British navy to be of equivalent strength in battleships to that of the combined navies of France and Russia, which was the basic belief of the 'blue water' school. This was opposed to the views of the military, who argued that the fleet should be kept in home waters to resist the possibility of a sudden invasion, the so called 'bolt from the blue.' The fear of invasion had been present ever since 1888, when the prospect of a sudden steam powered cross-Channel assault was seen as a very real possibility. In 1890 the publication of Alfred Mahan's persuasive book *The Influence of Sea Power upon History 1660-1783* lent considerable support to the contentions of the 'blue water' school of theorists.

Naval writers of this period devoted a lot of time and effort to extracting from the experience of recent wars some indication of the tactical lessons to be learned from them. One issue that occupied much attention was the advantage of a homogeneous fleet. H W Wilson, in *Ironclads in Action*, wrote:

> It looks as though fleet to fleet actions make uniform battleships as necessary as in the past. Again, cruisers, being longer in proportion to their beam, are not generally so handy at a moderate speed as the shorter and broader battleship. Their

19 Ibid., p. 214.
20 Theodore Ropp, *The Development of a Modern Navy* (Annapolis, Maryland), p. 166.

> inclusion in the line will thus reduce the manoeuvring power of the battleship. The best solution of the difficulty would seem to be the sharp separation of cruisers and battleships.[21]

Wilson was able to show just how conclusively the British 'two power standard' had been carried into effect, and that at the same time the homogeneity of the fleet had been greatly enhanced by the commissioning of larger classes of battleships. Noting that Britain in 1897 possessed 31 battleships comprising six classes built, building and projected, he recorded the French as having 13 battleships, of seven classes:

> Of the Russian ships five, and of the French one, are of comparatively small size, and of the English two are very feebly armed. The immense advantage of uniformity which the British first class possesses leaps to the eye. Ready for sea in the above class the numbers were, in 1897, England nineteen, France four and Russia eight. The *Canopuses*, *Majestics*, and the *Royal Sovereigns* form three homogeneous squadrons, in which each individual ship is equal to any that France possesses. Eight indifferent but closely similar ships would probably be found superior in war to eight ships, each of which was better than those of the homogeneous squadron, but each of which was at the same time different from the other.[22]

His figures excluded older and smaller battleships which, having a fair speed, could still take their place in the line of battle. Of these, Britain had eleven, France seventeen and Russia ten. Next, he noted several still older vessels which, if completely refitted, might be capable of much hard work; Britain had eight and France five of these. Finally, there remained quite large numbers of old ships which had not been refitted or rearmed, and which were of negligible value.

In Britain, the Liberal government had fallen in June 1895, and the incoming Tory administration was viewed with great approval by those favouring a strong navy. In fact the two main parties vied with each other at this time to be seen as pro-navy, which was good news for the Admiralty at a time when the international situation remained unsettled. The 1897 Programme of ship building included three battleships considerably larger than the *Canopus* class, displacing 15,000 tons, and armed with longer and heavier 12-inch guns. The increase in size had in part been prompted by the latest battleships ordered by Japan, the *Shikishima* and *Hatsuse*, displacing 15,000 tons and possessing a heavy secondary battery, and also by the announcement that the new French battleship *Iena* was to be larger than originally planned. The new British ships comprised the *Formidable* class, laid down in 1898 and completed in late 1901 and early 1902.

21 H.W. Wilson, *Ironclads in Action* (London, 1897), II p. 144.
22 Ibid. II, p. 271.

Before their construction had been far advanced, there occurred the Spanish-American War of 1898, which did not offer a great deal of practical guidance to naval architects. The battle of Manila Bay, in which an American squadron under Dewey had no difficulty in destroying a pitifully weak Spanish squadron, was later followed by the battle of Santiago. In this battle a squadron of Spanish armoured cruisers, which was blockaded by a powerful American battle squadron, found itself obliged to leave harbour and face overwhelming odds. Within hours, all four Spanish vessels had been destroyed. The American gunnery was no better than adequate, but the power of the four battleships' guns and those of an armoured cruiser was quite enough to ensure a victory. One aspect of the battle was the outbreak of fires aboard the Spanish vessels due to the amount of wood in their construction, and this was certainly something to be taken account of; another was the effectiveness of quick firing guns. These issues had already been identified in the Sino-Japanese War four years earlier.

By 1896 the scale of the British battleship building programme had begun to demoralise French naval leaders, and the principles of the *Jeune École* enjoyed a renaissance. French ship building was again focused on cruisers and torpedo boats, and although it was claimed in France that it was the threat from Germany which was the primary concern there, it could not fail to be noted that the types of ships now planned were just those which would be suited to a war against England. The French were laying down armoured cruisers, and the British Admiralty called for the laying down of four large cruisers to match them. These were the 12,000-ton *Cressy* class, which it was argued were stout enough to participate in fleet actions, as was intended by the French. The threat of commerce raiding was one of the concerns that caused the Admiralty to be alarmed by the French armoured cruisers; another was the indication that the French aimed at cruiser supremacy in the Mediterranean.

The most powerful of the new French armoured cruisers was the *Jeanne d'Arc* of 11,000 tons, capable of 23 knots. To counter this, the Admiralty wanted to build four cruisers (the *Drake* class) of 14,000 tons. This was advocated by the Director of Naval Construction: 'If we outclass the *Jeanne d'Arc* in the new cruisers, we produce at once vessels capable of dealing with equally swift but less powerful cruisers while they will represent a step in advance costing our rivals so dearly that they may well hesitate to attempt to go beyond or even equal it.'[23] The Sea Lords were enthusiastically in favour and got their way. Sadly. by the time of the First World War, these ships were to prove particularly vulnerable.

In 1897 an entirely new threat emerged with a fundamental change in German naval policy. In March of that year a political crisis arose in Germany over the naval budget proposed by the State Secretary, Admiral Hollmann. The Reichstag cut 12m marks off the total of 70m marks requested; the Kaiser, whose ambition to create a strong navy was boundless, was finally able to rid himself of Hollmann, and after a lengthy period of political dispute with his Chancellor, Prince Chlodwig von

23 Quoted Marder, *Anatomy*, p. 283.

Hohenlohe, succeeded in getting Rear Admiral Alfred von Tirptiz appointed as State Secretary in June 1897. His mission would be to pilot a fixed Navy Law through the Reichstag. 'The trident must be in our fist,' demanded the Kaiser, and in the autumn of 1897 the Navy Law was passed, fixing the strength of the German Navy at 19 battleships, 8 armoured coast defence vessels, 12 large and 30 small cruisers. To attain this, a large construction programme, including 7 battleships, would be necessary. Some elements of the British press were immediately hostile to this development. The *National Review* of January 1898 trumpeted: 'The British public are being daily taught to regard the Kaiser as the implacable and vigilant foe of their country ... We clearly cannot afford to allow the German Emperor to hold the balance of sea power in Europe in the early years of the twentieth century.'[24]

The great fear was that with Germany allied to France and Russia the odds against Britain were substantially changed. The German navy was already highly regarded; one British publication asserted that 'ship for ship and man for man it is as good as our fleet,' while H W Wilson observed:

> The additions sanctioned by the Reichstag will make the German navy the third in Europe in point of numbers. In quality it is already second to none. Perfect organisation, clearly defined responsibility, good material cheaply constructed, admirable and zealous personnel are its chief characteristics, 'full steam ahead' its watchwords.[25]

Against a background of rising Anglophobia in Germany, there followed in 1900 a revised Navy Law, which prescribed a huge increase in the ultimate size of the German fleet. It was now intended to comprise a battle fleet of 2 fleet flagships, 4 squadrons each of 8 battleships, 8 large cruisers and 24 small cruisers, with an overseas fleet of 3 large cruisers and 10 small cruisers. There would be a reserve of 4 battleships, 3 large cruisers and 4 small cruisers. Battleships would be replaced after twenty-five years and cruisers after twenty. At a stroke, the balance of naval power had been fundamentally altered, with an inevitable consequence of increased international tension. The preamble to the second Navy Law spelled out the 'risk theory' on which Tirpitz's use of sea power was intended to be based; that Germany's fleet should be 'so strong that a war even for the strongest sea power, would contain so much danger that through such a war its own existence would be put into question. For this purpose, it is not unconditionally necessary that the German battle fleet be as strong as that of the greatest sea power.'[26]

24 Ibid., pp. 292-293.
25 Ibid., p. 293.
26 Patrick J Kelly, *Tirpitz and the Imperial German Navy* (Bloomington, Indiana), pp. 185-186.

Meanwhile the navies of Europe, the United States and Japan continued to receive new battleships from the hands of the shipbuilders. Whatever might be the views of the adherents of the *Jeune École*, in the last analysis it was the battleship that remained as the principal yardstick of a nation's sea power, and around which its naval strategy revolved. In Britain, the *Formidable* class was followed by the five ships of the *London* class, which were laid down between December 1898 and March 1901. The last two joined the fleet in March 1904; the cost of the latest, the *Prince of Wales*, had now risen to £1.2m. These had then been overtaken by the six ships of the *Duncan* class which, laid down in 1899, joined the fleet in 1903 (apart from the *Cornwallis*, which arrived in the following year). All these classes retained what had become the standard main armament for battleships worldwide of four 12-inch guns in two turrets; ship designers everywhere, anxious to improve hitting power, concentrated on strengthening the secondary armament:

> For some time, past British battleships had been criticised on the grounds of being under-gunned, and it was their designer who was held to blame rather than the Board. Secondary batteries had been augmented abroad by the introduction of guns of an intermediate calibre, and in both Italy and America the construction of ships carrying four or eight 8-inch guns in addition to a standard *Majestic* armament on about the same or even smaller displacement had lowered the prestige of our designs.[27]

Typical of these foreign vessels were the American *New Jersey* and the Italian *Benedetto Brin*; the latter achieved a high speed as well as carrying a powerful secondary armament, but at the expense of protection.

Sir William White had been Director of Naval Construction since 1886; he finally retired in 1903. The last class of battleships built according to his designs was the *King Edward VII* class of eight ships laid down in 1902-1904 and completed in 1905-1907. Costs were still rising; these vessels cost between £1.4m and £1.45m. In response to the call for a stronger secondary battery, they carried four 9-2-inch guns in single turrets as well as ten 6-inch. Even so, at a displacement of 16,350 tons, they were thought by many in the British navy still to be carrying too few guns for their size, as well as too many types. The construction of this class reinforced, for the time being at any rate, the numerical superiority of the British fleet in battleships of the latest design. Maintaining this was a vital concern as Lord Selborne, the First Lord, explained in January 1903:

> This is a question of national existence. We must have a force which is reasonably calculated to beat France and Russia and we must have something in hand against Germany. We cannot afford a three Power Standard, but we must have

27 Parkes, p. 421.

> a real margin over the two Power Standard and this policy the Cabinet has definitely adopted.'[28]

It was against this background of quickening naval construction internationally that Britain and Japan concluded their alliance. In accordance with the terms of the alliance, in July 1902 a conference of British Admiralty and War Office representatives met with an equal number of Japanese officers of similar rank. The object of the meeting, which took place in London, was to draw up arrangements for concerted plans of action in the event of a war involving both nations:

> The proposals arrived at received the official approval and formed the basis of all preparations for carrying on hostilities in common. It was assumed that the most probable enemy forces against whom the alliance might be called to operate were the Franco-Russian forces in the Far East. The question of the German fleet in the Far East being ranged on the side of the enemies of the alliance was not considered, because that fleet did not hold the balance of power.[29]

28 Selborne to Curzon, January 3, 1903, quoted Boyce, p. 154.
29 Marder, *Anatomy*, p. 430.

3

The Naval Attaché

The role of the military and naval attaché stretches far back in diplomatic history, but it was only formalised during the nineteenth century. Alfred Vagts in *The Military Attaché* identified 'observation of the armed forces of a foreign country, their readiness or unreadiness for war, and the country's war power in general' as always having been one of the principal responsibilities of ambassadors and other diplomats.[1] For centuries the relatively simple nature of warfare was such that special expertise was not required to discharge this function, but by the end of the Napoleonic Wars it was becoming clear that the gathering of military intelligence and its assessment required more expert knowledge.

As a result, the fashion began for major embassies to be strengthened by the appointment of experienced officers. Gouvion St Cyr, responsible for reorganising the French army after the Bourbon restoration, wanted to station officers in a number of embassies and legations 'in order to reconnoitre and study the state of the military arts among the various powers by comparing it with the state of the same art as existing in France.'[2] This was a proposal about which the French foreign ministry felt extremely uneasy, since it would serve as a reminder of a system which Napoleon had employed to considerable effect, and was something which foreign powers would see as designed to keep the French government informed about their military state – which was of course, the object of the exercise.

The outbreak of war between other states was naturally the occasion for a Great Power to wish to follow the campaigns as closely as possible, in order to be able to draw conclusions about the military capabilities of the countries involved, and of the developments that had taken place in the art of warfare. Permission was usually, though not invariably, granted for officers to accompany headquarters in the field. These observers were accorded generous privileges, enabling them to make first hand reports of the events of the campaign.

1 Alfred Vagts, *The Military Attaché* (Princeton, Massachusetts, 1967), p. 3.
2 Ibid., p. 17.

Apart from arrangements of this kind, however, it was for some time relatively unusual for such officers to be permanently attached to embassies and legations. Vagts notes that the term 'attaché' was at first applied to civilian staff and did not appear in English usage before 1835.[3] When military officers were so attached, it was usual in France for them to be detached from the army and to enter the Foreign Service, and this practice was followed by other Great Powers. Not surprisingly, however, they were very much inclined to retain a loyalty to their original service. The Prussian military attaché in Vienna during the Crimean War, Prince Kraft zu Hohenlohe, addressed his reports both to the Ministry of Foreign Affairs and to the Ministry of War.[4]

Later in the century the issue of control over the attaché became a contentious issue in Germany. After Bismarck's departure from office his successor, General Leo von Caprivi, overcame the objections of the Chief of the Great General Staff, Alfred von Waldersee, and insisted that the attachés were responsible to their mission chiefs. Interestingly, in view of the espionage activities which inevitably grew out of the attaché's function, he banned the active procurement of information 'from a sordid source,' as being likely to endanger the reputation of German officers.[5]

The nineteenth century historian Lorenz von Stein, writing in 1872, assigned particular importance among the duties of the attaché to the collection of military statistics. He explained, however, that the scope of this was much broader than the mere assembly of data:

> True statistics must elevate itself beyond statistics of forces which find their expression in numbers. The institution without which the latter task would be fundamentally worthless is that of the military attachés of the legations; they are even more the statisticians of the spirit than of the facts of the foreign army in question. These statistics must not remain restricted to the simple facts which refer directly to the military institution; they will be the better the more they extend into the statistics of the material, and in particular the economic, condition of the army and its warlike activity.[6]

By the middle of the century the practice of appointing military attachés had become much more prevalent. This was due in particular to the significant acceleration in military technology; all war ministries were under pressure to keep pace with what was going on elsewhere. Alfred Vagts records that the first naval attaché was appointed in 1860; prior to this, a military attaché had also been required to report on naval affairs, but rapid technical progress made specialisation inevitable. This appointment came

3 Ibid., p. 18.
4 Prince Kraft zu Hohenlohe, *Aus Meinem Leben* I (Berlin, 1879), p. 242.
5 Vagts, p. 23.
6 Quoted Vagts, p. 31.

about when the Emperor Napoleon III decided that 'it would be useful and to the good of the service to place near the ambassador of France a higher-ranking naval officer, in the quality of naval attaché'. He proceeded to appoint a *capitaine de fregate* to the post. This was not well received by the ambassador, who was markedly unenthusiastic about the plan to send military and naval attachés to his embassy. There had been also some concern that the British government might not approve, but this proved not to be the case; the response was to send a naval captain to Paris to support Colonel Claremont, the military attaché there.

Across Europe, the deployment of naval attachés was at first somewhat haphazard. Germany maintained a naval attaché in Washington as early as 1873, but it was not until 1889 and 1894 respectively that similar appointments were made to the London and Paris embassies. The British government took the view right up to the end of the century that two itinerant naval attachés were quite sufficient to cover the whole of Europe. These undertook periodic visits to the naval offices and shipyards across the continent. It was, though, thought necessary to send a permanent naval attaché to Washington and another to Tokyo. So far as Germany was concerned, the information from the naval attachés there was supplemented by reports from the British Ministers accredited to the courts of the move important states of the German Empire: 'all of these diplomats were experienced observers of German affairs and, as such, represented a substantial pool of knowledge on the Reich that the Admiralty was able to tap.'[7] In addition, there were the members of the British Consular Service, many of whom were based in German ports. It was not until after the turn of the century that Captain Reginald Allenby was appointed as Naval Attaché in Berlin.

Vagts suggests that this rather casual approach to the appointment of naval attachés, at a time when there were a considerable number of foreign naval attachés stationed in London, 'was a clear expression of British naval supremacy.' The United States had at the end of the century one such attaché to cover Berlin, Vienna and Rome; Commander Barber, the holder of that post, was in no doubt, though, that the moment had come for the United States to have a naval attaché in each of the capitals concerned following the Spanish American War of 1898. In putting forward this view he allowed himself to speak in strong terms about the way in which his British naval colleagues discharged their professional duties:

> England is the only European nation that has itinerant naval attachés: but they are full captains because England wants them treated with consideration – and they are. English naval officers, however, have a fine large contempt for the navies of other nations (which they will some day regret) and their captains go around with their noses in the air principally when inspecting ships instead of looking after the details. [During Barber's Berlin stay the newly appointed British naval attaché had come to him for information which his predecessor had failed to

7 Matthew S. Seligman (ed.), *Naval Intelligence from Germany* (Aldershot, 2007), p. xvi.

> collect.] I mention these matters because I think that we are too prone to follow the example of the English Navy in preference to others especially in these days of 'tommyrot' about an Anglo-Saxon alliance. Someday when we ask England to give us Bermuda as proof of this new-found affection, we will see the cloven hoof. Our changed position in world politics makes it all the more necessary to credit our naval attachés to only one great nation.[8]

During hostilities there was naturally a greater tension between observers and the observed. If the host country perceived that the government sending an observer was displaying anything less than strict neutrality, considerable resentment could be caused. During the Russo-Japanese War the Russians were greatly affronted by the apparent sympathy shown by the American press towards Japan, which they regarded as a sign of ingratitude to an old friend. More serious than this was the opposite situation, where an observer so far identified himself with his hosts as to be seen to be playing an active part in the war. One instance of this was in the Russo-Turkish War of 1877-1878, where General Sir Arnold Kemball, accompanying the Turkish army on the Caucasus front, was alleged to be advising Moukhtar Pasha, the Turkish commander in chief. Had he been captured, it was said that he would have been treated as a Turkish prisoner of war, and not as a neutral military attaché.

On the other hand, benevolent neutrality was well received by a host country. Sir Arnold Kemball was received with considerable respect by his Turkish hosts, while during the Russo-Japanese War Captains Troubridge and Pakenham and other British observers were accorded exceptional treatment, as a result of the Anglo-Japanese alliance. Alone among the naval attachés and observers they were allowed to embark on Japanese warships, and to remain aboard during battle. Both Troubridge and Pakenham were to rise in their profession and play a significant part during the First World War, and the same was true of a number of others, such as General Sir Ian Hamilton, who would go on to command the British expedition to the Dardanelles; Captains Peyton March and Pershing, United States military attachés in Tokyo, who became Chief of Staff and Commander in Chief respectively of the American Expeditionary Force; and Max Hoffman, the influential chief of staff of Germany's army on the Eastern front, who was attached to Russian headquarters.

During the Russo-Japanese War the existing military and naval attachés were in many instances supplemented by the sending of observers, many of senior rank. Considerable importance was attached by the Great Powers to obtaining a comprehensive picture of the war as it unfolded, since it was conducted on a larger scale than any during the preceding three decades. The rapid progress of military and naval technology, and in particular the consequent influence on tactics, made the gathering of reliable information essential. It was not always the case, however, that governments took sufficiently seriously the reports which were received to apply

8 Quoted in Vagts, pp. 196-197.

in practice the conclusions which their observers had reached. There were a number of important lessons to be learned from the military campaign in Manchuria, for instance, that were entirely relevant to the conduct of the First World War. On the other hand, the reports by Troubridge and Pakenham and their colleagues received careful attention at the British Admiralty.

There was one aspect of the role of the attaché which was a cause for concern, and this was the tendency for them in effect to go native, especially if they were in post for any length of time, which could be a distinct handicap to any subsequent career as a commander:

> The attaché, originally a technician chosen for his language knowledge, his good manners, his ferreting abilities, too often became obsessed with politics, particularly foreign politics. While a certain amount of political judgement and talent proves helpful to the officer placed in positions such as war minister and chief of staff, particularly in his unavoidable dealings with civilian politicians, it has seldom improved commandership – except where a gift for politics and diplomacy could be helpful in circumstances those of coalition warfare.[9]

Admiral William S Sims, the commander of the United States naval forces in Europe during the First World War was a good example of the latter advantage, operating with considerable success among the complex problems of allied naval policy. He had spent only nine of his twenty-five years' service at sea; throughout much of the rest of this period he served as a naval attaché, a circumstance which led the US Navy Secretary Josephus Daniels to be extremely suspicious of him. However, it must be said that during the Russo-Japanese War the British Admiralty was to be extremely well served by Troubridge and Pakenham in Tokyo who, although very different personalities, understood and discharged their responsibilities to great effect.

Because, as has been seen, warship design had reached a crossroads at the time of the outbreak of the Russo-Japanese War, it was particularly important that the fullest information about its conduct should be available, A number of important issues were the subject of vigorous debate, of which perhaps the most important was the question of gunnery. There were many in the Royal Navy who were profoundly discontented with the performance of naval gunnery, Fisher and Captain Percy Scott among them. The latter was appointed as Captain of *Excellent* in April 1903, but he had long been severely critical of the way in which gunnery was taught and its consequent inaccuracy. He had worked hard when in command of the *Terrible* on the China Station to establish a system which greatly impressed Vice Admiral Sir Cyprian Bridge when he became Commander in Chief there, reporting to the Admiralty on Scott's method:

9 Vagts, p. 269.

> It is based on recognition of certain fundamental characteristics of human nature. It allows for excitability and moments of exaltation in men loading, aiming and firing; and goes a long way to neutralising both by making provision for an immediate sedative. In my opinion it is, in the highest sense of the term, scientific. Therefore, it is widely different from ordinary systems of training men to shoot, which consist essentially of mere repetitions sure to degenerate in time into formalism. Captain Scott's system is devised to put drill in its proper place; to make it an assistant in attaining efficiency, not a master.[10]

Scott was principally concerned with accuracy and was initially somewhat concerned that this might be lost sight of as a result of the growing demand for an effective increase in the battle range of naval gunnery. The standard armament of the pre-dreadnought battleship consisted of four 12-inch guns and twelve 6-inch guns. The maximum range at which it was said that the enemy should be engaged was 2,000 yards, although the 12-inch guns could throw a projective considerably further. Pressure to make use of this capability began to develop as a result of the increasing speed and range of torpedoes. In 1898 experiments in long range firing began in the Mediterranean, which, when he became Commander in Chief there, Sir John Fisher continued. He had been closely involved with questions of gunnery throughout his career; it has been written of him that 'in September 1899 it could fairly be said that no individual bore a greater responsibility for the state of gunnery in the Navy as a whole than Fisher himself.'[11]

Maurice Hankey, who was at that time serving as a captain of Marines in the Mediterranean Fleet, recorded with satisfaction Fisher's initiative:

> We have at last had some gunnery experiments of a useful character. I dare say you remember how continually I have railed against the Navy for their want of long-range firing. Well, at last, the present Admiral (whom nearly all naval officers revile because he goes on lines of his own – fools, they hate anyone not hidebound by their own ridiculous traditions!) who took the advice of the much derided 'New Navy,' including, I am happy to say, our Gunnery-Lieutenant Webb, carried out a practice at 6,000 yards, a most valuable and in every way instructive lesson.[12]

Firing at long range required accurate observation of the fall of shot and the correction of the elevation and training of guns to bear on the enemy. Range finders were therefore necessary, and arrangements made for the information to be passed to the guns. In 1903 experiments were carried out aboard the *Venerable* in the Mediterranean

10 Quoted Peter Padfield, *Aim Straight* (London, 1966) p. 124.
11 Ruddock F. Mackay, *Fisher of Kilverstone* (Oxford, 1973) p. 226.
12 Quoted Mackay, p. 229.

Fleet and *Victorious* in the Channel Fleet, which led to the conclusion that in ideal conditions, with the necessary equipment, guns could be effective at a range of up to 8,000 yards.[13]

Accuracy at longer ranges meant that a system of fire control, from broadside fire in slower, more deliberate salvos rather than rapid independent fire, would be necessary, and Scott strongly argued for this to be adopted, even before reports of the experiments with *Venerable* and *Victorious*. Alfred Chatfield, who was serving as commander in *Venerable*, summed up the effect of the experiments:

> Hundreds of salvoes of ammunition had been fired, and much coal and energy expended to prove what to many was a self-evident fact, i.e. that you could not efficiently fire the powerful and long ranged batteries of a modern man-of-war by the old plan of go as you please. Scientific, centralised control alone could meet modern needs. To adopt it as the standard method in the fleets meant for the Admiralty and the gunnery schools new plans for the design and equipment of ships, new methods of training, new and better instruments, an accepted gunnery revolution.[14]

The increasing range of the main armament and the use of salvo firing raised questions about the secondary armament; less effective in any case at longer ranges, its use would hamper accurate spotting of the fall of shot. This led to the advocacy of the 'all big gun' ship. The chief constructor for the Italian navy, Colonel (later General) Vittorio Cuniberti, published an article in *Jane's Fighting Ships of 1903* proposing a design for a 17,000-ton battleship carrying twelve 12-inch guns, to be capable of 24 knots and protected by 12-inch armour This was, however, criticised on the grounds of extravagance.

In the course of discussions about the design of the next generation of battleships for the British navy, serious consideration was given to the possibility that they should carry a greater number of guns of a smaller calibre. Among the outline designs for the two ships of the *Lord Nelson* class produced during 1902-1903 were sketches for ships mounting a uniform armament of twelve 10-inch guns, while other designs with sixteen 10-inch guns were also produced. The 10-inch gun being considered was a new weapon designed by Armstrong of 50 calibre, of substantial power and a higher rate of fire than the 12-inch gun, but with a lighter shell. Against the background of this ongoing debate, information from the Far East about the effectiveness of ordnance of different sizes during the Russo-Japanese War was always going to be enormously important.

13 John Roberts, *The Battleship Dreadnought* (London, 2004), p. 8.
14 Admiral of the Fleet Lord Chatfield, *The Navy and Defence* (London, 1942), p. 60.

4

Countdown to War

The ultimate outcome of the Sino-Japanese war had left Japan, and especially its military and naval leaders, outraged and humiliated. In spite of their successes, they were forced to surrender Port Arthur in the face of irresistible pressure from Western governments, each of which pursued its own aggressive diplomatic policy for national advantage, exploiting the weakness of the Chinese Empire. The subsequent acquisition in 1898 by Russia of a lease of Port Arthur and its environs for a term of 25 years caused a special bitterness. During the next six years there developed many reasons for conflict; neither in Russia nor Japan were there sufficiently strong influences to check the accelerating slide to war.

The behaviour of the Western Powers towards China in their own self-interest was disgraceful. Germany had acquired Kiaochow; Britain seized the moment to acquire not only Weihaiwei, but also the New Territories opposite her colony of Hong Kong; and France demanded and obtained a lease of Kuangchonwan. These acquisitions, on the back of Russia's expansionist Far Eastern policy, amply justified William L Langer's comment on the behaviour of European diplomats at this time:

> Europe's treatment of China in the whole period from 1895 to 1900 had been devoid of all consideration and of all understanding. The Celestial Empire to them was simply a great market to be exploited to the full, rich territory to be carved up like a sirloin steak. Hardly anywhere in the correspondence does one find any appreciation for the feelings of the Oriental or any sympathy for the crude efforts made at reform. The dominant note was always that force is the father of peace and that the only method of treating successfully with China is the method of the mailed fist.[1]

The Boxer rising, which was principally a protest at the conduct of the Western Powers, began in 1898 as a movement against native Christians, and escalated during

1 Langer II, p. 704.

the following year, spreading throughout northern China and increasingly directed against all foreigners. It was in the spring of 1899 that the southern branch of the Chinese Eastern Railway, from Harbin to the Liaotung Peninsula, was begun. It was in the building of the trans-Siberian railway that Russia's Far Eastern policy achieved reality, linking Vladivostok with the rest of the Empire. It was not, however, an ice free port, which was why the acquisition of Port Arthur was so important. In its turn, the linking of that harbour with the trans-Siberian railway had enormous strategic importance. Known as the South Manchurian line, the significance of the 772 kilometres of track was not lost on neighbouring countries, and contributed to the raising of tension in the region.

The threat from the Boxers in northern China culminated in attacks in 1900 on foreigners in and around Peking, where from June 4 to August 15 the foreign delegations were besieged. On June 20 the German minister, Baron von Ketteler, was murdered by the Boxers. An attempt by a combined force of the Western Powers and Japan to relieve the allegations opened with the seizure of the Taku forts; then, under the command of the British Admiral Seymour, a force of 2,000 men advanced from Tientsin, but was obliged to fall back after a week of heavy fighting. In the end, a relief force raised the siege of the legations on August 15, by which time the Russians had serious problems in Manchuria, where Chinese forces had begun to attack the railway. At this point the Russians had only 6,000 men in the region to protect their interests and these were besieged in Harbin and at Blagovestchensk; in response to these developments, the Russian government mobilised substantial forces to advance into Manchuria from the north, south and east. By mid October Russian forces controlled the whole of Manchuria.

There was, however, a profound difference of opinion in the Russian government. Count Sergius Witte, the influential Finance Minister, and the Foreign Minister Nicolas Lamsdorff were absolutely opposed to the views of General Kuropatkin, the War Minister, who had greeted the news of the Boxer rising as a splendid opportunity: 'I am very glad. This will give us an excuse for seizing Manchuria … We will turn Manchuria into a second Bokhara.'[2] Witte, who still enjoyed the support of Tsar Nicholas II, set out in a report to him on August 24 the danger of Kuropatkin's policy; if Russia seized Manchuria, other Powers would likewise help themselves to parts of China, while Japan would take Korea. The result would be that instead of weaker neighbours in the Far East, Russia would have strong Powers on her flanks. Witte was angry about the demands of the military, writing: 'There is no definite policy, no firmness, no adherence to one's word – and Kuropatkin is in a state of chronic rage … I have done all I could to prevent a disaster.'[3] Admiral Pavel Tyrtov, the Navy Minister, was also in favour of a forward policy in the Far East, although he was more interested in Korea than Manchuria. In his view 'Russia can only keep Japan in check

2 Quoted Langer II, pp. 695-696.
3 Ibid. II, p. 698.

by the threat of effective force,' and although he desired no territorial acquisitions, he did argue for obtaining a port in southern Korea, with Masampo as the best choice: 'If the occupation of such a port cannot be realised at the present time … it is necessary to proceed with the acquisition of it gradually by diplomatic methods.'[4] The need for such a port was explained as being for the support of the Far Eastern fleet which was to be 30% larger than the Japanese fleet.

The relief of the legations in Peking had only come about after the Allied forces at Tientsin had been reinforced by the arrival of two Japanese divisions. Russia observed this with deep suspicion; it seemed that this, encouraged as it was by Great Britain, was designed to forestall Russian plans. However, after Peking had been occupied, it was Russia who urged that it should be evacuated, evidently at the behest of the Tsar; out of a mixture of idealism and self-interest, the Russians wanted Peking to remain as the centre of Chinese administration. If that collapsed, and power passed to the Yangtse viceroys, Russian interests would suffer. The pliable Li Hung Chang was a known quantity with whom Russia could do business, while it was in Manchuria that her real interests lay. Japan, anxious to end the drain on her resources by the stationing of large forces in China, was glad to pull her troops out as soon as she could.

However, that still left the question of the increasingly strong Russian presence in Manchuria. The Japanese Cabinet was uncertain as to the line to take. One option was to take advantage of the current situation to consolidate the Japanese position in Korea, although this was opposed by Prime Minister Yamagata, who argued:

> Even if Britain privately agreed to it and the United States raised no objection, Russia, Germany and France would join together and oppose [Japan's taking Korea]. In the event of war, would Britain still help us with her military- naval forces? If we cannot rely with confidence on Britain allying with us, we will be forced to fight alone against a threefold enemy.[5]

With Britain heavily committed to the South African war, it was certainly the case that not much help was reasonably to be expected at that time.

The Russians, meanwhile, had been secretly negotiating with the Chinese. Witte had refused to pay a huge bribe to Li Hung Chang until it was clear that he could deliver an acceptable deal, and in the meantime Admiral Alexeiev, the Governor of Kwantung, reached an agreement on the spot with the Tartar commander at Mukden, Tseng Chi, whereby the civil administration of Manchuria was to be restored to the Chinese but that Russian troops should be stationed at key points and all Chinese troops disarmed. Witte disliked this arrangement, because he was still opposed to the extension of Russian power in Manchuria, and so did Li Hung Chang, because it deprived him of the chance of a massive bribe.

4 Ian Nish, *The Origins of the Russo-Japanese War* (Harlow, 1985), p. 64.
5 Ibid., p. 79.

This was followed by the submission of a detailed draft agreement on February 20, 1901 to the Chinese minister at St Petersburg; the Alexeiev-Tseng agreement had been ratified by neither side. There was considerable international concern, with good reason, about Russian intentions in Manchuria, not least in Japan, where anti-Russian feeling was strengthening. The suggestion put forward by Isvolskii, the Russian minister in Tokyo, for the neutralisation of Korea was refused by Kato, the new Japanese Foreign Minister, who said it could not be considered until Russia left Manchuria. News of the latest Russian draft further exacerbated Japanese public opinion, and a serious political crisis ensued. In the end, though, Kato's firm line paid off and the Russians backed down; Lamsdorff announced on April 5 the withdrawal of the draft, which defused the crisis in Tokyo. Isvolskii reported that:

> the most dangerous and hot-headed member of the Cabinet is Naval Minister Admiral Yamamoto ... The Navy is in almost full fighting order and is already distributed among the south-western ports lying nearest to the area of possible hostilities. With the arrival of the last battleship but one ordered from England, Japan's programme of naval armament can be regarded as almost completed ... The War Ministry has not made any special preparations and would require one year to come to a state of readiness.[6]

This may have been an overstatement of the navy's position, but there is no doubt that, for a moment, the danger of war had been acute.

Certainly there were reservations about whether Japan could take on Russia. The influential Field Marshal Yamagata wrote in a paper of April 24 that 'relations between Japan and Russia have not yet suffered a major upset but sooner or later a serious collision is inevitable ...If we are to prevent war, we must secure the help of other Powers to arrest Russia's southward advance.'[7] The political crisis in Tokyo was not yet over, however; the Ito ministry resigned, to be succeeded on June 2 by a government led by General Katsura, in which the new Foreign Minister was Komura Jutaro. The latter did not take up his post until September 21.

The last of the Allied troops left Peking in mid-September, and the Chinese court, which had been in Sian, finally returned to the capital on January 7, 1902. This was important to the Russians, who had been considering their position throughout the summer and autumn of 1901. Lamsdorff had argued that the best way out of the existing situation, in which Russia's military and naval position was weaker than that of Japan, 'would be as soon as possible to carry out the Tsar's will and prepare to evacuate Manchuria before international pressure forces that course upon us.' Witte supported this; Kuropatkin advocated only a partial evacuation, proposing for the moment that possession be retained of northern Manchuria. There was, however, a

6 Quoted Nish, p. 105.
7 Ibid.

considerable difference of view between the government in St Petersburg and those on the spot. Alexeiev's conduct of affairs there made it plain that he had little intention of pulling out of Manchuria, and the response of the British government was to make a point by stationing a gunboat at Newchwang. This was followed by the arrival there of a warship from each of the United States and Japan, so the three nations insisting on the 'Open Door' in China were represented in an effort to prevent the Russians taking possession of this treaty port.

It was during this period that discussions were taking place which were to lead to the Anglo-Japanese alliance, and this was in spite of the contacts being made by the peace loving former Prime Minister Ito with Witte and Lamsdorff in the course of his unofficial visit to Russia in the autumn of 1901. Witte and Ito were, for the moment, of much of the same mind; Witte wrote: 'it may be advisable to give up Korea altogether ... Between the two evils, an armed conflict with Japan and the complete cession of Korea, I would unhesitatingly choose the second.' Ito, who rejected a proposal that Russia should have a small possession on the south coast of Korea, was nonetheless prepared to indicate that perhaps Russia could do as she wanted in China if Japan could have Korea. There were disagreements in St Petersburg; the Navy Ministry objected to the entire proposal, while Kuropatkin insisted that Japan should not bring troops into Korea without agreement with Russia. It was, however, now too late to interfere with the Anglo-Japanese alliance; the negotiations with Britain had gone too far, and these effectively killed off the hope of an agreement between Japan and Russia, at least for the time being.

The discussions between Russia and the Chinese government, represented by Li Hung Chang, had been going on at the request of the Chinese, and had seemed to be making progress. Russia was prepared to evacuate Manchuria, where Chinese troops were to be permitted, and the Chinese Eastern Railway was to be restored to its Chinese owners. A separate and private agreement that China would award no railway or other concessions in Manchuria to foreigners other than Russians was objected to by Li, but a promised bribe of 300,000 roubles brought his assent; but then, on November 4, before the agreements could be signed, he died, and the negotiations came for the moment to an end.[8]

Although Ito's negotiations with the leaders of the Russian government had brought no results, they did indicate that on both sides there was a clear recognition of the risk of war, and a sincere attempt to avoid it. Ito had achieved an important result when he obtained an assurance from the British government that there would be no objection to formal negotiations between Japan and Russia notwithstanding the Anglo-Japanese alliance. The next phase in the Japanese diplomacy would be conducted by Kurino Shinichiro, who was posted as Japan's ambassador to St Petersburg. He disapproved of the British alliance, but it was his painful duty to break the news of it to Lamsdorff, who was taken completely by surprise.

8 Langer II, p. 751.

Some Russian historians have argued that the effect of the Anglo-Japanese alliance was a positive encouragement to Japan to go to war with Russia. Ian Nish, in his analysis of the origins of the war, rejects this, arguing that Britain had made it clear during the treaty negotiations that she did not discourage Japan from discussions with Russia. At the same time, the fact of the alliance had become an important consideration in the diplomacy between the Powers, as Lord Lansdowne observed in a letter to the King:

> The Anglo-Japanese alliance, although not intended to encourage the Japanese government to resort to extremities, had, and was sure to have, the effect of making Japan feel that she might try conclusions with her great rival in the Far East – free from all risk of a European coalition such as that which had on a previous occasion deprived her of the fruits of victory [the coalition of Russia, France and Germany in 1895].[9]

Somewhat to Russia's disappointment, the furthest that France was prepared to go in response to the Anglo-Japanese alliance was to agree on the issue of a bland statement accepting it as reaffirming the essential principles on which their policy was based. Since the two allies might have had rather more to say, the British reaction to the statement was that it seemed anodyne enough, although it did in one sense link the two allies in their Far Eastern policy. For the moment, though, there was no immediate sense of imminent crisis, and the Anglo-Japanese alliance had not had the effect of increasing tension in the region. Having got the alliance, the two parties were cautious as to how far it could be taken; neither was wholly confident about it, as William L Langer observed:

> Throughout the discussions a distinct note of distrust could be heard. The Japanese were not certain how much England could be depended upon to do, and the British on their side were more than a little suspicious of the use Japan might make of the treaty once she had got it. As a matter of fact there was no ground for the suspicion on either side. War was not nearly as close as many people thought. Russia could not afford it and was anxious to avoid it. France was even more eager to prevent friction, and would have been only too glad to see England brought into an agreement with Russia, or, failing that, to have the Russians and the Japanese make up their differences. But even the Japanese and the British were still hoping to make arrangements with Russia that would obviate the need of war.[10]

9 Nish, p. 131.
10 Langer II, p. 783.

During 1902 there were sporadic contacts between the Japanese and Russian governments with a view to arriving at a modus vivendi. Isvolskii, apparently thought to be too conciliatory to Japan, was replaced as Russian minister in Tokyo by Baron Roman Rosen, who had previously held the post, and who was supposed to be *persona grata* to Japan. Japanese public opinion continued to be hostile to Russia, and during the year the Japanese government had taken a number of steps to strengthen its position in Korea, but overall relations between the two countries somewhat improved.

The government of Korea revived, during the autumn, the proposal for the country to have an international guarantee. It was not a proposal that would go down well in Japan, except possibly as part of a wider deal covering Manchuria; as the French minister observed, 'whenever the question of Korea is brought up in conversation, Japanese statesmen slip away and become silent.' Certainly Japan would not be prepared to surrender its position in Korea lightly; the Koreans will have well understood what Japan's long-term intentions towards their country were likely to be.

For its part, Russia returned to the question of its relations with China. Li Hung Chang's successor was Prince Ching, who was a good deal more concerned with the future of his homeland than Li. In April 1902 a Russo-Chinese convention was signed dealing with the evacuation of Manchuria. This was to take place over a period of 18 months (the Chinese had wanted 12 months), while the railways would be returned to China; there was, however, a proviso that the evacuation should take place only if no disturbances arose and there should be no action by other Powers to prevent it. This had been included at Witte's suggestion. The news of the convention was welcomed as a success for the Open Door policy espoused by Britain, Japan and the United States. It has been questioned, however, just how sincere Russia was in signing the convention. The proviso gave them plenty of excuses to drag their feet in evacuating Manchuria; and in 1904, by which time he was out of office, Witte admitted that there had been no serious intention of carrying out the treaty. One well-informed British observer commented on Russia's attitude to international commitments of this kind:

> When inconvenient to Russia she simply cancels [agreements]; because, as she says, can you expect to bind the will of our great Emperor or criticise his actions? The Empire is above the law as well as morality, and I am sure this most estimable Monarch here thinks so.[11]

Perhaps not much changes in Russia.

The first stage of the evacuation was however due to be completed by October 1902; this covered the south-western part of the province of Mukden up to the River Liao, excluding Newchwang. In early autumn Witte had made an extended visit to Manchuria, returning to write a report asserting that a full evacuation was essential, since Russia had its hands full in colonising Siberia, and that it was the only way to

11 Sir Cecil Spring-Rice, quoted Nish, p. 142.

overcome international opposition and domestic hostility. A meeting with the Tsar, at which Lamsdorff, Kuropatkin and Plehve, the new Interior Minister were also present, was inconclusive, although there was apparently agreement that in the long term Manchuria should be annexed. Witte's power was waning; among those who opposed his views was General Alexander Bezobrazov, an entrepreneur who had succeeded in negotiating the purchase of a timber cutting concession on the River Yalu. Bezobrazov was sent to Manchuria on a mission from the Tsar, equipped with substantial funds. He was now of considerable significance in the making of Russian policy. He had apparently won the good opinion of the Tsar by his 'bluff soldierly manner' but had been seen by Witte, Lamsdorff and Kuropatkin as 'vain, self-centred and difficult to handle.' They had been opposed to him since he first became involved in the Korean timber concession in 1898, and Witte had for a while been able to check his activities by refusing to allow independent projects outside the control of the finance ministry.[12] Bezobrazov could, however, be very persuasive, and much of what he wrote and said about Russian prospects in the Far East appealed to the Tsar. At all times he had advocated a strong line:

> Russia should demonstrate her energy and determination. Withdrawal of Russian forces from Manchuria is out of the question. A problem such as this concerns only Russia and China and should not be made a subject for international negotiations. Russia should increase her forces in the Far East with a view to silencing any opposition. She should construct defence works on the Yalu River with the object of forestalling a Japanese attack on Manchuria's flank and making it possible for her to threaten Japan from that region in case Japan attacks. Russia should discard Witte's timid policy which will only lead her into difficulties.[13]

Lamsdorff held a meeting with the relevant Russian diplomats in January 1903, at which, although it was agreed that the evacuation should continue, it might be delayed until China accepted fresh conditions. This was followed by a meeting at which the diplomats were joined by Witte, Kuropatkin and Tyrtov. At this, Witte's more pacific line appeared generally to be accepted, and it was agreed that an attempt should be made to negotiate a deal with Japan. Kuropatkin differed, arguing that the whole of northern Manchuria should be absorbed into Russia, while the south was surrendered. In the meantime the fresh terms to be put to China, drafted by Lessar, the minister to Peking, were agreed.

These were presented to Prince Ching by the Secretary in charge of the legation, Grigorii Planson. The 'Seven Demands' would impose restrictions on Chinese freedom to a considerable extent, forbidding the establishment of free ports or foreign consulates as well as the employment of non-Russian nationals; various administrative

12 Nish, p. 165.
13 Ibid., p. 166.

requirements were also made. Not surprisingly, Japan urged China to reject the demands, while expressing concern about the effect on the evacuation schedule. China duly did so; Lamsdorff, for public consumption, partially retreated, suggesting that Planson had exceeded his authority. Privately, however, he went along with the hardliners in the Russian government, as did Witte.

In Japan, the Katsura government was experiencing considerable political difficulty. Although Admiral Yamamoto, the Navy Minister, prevailed on the Diet to approve a bill to expand the Navy by the building of three battleships and five cruisers, an important land tax bill was rejected. In its domestic political situation, the government could not be seen to take a timid line with Russia, and Katsura and Komura, at a meeting with the elder statesmen Ito and Yamagata, settled the policy to be adopted. A Russian failure to comply with the Russo- Chinese convention should be followed by protest; negotiations to settle the Korean question should begin, with the aim of obtaining recognition of Japanese rights there, with no concessions to Russia. At the same time as settling the Korean issues, Russia's rights over Manchuria should be acknowledged.

Behind this statement of government policy there were a number of voices calling for action against the continued Russian occupation of Manchuria. The Black Dragon Society, for instance, was founded to drive Russia back to the River Amur and out of Manchuria altogether, and was ready to urge Japan to go to war if necessary. Military and naval opinion, too, was in favour of a hard line; it was believed that war with Russia was ultimately inevitable, and the sooner it began, the better it would be for Japan in military terms. Within the Cabinet, Katsura and Yamamoto were not ready to be pushed into war; Komura, General Terauchi, the War Minister, and General Kodama, the Interior Minister, were more prepared to accept the arguments of the pro-war factions.

While Japan was in this way moving towards a firmer line, Russia was responsible for a forward movement in Korea, seeking a railway concession from Seoul to Viju; Japan objected to this. Meanwhile, on the Yalu, Bezobrazov's timber interests had led to the establishment of a Russian settlement at Yongampo, some 15 miles upstream from the mouth of the river. By May 1903 serious concern was felt in Tokyo about Russian intentions. Based on reports from the military attaché in Seoul, the army Chief of Staff, General Oyama, on May 22 presented a report to the Emperor which concluded that Russia aimed to occupy both banks of the Yalu, then invade northern Korea, and to prepare for war with Japan. The Foreign Ministry, on the other hand, had received a report from the consul in Newchwang to the effect that Russian actions were not preparatory for war but were directed to obtaining mining and forestry rights throughout Manchuria and on both banks of the Yalu.

For the moment at any rate Kuropatkin had accepted that the evacuation should proceed, authorising the building of barracks between Khabarovsk and Vladivostok to accommodate the troops pulling out of Mukden. However, the process was halted by order of Admiral Alexeiev, apparently under the influence of Bezobrazov. The latter, on his visit to the Far East, had liberally dispensed largesse to ensure the success of the commercial activities of the timber company. On his return to St Petersburg he at once stood out as one of Witte's chief opponents, and was supported by Plehve. Kuropatkin, meanwhile, had himself set off on a tour of the Far East, intending to visit Vladivostok and Port Arthur, and hoping to visit Japan as well. This was duly arranged, and he had the opportunity of lengthy discussions with Katsura and Komura, which appear to have been very candid, though the atmosphere remained cordial. He left Japan on June 28, and travelled to Port Arthur, having formed a favourable opinion of the effectiveness of the Japanese army.

Behind him he left a Japanese government in some disarray. The army had hoped for support from the navy for its view that Korea was an essential lifeline for Japan. Yamamoto, however, took a different view, dismissing the army view, and asking 'what if Korea is lost to Japan? It will suffice if Japan secures her own inland territories.'[14] Katsura and Komura sought imperial approval for a moderate position to be taken, advocating negotiations with Russia. A paper arguing for this was, however, written in strong terms; Japan could never endure the possession of Korea by a foreign power, and 'in order to ensure Korean security, Japan should limit Russia's activities in Manchuria to those permitted under existing treaties.' Komura, who wrote this document, was nonetheless perfectly aware that it would be hard to get Russia to agree, 'so it is essential, for embarking on negotiations, we are fully determined to secure objectives regardless of the ultimate sacrifice.'[15] In the end the council meeting held on June 23 broadly adopted the position which Katsura and Komura agreed on April 21 with Ito and Yamagata. Mindful of keeping its ally informed, Japan notified Britain of the intended approach to Russia, asking to be allowed to proceed on its own with these negotiations, and that neither Britain nor the United States should become involved. Ito hinted to the British minister that Japan would adopt the *ManKanKokan* formula, whereby Russia and Japan would have more or less a free hand in Manchuria and Korea respectively. This, however, was firmly denied by Komura, who instructed Hayashi in London to put the record straight; Japan's policy 'would be based on the principle of maintenance of integrity of China and Korea and of the Open Door and commercial equality for all.' After a further government crisis, in which Katsura briefly resigned, Komura was able to inform the Russian government on July 28 of Japan's wish to commence negotiations; three days later Lamsdorff agreed to the starting of talks.

While this was going on Kuropatkin had arrived in Port Arthur to meet with Alexeiev and Bezobrazov. He had left Russia under the impression that the more moderate line of Witte and Lamsdorff had been adopted as the basis of Russian policy; but behind his back Bezobrazov, who on May 15 had been appointed as State Secretary, had persuaded the Tsar to send two additional brigades of infantry to the Far East, while news of the formation of a new company, in which the Tsar,

14 Nish, p. 159.
15 Ibid.

Grand Duke Alexander, Count Alexei Ignatiev and others were private investors, sent shockwaves through Tokyo. Kuropatkin warned Nicholas of the effect:

> I do not dare conceal from your Imperial Majesty my apprehensions that now that our enterprise in the Yalu region has become known to the whole world and that the high interests of the Autocrat of Russia have also become a matter of common knowledge, both at home and abroad, it is no longer possible to present this enterprise as a purely commercial venture, and in the future it will inevitably preserve a great and alarming political importance.[16]

The conference at Port Arthur was also attended by the Russian ministers in the region; Pavlov, from Seoul, Lessar, from Peking, and Rosen from Tokyo. Also present were the local army commander, General Chekhov, the head of the Russian civil administration in Newchwang, the commander of the railway police, the military attaché in Peking and Dmitri Pokotilov, the Director-General of the Chinese Eastern Railway. Writing of the latter, Dr George E Morrison, *The Times* correspondent in Peking, observed that 'probably no abler servant of the Russian government ever came to the Far East.'[17]

The Port Arthur conference in the end was held in five sessions, in the course of which there were outspoken disputes between the various points of view. Overall, the conclusions were not favourable to Bezobrazov, resolving that military-political activity in connection with the Yalu timber project should come to an end; it should thereafter merely be a commercial operation. Furthermore, it was resolved that the evacuation of Manchuria should proceed, provided China accepted the ten new conditions upon which the conference agreed. However, the conference was more remarkable for what was not discussed. On his way by special train for the Far East Bezobrazov had received further instructions from the Tsar, to the effect that Russia would permit Japan to occupy Korea up to the limits of the timber concessions. This would be disclosed to Japan after the Russian forces in the region had been strengthened. Bezobrazov, however, did not disclose this crucially important telegram to his fellow delegates in Port Arthur, evidently because he disapproved of its contents. He argued against any retreat from Korea, and was in favour of war rather than doing so. Kuropatkin and Alexeiev strongly opposed this position, and seemed to have carried the majority of those present with them.

Kuropatkin was recalled to St Petersburg, but on his way carried out inspections at Dalny, Liaoyang, Mukden and Harbin. Bezobrazov left after him, but got back to St Petersburg before him and at once began to argue for a reversal of the decisions reached in Port Arthur. In this, however, he failed. Witte and Lamsdorff met with Kuropatkin on August 14, and agreed to reduce the demands to be put to China from

16 quoted Denis and Peggy Warner, *The Tide at Sunrise* (London, 1974), p. 152.
17 Nish, p. 167.

ten to five. Bezobrazov had ceased to cut much ice with the Tsar, and later in the year became ill and retired from the centre of the stage, apparently depressed by the failure of his schemes on the Yalu.

This did not mean, however, that the conduct of the Russian government had returned to normal. The reverse was the case. On August 12 Tsar Nicholas startled Russia with an announcement of the creation of a Far Eastern viceroyalty, a decision of which Lamsdorff, among others, learned only when he read of it in the newspapers. Effectively, it removed all power over Far Eastern policy decisions from Kuropatkin and Lamsdorff, and invested it in Admiral Alexeiev, whom the Tsar appointed to the new post. It carried with it authority over all diplomatic, military and economic administration to the east of Lake Baikal. The Viceroy would be based at Port Arthur, but his precise functions were unclear; a special committee at St Petersburg, consisting of the Tsar, and the War, Foreign, Interior and Finance ministers would supervise Alexeiev. The move was heavily influenced by the two naval grand dukes, Alexis and Alexander, who were hostile to Witte and who advocated a strong policy in the Far East.

The Tsar had not yet finished. On August 29 he dismissed Witte, appointing Eduard Dmitrievitch Pleske, as his replacement. Witte was shunted upstairs to the figurehead post of chairman of the committee of ministers. These changes undermined Kuropatkin's position, and he offered his resignation in protest against the transfer of responsibility for security from the War Ministry to the viceroyalty. The Tsar prevailed on him temporarily to withdraw his resignation, and Kuropatkin agreed to continue in post in the course of a meeting between the two men on September 12. These upheavals, however, left the consistent conduct of Russian policy in an even more uncertain state than had previously been the case.

The choice of Alexeiev was made by the Tsar personally. Alexeiev had first come to prominence as commander of the Russian naval forces in 1895. After the acquisition of Port Arthur and the Liaotung peninsula he was appointed as Governor of Kwantung, and retained his naval command. During the Boxer rising he was appointed by Kuropatkin as a corps commander since he was the man on the spot. He was not, however well regarded by the leaders of the Russian army. He was seen as a rather remote if hard-working administrator. During the Port Arthur conference he and Kuropatkin had discussed the possibility of their assuming command of the naval and military forces in the region, but this was not pursued.

The proceedings during the Port Arthur conference had naturally been of considerable interest to the Japanese government, which eagerly fed on all the scraps of intelligence it could collect. This was enough to give a fairly accurate picture of what had transpired. The Japanese consul at Newchwang reported:

> According to private information from Port Arthur, in conference which was held there, Russian Minister of War, and most of military and naval officers insisted upon peace. Imperial messenger [Bezobrazov] and most of civil officers insisted upon war, but the latter were not successful. In Port Arthur Minister

> of War intended to leave on Wednesday, but having received telegram from St Petersburg, he has left on Monday in haste.[18]

Alexeiev's appointment as Viceroy clearly changed the way in which Russia would now approach the negotiations with Japan, and not for the better. The draft articles of an agreement between Japan and Russia were presented to Lamsdorff on August 12. On August 23, not having been able to consult the Tsar who was absent attending military manoeuvres, Lamsdorff proposed that the ensuing negotiations take place in Tokyo. He had now, of course, to consult with Alexeiev as well. The Japanese greatly resented this suggestion, but reluctantly agreed that the talks should take place between Rosen and Komura. However, the former was hampered by an inability to get any clear instructions from Alexeiev, and as a result was obliged to sail to Port Arthur to meet the Viceroy to settle the Russian reply. Japan's proposal had been effectively to bring Korea completely under her influence, while limiting Russian forces in Manchuria, which were to be withdrawn after their mission was concluded. It was scarcely to be expected that such a deal would be acceptable to Russia, and the counterproposal which Rosen brought back from Port Arthur was to the effect that no part of Korea should be used for military purposes; that Japan's position in southern Korea was recognised provided that the territory north of the 39th parallel be treated as a neutral zone; and that Manchuria was to be regarded as outside Japan's sphere of interest. Nothing was said about evacuation. It was obviously unacceptable; but Komura held five meetings with Rosen in in October to discuss possible amendments.

These were summarised in a document handed to Rosen on October 30, which was copied to St Petersburg. Japan now proposed a 50 kilometres neutral zone either side of the Yalu, and while recognising the priority of Russian commercial interests in Manchuria sought assurance about the protection of her existing treaty rights. Alexeiev showed his view of this by reoccupying Mukden with 1,000 troops, while in St Petersburg the proposal languished due first to Lamsdorff's absence and then to the unavailability of the Tsar due to the Tsarina's illness. Not everyone in high places in Russia thought that a hard line should be taken; there was a substantial party favouring evacuation; for instance, the prominent General D I Subbotich advised Kuropatkin that the best course would be to give up southern Manchuria in exchange for keeping the north of the province. Kuropatkin himself urged the Tsar to surrender Kwantung, including Port Arthur, and the southern part of the Chinese Eastern Railway, in exchange for rights in northern Manchuria and a compensation payment of 250 million roubles. It was, as has been remarked, a 'strange and pessimistic proposal' which was not taken up.[19] It was, though, a realistic appraisal of the real cost/benefit of fighting a war over the issues that confronted Russia.

18 Ibid., p. 173.
19 Ibid., p. 187.

Alexeiev, in addition to reoccupying Mukden, had staged a provocative military parade in Port Arthur, and the Tsar found it necessary to send him a cable telling him that he did not want war with Japan, and reminding the Viceroy that his authority did not extend to ordering mobilisation. That was, no doubt, a sincere attempt by Nicholas to reduce the risk of war; but like much of what he did, it was ineffectual. If he wanted to avoid war, he could have grasped the nettle more firmly and, whatever might be seen to be the domestic consequences of backing down, given his ministers some clearer direction. He told his cousin, the German Emperor, that there would be no war because he did not wish it, a demonstration of his inability to recognise the tenuous grasp which he had on his government.

It has been pointed out that 'almost without exception those with most immediate access to the Tsar were monumentally ignorant.' Kuropatkin later mournfully reviewed the state of Russian understanding of Japan:

> We were fond of their productions, of which the delicate workmanship and brilliant colour enchanted us. Our services spoke with appreciation of the country and its inhabitants and were full of pleasant reminiscences of their visits, especially of Nagasaki, where they appeared to be popular with the inhabitants. As a military factor Japan did not exist. Our sailors, travellers, and diplomats have entirely overlooked the awakening of an energetic independent people.[20]

One of the least well-informed, for which he had the least excuse, was Colonel Konstantin de Vogak, the Russian military attaché in Peking and Tokyo, whose opinions were recycled by men such as Bezobrazov in their advice to the Tsar. He was contemptuous of the Japanese army, and his opinions appear to have heavily influenced Alexeiev, with unfortunate results. He had told Kuropatkin, when the latter visited Japan, that only 10 of the army's 13 military divisions could be put in the field, and he apparently knew nothing of the strength of the Japanese reserves.

On October 1 occurred an event which altered the balance in Tokyo between peace and war, when General Tamura Iyozo, the Deputy Chief of the General Staff, died suddenly. He was succeeded by General Kodama, the interior minister and former Governor General of Taiwan. Although accepting an apparently lesser post, Kodama took up the challenge. His appointment enormously strengthened the strategic capacity of the General Staff, and by October 23 he had drafted his first strategic plan, which involved an invasion of Korea. It also strengthened the hand of the pro-war party; Kodama was firmly of the view that war must come, and strongly advocated this not only to the Cabinet and to the elder statesman of the *Genro*, but also to businessmen and the press to which he leaked damaging anti-Russian information. To foreign observers in Tokyo, such as Baroness d'Anethan, the wife of the Belgian Minister, war seemed inevitable:

20 Warner, p. 159.

> It is difficult to see how it can be averted. It does not look as though Russia, in spite of her promises, seems inclined to give up the occupation of Manchuria … The Japanese are most bellicose and equally indignant. Russia thinks the latter are playing a game of bluff, but they are mistaken, and there is not the slightest doubt that the Japanese are in deadly earnest.[21]

Rosen, who was well placed to disabuse the Russian leaders of any conception that the Japanese were bluffing, clung to the hope that the Katsura government could hold back extremist feeling, drawing some comfort from the restraint of the Japanese press, which appeared ready to take its cue from the government's lead. On December 11 he delivered Russia's latest proposals, which showed little movement; this was in large part due to the hard line that Alexeiev was taking, in response to what he understood to be the Tsar's position. In fact, he was being gravely misled by Admiral Abaza, serving as secretary of the Far Eastern Committee. He was Bezobrazov's cousin; when Alexeiev made known his views, he represented them to Kurino, the Japanese minister in St Petersburg, without troubling to consult Lamsdorff.

The Japanese response to the latest Russian proposals was to stand firm; the attempt to exclude Manchuria from discussion was rejected, and Russia was asked to reconsider her position. Meanwhile military preparations continued; the General Staff were carefully assessing the likely scale of Russian reinforcements and the capacity of the rail system for bringing them to the East. The army now felt that it was time for the leaders of the armed forces to meet to hammer out a common position. The Naval General Staff was anxious about the tasks which must be carried out. Although the First and Second Fleets had been amalgamated to form the Combined Fleet under Admiral Togo Heihachiro, the concern was whether the navy could transport the invasion fleet to Korea. At the end of the year there was a crucial meeting attended by Ito, Yamagata, Matsukata and Inouye of the *Genro*, Katsura,Komura, Yamamoto and Terauchi of the Cabinet, Oyama and Kodama of the Army General Staff and Ito and Ijuin of the Navy General Staff. Yamagata argued for the sending of two divisions to Korea forthwith; Yamamoto was opposed to this, because Japan was not yet ready and in any case the taking of such a step was improper while negotiations continued. In the end it was agreed to send one mixed brigade.

The Cabinet was now meeting very frequently. It decided on December 30 that if war did break out, China should be kept out of hostilities, since if she became involved it would be difficult if not impossible to limit the scope of the war. China must therefore be encouraged at all costs to remain neutral, and on January 7, 1904 this was strongly recommended to the Chinese government by the Japanese Minister in Peking.

In St Petersburg, meanwhile, similar meetings were taking place, but these were conducted with less clear-sightedness. On December 28 the Tsar met with Lamsdorff,

21 Quoted Warner, p. 162.

Kuropatkin and Grand Duke Alexis; neither Plehve nor Pleske attended the meeting, but Abaza did. It was agreed not to break off negotiations; this meant that the question of Manchuria must be addressed. Kuropatkin held to his view that Russia should concentrate on holding northern Manchuria, and not fight a war for the south. Abaza put forward Alexeiev's view, which was that Russia should not be a party to Japanese advances in Korea, which would be unpopular internationally and would in any case not profit them much. The Tsar was sympathetic to this view; but all were agreed on the importance of avoiding war. The Russian reply, handed to Komura on January 6, included what was hoped to be a sufficient sop to the Japanese demand that Manchuria be discussed; Japan was to acknowledge that Manchuria was outside her sphere of interest, while Russia would not impede Japanese rights within the province under existing treaties. It was something; but it was not enough.[22]

The Japanese had by now abandoned practically all hope of a peaceful settlement. The Cabinet, and the military leaders, were convinced that their duty lay in fighting; only the navy's reluctance to see war declared stood in the way. A further important meeting was held in the presence of the Emperor on January 12 when it was resolved that Russia had made no adequate concession over Korea, was refusing to discuss Manchuria, and was building up a military strength. Ito, who of all Japan's leaders had taken the most conciliatory line, wrote later of the breakdown in effective negotiation:

> There is no question but that Russia's aim was from the start to increase her military and naval forces and then reject Japan's demands. In this way she could fulfil her ambitions in Manchuria and Korea without interference. This being so, if Japan does not now go to war and defend her threatened interests, she will eventually have to kowtow to the Russian governor of one of her frontier provinces.[23]

This view, of course, ascribed to Russian policy making a much more consistent and logical structure than was in fact the case. It also set out starkly the obligation which Japan's leaders felt; whatever the consequences, in loss of life and wasted resources, it was their duty to go to war.

By now each side had effectively reached what was its final position. The parties were still too far apart for there to be any realistic hope that an agreement could be reached. In that situation, the leaders of Russia and Japan must now face the reality that war was almost certainly inevitable. They did so in very different states of mind as to the prospect of success. Thanks to arrogance and incompetence, Russia's military and naval leaders blundered forward in the conviction that success was certain. Kuropatkin, at least, was an honourable exception to this. The extent to which he may have influenced Tsar Nicholas II is not clear; what is certain is that however sincere the Tsar may have been in his desire to avoid war, he lacked the confidence

22 Nish, p. 203.
23 Ibid., p 207.

and authority to impose on his advisers an insistence that ground must be given in the negotiations with Japan in order that war could be averted.

On the Japanese side there was a more sober realisation of the risks of war. Among those arguing for it, Kodama made his views clear. To Ito, who was still expressing anxiety about the prospect of war, he was firm: 'I told him that if we lack certain things, I suppose that the opponent lacks some other things. We cannot say with certainty that with our present military power we cannot win against Russia. I told him this and urged him to make up his mind.'[24]

Notwithstanding that the endgame had finally been reached, the Japanese sent a final ultimatum. Although not incorporating a deadline, Kurino was instructed to say that there should be no unreasonable delay in replying. It was presented in St Petersburg on January 16. Couched in courteous terms, it may not have been evident that it was the last chance for Russia to avoid war. It rejected the Russian proposal for a neutral zone, and insisted that Russia must accept Korea as being outside her sphere of interest. To this Russia responded by referring the matter to a special conference in St Petersburg, indicating that the decision-making process had moved back from Port Arthur; confidence in Alexeiev had ebbed, although he was still to be consulted. The meeting took place on January 28, attended by Lamsdorff, Kuropatkin, Admirals Avelan and Abaza, and Grand Duke Alexis. Subject to obtaining the approval of Nicholas, it was agreed to omit any reference to Chinese territorial integrity in Manchuria, to abandon the demand for a neutral zone in Korea, but to insist on a guarantee that Korea not be used for strategic purposes. The Tsar approved the proposals on February 2, and they were telegraphed to Alexeiev for transmission to Tokyo. In fact they did not reach Tokyo by this route until February 7, but Kurino had been informed of the terms on February 5 and reported them at 5:15 pm that day. In any case, however, the response was too little and too late; on that day, at 2.00 pm, the Japanese telegram breaking off diplomatic relations had already been sent. Thus ended the lengthy negotiations that might have avoided war. There had been considerable hope internationally that the negotiations would succeed. Balfour, the British Prime Minister, thought that both sides were wrong in treating their immediate objectives as justifying war. Even if Russia occupied Masampo, which it was assumed would be an objective, Balfour did not suppose that this would be so fatal to Japan or as advantageous to Russia as was believed; it was the same distance that Antwerp was from the Thames, and while he did not want to see that port occupied by a Great Power, he did not think it would be fatal to Britain.[25]

Above all, however, the British concern was not to be seen to have encouraged Japan to go to war. Selborne, the First Lord, was probably expressing the views of many in the Cabinet when he replied to Balfour that 'if the Japs win all is for the very best, and a long drawn indecisive struggle is also excellent for us because weakening to

24 Quoted Warner, p. 162.
25 Boyce, p. 165.

Russia.' On the other hand, he thought that, if Japan was beaten at sea, Britain must either intervene to save her or allow her to disappear as an effective naval power. He considered, though, that this would not happen, and told Bridge on January 11 that no action need be contemplated 'other than that of faithful allies who will prevent the intervention of a third power and meanwhile observe strict neutrality.'[26]

International efforts to maintain the peace were not inconsiderable, but were completely ineffectual. Anglo-French efforts to set up a mediation process stood little chance of success, while the hypothetical possibility that France and Britain could have stopped their respective allies from going to war was based on illusions; in reality, neither would have been prepared to go far enough to prevent it. In practice, although Britain was innocent of the charge of having encouraged Japan to go to war, the cynical view that anything that weakened Russia was all to the good would certainly have inhibited any really effective peacemaking.

When it came to it, although Japan's policy was by no means wholly defensive in nature, it was at the apex of power in Russia that responsibility for the conflict ultimately rested. William L Langer was in no doubt about this:

> The Russians had only themselves to blame for the war of 1904-1905, and when we say the Russians we need not include either Witte, who fell from power in 1903, or Lamsdorff, who favoured conciliation from the outset. We refer simply to the military and naval cliques and the Korean adventurers who captured the imagination of Nicholas II and lightheartedly took up the struggle with Japan. No statesmanship can reckon with the ignorance and blindness of groups like these.[27]

In assigning the blame for the outbreak of war, Hugh Seton Watson took a similar view:

> It can be argued that in the last months of peace it was the Japanese who were pushing towards war, and the Russians who were retreating. Indeed Russian policy at this time was marked by incompetence and confusion rather than by aggressive intentions. But it is equally arguable that the Russian seizure of the Liaotung Peninsula in 1898 was not only an act of aggression but an unforgivable insult to Japan, from which – despite some temporary relaxation of tension - only war could come. To those living more than half a century later, the most fantastic feature of all was the belief, then held by all concerned, that it would be possible to act as if the Chinese giant did not exist. In 1905 Japan seemed to have prevailed, forty years later Russian supremacy appeared restored, yet it was not long before both victories were shown to be equally illusory.[28]

26 Ibid., p. 168.
27 Langer II, p. 784.
28 Hugh Seton-Watson, *The Russian Empire 1801-1917* (Oxford, 1967) p. 59.

5

The Imperial Japanese Navy

The navy with which Japan prepared to go to war in 1904 was, in practically all its aspects, the creation of Yamamoto Gombei. It was he who, while still holding the post of Chief of the Naval Affairs Bureau of the Navy Ministry, prepared the programme for the expansion of the navy after the Sino-Japanese war and the regrettable diplomatic events which had followed the Japanese victory. His objective was to build a balanced fleet, based on homogeneous squadrons of battleships and armoured cruisers, supported by protected and unprotected cruisers, destroyers and torpedo boats. Its objective would be to gain command of the sea in the waters around Japan. The fleet must be prepared for all eventualities, but by far the most likely opponent it would have to face was the Russian Pacific Fleet. The lessons of the Sino-Japanese war had been carefully considered; these included making extensive use of the smaller units as well as auxiliaries capable of cooperating with the army.

The deteriorating political situation had demonstrated in 1903 the need to supplement the existing fleet; the building programme was ultimately expanded to provide four additional battleships and four armoured cruisers, although naturally none of these would be available for a war breaking out in 1904. Japanese shipyards, which had developed sufficiently to build small warships, had not yet reached a capability of building larger units, which must still be ordered from foreign shipyards. 90% of the tonnage ordered under the 1896 programme had been built abroad, the bulk of it in Britain.[1]

Under Yamamoto's leadership, the Japanese Navy Ministry followed closely the developments in warship technology, for instance insisting on the equipment of new cruisers with Elswick quick firing 8-inch and 6-inch guns, and embodying the latest advances in armour protection in their new ships. It has been pointed out that it was in the area of naval explosives and ammunition that the Japanese navy was able to progress the furthest. By 1897 the Kure Arsenal, located on the Inland Sea, was turning out all kinds of projectiles based on the most modern designs, with innovative

1 Evans and Peattie, p. 60.

shell casings, explosives and fuses, which were to prove 'awesomely destructive' in the naval combat of the Russo-Japanese war.[2]

By the time the long-awaited conflict finally arrived, Japan stood fourth in the list of the world's naval powers. It had been a remarkable progress from the limited weaponry with which it had fought the Sino-Japanese war. It was not, however, merely in hardware that the navy had advanced; the training of Japanese officers and men ensured that they would be well able to make the most of the powerful fleet which Yamamoto had created. Fred T Jane, reviewing the Japanese fleet in a book published in 1904, remarked on the background from which officers were selected:

> Theoretically, the Imperial Japanese Navy is a democratic institution; actually, it is no more so than the British Army. All classes are eligible for commissions, but owing to the low rate of pay, only those with some private means care to become officers. 85% or so belong to the old fighting class, the Samurai.[3]

Jane observed that although conscription by ballot applied to every man of the age of 20, there were relatively few conscript sailors in the Japanese navy, because young Japanese volunteered for the service in large numbers. Volunteers signed on for six years; conscripts served for four years. They were not, however, eligible for promotion to commissioned rank. Class distinctions were strictly observed. Jane concluded, however, that Japanese officers 'would fight harder and die harder than any Westerner.'

In the closing years of the nineteenth century the Japanese navy made great strides in evolving an advanced tactical doctrine based on the establishment of the Naval Staff College. The president of the college in the years 1902-1904 was Sakamoto Toshiatsu, who comprehensively reformed the college so that the curriculum reflected a shift from technical and scientific studies to the study of strategy and tactics. Sakamoto ensured the success of the college by recruiting some of the ablest officers in the Navy as instructors. The most influential of these was Lieutenant Commander Akiyama Saneyuki, who during a two-year tour of duty in the United States was able to serve as a foreign observer aboard one of the ships of the American fleet at the Battle of Santiago in 1898 during the Spanish-American war. He became instructor on tactics and strategy at the Staff College in July 1902 at the age of 34, barely a year older than his most senior students. Based on his American experience, he introduced wargaming as the basis for teaching strategy and tactics and for testing plans and doctrines.[4]

By 1904 Yamamoto's programme of expansion of the Japanese fleet had been completed. The fleet now had six modern battleships. The first two of these which had been built in Britain had joined the fleet in 1898. Displacing 12,300 tons, the *Fuji* and *Yashima* had roughly similar protection to the ships of the *Royal Sovereign* class,

2 Ibid., p. 63.
3 Fred T. Jane, *The Imperial Japanese Navy* (London 1904), p. 257.
4 Evans and Peattie, p. 72.

but were armed with four 12-inch guns rather than the 13.5-inch guns of the British ships. They were 390 feet long, with a beam of 73 ¾ feet. In addition to their main armament, they mounted ten 6-inch guns, and sixteen 12-pounders. On their first trials they attained a speed of 19 knots. They carried a crew of 600 men.[5]

They were followed by the *Shikishima* and *Asahi*, built by Thames Ironworks and Clydebank respectively. They displaced 15,000 tons, with a length of 415 feet and a beam of 76 feet. They were armed with four 12-inch, fourteen 6-inch and twenty 12-pounder guns. Their armoured belt was 9 inches amidships, with 10-inch armour to the turrets. Their designed speed was 18 knots. The total complement was 741 men. They were completed in 1900 and 1901 respectively. Unlike the other battleships, the *Shikishima* could be distinguished by having a third funnel.

The last two battleships to join the fleet before the outbreak of war were the *Mikasa* and *Hatsuse*. Also built in Britain, they were completed in 1902. They displaced 15,200 tons but in most other respects their design followed that of their immediate predecessors with similar armament and armour protection. Their arrival meant that the battle squadron of the combined fleet consisted of six homogeneous vessels, giving a not inconsiderable tactical advantage in a fleet action. They were organised as the 1st Division of the First Squadron. The Japanese had one other battleship, the *Chin Yen*. This had been captured from the Chinese in 1895. She displaced 7,350 tons, with a length of 308 feet and a beam of 59 feet, and was armed with four 12-inch and four 6-inch guns. She had undergone considerable reconstruction, but her low speed (she could do no more than 11 knots) meant that she could not take her place in the main line of battle, and she was assigned to the Third Squadron, where she joined the veterans of the Sino-Japanese war *Itsukushima*, *Hashidate* and *Matsushima*. These were the French-built 'Sankeikan' class. Usefully employed against the Chinese, they were by now obsolete.

As has been seen, Yamamoto's original programme had called for the construction of four armoured cruisers and four protected cruisers as part of a balanced fleet, and he planned also for the construction of 23 destroyers and 63 torpedo boats. In 1897, however, the plan was reviewed in the light of concerns that six battleships might not be enough if Russia concentrated the bulk of her fleet in the Far East. Since the cost of an additional battle squadron was prohibitive, it was decided to delete the plan for four protected cruisers and to build in their place two more armoured cruisers. With the latest armour protection it was reckoned that these would be fit to lie in the line of battle.[6]

The six armoured cruisers which were built under the revised programme were, in order of their completion, the *Asama, Tokiwa, Yakumo, Azuma, Idzumo* and *Iwate*. They were all of about 9,800 tons displacement and all had a main armament of four 8-inch guns. All except *Azuma* and *Yakuma* had in addition fourteen 6-inch

5 Fred T. Jane (ed.), *Jane's Fighting Ships 1906/7* (London, 1906) p. 200.
6 Evans and Peattie, p. 60.

guns; these two each had twelve. The 8-inch and 6-inch guns, with which all six vessels were equipped, were Elswick quickfirers. In addition they carried twelve 12-pounders. Their armoured belt was 7 inches thick. They had an operational speed of 21 knots, though the first two attained 23 knots on their trials. The *Azuma* was built at St Nazaire and the *Yakumo* at Stettin; the rest were all built at Elswick. They represented a well-designed and effective group of warships and, in the days of the pre-dreadnought, were capable as intended of supplementing the battle line.[7] They were organised as the 2nd Division.

As the likelihood of war increased, the Navy Ministry began to look around for ways of strengthening the fleet. One way of doing this would be to acquire vessels from abroad, and suitable candidates were identified in a pair of armoured cruisers being built by Ansaldo in Italy for Argentina. These were purchased at a cost of £760,000 each at the end of 1903, and represented a valuable addition to the fleet, which they joined in April 1904. They were of typical Italian design; displacing 7,700 tons, they were 357 feet in length, with a beam of 61 ½ feet. The *Kasuga* was armed with one 10-inch and two 8-inch guns; the *Nisshin* with four 8-inch. They each carried in addition fourteen 6-inch and ten 12-pounder guns. Their armoured belt was 6 inches, with 5 ½ inches to their turrets. Their designed speed was 20 knots, which they were able to attain operationally. Their complement was 525 men.[8]

The Japanese navy was also well equipped with a number of relatively fast protected cruisers. This group of vessels included the 'Sankeikan' ships, referred to above, together with thirteen others; in addition there were four other older protected cruisers of low speed, plus two fast unprotected cruisers, and seven other still older vessels. The navy possessed nineteen destroyers, of which fifteen had been built in Britain, and the remainder in Japan from British designs and materials. These were all of the British '30 knotter' type There were 58 first-class torpedo boats; the 16 most recently built were capable of 29 knots, while there were 37 relatively modern boats capable of between 22 and 25 knots, and five older vessels. There were also 27 second-class torpedo boats. Finally there were 26 old cruisers, sloops and gunboats of no real fighting value but which would be of use in covering landing operations and assisting the army once command of the sea had been assured.

Considerable progress had been made with the development of dockyards in Japan, which it was intended should in due course be able to build warships of the largest type. The principal yards in 1904 were at Yokosuka and Kure, with lesser facilities at Sasebo and Tokyo. The major naval harbours were at Nagasaki, and at Takeshiki on the island of Tsushima, while there were also bases at Ominato, Kobe and Kure.

In planning the expansion of the Japanese navy, Yamamoto had taken account of the technological developments which bore upon the future conduct of naval warfare. The new Japanese battleships were at the cutting edge of warship design, but it was

7 *Jane's Fighting Ships*, pp. 206-209.
8 Ibid., p. 210.

perhaps the destructive possibilities of the self-propelled torpedo which had most caught the attention of Japanese planners. This accounted for the large number of destroyers and torpedo boats included in the expansion programme. The development of the torpedo boat as a weapon that was cheaper and more adaptable than any other was central to the precepts of the *Jeune École*, and it was obviously of particular value to a navy like that of Japan seeking to catch up a more powerful adversary. Nevertheless, Japanese awareness of the effect of rapidly changing technology was sufficiently sensitive for them to cancel the order for 26 of the torpedo boats originally planned, and to substitute a lesser number of the larger and more powerful destroyers.[9]

In the years before the outbreak of war, the navy monitored as closely as possible the developments in all other navies, even to the point of smuggling secret advanced technological information from out of Britain. It was largely as a result of the navy's wish that this successful espionage should not become known that it felt unable at this time to employ British instructors at the Staff College, who might pick up on these activities. In the opinion of Fred T Jane, the Japanese navy possessed the best intelligence service in the world, considerably superior to its Russian counterpart, which failed lamentably in its task of collecting information:

> The Japanese, on the other hand, manage to find out nearly everything. They have to a marked degree men eminently qualified for the task. Where other nations employ agents, Japanese naval officers have always been found ready to serve in the most menial capacities. Both at Port Arthur and Vladivostok officers served as coolies, or as native servants, being Japanese, Chinese, or Koreans, as it suited their book. Whether any one man secured really valuable information is doubtful; the benefits were secured rather by the patient sifting of everything at Tokyo.[10]

Perhaps the most important decisions which Yamamoto had to make concerned the choice of the fleet's leaders. The Combined Fleet was designated as the main battle force on December 28, 1903, consisting of two fleets each of two divisions. The First Fleet consisted of the six battleships, with four protected cruisers, while the Second Fleet comprised the six armoured cruisers, and four other cruisers. The Third Fleet, which was not part of the Combined Fleet, consisted of the older or smaller warships. Yamamoto's choice of Vice Admiral Togo Heihachiro had not been expected; general opinion was that the commander-in-chief would be Admiral Hidaka Sonojo or Admiral Shibayama Yahachi, both of whom had a reputation for boldness. By contrast Togo was seen as less outstanding, though a competent but rather taciturn officer. The

9 Evans and Peattie, p. 62.
10 Jane, *Imperial Japanese Navy*, p. 255.

Emperor apparently asked Yamamoto why he had chosen Togo; the Navy Minister is said to have replied: 'Because Togo is lucky.'[11]

Yamamoto rated Togo highly because he had shown himself to be composed and calculating when it came to decision-making. His conduct during the Sino-Japanese war, when in command of the *Naniwa*, had shown his ability to keep a cool head, when he decided to sink the British merchant vessel *Kowshing* carrying Chinese troops to Chemulpo in Korea. In that incident he had drawn on his expert understanding of maritime law. Among his colleagues, as his career progressed, he had a reputation as a quiet, dedicated, practical and stubborn officer. Born in 1848, the 15-year-old Togo had, with his father and two brothers, served in the garrison of Kagoshima when it was bombarded by the British squadron under Vice Admiral Kuper. He joined the Navy in 1866, his first seagoing assignment being aboard the *Kasuga* during the civil war that followed the accession of the Meiji Emperor. In 1871 he was sent with 11 other young officers to England where, after some delay, he was accepted as a student at the National Training School based on the aged warship *Worcester*, where he formed a lasting admiration for Horatio Nelson. After graduating, he was assigned to supervise the building of the *Fuso*, under construction for the Japanese government at Thames Ironworks. Thereafter returning to Japan, he progressed through the ranks of the navy until he took command of the *Naniwa*.[12]

He was promoted to rear admiral in February 1895; he subsequently took part in the operations at the Taku forts during the Boxer rising in China. In 1901 he was appointed to command the Maizuru naval station. Yamamoto was impressed by Togo's response to a memorandum which he had circulated in early 1903 to all fleet and base commanders asking for opinions on prospective naval operations against the Russian fleet. In his reply, Togo was one of the few admirals to be optimistic; but he urged caution, arguing that war should only be declared after a thorough assessment of the relative strengths of the two fleets.[13]

The division which comprised Togo's battleships was led by Rear Admiral Nashiba Tokichi. The cruiser squadron of the First Fleet was assigned to Rear Admiral Dewa Shigeto, who had been captain of Admiral Ito's flagship at the battle of the Yalu. The Second Fleet would be led by Vice Admiral Kamimura Hikonojo; with a considerable reputation in the navy for his fighting ability, he had, like Togo, served in the Restoration battles and the Sino- Japanese war with considerable success. He was known as a bold and determined leader. The two squadron commanders of the Second Fleet would be Rear Admirals Miso Sotaro and Uriu Sotokichi. Togo chose as his Chief of Staff Captain Shimamura Hayao, a pioneer in the development of Japanese

11 Evans and Peattie, p. 82.
12 Vice Admiral Nagayo Ogasawara, *Life of Admiral Togo*, translated by Jukichi Inouye (Tokyo, 1934), pp. xxviii-xxxviii.
13 Evans and Peattie, p. 83.

tactical doctrine, who had been an adviser on Ito's staff in 1894-1895. Commander Akiyama was appointed as a special staff officer responsible for operational planning.[14]

Togo hoisted his flag aboard the *Mikasa* on October 28, succeeding Hidaka in command of what was still designated the Standing Squadron. He immediately began a programme of gunnery and torpedo firing training and consulted closely with Yamamoto and with Ito, as Chief of the Naval General Staff on questions of tactical planning. Ito wrote to Togo on December 15 with an outline of a proposed operational plan. Togo replied on December 20:

> I am waiting fully prepared to see that the negotiations on the situation are steadily progressing. Since I came here on my appointment, I have been daily engaged in training of all kinds, and the gun practice which lately took place gave very good results … The spirit is growing very high.[15]

He accompanied his reply with a plan of his own ideas of the operations that should be conducted.

With his staff and senior commanders, Togo remained cautious, as the diplomatic situation continued to deteriorate. This did not always go down well:

> The more impetuous among the commanders of the warships would, losing patience, come before him and argue that war was inevitable and warned him not to let slip an opportunity. One commander, who was regarded as a leader among those zealous for war, argued with such vehemence that his language became violent. Togo, who had been listening with a smile, now looked serious and said to him: 'Have confidence in Togo.' The calm dignity with which he spoke these words silenced the other, who thereupon withdrew without further argument. After that, no one criticised the Admiral.[16]

14 Ibid.
15 Ogasawara, pp. 191-192.
16 Ibid., pp. 192-193.

6

The Imperial Russian Navy

Geography determined that the Russian navy should be organised in three separate fleets. The Pacific Fleet would of course be Japan's adversary in the event of war, but there were two other components of the navy - the Baltic Fleet and the Black Sea Fleet. The latter, developed in recent years, was more or less confined by treaty obligations to the Black Sea. The Baltic Fleet, however, could be a crucially important source of reinforcement for the Pacific Fleet, a factor of vital strategic significance. Any losses which Togo might sustain could not be replaced during the course of the war, necessitating caution on his part at all times, whereas the Russians could, in theory at any rate, make good any losses from the Baltic Fleet.

Quite apart from this the Pacific Fleet had on paper quite a lot going for it. The most modern units in the Russian navy had been assigned to the Far East; the battleships, armoured cruisers and protected cruisers had all joined the fleet recently, while the destroyers were less than five years old. In numbers of battleships available to face the Combined Fleet, the Russians outnumbered their adversary, while there were ships being built that might join the fleet during the course of the war; the Japanese, on the other hand, could look only to add the *Nisshin* and *Kasuga* and two protected cruisers. The Russians had no money to buy more, if any were available.[1] In fact the only two major warships to come on the market were two small battleships, *Constitucion* and *Libertad*, being built in Britain for Chile; to prevent these being snapped up by the Russians, the British government bought them and they entered service as *Triumph* and *Swiftsure* in 1904. Although reasonably fast - their design speed was 20 knots - they were lightly armoured and carried only four 10-inch guns as their main armament.

At the beginning of January 1904 the Russian navy in all three of its fleets comprised seventeen battleships, eight coast defence ships and eight other turret ships; ten armoured cruisers; twelve protected cruisers, with five others under construction; and nine very elderly sloops and protected cruisers; 35 gunboats of various kinds; 49

1 Evans and Peattie, pp. 92-93.

destroyers, with 11 under construction; and 90 torpedo boats, some of which were very old. The Pacific Fleet could dispose of seven battleships, four armoured cruisers (three of these were based at Vladivostok), five protected cruisers (one at Vladivostok and one at Chemulpo), eight old protected cruisers, eight gunboats (one at Chemulpo), 25 destroyers and 11 torpedo boats (all of which were at Vladivostok). In addition a squadron of reinforcements, commanded by Rear Admiral Virenius, was on its way from Europe. It consisted of the battleship *Oslyabya*, the cruisers *Dmitri Donskoi, Aurora* and *Almaz*, with seven destroyers. It got as far as the Red Sea, but in part due to obstruction on the part of the British authorities in Egypt it ultimately turned back.[2]

The newest battleships in the Pacific Fleet were both foreign built. The *Retvizan* was built by Cramp's Yard in the United States, and the *Tsarevitch* by La Seyne in France. They were similarly armed, carrying four 12-inch, twelve 6-inch quickfirers and twenty 12-pounders, but their overall design was very different.The *Retvizan* displaced 12,700 tons, was 376 feet long and 72 feet in the beam. Her armour consisted of a belt some 9 inches thick over a length of 250 feet, with a 3-inch armoured deck. The turrets carried 10-inch armour. Her design speed was 18 knots. She carried a complement of 750 men. The *Tsarevitch* was somewhat larger, displacing 13,000 tons, with a length of 387 feet and a beam of 75 ½ feet. Her armoured belt was 10 inches amidships reducing to 4 inches at bow and stern, with a 2-inch armoured deck. The turrets carried 11-inch armour. Her 6-inch guns were carried in pairs in six turrets with 7-inch armour. Her design speed was 18 knots, but she reached 19 knots on her sea trials. Her complement was also 750 men. [3]

Of the remaining five battleships of the Pacific Fleet, the oldest were the three vessels of the *Poltava* class. The building of these commenced with the laying down of the *Poltava* in 1892, followed by the *Petropavlovsk* and the *Sevastopol.* It took seven years to complete them. They displaced about 11,000 tons, were 367 feet long and 69 feet in the beam. The armoured belt, covering about three quarters of the hull, was up to 16 inches thick; the armoured deck was $2^1/_2$ inches thick. They mounted four 12-inch, twelve 6-inch quickfirers and thirty six smaller quickfirers. The main turret armour was 12 inches thick. On their trials they attained over 16 knots. This class was followed by the *Peresviet* class of three ships, laid down in November 1895. The *Peresviet* and *Pobieda* were with the Pacific Fleet, and it was intended that they be joined by the *Oslyabya*. This class displaced 12,674 tons, being 436 feet long and over 71 feet in the beam. They carried four 10-inch, eleven 6-inch, twenty 3-inch and twenty six smaller guns. They were less heavily armoured than their immediate predecessors, with a belt of 9 inches tapering to 6 inches at the ends; a curved deck

2 Donald W. Mitchell, *A History of Russian and Soviet Sea Power* (London, 1974) pp. 206-208.

3 Fred T. Jane, *The Imperial Russian Navy* (London, 1904), pp. 417-421.

was of $4^1/_2$ inch armour. They were estimated to reach a maximum speed of 19 knots. Jane called them 'armoured cruisers masquerading as battleships.'[4]

Of the four armoured cruisers, one, the *Bayan*, was sometimes described as a protected cruiser. Jane thought her, for her size, 'one of the best designed warships afloat.' She displaced 7,800 tons, was 443 feet long and 55 ¾ feet in the beam, and mounted two 8-inch and eight 6-inch quickfirers, with twenty 12-pounders. She had an armoured belt of up to 8 inches, and a 2-inch armoured deck. She was designed to attain 21 knots, but exceeded this on her trials. Jane thought her a credit to her French builders: 'it cannot be denied that in the *Bayan* France exemplified that her old fame for design and speed is still with her.'[5]

There were five protected cruisers with the Pacific Fleet at Port Arthur; these were the *Askold, Diana, Pallada, Novik* and *Boyarin*. The first three of these displaced 6,350 tons, and carried eight or twelve 6-inch as principal armament; the last two were smaller, of about 3,000 tons, armed with six 4.7-inch. At Chemulpo there was a further cruiser, the American built *Varyag*, of 6,500 tons, mounting twelve 6-inch. The design speed of these vessels was 23 knots, but all had exceeded this on their sea trials.

The squadron at Vladivostok comprised three armoured cruisers and one protected cruiser. The armoured cruisers were the *Rossiya*, *Gromoboi* and *Rurik*, all Russian built. The first of these to be completed was the *Rurik*, and her design attracted a good deal of international interest since she appeared, as Jane put it, to represent 'the maximum of offence with the minimum of defence.' She displaced 10,950 tons; was 426 feet long and 67 feet in the beam; and carried four 8-inch, sixteen 6-inch quickfirers and six 4.7-inch quickfirers, with a large number of smaller guns. She was armoured with a belt of 8 to 10 inch steel, with an armoured deck of two and three-quarter inches. Her guns were only lightly armoured. Her speed was 18 knots. The *Rossiya,* launched in 1896, was larger, displacing 12,100 tons with a length of 480 feet and a beam of 68 feet. She was armed with four 8-inch, sixteen 6-inch quickfirers and twelve 3-inch quickfirers with a host of smaller guns. Her speed was about 19 knots. Her armoured belt extended just under 360 feet, with a thickness of 9 $^3/_4$ sheet steel. There was a 6-inch bulkhead to the central battery fore and aft. She was regarded as greatly superior to the *Rurik.* She was followed by the *Gromobo*i, launched in 1899, which was an improved version of the *Rossiya*, slightly larger, with similar armament and somewhat improved protection especially to the guns, and was also slightly faster at 20 knots. The Vladivostok squadron also included the protected cruiser *Bogatyr* of similar specifications to the *Askold* though with only three funnels rather than that vessel's distinctive five funnels; both had been built in German yards.

The size and effectiveness of the Russian Navy had, since the days of Peter the Great, waxed and waned in accordance with the international and domestic political

4 Ibid., pp. 307-324.
5 Ibid., p. 322.

situation. Following the successful outcome of the Russo-Turkish war in 1878, the government's naval policy was essentially defensive. The shipbuilding programmes at the start of this period featured coast defence ironclads and large, fast cruisers, the assumption being that in a war the Russian coastline would be blockaded by a stronger naval power. At that time it was the Baltic and Black Sea with which naval planners were principally concerned. However, in 1881 Tsar Alexander III approved a 20 year naval programme intended to produce 19 first-class or second class battleships, with 25 cruisers.[6]

The implementation of this programme in the 1880s was erratic; the battleships of this period were based on a series of very different designs. Neither in the Baltic Fleet nor the renascent Black Sea Fleet was there uniformity in speed, armament or armour, and the ships built were decidedly unsatisfactory. Russian planners did, however, begin to take a keen interest in torpedo boats, and built a large number of these vessels. A number of small submarines was also ordered, though they enjoyed only limited success. Although the overall effect of the shipbuilding policy did not produce a very satisfactory fleet, it has been pointed out that 'the efforts expended in its creation had far-reaching effects on the Russian economy.' The shipyards, factories and railways necessary to sustain such a programme contributed to the development of the industrial revolution in the country, even though the domestic shipbuilding capacity meant that some ships must be built abroad.[7]

The fleet that Russia possessed in 1904 was the product of a significant change in government policy from the mid-1890s. The Far East expansion that had been revived during the reign of Alexander III was continued under Nicholas II, and the development of this Russian sphere of influence was soon seen as necessitating a different kind of fleet. The occupation of Port Arthur and the Liaotung peninsula demanded the strengthening of the Pacific Fleet, particularly as to first class battleships. The powerful international influence of the works of Captain Alfred T Mahan had its effect in Russia as well as in the United States, Britain, Germany and Japan. Mahan's Russian counterpart was Nicolai Klado, a young naval officer who wrote widely on the subject of sea power, and was a powerful advocate of the need to build up a blue water navy. The new Tsar was already a naval enthusiast, and Klado was pushing at an open door, not least in his support for Far Eastern expansion.

By the end of the nineteenth century Russia was rated third among the world's naval powers, having built up a fleet which was recorded in *All the World's Fighting Ships* of 1898 as possessing 20 battleships, 22 coast defence ships, 11 armoured cruisers, 2 protected cruisers, 20 smaller cruisers, 9 torpedo gunboats, 54 destroyers and about 75 torpedo boats. The policy had now been adopted to build battleships in classes, in order to improve uniformity. It was also now settled policy to send the latest ships to the Far East.

6 Mitchell, p. 192.
7 Ibid., p. 197.

Outstanding among the leaders of the new Russian navy was Vice Admiral Stepan O Makarov. Born in 1849 of modest parentage, he was able to become an officer by reason of his personality and outstanding abilities. He joined the navy as a cadet in 1863, and rose quickly. In 1870 he was the inventor of a collision mat, displayed at the 1873 World's Fair in Vienna. During the Russo-Turkish war of 1877-1878 he served as captain of a torpedo boat tender, and in 1878 took command of a torpedo boat which sank the Turkish *Intibakh* at Batoum, the first success for the Whitehead self-propelled torpedo. As captain of the corvette *Vityaz* he conducted a world-wide oceanographic expedition in 1886-1889, and in the following year was promoted to Rear Admiral. He was chief inspector of naval ordnance between 1890 and 1894 and while holding this post invented an armour piercing shell known as the 'Makarov's Little Cap.' After a spell as commander of the Mediterranean Squadron he was Director of Naval Training, becoming a vice admiral in 1896. He was responsible for the design and construction of the *Yermak*, the world's first icebreaker. He commanded this vessel on her maiden voyage in 1899, and again in 1901 on an Arctic surveying expedition. He also designed two icebreakers to be used to connect the trans-Siberian railway across Lake Baikal.

In 1898 he designed a class of six minelayers. These were the first purpose-built vessels of their kind, and reflected the strong interest of the Russian Navy in the use of mine warfare. In addition, however, to the many practical products of his fertile brain, Makarov became noted for his extensive writing on naval questions. He was committed to the tactical offensive, writing that 'a good gun brings victory while armour only postpones defeat.' His most famous book was his *Discussion of Questions in Naval Tactics*, which reached a worldwide naval readership. It was translated into English by the American Lieutenant John B Bernardon and published by the United States Office of Naval Intelligence in April 1898, on the eve of the Spanish-American war. Quoted with approval was his summary of the role of strategy and tactics:

> Above strategy is to be placed imperial policy, which determines whether an end sought may be obtained without war or not – whether a demonstration will suffice, or whether military operations must be undertaken. When war is begun, strategy shows where it is to be carried on, and tactics how to conduct it so as to defeat the enemy with the least loss.[8]

Makarov was a realist. He foresaw the advent of war with Japan, and argued that for success the Russians must aim at a margin of at least 20% over the Japanese. In his introduction to a recent edition of Makarov's book, Captain Robert B Bathurst of the U.S. Navy wrote that the work was 'as modern, concrete, practicable, and creative as can be found among any of the tactical thinkers of the turn-of-the-century, a period

8 Vice Admiral S.O. Makarov,*Discussion of Questions in Naval Tactics* (Annapolis, Maryland, 1990) p. 1.

distinguished by the quantity of writing on the subject.'[9] Bathurst's conclusion is that the Imperial Russian Navy had needed more than one Makarov. The empire's national security was, he finds, endangered by the 'indolent Russian naval staffs, and the even more lethargic naval ministry' which responded inadequately to technological change.

The outbreak of war did not, however, find Makarov at the sharp end of the Russian navy in the Far East; at that time he was serving as Port Admiral at Kronstadt, and the command of the Pacific Fleet was in less capable hands. Admiral Yevgeny Alexeiev had been its commander until his appointment as Viceroy, and he was succeeded by Vice-Admiral Oscar V Stark. Stark was born in 1846, graduating from the Sea Cadet Corps in 1864. He commanded a gunboat during the Russo-Turkish war. He had joined the Pacific Fleet in 1898, where he took command of the naval base at Port Arthur, and assumed command of the Pacific Fleet as well on February 7 1902, becoming a vice admiral in December of that year. He was also the commander of the first division of battleships, which comprised the *Petropavlovsk*, *Retvizan*, *Pobieda* and *Tsarevitch*. The second division, which comprised the *Peresviet*, *Poltava* and *Sevastopol*, was led by Rear Admiral Prince Paul Ukhtomski. Born in 1848, he had graduated from the sea cadets in 1867, and become a specialist in mine warfare; he reached the rank of captain in 1894, and that of rear admiral in 1901 when he served as chief of staff of the Kronstadt naval base. He then joined the Pacific Fleet, where he was second-in-command.

Chief of Staff of the Fleet was Rear Admiral Wilhelm Vitgeft, who had held that position under Alexeiev, and continued to do so when the latter became Viceroy. He was born in 1847; he graduated from the sea cadets in 1868 and became a specialist in naval artillery and mine warfare. He was promoted to captain in 1894 and commanded a cruiser before reaching the rank of rear admiral and joining the Pacific Fleet in October 1899.

It was not a very convincing group of senior officers. A former commander of the Pacific Fleet, Rear Admiral Dubasov, had been much abler. In 1898, by which time the fleet was already at Port Arthur, he had strongly argued that on all principles of strategy the fleet should be based on the Korean coast 'where it would give control of the Japanese communications with Korea and China.' It would also cover the Russian Maritime Province. His objection to Port Arthur was presciently expressed in his report:

> Port Arthur, with its difficult and narrow entry is likely to become a trap for any squadron that seeks refuge there, because it is so easy to blockade. To break such a blockade will be impossible, especially if it be borne in mind that ships can only leave the inner road one by one and very slowly.[10]

9 Ibid., p. xxvi.
10 Quoted Julian S. Corbett, *Maritime Operations in the Russo-Japanese War 1904–1905* I (Annapolis, Maryland 1994), p. 14

It was a view that was widely shared within the Russian navy; but political considerations made it impossible for Port Arthur to be abandoned. It was central to Russian Far Eastern policy, and to let it go would be a crushing blow to Russian ambitions there. The local staffs in the East were adamant that if it were not properly defended, it would expose the Russian position in Manchuria to defeat.

By 1904 there was, however, a fuller understanding of the vulnerability of Port Arthur. When Kuropatkin visited the place in 1903, Alexeiev had submitted to him a paper showing that the fortress was at the mercy of Japan, not least since the kind of numerical superiority which Makarov had pointed out as essential was not in place. This was not the only problem facing the Pacific Fleet:

> Nor was it only in materiel that the Russian inferiority was felt. Since Admiral Stark had been in command the squadron by general testimony had been going steadily downhill. The new Admiral lived ashore and seems to have set a bad example in keenness. There was, moreover, a continual shifting of officers that broke the *esprit de corps* which Admiral Dubasov had fostered and the demoralisation was serious and patent.[11]

The key problem for the Russian commanders was that a concentration of all their forces in the Far East would have to be at either Port Arthur or Vladivostok, but for all practical purposes the latter simply would not do. In some respects it was superior to Port Arthur as a base; its docking accommodation was better, it had a larger and more open roadstead and its double entrance made it difficult to blockade. But it was in the wrong position to concentrate the fleet if the object was to be ready to deliver a decisive stroke. If it was based there, the fleet must put to sea the moment the war began, and it was too far from the Yellow Sea to be able to intervene at once in any Japanese amphibious operations. Thus it was settled that the fleet must be based at Port Arthur, save for the armoured cruiser squadron at Vladivostok, which at the start of the war was commanded by Rear Admiral Stakelberg. A further disadvantage of the northern port was of course that it was not ice free; only by the constant use of icebreakers could access to Vladivostok be kept open from December to March.

11 Ibid., p. 39.

7

War Planning

In September 1901 a Russian war plan was approved by the Tsar to take account of the current political situation. Corbett noted that 'it rested for its effect entirely upon the power of the Pacific Squadron to dispute the local command with Japan. It turned, in fact, upon the sea factor.'[1] The plan assumed sensibly enough that Japan would open hostilities by seizing Korea without a declaration of war. Thereafter, the question was whether she would use it as a base for further operations, which might be directed towards Manchuria, or Port Arthur, or Vladivostok and the Maritime Province. The naval aspects of the plan concerned Port Arthur in particular, since it was not thought that Vladivostok would be a target. As to Port Arthur, Alexeiev was firmly of the view that the Japanese would not dare to move troops by sea in the face of the Russian fleet. The plan, therefore, concentrated on the military aspects of an invasion of Manchuria. Crucial to its defence was the necessity of delaying the Japanese advance for as long as possible to enable reinforcements from Europe to arrive, and this depended on what the navy could do. At that time, the Pacific Fleet was below strength; but although not strong enough to achieve a general command of the sea it could deny that to Japan 'and expose her to all the risks, delays and drawbacks of an invasion over an uncommanded sea.'[2]

Alexeiev and his staff, aiming at imposing as much delay as possible upon the Japanese, concluded that although the naval operations must be defensive in character, they should aim at winning local control of the Yellow Sea. This determined the deployment of the fleet in two parts; the bulk of it would be based at Port Arthur, with the cruiser squadron at Vladivostok, which would threaten the Japanese communications and harass the enemy's trade and coastline, and thereby compel the enemy to transfer forces from the Yellow Sea. This plan, however, had to be extensively revised when news came of the Anglo-Japanese alliance, which fundamentally altered the assumptions on which it had been based:

1 Corbett I, p. 23.
2 Ibid., p. 24.

> The Japanese would now be assured that they would never be suffered to lose entirely the command of the sea, and they would thus be able to hazard a vigorous offensive. Even if England remained neutral the situation would be as bad. As soon as the war opened her squadron would begin to shadow that of Russia, and by being in a position to commence hostilities at any moment it pleased, it would practically paralyse the operations of the Pacific Squadron.[3]

It was enough, at that time, to cause Russia to back down and promise the phased evacuation of Manchuria.

By the autumn of 1903, when Kuropatkin paid his visit to Port Arthur, it was made clear to him by the staff there that the fortress itself was extremely vulnerable. The reinforcement of the Pacific Fleet that had taken place had not created the kind of superiority that would be necessary to win command of the sea. Port Arthur was without adequate land defences, and there were insufficient facilities for docking the fleet. For this reason Alexeiev wanted to see a concentration of the principal forces in Manchuria much further south than had been proposed; the general staff in St Petersburg were firmly against this, since a position at Liaoyang would be dangerously exposed to envelopment.

On the other hand, the confidence of the local naval staff had increased in one respect; it was now believed that the continued existence of the Pacific Fleet at Port Arthur meant that no Japanese landing at Newchwang or in the Bay of Korea was possible. Vitgeft expressed the view that, in the existing state of the forces, 'the Russian fleet could not be beaten by the Japanese in the Bay of Korea, or indeed anywhere in the Yellow Sea'.[4] It was an optimism that could not be justified; indeed, the Japanese seem to have had a clearer understanding of the state of the Russian fleet than its commanders. One Japanese naval officer wrote in his diary:

> Certainly at sea we shall give a good account of ourselves, for although they are good fighters they possess little practical experience, and their ships, with a few exceptions, are not worth much. An officer of our general staff was in Port Arthur a short time ago as a spy – we have been practising espionage for some time now – and is sure the Russians do not believe in the proximity of war … They do not manoeuvre, they do not carry out any gunnery exercises, and in a corner of the arsenal there are goodness knows how many torpedoes, quite neglected. For months they have not been inspected by either officers or engineers. What a state they must be in – covered with rust.[5]

3 Ibid., p. 26.
4 Ibid., p. 42.
5 Quoted in Mitchell, p. 211.

The assumptions made by the Russians in 1901 as to what the Japanese might do remained unchanged. The military staff advised that since the enemy outnumbered the Russian forces immediately available by two to one, an advance into Manchuria and the Liaotung peninsula would follow the occupation of Korea. This meant that the more southerly concentration of the army was essential if Port Arthur was to be saved from a decisive stroke:

> If the fleet could really deny to the Japanese the quick route over the Yellow Sea and force them to use the long and difficult line through Korea and the mountainous region of Southern Manchuria there would be just time. Liaoyang had at any rate too many advantages as a concentration zone for the attempt not to be made on any reasonable chance.[6]

A large part of the difficulty in producing a coherent plan arose from the lack of any naval war staff at the Admiralty, which had not therefore the means of making a proper study of the issues. Alexeiev's appointment as Viceroy made him independent of the Admiralty, which then lacked the essential understanding that the general plan depended absolutely on the command of the sea. It was for this reason, as was subsequently explained, that the Pacific Fleet did not receive the further reinforcements it so desperately needed. Absurdly, a conference of flag officers at the Admiralty convened shortly before the outbreak of war concluded that in their opinion it was not necessary for success in naval warfare to draw up an operations plan beforehand.

It was down to the local naval staff, therefore, to take such decisions as it could about the immediate conduct of hostilities. No change was made in the essential division of the Pacific Fleet, with the main body at Port Arthur and the cruiser squadron at Vladivostok. The latter base would be quite unsuitable for operations directed at preventing Japanese use of the Yellow Sea; but the subordinate objectives of the cruisers were still considered of sufficient value to warrant the continued division of the fleet. Stakelberg's orders, therefore, required him to proceed at once on the outbreak of war to the Japanese coast, and thereby deny the enemy a safe crossing of the Sea of Japan. His orders required the squadron to be ready to move immediately. It was to commence its operations on the north-west coast of Yezo and the west end of the Tsugaru Strait and then proceed down the coast destroying all pilotage marks and signal stations and capturing or sinking all the transports that it encountered carrying troops or war materiel and generally wrecking the coast wise traffic.[7]

This division of the fleet has been much criticised by historians. Donald Mitchell, remarking that 'the Russian leaders displayed little evidence of talent for strategic planning,' is particularly critical.. The Russian distrust of sea power was almost certainly, he thought, based in part on the fleet's tactical unpreparedness for any role,

6 Corbett I, p. 43.
7 Ibid, p. 47.

as a result of which the navy 'had virtually no design for the conduct of the war.'[8] Corbett, however, took a different view; by massing the cruiser squadron with the rest of the fleet at Port Arthur the real benefits that they were able to achieve would all have been lost. For the moment, therefore, the Russian Pacific Fleet must await events with the resources it actually had; no reinforcement was now likely to arrive before war broke out.

During 1903 the Russian Admiralty had taken some steps in the direction of Makarov's suggestion of the need for a margin of superiority over the Russian fleet of 20%. The squadron of reinforcements for the Pacific Fleet under Rear Admiral Virenius had been dispatched. However, the squadron's proceedings in the Mediterranean as it sailed eastwards provided an instance of the poor staff work and lack of urgency that characterised the Russian Admiralty. All told, Virenius had with him two battleships (*Tsarevitch* and *Oslyabya*) three cruisers (*Dmitri Donskoi, Aurora* and *Bayan*) and seven destroyers. These moved individually to Bizerta, where the squadron was concentrated before setting off again for the Suez Canal. Unfortunately, the *Oslyabya* ran aground in the Straits of Gibraltar and having suffered some damage proceeded to La Spezia in southern Italy for repairs. The *Tsarevitch* and *Bayan* continued their journey to the Far East, arriving at Port Arthur on December 2

The continued presence of the rest of the squadron in the Mediterranean was not without significance for the Japanese, who were concerned that the recently acquired armoured cruisers built in Genoa and now named *Nisshin* and *Kasuga* should be able to make their way unmolested to the Far East. An abortive attempt was made to persuade the British authorities to allow them to sail under the British flag, as they carried a largely British temporary crew, but this was firmly refused. They accordingly hoisted Japanese colours when they sailed for the Suez Canal, arriving to find that part of Virenius's squadron had preceded them. The *Dmitri Donskoi* went on through the canal to Suez, where the Japanese cruisers passed her at anchor on January 15.

Virenius had spent the autumn hanging around in the Mediterranean, and even after passing through the canal the squadron dawdled in the Red Sea, apparently awaiting pilots. It had been now joined by the *Oslyabya*, the damage to which was less serious than supposed. Had hostilities commenced at this time, the *Nisshin* and *Kasuga* would have been at serious risk from the obviously superior Russian squadron. As it was, they had by January 28 safely passed Colombo en route to Japan.[9]

The margin of 20% advocated by Makarov could certainly have been attained quantitatively in battleships, but in terms of quality the Russian vessels were not the equal of their opponents. The Japanese battleships were larger, faster and more heavily armed, and some of them enjoyed greater armour protection. It has been calculated that in terms of battleships and armoured cruisers in the war zone the Japanese had a superior ratio of fourteen ships with a total broadside of 37,600 pounds to eleven

8 Mitchell, pp. 211-213.
9 Corbett I, p. 58.

Russian vessels with a broadside of 26,500 pounds. The Japanese ships were generally more modern, and were homogeneous in design, equipment and performance.[10] The failure of the Russians to reinforce the fleet in Port Arthur when it had the opportunity to do so was disastrous, but was all of a piece with the confused and divided thinking that had dogged their planning from the outset.

At the beginning of 1904 Russian war planning for their forces in the Far East, both naval and military, had become decidedly uncertain. The general strategic direction originated from St Petersburg, but the terms in which it was now communicated to Alexeiev bewildered him. He had asked what he was to do if the Japanese attempted to land in Korea. In reply, he was told, on January 27, that Russia would shut her eyes to a landing either in the southern part of Korea or on the east coast below the latitude of Seoul. This instruction was decidedly vague, and made no mention of the west coast, where Chemulpo was the most obvious Japanese objective. Alexeiev asked for clarification; on January 29 he got orders which illustrated the extent to which, far too late, the Russian government was prepared to go to avoid hostilities:

> In the first place a landing of the Japanese will be permitted on the whole extent of the western coast of Korea as high as Chemulpo inclusively. In the second place the northern limit of the Japanese occupation will be determined exactly by negotiations which are now in progress here.[11]

This was to abandon completely any hope of preventing a general occupation of Korea by the Japanese, and with it to lose any chance of establishing a naval base on the peninsula that would be so much better than Port Arthur as a point from which to threaten the Japanese mainland. It might, though, have had some considerable effect on Japanese actions – if, that is, this extraordinary departure from what had been settled Russian policy had been made known to them. However, it obviously was not.

At the same time, at the eleventh hour, the Russians had begun to make some preparations. Large numbers of troops began to move eastwards along the railway and when disembarking, were directed towards the Yalu. In St Petersburg the voice of Kuropatkn had begun to be heard again and what he was saying was a stark warning of what war would mean. The resources available to fight such a war were inadequate. With Japan in possession of Korea such a war would, in the end, be unavoidable, and Russia's policy would have to aim at driving the Japanese not only out of Manchuria, but Korea as well, and then would come the problem of invading Japan itself. As the crisis deepened, he wrote another memorandum, bluntly pointing out that Russian interests in the Far East were negligible and not worth the war. Manchuria was not needed either for trade or immigration; Port Arthur had no real value, and could only be defended if heavily fortified, with a strong garrison and a large fleet. The proper

10 Mitchell, pp. 209-210.
11 Corbett I, p 57.

course, he urged, was 'to restore Kwantung to China, sell the southern branch of the railway, and fall back on the original position.'[12] Kuropatkin was a clear-sighted and able soldier, who had demonstrated outstanding qualities as early as the Russo-Turkish war; but the Tsar and his advisers would not, or could not, grasp the need to make an immediate change of course if disaster was to be avoided. Ironically, when war broke out, it was Kuropatkin who produced the basic plan.

Such as it was, he set down in summary form the overall plan in a memorandum written on February 15, by which time the Japanese had already established a force at Chemulpo:

> The plan of campaign should be simple:
>
> 1. Struggle of the fleets for command of the sea.
> 2. Landing of the Japanese – operations to obstructed.
> 3. Defensive operations with extensive use of the action of irregulars until the concentration of sufficient forces.
> 4. Assumption of the offensive –
>   a. Expulsion of the Japanese from Manchuria.
>   b. Expulsion of the Japanese from Korea
> 5. Landing in Japan. Defeat of the Japanese territorial forces. Struggle against a popular rising.[13]

All of that would have been a very tall order indeed. Kuropatkin was a realist; and he cannot have supposed it to be probable that the war would pass through all those stages before common sense brought it to a conclusion. However, getting his colleagues in the Russian government to understand just what they had brought on their country was always going to be difficult.

The Japanese Admiralty was presided over by Yamamoto in his capacity as Minister of Marine. He was not directly involved in the conduct of the war. Responsibility for drafting the naval war plan rested with Ito, as Chief of Staff; his deputy, Vice Admiral Ijuin Goro, took a leading role in operational planning. In time of war, the supreme authority for advising the Emperor was the *Dai-hen-yei*, or Imperial Headquarters Staff, formed by the transformation of the 'Board of Marshals' (composed of the most senior generals and admirals) into the 'Grand Council of War' by the addition of the ministers of the army and Navy, and the chiefs of staff, and their staffs. The Imperial Headquarters Staff only came into existence on the outbreak of war, so the planning process went on under the aegis of the Grand Council of War. It was certainly a mechanism which enabled a wide range of knowledge and experience to be available; but it could also have been unwieldy if it became directly involved in war planning. It

12 Ibid, p. 53.
13 Quoted Corbett I, p. 63.

was essentially a consultative body. The Japanese attributed the harmonious working of the two armies to the existence of the Imperial Headquarters Staff.[14] Since it was the body that actually issued the necessary orders to the various commanders in chief, it did no doubt ensure the compatibility of the directions which each service wished to see embodied in those orders.

There was at least no doubt in the minds of both the military and naval planners that the first objective must be the seizure of bases on the western coast of Korea, from which the necessary operations for the occupation of the country would be launched. The Russians expected that the bulk of the Japanese invasion force would land at Fusan, at the southern end of the Korean peninsula, from where they would have a lengthy march northwards to Seoul. The Japanese told British military observers that this would probably be necessary, and that the most that could be hoped for was that the invading army would get far enough northwards to meet the Russians in the area of the capital.

For the naval planners it was evident that it would be the fleet that would be responsible for achieving the best possible result, and that task depended entirely on the way the Russians behaved. If the Pacific Fleet did come out and make an attempt to disrupt the Japanese troop movements, then a fleet action would have to be fought to determine the command of the sea. This was not, however, the only scenario that must be considered.

In evolving the Japanese naval war plan, the Naval Staff had invited Togo's comments on a number of assumptions which they suggested could be made. The first was that the Russians would concentrate at Port Arthur, choosing a favourable time and place to come out and fight, but that they would not come as far as the south of Korea. The second assumption was that the Vladivostok squadron would be used to create a diversion by harassing Otaru and Hakodate and compel the Japanese to divide their fleet. Finally, it was suggested that the Russians would seek an opportunity to reunite their forces. Since the first and crucial task for the Combined Fleet would be to cover the transport of the army to Korea, it appeared that to obtain the necessary command of the sea regular operations leading to a fleet action would be required.[15]

Togo took a somewhat different view. He did not disagree with the first two assumptions, but as to the Russians combining their squadrons, he replied that it was his hope to decide the control of the sea more quickly. He was relying on the doctrine that it was enough to secure the necessary local control defensively, provided that the enemy was not so strong as to be able to defeat the defending fleet decisively. This perhaps contributed to the curious suggestion made by Alexander Kiralfy in 1943, in an essay on Japanese naval strategy published in *Makers of Modern Strategy*, that Japanese naval thought was quite different from that of Western powers. He

14 Ibid., pp. 68-69.
15 Ibid, p. 72.

contended that the Japanese navy did not accept the idea of command of the sea nor that its objective should be the annihilation of the enemy fleet.[16]

In fact, the thrust of Japanese planning in 1903-1904 certainly did not support Kiralfy's thesis. All that Togo was doing was expressing his conviction that the Russian fleet would not oblige the Japanese by coming out at once for a decisive encounter, so that it would be necessary to commence the military movement without having first defeated the enemy fleet. He planned, therefore, to cover the troop transports by concentrating the fleet at Asan Bay, just south of Chemulpo, with a destroyer base 75 miles to the north-west. Strong patrols would escort the transports on their journey to Korea. In this way, he made it impossible for the Russians to interfere with the landings without first defeating the Combined Fleet. So far as the Vladivostok squadron was concerned, he took a relaxed view, saying 'We should let the enemy do as he wishes at Otaru for a while.'[17]

Nevertheless, it was desirable to obtain effective command of the sea, and to do so as soon as the Russians made it possible by emerging to fight a fleet action, or by commencing operations to take it out if it failed to do so. In any event, a degree of caution was unavoidable, since Togo was obliged carefully to husband his irreplaceable battleships and armoured cruisers. He was no doubt perfectly correct in his opinion that the Vladivostok squadron could be ignored for the time being. The likelihood of its attempting at an early stage to force the Korea Strait was not great, and in any case if it did so it would provide just the sort of opportunity needed, particularly if it meant the Port Arthur forces emerging in support.

It did not therefore take second sight to calculate that the Russians would probably remain in Port Arthur as a 'fleet in being' hoping that their presence would deter the Japanese from launching the expected invasion of Korea. The temptation to remain there, in the hope of reinforcements from the Baltic Fleet, was obvious. Togo had no problem with that; but to obtain and keep sufficient control of the sea to enable the troop movements to be completed, steps should be taken to ensure that in fact the enemy fleet did stay put in Port Arthur. He was entirely prepared to offer battle, but did not expect the Russians to come out. That being so, he considered it better to make sure that they should stay in, thus ensuring the success of the defensive action of the fleet on which the military invasion depended. Accordingly he proposed a dramatic action to achieve this.[18]

This was the delivery of a surprise attack, in advance of a declaration of war, by his destroyers on those units of the Russian Pacific Fleet as might be found lying outside Port Arthur or Dalny. This would be supplemented by sinking a block ship in the mouth of the Gut at Port Arthur. This view of his responsibilities was, as Corbett

16 Alexander Kiralfy, 'Japanese Naval Strategy' in Edward Mead Earl (ed.), *Makers of Modern Strategy* (Princeton, Massachusetts 1943), pp. 457-477.
17 Evans and Peattie, p. 87.
18 Corbett I, p. 75.

wrote, 'characteristic of his unfailing grasp of a combined problem and was in full accordance with our own traditional practice.' Where the principal offensive was to be undertaken by the army, it was inevitably necessary for the fleet's function to be defensive.

It was as late as the end of January that Togo finally made up his mind to launch the surprise attack. Intelligence reports reaching Japan confirmed that the major units of the Russian Pacific Fleet remained at anchor in the roadstead outside Port Arthur, making them a vulnerable target. He was by now convinced that this was the only way to get at his adversary, since the Russians would not venture out to risk a major fleet action. Accordingly he asked for approval of his plan, though adding that he would prefer not to attempt the blocking operation at that time.

While Russia, therefore, was planning to stand on the defensive, Japanese war planning proceeded on the basis that, from the outset, they held the initiative. The principal author of the Combined Fleet's own operational plan for a fleet action was Akiyama, who completed it on January 9, 1904; it was circulated to all units of the fleet.[19] It was published over Togo's name, and set out the tasks assigned to each unit of the fleet. For the 1st and 2nd Divisions, the principal elements of the battle fleet, the objective would be the destruction of the enemy's battleships, armoured cruisers and protected cruisers. The 3rd and 4th Divisions were to deal with the remaining Russian cruisers and destroyers, while the destroyer and torpedo boat flotillas would be launched at what was assumed would be a retreating enemy fleet.

Tactically, the battleships should aim to cross the enemy T:

> The 1st Division will choose the formation of the enemy that is easiest to attack, forming a line against it, a 'T', … manoeuvring so as to put as much pressure as possible on the enemy's leadership; it will make efforts to maintain the T formation with respect to the enemy by carrying out simultaneous turns as appropriate.[20]

The 2nd Division would seek to take advantage of any opportunity to launch a 'cross firing or scissoring attack' on the enemy's battle fleet, either following the 1st Division or taking an opposite course to form the letter 'L'.

In the last weeks before the outbreak of war, Togo was visited by H C Seppings Wright, a British war correspondent. The Japanese Admiralty granted him permission to go on board the *Mikasa*, and Togo allowed him the run of the whole ship. Wright wrote a detailed description of Togo as he saw him on the eve of his greatest achievements:

19 Evans and Peattie, p. 87.
20 Quoted Evans and Peattie, p. 85.

> The admiral has a pleasant face, marked by lines of thought ... The face might be that of any man of studious habits, yet there is something impressive in its expression. The eyes are very bright, like those of all Japanese, with a slight fold at the corners, which hints at humour. The nose is fine and curving downwards, the mouth well shaped, the lower lip somewhat prominent. The head is strong and shapely, the hair fine and cut very close. The face is framed by a sparse beard, turning grey at the chin. The moustache is thin and black.[21]

The plan to launch a destroyer attack was a last-minute decision, but the crews of Togo's destroyer flotillas were not unprepared. Since 1900 a lot of work had been done to determine the tactics to be employed in a destroyer attack launched against the major units of the Russian Pacific Fleet. Exercises had been undertaken which showed that the increased speed and range of the latest torpedoes meant that an attack could be launched at a greater distance from its target. The current weapons had a range of 600-800 metres at a speed of 26 or 27 knots; to achieve a range of 2500 metres the speed had to be reduced to 10 to 11 knots. In Russia it had been Makarov who advocated the greater range and slower speeds; the adoption of this policy by the Japanese navy had not been well received by its torpedo specialists.[22] The actual plans for the torpedo attack on Port Arthur were worked out by the Naval Staff, rather than by Togo's staff. The Naval Staff also worked on the proposal for a blocking operation in the Gut. The plan for this had now developed well beyond Togo's suggestion of one block ship; five merchant vessels had been identified to carry out the operation.

The most important consideration was of course the timing of the proposed attack. On January 30 the Naval Staff asked Togo to report exactly what he proposed to do. In his response he gave a clear indication of what he thought might happen. He intended to send forward two destroyer divisions with their parent ships and his dispatch vessel to Hakko two days in advance of the fleet's sailing and he asked if there was any objection to this. He also said that Port Arthur should not be blocked at the outset, which suggests that he still hoped for a decision after the torpedo attack, and advised that the army should be landed at Asan.[23]

The really ticklish question that had to be addressed was the timing of the Japanese moves. By January 30 no reply had been received from Russia to the last Japanese Note of January 13. Kurino was therefore instructed to ask Lamsdorff on what date the Russian reply was to be expected. Togo's answer to the question as to what he intended was considered by Yamamoto and Ito on January 31, and he was told that there would be no objection to sending the destroyers forward in advance of the main fleet, and that it was believed that he could be given the two days' notice that he required

21 Quoted Georges Blond, *Admiral Togo* (London, 1961) p. 155.
22 Evans and Peattie, pp. 89-90.
23 Corbett I, p. 80.

This, though, was the navy's view. The army wanted the landing to be at Chemulpo if possible. They had also wanted 24 hours' notice before the fleet was to sail. A landing at Asan Bay meant a four-day march to Seoul, where the political situation was extremely volatile. Togo could not guarantee that a landing at Chemulpo would be feasible, so Asan Bay was to be the first objective, with Chemulpo to be attempted if possible.

The Foreign Ministry raised more difficult concerns, pointing out that while from the strategical point of view a surprise attack was essential, it was diplomatically necessary that nothing should be done to attract criticism from other countries before relations had been broken off. The attack must be carefully timed, and Togo should be asked to refine his plan still further.[24]

The original approval which had been given by the Naval Staff to Togo's plan was accordingly followed by an anxious enquiry from Ijuin as to the time that would elapse between the order for the destroyers to start and the actual delivery of their attack. Ijuin also asked what flotilla Togo would use for a second attack if the first was prevented by bad weather, and how soon it would be made. Togo replied that the attack would be between sunset on the second day after the order was given and dawn the next day. If bad weather prevented the attack, the same flotilla would make another attempt.

This response was by no means satisfactory. Ijuin told Togo that the date of the attack must be determined 'by the last word of the negotiations.' If the weather caused the destroyer attack to be postponed on the night for which it was planned, he asked if in those circumstances Togo could use his main fleet to launch an attack on Port Arthur. This, Togo was not prepared to consider. The battle fleet could not be used in an attack on the Russian fleet while it lay under the protection of the forts. To risk the fleet in this way was, he thought, 'the last expedient from the point of view of strategy.' If an attack on the second night was not possible, it could take place on the following night; this, he hoped, would be near enough.[25]

The government's reaction was that it was not. On February 3 an officer from the Naval Staff was sent down to Sasebo with explicit orders, and an instruction that it was considered too dangerous to send the destroyers alone; they were to be escorted by the battle fleet, and not have any discretion about the timing of the attack until they were within striking distance. Politics was now playing a major role in determining strategy.

What was even more serious was that the nature of the attack was being completely changed. According to the Japanese confidential history of the war, the intention was that the attack should be 'a lightning stroke on the enemy's squadron in the Yellow Sea.' What Togo had proposed as a defensive holding operation was now being converted into a major offensive. On February 4 the final decision was embodied in

24 Ibid, p. 81.
25 Evans and Peattie, pp. 89-91.

a positive order: 'It has been decided to give the fleet sailing orders at the same time that we break off diplomatic relations. It is therefore necessary to change your plan of sending the flotilla to Hakko two days in advance.'[26]

At the beginning of February everything pointed to the need to act quickly. No reply had been received from Russia, and it would be good to be able to move before it came. The *Nisshin* and *Kasuga* were well on their way, but Virenius had got as far as Djibouti. There were Russian troop movements towards the River Yalu. On February 3 there had been a false alarm which suggested that the Pacific Fleet had put to sea from Port Arthur; if true, it would have meant that the Russians had seized the initiative. For the Japanese, it was now essential to coordinate the breaking off of diplomatic relations with the sailing of the fleet and the readiness of the army to embark their leading units.

By 6.00am on February 5 the troops were moving to the transports at Hayagi, close to Sasebo, which were to take them to Korea. Sealed orders went to Togo that afternoon. Reports suggested that the Pacific Fleet had returned to Port Arthur, but one report was to the effect that three battleships had again put to sea. None of these were correct, but it was obviously a matter of profound concern. Finally, as the troops began to board the transports, Togo was instructed to open his sealed orders, the decision to break off diplomatic relations having been finally taken that day.

At 2.00pm Togo summoned all his commanders to the *Mikasa*. When all were present, he said quietly: 'We sail this morning. Our enemy flies the Russian flag.' He went on to read the orders that he had received. The Imperial order to the whole of the Japanese armed forces was to the effect that the Russian government did not genuinely wish to maintain peace. Negotiations had been broken off. The Emperor counted on the loyalty and courage of all concerned to take action to safeguard Japan's independence. General Fleet Order No. 1, which Togo also read to those assembled, was as follows:

> The fleet will sail at nine this morning and will steer a course for the Yellow Sea to attack the enemy squadrons at Port Arthur and Chemulpo. Rear Admiral Uriu, commanding the Second Squadron, will take command of the 4th Division, reinforced by the armoured cruiser *Asama* and by the 9th and 14th torpedo boat flotillas. He will attack the enemy ships moored at Chemulpo and will cover the landing to be made at the same place. The 1st, 2nd and 3rd Divisions, and all other torpedo boats, will make directly for Port Arthur. The torpedo boats will go forward in advance and they will attack the enemy on the 8th under cover of darkness. The squadron will follow up the attack on the following day. The salvation of our country depends on this war. We shall work

26 Corbett I, p. 82.

together with all our strength to break the enemy, without losing heart, for the satisfaction of his Majesty.[27]

27 Quoted Blond, pp. 156-157.

8

Chemulpo & Port Arthur

Once war became inevitable, the Japanese Admiralty imposed a ban on all foreign naval attachés and observers, none of whom were permitted to go to sea with the fleet, with the sole exception of the British. In deference to the special relationship arising from the Anglo-Japanese alliance, the British officers were given unrestricted access to the Japanese navy at war, serving aboard warships in the war zone. They enjoyed a candid relationship with the officers and men of the fleet, which enabled them to send back comprehensive reports of all aspects of the Japanese naval war effort, including descriptions of the actions which were fought.

When war broke out, the British Naval Attaché in Tokyo was Captain Ernest Charles Thomas Troubridge. He had been in post since September 18, 1901. Born on July 15, 1862 into a well-known naval family, he entered the Royal Navy as a naval cadet at Dartmouth on his thirteenth birthday. He did well there, passing out second in his term. After going to sea he reached the rank of lieutenant in September 1894, and was appointed to the turret ship *Agamemnon*, at that time serving on the China Station. In 1895 he was promoted to the rank of commander, and early in 1896 received his first command when he was posted to the newly completed destroyer *Shark*. This command, however, lasted only four months before it was followed by a shore based posting, and it was not until August 1900 that he took up his next seagoing command. This was the small protected cruiser *Pelorus*, completed in 1897. This appointment also was not destined to last long. After ten months he was promoted to the rank of captain, and went on shore again. He had been earmarked to take over the post of naval attaché in the British Embassy in Tokyo, and in September his appointment took effect.

In February 1904, as the war clouds gathered, Troubridge was kept informed by his hosts of the developing situation. As soon as he was told that operations were imminent, he hastened from Tokyo to the Combined Fleet's base at Sasebo, after an unbroken rail journey of 36 hours. As soon as he reached the base he went on board the dispatch vessel *Genkai*, where he learned that war had now been declared. He had no opportunity to send a report of his arrival, as the *Genkai* put to sea almost at once. He noted that preparations for war were well advanced:

> Day was breaking as we proceeded out of harbour, and I was able to see that the port was in a thorough state of defence. Seamen were covering the electric lights and falling in from around the light batteries, adjacent to which were the tents in which they had been sleeping. All guns in forts were uncovered. Two torpedo boats from patrol duty entered the harbour, joining four others in a small bay at west side of entrance. In fact the harbour is in complete preparation for war.[1]

The *Genkai*, having put to sea, remained off Sasebo to await dispatches, which enabled Troubridge to witness the arrival of Russian prizes:

> At 10.00am the first sign of war appeared, the *Saiyen*, third class cruiser, escorting into harbour a large Russian steamer of 6,000 tons, of the Russian Volunteer Fleet, a prize, with the Japanese man-of-war flag flying on board of her. Her name was painted out. Closely following was the *Heiyen*, second-class battleship, with another Russian steamer, a prize, about 2,500 tons.[2]

The *Genkai* then headed for Hakko, the advanced base of the Combined Fleet; the name literally means eight entrances. The enclosed anchorage was about 12 miles west of Mokpo. The *Genkai* arrived at 10.00am on February 8, and Troubridge was able to see that a number of fleet auxiliaries were already ensconced in a base which he thought admirably suited to its purpose. After a four-hour stay, during which news came confirming that the Russian cruiser *Varyag*, the gunboat *Koreetz* and a merchantman the *Sungari*, were still anchored at Chemulpo, the *Genkai* sailed again. She headed for Asan Bay to join the the squadron of Rear Admiral Uriu. She arrived in time for Troubridge to witness personally the operations against the Russian vessels at Chemulpo.

Uriu had sailed from Sasebo early in the afternoon of February 6. He had with him the cruisers *Naniwa, Takachiho* and *Niitaka*, together with the armoured cruiser *Asama*. Off the port he was joined by the three troop transports carrying the units which would be landed at Chemulpo if possible, or otherwise at Asan Bay. The 47-year-old Uriu was one of the most highly regarded admirals in the Japanese navy. He had served a term as Chief of the Naval Staff in the years before the war. Now it was his responsibility to undertake the crucially important task of covering the landing of the first wave of Japanese troops in Korea, unmolested by the enemy. As he

1 Reports from Naval Attachés, *The Russo-Japanese War 1904-1905* (Nashville, Tennessee 2003), p. 1.

2 Ibid., p. 2.

made his way towards his destination he was met by the *Akashi* and by two flotillas of torpedo boats.

In addition to the *Varyag* and *Koreetz* in the harbour at Chemulpo there were a number of neutral vessels, as well as the Japanese cruiser *Chiyoda*, which was there to watch the Russians, as well as to protect the 10,000 Japanese nationals estimated as living in Korea. In the first week of February the *Chiyoda's* Captain Murakami did his best to prepare his ship for war without the Russian vessels becoming aware of this. On February 6 he was ordered by the Admiralty to leave port and meet Uriu's squadron off Baker Island on February 8. At 11:30pm on February 7 the *Chiyoda* crept silently out of the harbour, past the British cruiser *Talbot*, and set off for the rendezvous. Once she had reached the squadron at 8.00 next morning, Uriu called his commanding officers together; Murakami reported on the situation inside Chemulpo harbour, and confidently advised that there would be little to fear from the Russian warships. He also brought with him news from Seoul. The Japanese Naval Attaché in the Korean capital had sent disturbing information. His military colleague had asked that the troops be landed at Chemulpo without delay, because the political situation was becoming unsettled. In the harbour at Chemulpo, in addition to the *Talbot* were three other neutral warships, the *Pascal* (French), *Elba* (Italian) and *Vicksburg* (United States).

Uriu lost no time in deciding that the troops should be landed at Chemulpo without delay. The *Varyag* and *Koreetz* were lying at anchor with the neutrals in an anchorage six or seven miles up the channel leading to the landing place. Uriu calculated that if the Russian vessels stayed where they were among the neutrals, they could scarcely attack the transports, and if they came out his force was ample to deal with them. In giving his orders, he stressed that if the Russians appeared outside the channel, they would be destroyed, but they were not to be fired on if they remained at anchor and took no hostile action. As the squadron neared the harbour it was seen that the *Koreetz* was putting to sea; she was carrying dispatches from the Russian Minister at Seoul to Port Arthur. She passed Uriu's squadron, saluting; her captain realised that the Japanese presence could only mean war, and she turned about and headed back to harbour. Whether she fired a shot is unclear; three torpedoes were fired by the Japanese flotilla but all missed, as did the subsequent shots fired in reply by the *Koreetz*.[3] Seeing what was happening, the captain of the *Asama*, which was some 5,500 yards up-channel with the transports, turned and began to bring them back until the *Koreetz* had begun her run back to Chemulpo. The transports proceeded to the landing place and began disembarking the troops at 6:15pm.

For Captain Rudnev, of the *Varyag*, the situation was extremely difficult. His orders were not to interfere with any troop landing until after a declaration of war, and that he was not to leave Chemulpo until ordered to do so. Beyond that, he had no instructions. The disembarkation of the troops was completed in the early hours of

3 Warner, pp. 189-190.

the morning of February 9, and by 9.00am the transports and all of Uriu's squadron except the *Chiyoda* left the harbour. Murakami was ordered to deliver an ultimatum to Rudnev; he must leave port by noon, or he would be attacked at 4.00pm. To the neutrals went letters informing them that war had begun, advising them to clear the port for their own safety. Rudnev went on board the *Talbot* and met the neutral captains, apart from Captain Marshall of the *Vicksburg*. The neutral captains protested to Uriu about the Japanese violation of Korean sovereignty, but privately told Rudnev that if he did not leave the harbour by noon as required, they would themselves be obliged to leave the anchorage. The Russian commander felt that he now had no option but to go out to face Uriu's overwhelming force, and the crews of the two Russian ships hastily prepared for battle.

Shortly after 11.00am the *Varyag* weighed anchor and followed by the *Koreetz* made her way down the channel. As they passed, the crews of the *Talbot, Pascal* and *Elba* lined the decks and rigging and cheered them, waving their caps and wishing them luck. Captain Lewis Bayly of the *Talbot* wrote in his ship's log:

> Here were 694 Russian officers and men going to almost certain death – for no one expected them, or at any rate very many of them, to survive the most unequal conflict – and yet they had their bands playing and were cheering, and their cheers being heartily returned by about 400 British officers and men, who felt very sorry for them, and admired their pluck in giving battle.[4]

It was a clear bright day. The sea was calm and the visibility excellent. The Japanese cruisers were disposed in line abreast outside the entrance to the channel; Uriu had not really expected the Russians to come out. He was working out how to sink them without harming the neutral vessels, and in the meantime had given orders for a close blockade of the harbour entrance. Just before noon, the *Asama* signalled that the Russians were coming out. Uriu gave the necessary orders to his squadron to cut off the enemy, and it was at about this time that Troubridge, in the *Genkai*, came in sight, in time to witness the opening of the action, as he reported:

> At 12:30pm we passed White Rock Lighthouse, and I then observed that the *Asama* was separated from the remainder of the squadron and steaming at full speed directly towards us in the *Genkai*. When she was about one and a half miles ahead we altered to eastward to keep out of her way, when at 12.35 she suddenly opened fire with her whole port broadside, at an object which the configuration of the land prevented our seeing from the *Genkai*; she then turned to starboard and the fire was taken up by all ships except *Takachiho* and *Akashi*. We followed up in *Genkai*, and all the squadron turned to eastward and chased

4 Quoted Warner, p. 192.

> towards Chemulpo into which we saw the two Russian ships disappear, from two to three miles ahead of the squadron.[5]

The *Asama* opened fire at a range of 7,700 yards with her 8-inch guns, and almost at once began to score hits on the *Varyag*. As the range closed, her 6-inch guns opened fire, and soon the other Japanese cruisers joined in. The *Varyag* replied, but to little effect, no hits on her targets being recorded. After fifteen minutes, with her steering gear damaged, on fire in several places and with most of her guns put out of action, the *Varyag* made for the shelter of Yodolmi Island, where she hoped to repair some of the damage. Rudnev had been severely injured by shell splinters. As the *Asama* closed in, and the other cruisers also began to score hits, the *Varyag* turned and made her way back to the anchorage at Chemulpo, followed by the *Koreetz*. By now both the *Varyag's* range finding stations were gone; an 8-inch shell had opened a huge hole below the waterline, and collision mats were put out; she had only two guns remaining. The *Koreetz* had also been seriously damaged.

In Chemulpo, the Russians were sympathetically received. The foreign warships sent off boats with medical staff to assist the wounded. All told, 31 Russians had been killed and 193 wounded, and it was clearly impossible to renew the action. It was decided to destroy both vessels; all the neutrals, except the *Vicksburg*, agreed to receive their crews, and by 4.00pm the *Varyag* was scuttled and the *Koreetz* blown up. Outside the port Uriu, at first not aware of the completeness of his success, was preparing to renew the action next day, but then sounds were heard of the explosions. The cruiser which he sent in to investigate reported that the enemy ships were destroyed.

Troubridge interviewed Uriu and other Japanese officers, finding that no hits at all were sustained by the Japanese vessels, 'which seeing that there were six of them in such narrow waters, does not speak well for the Russian gunnery.'[6] The captain of the *Asama* told him that he aimed to engage at long range to keep the advantage of his 8-inch guns and his armour. He had intended if necessary to attempt to sink the *Varyag* by ramming her, but she had by then returned to a position among the neutral ships in the harbour. Corbett was unimpressed by the way in which Uriu had dealt with the matter: 'seeing how delicate was the situation the affair could scarcely have been more unskilfully managed.' He considered that the Russian vessels should have been allowed to get well out to sea, and there destroyed. As it was the Russian vessels had simply been driven back among the neutrals.[7] However, the job was done, and with the landing completed, Uriu was able to return to the general rendezvous at Asan Bay, where he was soon to learn of what had been happening at Port Arthur.

Togo, with the battleships of the Combined Fleet, had cleared Sasebo harbour at noon on February 6, having been preceded first by Dewa, with the cruisers, destroyers

5 Naval Attaché Reports, p. 7.
6 Ibid., p. 8.
7 Corbett I, p. 118.

and gunboats, and then by Kamimura with the armoured cruisers which made in the first instance for the anchorage at Hakko, located in the Naju group of islands. By 3.00pm on February 7 Togo had concentrated his fleet at Single Island, midway between the Mackau group and the Naju group. In issuing his final instructions he was hampered by the continuing uncertainty which appeared to exist about the location of the Russian battleships. At 4:15pm he sent Dewa with his cruiser division to reconnoitre the area of the Sir James Hall group of islands and at 5.00pm sailed with his battleships, armoured cruisers and five flotillas of destroyers. Cautiously, he made for Rooper Harbour, where he would be only 60 miles from Uriu's squadron off Baker Island outside Chemulpo, within wireless range, so that he could get the latest information. At 10:30am on February 8 he received news that Dewa had completed his search of the islands and all was clear. There was no news of any problem at Chemulpo, so Togo carried on for Round Island, which was to be the fleet's final rendezvous before an attack was launched.

It was something which the Russians should have seen coming. On February 7 Makarov had warned the Admiralty of what to expect:

> Supposing that the Japanese fleet possessed no closed roadsteads, and were fated to lie in full strength off an exposed shore, our tactics ought to consist in carrying out on the first night after the rupture of negotiations the most energetic attack on their fleet. The Japanese will not allow so unparalleled an opportunity to pass of striking us a damaging blow.[8]

In fairness to Stark, he had asked Alexeiev for permission to put his fleet on a war footing, and had been refused. He had, however, ordered the fleet to prepare to repel torpedo attacks, but this seems to have been taken by the units of the fleet as a peacetime exercise, and those ships that did anything about it did not do very much. Even after it was known that diplomatic relations had been broken off, no precautions were taken. All the battleships and cruisers were in the outer anchorage; the destroyers, with the exception of the *Rastoropni* and *Bezstrashni* were inside the harbour. These two vessels were assigned on February 8 to patrol to seaward for a distance of 20 miles, cruising together, with orders to return and report anything suspicious to the flagship. Aboard the ships lying at anchor, a searchlight roster was instituted. Any ships observed were to be boarded by an officer, but nothing was said about firing on them.[9]

At Round Island Togo issued his final instructions. The destroyers were to proceed in two groups. The first group, of ten vessels, comprising the 1st, 2nd and 3rd Divisions, had as its objective the anchorage at Port Arthur. The second group of eight vessels would attack the Russian warships which the Japanese incorrectly believed to be lying

8 Ibid., p. 92.
9 Committee of Imperial Defence, *British Official History (Naval and Military) of the Russo-Japanese War* I (London 1910), p. 57.

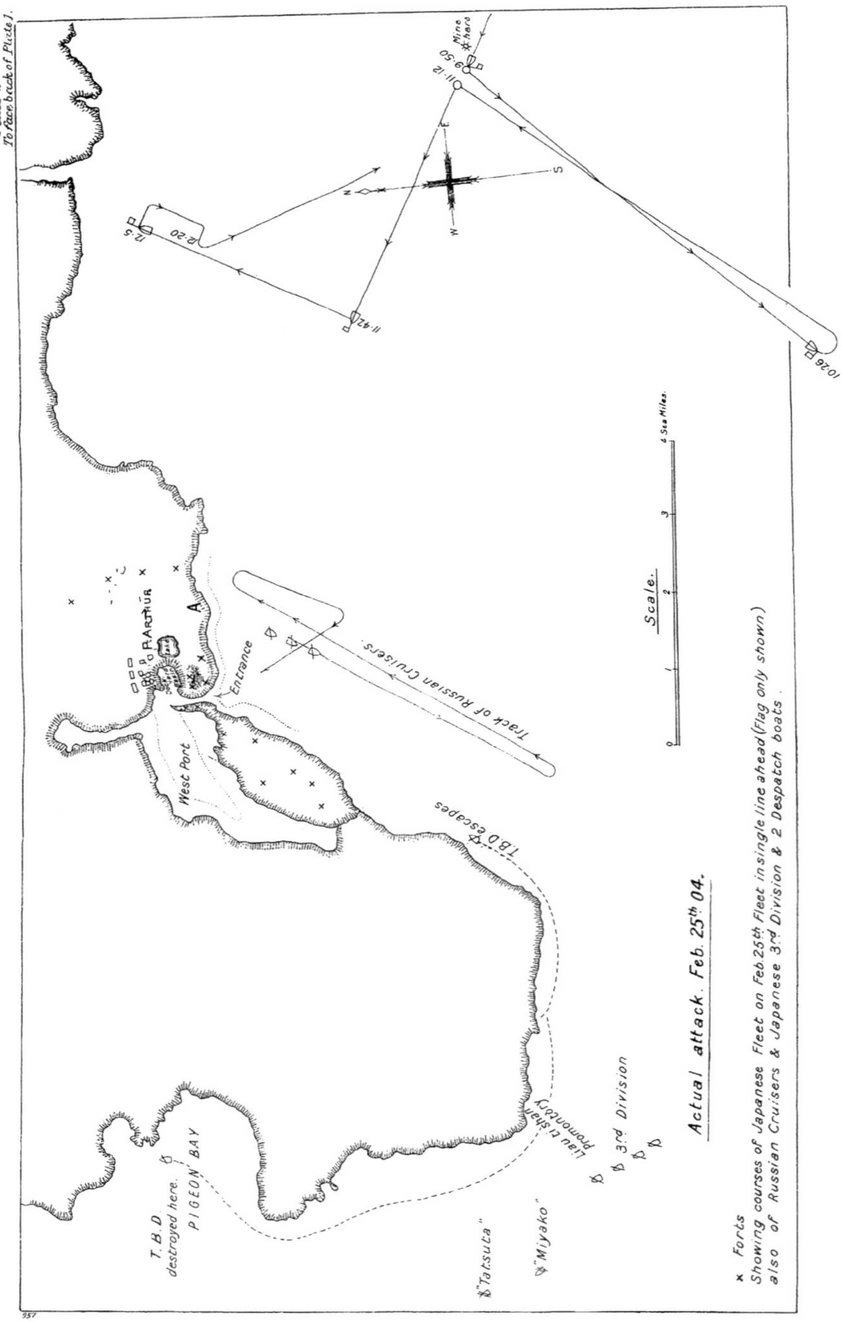

Sketch 1: Attack of February 25 1904

at Dalny. What Togo did not do, however, was to send with the destroyers a dispatch boat which could have reported to him the outcome of the attack; since by his orders from the Admiralty his next actions were to depend on how successful the destroyers had been, the omission was to lead to serious error.

Captain Asai, the senior officer in the group to attack at Port Arthur, agreed on the tactics to be employed with the other division commanders. They would carefully approach the anchorage to identify the positions of the Russian ships and then, between midnight and moonrise, at 1:40am would launch an attack at the first convenient moment. They would head straight for their target in line ahead and then turn, the 1st Division to port and the other two to starboard, and launch their torpedoes. The sea was calm, and there was little mist, but it was extremely cold. Soon after they set off, Asai's group was thrown into confusion when the Dalny group crossed its path, and it took some time to regroup. At about 10:30pm they saw a searchlight, suggesting that the Russians were on their guard, but a few minutes later the light was obscured by thickening mist. Just then lights were seen to port; it was the *Rastoropni* and *Bezstrashni* on patrol, and Asai reduced speed and turned to starboard to avoid them. The Russian destroyers crossed the path of the 2nd Division, and in the confusion the two leading vessels collided, while the 3rd Division stopped altogether. By 11.00pm the light at Liautishan became visible, enabling the Japanese to fix their position. Soon after midnight they were close enough to make out the Russian ships, anchored in four lines. At a distance of 660 yards Asai turned to port as arranged and launched a torpedo from each of his tubes and then wheeled away to the south at top speed. The rest of the division and the leader of 2nd Division followed suit; a number of explosions showed that several hits had been scored. Then two destroyers of the 3rd Division came up, and picking up one of the damaged destroyers from the 2nd Division went in to launch two torpedoes apiece. Then they too turned to the south in the direction of Round Island.

Meanwhile the other damaged vessel, the *Oboro*, which had been joined by the *Sazanami* which had got separated from the 2nd Division, pressed on to launch attacks independently, each firing two torpedoes at 1,300 yards and 770 yards respectively before themselves turning and heading back south. The *Oboro*, the last to attack, was illuminated by all the Russian searchlights and was the target for a hail of gunfire, but got away unscathed. The Russian ships made no attempt to pursue the retreating destroyers, with the exception of the cruiser *Novik*, which followed the Japanese for 30 miles before returning empty-handed. The assailants concentrated at Round Island before, at 5.00am, setting off for Rooper Harbour.[10]

A total of 19 torpedoes had been launched at the Russian ships, three of which found their target. In spite of the patrols, and the searchlights, the surprise was complete. Admiral Stark, who had just had a meeting aboard his flagship with the Chief of Staff and the Port Commandant, wrote: 'The attack was so unexpected and

10 Corbett I, pp. 94-95.

so inconsistent with the latest reassuring information that in my vessel the conviction at first prevailed that one of the *Retvizan's* torpedoes had exploded accidentally, since on this day they had been made ready for firing.'[11]

The ships on searchlight duty were the *Retvizan* and *Pallada*; not surprisingly they were the first to be hit. The *Pallada* was hit amidships on her port side, abreast of the coal bunker; the explosion caused a large hole and the coal caught fire. The *Retvizan* was struck on the port side forward, the hole measuring some 220 square feet. The *Tsarevitch* was torpedoed aft on her port side, abreast of the magazine compartment; the force of the explosion shattered the bulkhead and armoured deck, and flooded the steering compartment.

Nonetheless, all three vessels remained afloat, and got under way intending to reach shallow water. The *Pallada* grounded close to the lighthouse on the west side of the harbour entrance. The other two battleships endeavoured to enter the harbour but both went aground in the Gut.[12]

Meanwhile the destroyer group that had headed to Dalny found no targets. The Japanese were evidently completely misinformed about the possibility that Russian warships would be found at anchor there, with the result that nearly half of the destroyer force available to Togo was committed to an entirely wasted effort. As for the force at Port Arthur, gallantly though the later attacks were pressed home, it seems that only torpedoes fired by Asai's 1st division scored any hits. Once the Russian ships recovered from the surprise and opened fire on their attackers, no further hits were scored. The Russian account of the attack made this clear:

> In examining the operations of this night we see that it was due to our searchlights that the Japanese destroyers found our vessels. We see also that the three vessels damaged were hit by torpedoes discharged before we opened fire. The rest of the attack was ineffective. The Japanese torpedoes were fitted with net cutters which diminished their speed and accuracy. They were moreover fired from a very great distance although the range, according to the Japanese reports, was only a few cables.[13]

Reviewing the attack, Corbett regarded it as having been relatively unsuccessful when all the circumstances were considered: 'Such was the first great torpedo attack in naval history, made with all the advantages of weather as perfect as winter could offer, and at the outbreak of war high-spirited and devoted personnel against an enemy at anchor, demoralised, ill-prepared, and exposed as much as a fleet could be.'[14]

11 Ibid., p. 98.
12 *British Official History* I, pp. 58-59.
13 Corbett I, p. 100 n.
14 Ibid., p. 99.

When Troubridge joined the Combined Fleet, he took the opportunity of discussing the destroyer attacks with Captain Asai and a number of other officers, who were convinced that at least three Russian vessels had been sunk. Asai told him that he had heard seven explosions, while the commander of the *Akatsuki* told him that he had heard eight. Troubridge readily understood how hard it was to form an accurate opinion about the actual results, observing that 'the difficulty of reconciling the various accounts of torpedo attacks, even in peace manoeuvres, is well known.'[15]

Although Togo had no immediate information about the outcome he was soon to get a reliable report from Dewa, whose 3rd Division he sent to Port Arthur to reconnoitre the situation there. Coming in sight of the port at about 8.00am on the morning of February 9, Dewa counted about twelve Russian ships, 'all mixed together in no sort of order,' congregated under the guns of the forts. Two appeared to be damaged. Although he came within range to complete his reconnaissance, no shots were fired at him, and he signalled to Togo that there was a great opportunity to be had if action was taken quickly: 'I consider it would be extremely advantageous for the 1st and 2nd Divisions to come quickly and bombard the enemy outside port.'[16] Although he disliked the idea of exposing the principal units of his fleet to damage at the hands of the powerful shore batteries, Togo could see that he should seize the moment, and turning his fleet towards Port Arthur he led the way to attack the Russian fleet. At 11.00am he signalled: 'We are now on the way to attack the enemy's main force. Go to dinner. The rendezvous is Clifford Island.'[17]

As the Russian fleet came in sight, Togo ordered the Japanese fleet to engage the enemy, hoisting the signal: 'Victory or defeat will be decided by this one action. Let every man do his utmost.' Although obliged to take advantage of the opportunity which the stationary Russian fleet appeared to present, Togo was still not minded to take any unnecessary risks. As his fleet approached the Russian line at a range of 9,300 yards he turned five points westward to pass along the enemy line, and at a range of some 8,700 yards, at about noon, the *Mikasa* fired her first shot. Eight minutes later the Russians opened fire, and first the *Mikasa,* and then the rest of the Japanese battleships responded with every gun within range. The Russians formed a line to the eastward, so the two fleets were on opposite courses. As the range shortened, the Japanese began to score hits, but so did the Russians, now supported by the guns of the shore batteries. The *Mikasa* was the first to be struck, a heavy shell destroying the after bridge. For the Japanese, spotting the effect of their fire became difficult, as their Confidential History recorded: 'Our shells were bursting alongside the enemy and raising columns of water or hitting the ships and sending out black smoke all round. Volumes of it so concealed the enemy that it was extremely difficult to tell the range.'[18]

15 Naval Attaché Reports, p. 16.
16 Warner, p. 198.
17 Corbett I, p. 102.
18 Ibid., p. 104.

By about 12:20pm the *Mikasa* was approaching Liautishan, and Togo reckoned that the moment had come to turn away. The fleet altered course in succession eight points to the southward, giving the Russians the opportunity to concentrate their fire on the turning point as first the battleships, and then the armoured cruisers, came under a hail of fire. As the Japanese turned away the cruiser *Novik*, alone among the Russian vessels, steamed out to close the range. It was as the armoured cruisers turned that the *Novik*, at a range of about 3,000 yards, fired two torpedoes at Kamimura's flagship, the *Idzumo*. Interviewing senior officers some days later, Troubridge learned more about the incident:

> The Vice Admiral and Captain Kato, his Chief of Staff, and also Captain Tchigi, of the *Idzumo*, informed me that of these torpedoes, one passed about 30 yards ahead, and one about 30 yards astern of the *Idzumo*. Both had come to the end of their below water run and were leaping along the top of the water like dolphins, as the Vice Admiral expressed it. Both sank on the other side of the ship.[19]

The *Novik* retired, having suffered some damage. One of her officers, Lieutenant Andrew Petrovitch Steer, reckoned that an outstanding opportunity had been missed:

> The entire Japanese fleet steamed past us in one well-kept line ahead, the cruisers bringing up the rear, always following in the wake of their battleships, then very quietly steamed away, complete in numbers, after they had traversed the arc of fire of our guns ashore and afloat. Any sea officer with the slightest notion of what was meant, or simply possessing some energy, would not have hesitated to fall upon this tail of the line so as to cut it off, which would then have been obliged to turn back. Everybody was expecting this manoeuvre when the signal came in: 'Destroyers to attack the enemy.' This was sheer folly, seeing that it was impossible for the small flotilla we possessed to get unharmed within torpedo range in broad daylight. This signal, which was negatived after some moments of hesitation, before even our destroyers could get under way, had only served to furnish the proof that our leaders had on that day lost all judgement.[20]

Steer thought that with 'the slightest spirit of enterprise, things might have turned out to Russia's advantage.'

He was by no means the only Russian officer to despair of ineffective leadership. Commander Bubnov, aboard the coast defence vessel *Bobr*, observed:

> As our fleet had been ordered by the Viceroy not to go beyond the range of the forts, we were unable to pursue the retreating enemy. While the enemy sang

19 Naval Attaché Reports, p. 20.
20 Quoted in Warner, p. 200.

> triumphal songs and were thus able to stimulate the morale of the whole fleet, our petty officers and men, on the other hand, became obsessed with the idea that the Japanese were unconquerable.[21]

In fact, not everyone in the Japanese fleet appears to have had their morale stimulated to this extent. The purported diary of a destroyer captain, later posted temporarily to the battleship *Fuji*, recorded a good deal of discontent with Togo's caution:

> All the officers are complaining of the Admiral. They say, and I agree with them, that after the attack on the 8th, Togo ought to have sailed immediately with the whole of the squadron to the roadstead of Port Arthur, and when he had got as near as he could, to have opened fire. The Russians were not ready, and it is said that most of the officers were on shore. Togo did not know how to take advantage of the situation; he ought to have sent out to the fight not only his battleships, but also his destroyers. What could have stopped him? No Russian ship could have offered serious resistance. They would all have been taken by surprise, unprepared for the conflict and incapable of moving … It is probable that we should have been able to destroy the battleships and cruisers which were in the roadstead. What a glorious victory! Certainly it would have cost us dear. But why not? To win, in war, one must always risk something.[22]

This was certainly a view held by some Japanese officers. However, although historians appear to have accepted this diary as authentic, it is by no means certain that this is so. Captain Grant, the translator, recorded that it had been translated from 'a volume by a Spanish officer, described by him as a translation from the Japanese.' He had verified the names and dates so far as he was able, but could not hold himself 'responsible for the circumstantial accuracy of the narrative.' There are in fact a number of striking inconsistencies which cast doubt on the work. Although purporting to have been captain of the *Akasuki* (sic), and when saying goodbye to her crew to have observed that he hoped to be 'able once more to sail in her to meet the foe,' he makes no reference at all to her subsequent loss. The new destroyer of which he claims to have taken command, the *Osiva*, appears to have been entirely fictitious, as is the light cruiser *Katzumo* to which he also claims to have been appointed to command.The diary went on to express the hope that Togo's inactivity would not be repeated, commenting that naval history proved that only an attack delivered with energy and determination could succeed.

Corbett, however, rejected such criticisms. The fault was, he considered, in the 'neglect of certain fundamental principles of war, both in the design and the execution

21 Quoted in Ogasawara, p. 214.
22 Anon., *Before Port Arthur in a Destroyer*, translated by Captain R. Grant (London, 1907) pp. 81-82.

of the operation.' Togo had originally planned the attack by the destroyers as a holding operation, but his reluctance to expose the whole of his fleet unnecessarily was overridden, and he was ordered to attack if the destroyers failed. If the armoured ships were to go at all to Port Arthur, they should have been there to attack immediately after the destroyers had gone in. The success of the destroyers would have been the best reason for attacking with heavy ships, and not a reason for holding them off. The principle of sustained continuous effort in offence should have been applied. As it was, the result was a compromise, and 'when the truth was realised the best that could be asked of the commander-in-chief was the moral courage to break off.'[23]

Only if Togo had ignored his instructions could any decisive result have been obtained: 'But this Admiral Togo was unable to do. Clogged with the half measure, he could not rise to the height of casting himself free from it and taking the course which sound doctrine should have dictated.' What he could have done, Corbett thought, was to detail a cruiser to keep in touch with the destroyers so that he learned of the situation earlier than he had done from Dewa. Alternatively, he could have conducted the reconnaissance with his whole fleet. An attack soon after dawn would have found the Pacific Fleet hopelessly disorganised, as Russian accounts confirmed. Togo's caution is, of course understandable; the risk from the forts was considerable. That being so, however, it was surprising that he responded so hastily to Dewa's over optimistic assessment.

As it was, Togo made his way back to the rendezvous at Asan Bay with his whole force, and there met Uriu to hear of what had happened at Chemulpo. In the actions on February 8 and 9 the Japanese had lost a total of about 90 men killed and wounded; Russian casualties amounted to about 150. In addition to the three ships torpedoed on February 8, the *Novik, Askold, Diana* and *Bayan* suffered most from shellfire, but all were repaired quite quickly. Several of the Japanese destroyers had been damaged and a number of the heavy ships, but apart from the *Hatsuse* and *Iwate* none seriously. When Troubridge went aboard the *Asahi,* to which he had been assigned, he heard first-hand accounts of the actions on February 8 and 9, and took the opportunity of going aboard other vessels to inspect the damage. The *Hatsuse* for instance had suffered three hits, one from a 12-inch shell fired from a fort at a range of 8,000 yards. Pieces of the shell had penetrated six steel bulkheads, and inflicted a good deal of damage internally. Troubridge wrote that 'it is difficult to imagine anything more complete than the wreckage made by the passage of this shell, which killed three men and wounded 13 others.' A 4.7-inch shell damaged the fore funnel and ventilators; the signalman on the forward bridge was killed. In his reports of the actions Troubridge commented on what had been achieved:

> The Japanese fleet evidently withdrew on account of the tremendous fire to which they would have been subjected by the shore batteries had they closed

23 Corbett I, pp. 106-107.

> or even continued the action. It should be remembered that they are under the necessity of acting with considerable caution in this respect. They have no reserve battleships and cannot afford to engage shore batteries. On the other hand, what they have done is this: they have demonstrated the insecurity of the anchorage of Port Arthur; they have reduced their opponents' fighting strength, at the present moment certainly, in the future probably. But they entirely recognise that they are very far from having finished with the Russian fleet. They are much perplexed at seeing no Russian destroyers.[24]

Troubridge had evidently picked up to some extent the feeling of disappointment in the fleet that more had not been achieved.

He returned to the subject of the action of February 9 in a further report later in the month, to which particular attention was paid by the British Board of Admiralty when it was considered in late May-early June 1904. His conclusions were of considerable importance, addressing as they did the crucial question of the effective range of naval gunnery:

> What stands out very clearly, is the immense importance of long-range firing under conditions of modern warfare at sea. In the action off Port Arthur of February 9, the ranges were 6,000 to 7,000 yards, at which distance the Japanese fleet inflicted severe damage on the Russian fleet at anchor. In the action of Chemulpo on February 9, between Rear Admiral Uriu's squadron and the *Varyag* and *Koreetz*, the range was from 4,000 to 6,800 yards; the *Varyag* was driven back on fire, and suffered heavy loss in men. Eight thousand yards sounds a very long range at which to engage, but in actual fact, it did not at the moment of action appear a very long range ... The range is well within the capacity of the guns, and it is only a question of practice at long range at large targets to make the fire effective. The Japanese have, in anticipation of much long-range firing, been practising a great deal at 6,000 to 7,000 yards, and the gunnery officers assure me they could have destroyed [the three Russian cruisers outside Port Arthur] at that range.[25]

It was apparent that the events of February 8 and 9 had had generally a considerable effect, notwithstanding the disappointment which may have been felt by some officers. The British Official History observed that the comparatively insignificant losses were no real indication of what had been achieved:

> In the 18 hours which had passed Japan had vindicated her claim to be considered a first-class naval power, and her success had done much towards securing that sea

24 Naval Attaché Reports, p. 11.
25 Ibid., pp. 31-32.

> command upon which the result of the war was largely dependent. The strength of the Russian fleet, from which so much had been expected, was broken, and henceforth it was compelled to act entirely upon the defensive. But the moral effect of Japan's assumption of the offensive was even greater than the material results which were achieved, and in no way was it more clearly demonstrated than by the plain fact that the Russian ships elected to await attack under the guns of Port Arthur.[26]

Lieutenant Newton A McCully, the United States Naval Attaché, had not yet arrived at Port Arthur, but what he found when he did so left him in no doubt of the effect on Russian morale: 'For the Russians, their most serious loss was in their self-confidence, due to the dash and initiative of their enemy, and this was a loss from which they never recovered during the rest of the war.'[27]

It would take a commander of much greater charisma, and much greater ability, than Vice Admiral Stark to make good the damage to the fleet's morale.

26 British Official History I, p. 60.

27 Lieutenant Commander Newton A. McCully, *The McCully Report* (Annapolis, Maryland, 1977), pp. 67-68.

9

Makarov

Although the surprise attack by Togo's destroyers on the night of February 8/9 had caused a very considerable panic at Port Arthur, both the shore batteries and the fleet had recovered enough to put up a more or less creditable performance on the following morning. The gunners in the Russian forts had presented a real threat to Togo's armoured ships, while the fleet had managed to get itself into line, on a course opposite to that taken by the enemy. Once Togo had withdrawn, efforts were at once put in hand to repair the damaged ships, although the *Retvizan* remained aground in the entrance to the harbour.

Steps were also taken to protect Dalny, which was seen as an extremely vulnerable point. The mine layer *Yenisei*, escorted by the cruiser *Boyarin*, was sent to lay mines at Talien Wan, a task which she completed on the morning of February 11. Just as she was on the point of returning to Port Arthur, however, she struck one of her own mines, and sank rapidly, taking with her her captain, who refused to give up his ship, and 93 of her crew. At Port Arthur it was believed that she had been sunk by Japanese destroyers, and the *Boyarin*, with a division of destroyers, was told off to investigate. Unfortunately, she too struck one of the *Yenisei's* mines, and her captain ordered that she be abandoned and that one of the destroyers should torpedo her. The destroyer captain twice questioned this order before finally complying, but both torpedoes missed, and Captain Saruichev left and went back to Port Arthur. The *Boyarin* did not sink until a violent snowstorm on the night of February 12, after a destroyer division had visited her and removed a quantity of the mess room's silver plate. Captain Saruichev was later court-martialled for his 'irregular conduct.'[1]

For Togo, the primary responsibility remained unaltered. His task was to ensure that the Russian fleet could not interfere with the landing of Japanese troops in Korea. He was far from sure that his operations so far had removed the danger. At Asan Bay all hands were engaged in effecting repairs to the ships which had been damaged, and Togo published his plan for the next stage of his operations:

1 Corbett I, p. 121.

> I have considered the reports of the various sections of the fleet and judge that the enemy outside Port Arthur have undergone a heavy attack from our destroyers and battle squadron. Several of their ships have narrowly escaped sinking and have with difficulty been towed into port.[2]

He went on to identify his next objectives, which were to destroy the enemy ships still outside Port Arthur, to blockade that port and Dalny, and to construct a forward base at Asan Bay. All ships, he wrote, 'refusing to flinch in the extreme cold, must put their trust in the gods and courageously carry out their several duties and work to obtain a final decision.' The fleet must, however, remain strictly on the alert: 'The worst foe is negligence. Even in sleep there must be no forgetfulness.'

The task of finishing off any Russian ships outside the port was assigned to Dewa, with three cruisers and two destroyer divisions. Bad weather separated Dewa from his destroyers, but independently they struggled on through a mounting gale. In the end only two made it to Port Arthur, where they found Russian destroyers outside the entrance, which they managed to evade before launching their torpedoes under heavy fire. They then turned away, and made off at high speed. When receiving their report, it was obvious to Dewa that none of the Russian heavy ships remained outside the harbour, and he returned to the fleet. Kamimura, meanwhile, who had been ordered to reconnoitre the harbour, had abandoned this task due to the violent gale, and was heading back to Hakko.

Thwarted in his immediate plans, Togo now received news of a staggering change of plan on the part of the military high command. Emboldened by the apparent success of the naval operations, it was resolved to disembark the whole of the First Army at Chemulpo, rather than to use the much less risky ports of Gensan and Fusan, which would have required lengthy marches. On February 15 Togo got a reply to his anxious enquiry as to what was intended: 'The 12th Division will land at Chemulpo. Their dispatch began on the 10th … We have decided to take immediate advantage of the crushed state of the enemy owing to our naval victories, and are disregarding whatever danger there may be.'[3] In the light of this Togo prepared his next move, which would be to attempt to block the entrance to Port Arthur, to prevent the Russian fleet from emerging.

Meanwhile news of the outbreak of war had reached Vladivostok on February 9. The purpose of detaching a powerful cruiser squadron from the main fleet at Port Arthur had been to draw off a significant part of the Japanese fleet, and it was plainly essential to commence operations at once. Captain Reitzenstein put to sea with the *Rossiya, Gromoboi, Rurik* and *Bogatyr*, with the aid of icebreakers, and by 10.00am on the morning of February 11 was approaching the Japanese coast. Two small coasters were encountered; the *Nagonoura Maru* was sunk and the *Zensho Maru* escaped to

2 Ibid., p. 123.
3 Ibid., p 127.

Fukushima. Finding no other prey, Reitzenstein headed for the Korean coast before being driven back to Vladivostok by intense cold and heavy gales, arriving there on February 14.[4]

On the morning of February 19 Troubridge, aboard the battleship *Asahi*, watched as five steamers arrived and anchored near the fleet: 'They appeared to be old merchant tramp steamers, were but half rigged, and were painted black and dark grey. Shortly after their arrival I was made acquainted with the purpose for which they are intended.'[5] These were the block ships, of between 2,000 and 4,000 tons, deep loaded with stones, earth and other rubbish, which would be sunk if possible in the entrance to Port Arthur. The operation would be led by Commander Azima, of Togo's staff. Five torpedo boats would accompany them to attempt to rescue their crews of volunteers, while twelve destroyers would endeavour to distract the defenders when the attempt was made.

Careful precautions had been taken to prevent news of the intended blocking operation from reaching Port Arthur, but in spite of these some information did reach the Russians; although no special measures were taken, the garrison was on the alert. By nightfall on February 23rd the block ships and their escorts had assembled at Round Island, and the destroyers that were to lead the attack were ready to leave. In his diary the captain of the *Akatsuki* professed to be extremely sceptical about the operation, concluding that the blocking venture was 'impracticable and absurd,' reporting that the senior commander of the destroyers was also dubious, when he gave his explanation of the reasoning behind the attack:

> Admiral Togo has no appetite for a fight with the coast batteries; he wants, at all costs, to avoid weakening his squadron. But something must be done, even if for no other reason than to telegraph to Japan, and his Chief of the Staff has to think out the most extraordinary schemes.[6]

The destroyers led the way towards Port Arthur, followed by the block ships and the torpedo boats. As soon as the moon went down they crept towards the harbour undetected. At long range they launched their torpedoes at the *Retvizan* and, they believed, some cruisers, and then wheeled away under heavy fire. By now the searchlights were sweeping systematically, and both the shore batteries and the battleship could take advantage of their light. As the block ships came forward, they were dazzled by the beams of the searchlights and were met with a hot fire. The leading block ship, the *Tenshu Maru*, went aground three miles from the entrance. The next two kept more to starboard, but as they neared the Gut, a shot from the *Retvizan* smashed the steering gear of the *Hokoku Maru* and set her on fire. She went aground

4 *British Official History* I, p. 64.
5 Naval Attaché Reports, pp. 21-22.
6 R.F.S. Grant, *Before Port Arthur in a Destroyer,* p. 51.

outside the west of the entrance; the *Jinsen Maru* avoided her, but then hit a rock as she was turning towards the entrance, and was abandoned and blown up. The last two, unaware of the *Tenshu Maru's* mistake, believed that they had reached the entrance and blew themselves up in what would have been the correct position relative to her.

Thus the attempt had failed completely. Remarkably all of the courageous volunteers save one survived the operation; the torpedo boats rescued the crews of three of the block ships, and the crews of the other two made their way by sea to Chefoo. Troubridge debriefed Lieutenant Commander Hirose, one of the officers of the *Asahi*, who had commanded the *Hokoku Maru*. He told Troubridge that if all the block ships had steamed at full speed from the southward, direct for the entrance, at least one if not two would have succeeded in the mission. Troubridge concluded:

> If any lesson is to be learned from this operation, it is that all navigation questions should be, so far as possible, eliminated from the mind of the commanding officer, and his faculties thus left perfectly free for concentration on the primary object for which he set out. For in his own case, although many guns were firing at the *Hokoku* from all directions, and though, according to his account, she was shot through in many places, set on fire aft, and all her upper works destroyed, she was actually only stopped by running on the rocks.[7]

Next morning, being unaware of the outcome of the blocking operation, Togo sent Dewa in to reconnoitre. Dewa's impression was that two of the sunken ships were indeed blocking the entrance. He also noticed the *Bayan* outside the harbour, while the *Novik*, with five destroyers was sighted heading for the port. It was his opinion that the cruisers were unable to get back in; in fact, the *Novik* and her attendant destroyers had been sent out to collect a destroyer that had been posted in Pigeon Bay, on the other side of the peninsula, as a night guard, but seeing Dewa the Russian cruiser headed back to the harbour entrance.

Dewa's report prompted Togo to postpone his intended attack with his battle fleet, and instead to send in another destroyer attack on the night of February 24/25. If some of the Russian cruisers were indeed trapped outside the harbour, it was an excellent opportunity to catch them at a disadvantage. The destroyers succeeded in evading the guard boats, and in launching their torpedoes at what they supposed the positions of the cruisers, and then turned away without suffering any damage. The cruisers, of course, had gone, and only the *Retvizan* remained; no hits were obtained. Next morning the *Bayan, Askold* and *Novik* sortied in support of the Russian destroyers, sustaining Togo in his belief that they were still trapped outside, and he decided to combine a bombardment of the harbour and its installations with an attempt to destroy the cruisers. At about 11:45am on February 25th the battle fleet opened fire, and continued a bombardment of the Russian ships, the forts and the harbour, but to

7 Naval Attaché Reports, p. 31.

no significant effect, and after 45 minutes of this Togo withdrew. Dewa, meanwhile, had been sent to Liautishan, where he spotted the two Russian destroyers which had been on night patrol; the *Bezstrashni* got away, but the other, the *Vnushitelni*, was chased into Pigeon Bay and was there destroyed.[8]

Meanwhile, dismayed at the ineffective start to the naval campaign, the Russian Admiralty and government had taken a decision which ought to have been obvious, and ordered Makarov to proceed to Port Arthur and to take command of the Pacific fleet. The uninspiring Stark had been selected as the scapegoat for the events of February 8/9, and as a result had come in for much criticism, some of which was scarcely just. He vigorously denied the rumour that at the time of the destroyer attack he was entertaining guests onshore at a party, and this does seem to have been a canard put about without any foundation. Nor was he perhaps entirely to blame for the unprepared state of the fleet; his requests that it be put on a war footing had been turned down by Alexeiev. Stark appears to have insisted on retaining all his papers, since among them was his application to get the fleet ready, endorsed in the negative in the familiar green pencil of Admiral Alexeiev. With this in his possession Stark could feel confident that he would not be subjected to a court martial.[9]

Makarov left for the Far East on February 17, having three days earlier spelled out to a group of senior naval officers at the Admiralty the steps that should at once be taken. These related to questions of supply, and of intelligence gathering, and to establishing alternative communications with Port Arthur in case it should be isolated. As his train made its way eastwards, he remained in constant touch with the Admiralty; on February 19 he called for the eight destroyers recently completed to be dismantled and sent by rail to Port Arthur, and for forty small torpedo boats to be constructed and sent out in the same way:

> These small boats will serve the port at night. Leaving two hours before dark and steaming at 16 knots, they will be 100 miles from the port at 11.00pm. This will be their radius of action. During the night they will be masters of the sea in the waters allotted to them.[10]

Makarov also pressed for immediate orders to go to Virenius to resume his journey to Port Arthur. An additional battleship, two cruisers and seven destroyers would be an invaluable reinforcement:

> If the squadron of three ships and seven destroyers is unable to appear in the theatre of the war, it will be equally impossible for me to send out a similar detachment for any operations whatsoever. I consider it absolutely necessary that

8 Corbett I, p. 136.
9 McCully, p. 51.
10 Corbett I, p. 146.

> the squadron should proceed to the Far East, otherwise the moral effect would be most serious.[11]

Construction work did start on the torpedo boats, but this was the only one of Makarov's proposals to be implemented.

News that he was on the way had an immediate effect on morale at Port Arthur. When the Japanese heard the news, they took it very seriously. Makarov's reputation was internationally known, and Togo expected it to result in an immediate change in the way the affairs of the Russian fleet would be conducted. Specifically, he expected that Makarov would take out those ships fit for sea in a sortie as soon as he arrived, and this strengthened his usual caution. The 12th Division was by now ashore at Chemulpo, but it was only the want of sufficient transports that was delaying the movement of the rest of the First Army.

In addition, Togo was now called upon to do something about the Vladivostok squadron, which at the end of February was making its presence felt. On February 29 he was ordered by the Naval Staff, if possible, to 'detach a powerful portion of your command and send them to make a reconnaissance in force in the Vladivostok area.' This was asking quite a lot of a commander-in-chief whose principal concern was to cover the transport of troops to the west coast of Korea, but he thought that the Russians would not make a move until after Makarov arrived, and next day he dutifully ordered Kamimura to make the necessary demonstration. He was not, however, to remain in the area for more than three days, and he was to stay closely in touch by wireless.

Kamimura arrived off Vladivostok on March 6. It was his intention if possible to catch the Russian squadron in the harbour, which would be bombarded at long range. He avoided the fire of the shore batteries at the harbour entrance and steamed parallel to the shore in Ussuri Bay, firing into the harbour over the low hills from 1:50pm for three quarters of an hour. The Russian cruisers were, however, lying concealed from Ussuri Bay in the entrance to the harbour, and were untouched during the bombardment. By the time the Russian cruisers began to make their way out, between 3.00 and 4.00pm, the Japanese had already retired. Next day Kamimura again appeared, but there was no sign of the Russian cruisers, and he gave up. On his way back he looked into Possiet Bay and Gensan, but finding no enemy returned to join the Combined Fleet.[12]

Troubridge, meanwhile, had been musing on a subject of continuing concern to the Japanese, which was the possibility of a substantial fleet being sent out from the Baltic. After reviewing the high level of efficiency to which the Japanese had been performing, he was impressed by the way that they had been exercising day and night,

11 Ibid I, p. 147.
12 *British Official History* I, pp. 80-81.

in all weathers, with 'a single-mindedness of purpose and method that only those who know the Japanese well can realise:'

> The result is that this fleet is in a very remarkable state of efficiency for fighting purposes. All the several elements coordinate perfectly ... Wireless telegraphy, signalling, preparation for battle, the giving and receiving of orders, patrolling and defensive harbours, the management and order of fleet auxiliaries, and the thousand and one other matters, which, at the outbreak of war, from unfamiliarity and lack of experience, may cause difficulties, all these are worked with a smoothness and ease that indicate the precision of the teaching and the practice of the past six months. For these reasons it will be a very dangerous assumption on the part of those who direct the sending of a fleet from European Russia, if they calculate the strength of the Japanese fleet by its numerical composition.[13]

He went on to point out that if a Russian fleet made the long journey from European waters, it would be in a very poor state to meet a Japanese fleet operating to such a high standard of efficiency: 'even if some losses are incurred during the next few months, they will still be a most formidable force for any fleet, however constituted, to pass by or to engage.' It was a prescient assessment of the problems which the Russians would have to face.

The army, meanwhile, had been thinking hard about the progress of the advance in Korea. With control at least temporarily assured over the Yellow Sea, it seemed to the military planners that if at all possible the rest of the First Army should be landed at Chinampo in the Pingyang inlet, which would cut out hundred and fifty miles of difficult roads north from Seoul as it carried out the advance to the Yalu. It would not be possible to make the landing immediately; Chinampo was not yet free from ice. On March 2 Togo ordered Uriu to investigate the situation there. He was at this time with the battle fleet at Hakko, but he had sent Dewa to Thornton Haven to check that the Russians had not established an advanced base there. There had been rumours before the war that a torpedo base was contemplated there, which would be a considerable threat to transports heading for Chinampo. Dewa, however, found Thornton Haven abandoned, and headed south to Hakko to report.

Togo had been considering his own need for a more northerly advanced base. Asan Bay had proved much less convenient than Rooper Harbour; he now settled on Haeju Bay, 25 miles east of Rooper Harbour. This large inlet, much further up the Korean coast than Asan Bay, had the additional merit of being practically impenetrable to an enemy torpedo attack. Hakko, however, was not to be abandoned, since it was regarded as much too valuable, marking as it did the focus of the Japanese interior position and also for watching the approaches to the Yellow Sea.[14] Togo now had

13 Naval Attaché Reports, pp. 39-40.
14 Corbett I, p. 142.

placed under his command the ships of the Third Squadron, under Vice Admiral Kataoka, based principally at Takeshiki on the island of Tsushima. It would be these that escorted the troop transports carrying the First Army from its concentration point at Hiroshima to the designated landing at Chinampo.

On the morning of March 8 Makarov arrived at Port Arthur. His reputation as an energetic and scientific officer who had made a thorough study of his profession was not the only asset he brought; his personality was such that he had an immediate effect on all those in Port Arthur:

> Great confidence was therefore felt in him and his arrival did much to raise the spirits of his men. Hitherto the lack of enterprise displayed by the fleet had given rise to bitter recriminations, particularly among the dockyard hands, who complained that they were kept at work night and day repairing ships which never left the harbour. Now, however, it was felt that something would be done, and when Admiral Makarov hoisted his flag in the *Novik* it was believed that the fleet would very soon retrieve its reputation. With him came also numbers of skilled workmen from Kronstadt, whose services were very badly needed; and, on the very day of his arrival, the *Retvizan* was at last floated and taken into the harbour.[15]

Rather than mark his arrival with an immediate sortie of the fleet, as the Japanese supposed might be the case, Makarov made clear to his senior officers that his policy would be to husband the fleet until reinforcements arrived.

On the night of March 9/10 Makarov demonstrated his determination to respond vigorously to attacks by the Japanese fleet. That night the Japanese 1st Division of four destroyers arrived off Port Arthur, but at first found no enemy in sight. After patrolling off the port for some time, they suddenly encountered an unknown number of Russian destroyers near Liautishan. A confused and violent action began. There were in fact four Russian vessels, sent out by Makarov on news of the approach of the Japanese. In the course of the engagement, fought at close range, all the destroyers received serious damage before the Japanese drew off, and the Russians returned to port. Meanwhile the Japanese 2nd Division met two Russian destroyers that had been on a reconnaissance mission to Thornton Haven, and were now returning to Port Arthur. The *Ryeshitelni* escaped, but the *Steregushchi* was surrounded by the Japanese and subjected to a heavy fire. By now it was broad daylight; Makarov, seeing what was happening, at once put to sea in the *Novik* in an attempt to rescue the stricken destroyer, ordering the *Bayan* to follow.

The *Steregushchi* had been reduced to a silent wreck, and the Japanese endeavoured to take her in tow. They had been supported by the cruisers *Tokiwa* and *Chitose*, but these were soon obliged to steam out of range of the shore batteries. At this point

15 *British Official History* I, p. 82.

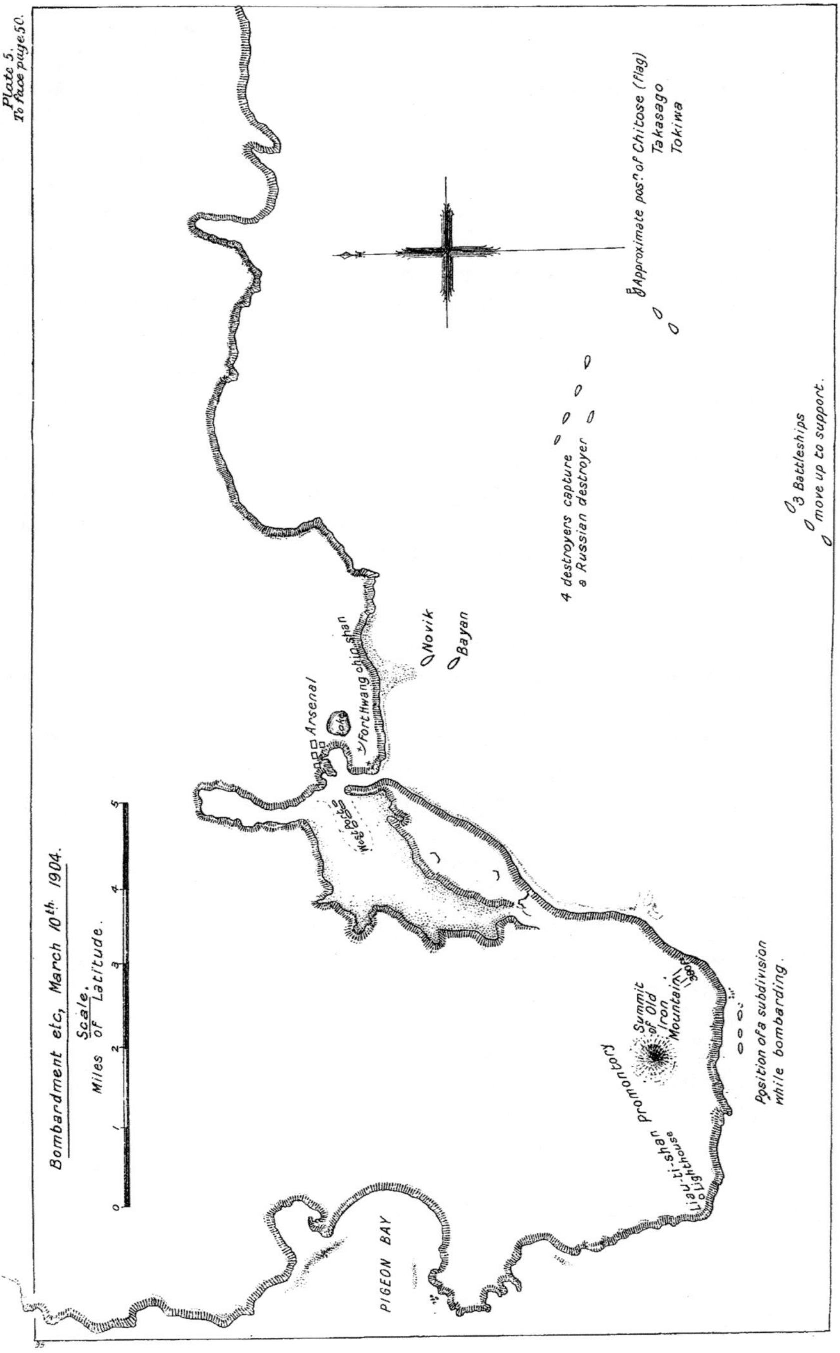

Sketch 2: Bombardment of March 10 1904

Uriu arrived on the scene, on his way to destroy Russian installations on the island of Sanshanfan, off Talien Wan, and he at once turned to engage the two Russian cruisers. Makarov paused under the shelter of the forts, and Uriu steamed off; thereupon Makarov moved out, but by now the unfortunate *Steregushchi* had sunk, taking with her the surviving members of her crew. It was then seen that Togo, with the battle fleet, was approaching; it was low water, and the Russian battleships could not in any case get out from the harbour, so Makarov had no choice but to re-enter Port Arthur himself.[16]

Covering the damaged Japanese destroyers with the remainder of his battleships, Togo sent forward the *Fuji* and *Yashima* under Rear Admiral Nashiba to bombard Russian positions from Liautishan lighthouse to Rotetsu Tau. At first these two ships were masked from the Russian batteries, but soon came within range of the Golden Hill fort, and Nashiba turned away. Togo now took his place with the rest of the battleships and commenced to bombard the harbour from a range of up to 15,000 yards. Although 150 rounds were fired, most falling into the Gut and the inner harbour, only two of the Russian ships were hit; these were the cruiser *Askold* which received only slight damage, and the *Retvizan*, where the coffer dam was struck. By now the tide had risen, and the Russian battleships had steam up and were moving out into the roadstead as Togo began to withdraw, enabling the Russians to treat the operation as having ended with a Japanese retreat.

Once Togo had disappeared, Makarov took the opportunity of leading out his fleet for a short cruise. He had succeeded in getting it out of port on one tide, which had never before been attempted, but he was profoundly dissatisfied with its performance of the various manoeuvres which he undertook. He reported to Alexeiev on the first conclusions he had drawn from the day's events. He had found only eight destroyers and two torpedo boats to be serviceable, having expected to be able to deploy twenty four destroyers. The captains of the larger ships had not previously steamed together in company, as was evident when they steamed out to carry out evolutions:

> The rapid departure of the squadron out of port and its return into port have not been practised, and today for the first time nine large vessels went out during one tide and returned on the next, but the port is by no means suited for this; at the same time I find it risky to leave any of the vessels at anchor for the night in the outer roadstead, while the sea is entirely in the hands of the enemy. It would be extremely desirable to deepen the entrance so that the vessels might go in at any minute, not only with their normal draught, but when they have been holed and are filling with water ... I am especially anxious with regard to the frequent damage to machinery of the destroyers. Every small expedition made by them at night is accompanied by certain breakdowns.[17]

16 Corbett I, p. 151.
17 Ibid, pp. 153-154.

Makarov went on, however, to make clear that he intended as soon as he could to undertake offensive operations. In spite of all the difficulties, he wrote that they 'might now risk an attempt to obtain command of the sea, although prudence dictates that the present time is too early to lay all at stake, and half measures are impossible.'

Alexeiev accepted Makarov's report, with two qualifications. The general action should only be fought if absolutely necessary, for instance if the Japanese landed large numbers of troops on the Liaotung peninsula. Otherwise it should be deferred until Russian troops had crossed the Korean frontier, by which time the Baltic reinforcements should have arrived. Secondly, he advised Makarov to attempt to concentrate his whole force by bringing back the cruiser squadron from Vladivostok. With this Makarov entirely agreed; when the main fleet moved out to oppose a Japanese landing, the Vladivostok squadron should also proceed to sea to join the main body. In the meantime it should undertake short cruises in the seas around Vladivostok.

The effect on morale of Makarov's sally in the *Novik* had been remarkable. Commander Vladimir Semenov described the scene as she re-entered the harbour:

> This return nearly became a triumphal progress. Thousands of men stood crowded on the decks of the ships, on the ramparts of the forts, and along the harbour embankments, and everyone anxiously followed the movements of the *Novik*. The fast little vessel manoeuvred cleverly through the narrow passages in the entrance; but the general attention was not fixed on the ship herself. Everyone wanted to see the proud flag of St Andrew, with an admiral's distinguishing marks, which the cruiser flew at her masthead ...The Admiral had conquered all hearts at one stroke.[18]

It was clearly impossible in a few weeks to make good the deficiencies in training that had accrued over years of neglect, but Makarov and his staff at once set about the task of raising the level of the fleet's efficiency. He abolished all ceremonies is a waste of time, cut through the Russian habits of bureaucracy, ordered constant drills and brought a vigorous energy to the repair of damaged ships. Repeated exercises in leaving and entering harbour reduced the process to a time of two and a half hours, albeit at the cost of collisions. One such, between the *Sevastopol* and *Peresviet* led to the replacement of the former's captain by Captain von Essen, hitherto captain of the *Novik*. Makarov also strengthened the shore batteries, creating a system of fire control, and adding guns which he found unused in storage. Within the fleet he was known as 'Little Grandfather' and 'Old Beardy.'[19]

Following the bombardment of March 10, Togo shifted his advanced base to the new anchorage at Haeju Bay, and began to prepare for another attempt at blocking the

18 Vladimir Semenov, *The Russo-Japanese War at Sea* (London, 2014), p. 70.
19 Mitchell, pp. 218-219.

entrance to Port Arthur. On March 15 he sent Dewa to reconnoitre the port. Next day, in spite of weather that was so foggy that Dewa was able to approach the harbour entrance unmolested, he was able to confirm that the Russian fleet remained in port, and returned to report this to Togo.

Troubridge reported on the considerable advantages which Haeju possessed as an advanced base for operations against Port Arthur, which was only about 240 miles distant:

> It will be recollected that in the discussions that took place between the general staff of the navy and myself, on the subject of combined operations, stress was always laid by the Japanese on the necessity of constantly shifting the base of the fleet nearer to Port Arthur, as the Russian fleet was weakened. My own impression is, however, that except in destroyers and *Varyag*, the strength of the Russian fleet will shortly be as it was before the war commenced. The arrival of ship constructors from Russia, the moving of the *Retvizan*, and the fact that the Russian fleet did not come out and engage on March 10, would rather seem to indicate that repairs will be effected on the injured ships.[20]

On March 21 Togo put to sea from Haeju to carry out another bombardment, arriving off Port Arthur at 8.00am on March 22. The *Fuji* and *Yashima* were detached, and took up a position in Pigeon Bay, from where they shelled the East Basin and the Arsenal. The bombardment began at 10.30 and lasted about an hour, during which about a hundred rounds were fired. No damage was done to any of the Russian ships, although the hospital ship *Kazan* was hit by a 12-inch shell which did not explode. Nor did the Japanese ships sustain any hits, though there were many near misses close to the *Fuji*. Before the bombardment commenced, Makarov ordered all ships to raise steam, and at about 7.00am the leading ships began to leave the harbour, though it was not until 11:30am that the last ship, the *Sevastopol*, reached the outer anchorage. They formed a single line, but remained under the protection of the forts; Togo's main fleet closed up but did not venture inside the range of the shore batteries. At about 1,00pm Togo ordered the whole fleet to withdraw.[21] It had not been much more than a reconnaissance in force, but the overall effect, if any, was further to raise the spirits of the Russian fleet, which had endured the bombardment unscathed.

In what was to be his last report, Troubridge commented on this operation, remarking that it showed the present strength of the Russian fleet ready for action, and proved the increased efficiency of the defences, both fixed and mobile. The range at which the Japanese fired had gradually increased since the first fleet action on February 9; on that day it had been 8,000 yards, but on March 10 it was 13,000 to 14,000 yards, and on March 22 the bombardment had been from Pigeon Bay, and no

20 Naval Attaché Reports, p. 56.
21 *British Official History* I, pp. 86-87.

attack was made on ships in the outer roadstead. While the defence was apparently growing stronger, the options for the attackers were more limited.[22]

22 Naval Attaché Reports, pp. 57-58.

10

Pakenham

Troubridge's successor as Naval Attaché was already en route. Captain William Pakenham arrived in Japan at the beginning of April, and sent his first report, describing his visit to the naval establishment at Kure on April 5. From there he proceeded to Sasebo, and thence to the Combined Fleet, where he took Troubridge's place aboard the *Asahi*.

William Christopher Pakenham was born in London to a well-known naval family on July 10, 1861. His father was Captain Thomas Pakenham, a son of Thomas Pakenham, the Earl of Longford. William entered the Royal Navy as a cadet aboard the training ship *Britannia* at the age of 13; on leaving her in 1876 he was posted first to the *Duke of Wellington*, then to the battleship *Minotaur* and finally to the turret ship *Monarch*. Pakenham was renowned for his swimming ability, which he put to good use in August 1879 when jumping into the sea to rescue a seaman who had fallen overboard as his ship was leaving the port of Larnaca in Cyprus. For this, he was highly commended for gallantry. Years later he repeated the feat when endeavouring to save a man who had gone overboard from the *Calypso* in Kiel harbour.

In 1883, as a sub lieutenant, he was appointed to the *Canada* on the North America and West Indies station. One of the junior midshipmen aboard was the later Admiral Sydney Fremantle, who apparently suggested that Pakenham had been expressly chosen for the posting due to the appointment of HRH Prince George to the vessel. Fremantle provided a glimpse of Pakenham this early in his career:

> He ruled us – one other sub lieutenant, a clerk, and seven midshipmen as a benevolent autocrat, and very strictly as regards personal appearance, demeanour and good manners. In the hottest West Indies weather we were not allowed in the mess without a jacket, while the midshipman in the other corvettes wore, after working hours, a vest and a towel.[1]

1 Fremantle to Baddeley, November 4, 1945, Baddeley Papers, National Museum of the Royal Navy, Portsmouth, MSS 264.

Pakenham's career was following an entirely predictable path, though his remarkable personality did mark him out as different from other officers. One story about him was to the effect that he played tennis in full evening dress, and it is certainly true that he had a marked sense of decorum. Commander Lowis described him:

> In all circumstances he remained well-groomed and immaculate in dress, so fastidious indeed that when wearing white tropical uniform he used two suits each day. His slim, well-proportioned body stood so upright that he gave the impression of being inches taller than his five foot ten inches. The clipped, polished speech would have sounded prim in anyone else. He seldom raised his voice, and every word was carefully chosen and grammatically correct. He was one of the most observant of men, but his whole attitude was one of complete aloofness – or even superiority. He bore, in fact, the burden of a terrific superiority complex which imposed on him a high standard of deportment, good manners and consideration for others.[2]

His reports exactly mirrored his personality as thus described, being both boundlessly self-confident and precisely drafted.

He was promoted to lieutenant in October 1883. He finally achieved his first command, that of Torpedo Boat *No 29*, which he commanded in the annual manoeuvres of 1887. This assignment did not last long. Pakenham now decided to qualify as a gunnery specialist, taking a gunnery course at *Excellent* before joining the *Calypso* in April 1888. He served aboard her for two and a half years as her gunnery officer, though temporarily transferred to the *Medusa* for the 1899 manoeuvres. The posting to the *Calypso* was followed by a further even longer posting to the *Garnet*, which he left in September 1894 to take another gunnery and torpedo course. At the beginning of 1895 he joined the *Sybille*, aboard which he served until August 1896, having been promoted to commander in June at the age of 35. His rise was fast enough to indicate that he was well thought of, as was his assignment to the Naval Intelligence Department, in which he served until March 1901. Thereafter he returned to sea to take command of the cruiser *Daphne*, serving on the China Station. His next posting brought him promotion to the rank of captain in June 1903, and the command of the new *Canopus* class battleship *Albion*. Later that year he attended the war course at the Royal Naval College, Greenwich; this had been established for senior officers in 1900, and eventually evolved into the separate Royal Naval War College. He was graded as First Class.[3]

At this time the First Sea Lord was Admiral Lord Walter Kerr, who would be succeeded in 1904 by Sir John Fisher. Kerr was sympathetic to Lord Charles Beresford, with whom Fisher was embarking on his notorious feud which was fiercely to divide

2 Commander G.L. Lowis, *Fabulous Admirals* (London 1957), pp. 143-144.
3 *Mariners Mirror*, November 2017, p. 473.

opinions among naval officers. For his part, perhaps not altogether surprisingly in view of his aristocratic connections, Pakenham was also sympathetic to Beresford, and he was not part of the 'Fishpond,' as the group of officers around Fisher became known. Pakenham's appointment in July 1903 as Naval Attaché in Tokyo, to take effect in succession to Troubridge in the following year was a considerable mark of the Admiralty's esteem. It took him away from the increasingly heated disputes between Fisher and Beresford; from Japan, he wrote to a relative, Jessica Sykes, that she should do all that she could to smooth matters over. In Pakenham's opinion, Fisher was so clever that he would be too much for Beresford, who as a result 'may ultimately suffer from the disagreement.'[4]

There was a short interregnum between Troubridge's departure and Pakenham's arrival. During this time Makarov had sortied with the Russian fleet as part of his programme to improve its battle readiness. On the morning of March 26, with his flag in the *Petropavlovsk* he led his fleet towards the Miao Tao Islands. At 10,00 a small Japanese steamer was captured by the *Novik* off the northernmost island; difficulty in towing the vessel meant that she had to be sunk. Just then a wireless message from Port Arthur reported that 14 ships were on the horizon, and Makarov turned to regain his base. It had, however, been a false alarm. The fleet was in the outer roadstead by 1.00pm and three hours later regained the inner harbour, albeit at the cost of a slight collision between the *Peresviet* and *Sevastopol.*

Meanwhile Togo had been planning a further attempt to block the entrance to Port Arthur. On this occasion four block ships were to be employed, each fully laden with stone and cement. It took some time to assemble and prepare the vessels, and it was not until nearly the end of the month that they were ready, and joined the fleet. They were to be commanded as before by Commander Arima. Togo now issued his orders for the operation: 'The Combined Fleet will again set out with the sole idea of blocking the entrance to Port Arthur in order to convert it into a lake, and thereby render useless the main force of the enemy and cause them to lose their base.'[5] His intention was that Kamimura and Uriu should remain on call at Haeju, while the rest of the fleet escorted the block ships. As they neared their target, they would be taken in by the destroyers, one division of which should go ahead to clear away the guard boats. The rest would engage the searchlights and endeavour to confuse the enemy while standing by to pick up the crews of the block ships.

The operation was delayed by the foggy weather and it was on the night of March 26/27 that the attempt was finally made. At 3.00am, after the moon had set, the block ships moved forward. They were picked up by searchlights at a distance of about two miles, and a heavy and accurate fire was opened on them. The leading ship nevertheless managed to reach the entrance, anchoring and then blowing herself up. The next, torpedoed by one of the guard destroyers, sank herself in the wrong position to the

4 Richard Freeman, *The Great Edwardian Naval Feud* (Barnsley, 2009) p. 99.
5 Corbett I, p. 163.

starboard of the leading ship; misled by this, the next ship took a worse position. It was left to the final ship, which had fallen behind, to realise what was wrong, and she headed for the middle of the channel; but her engines failed at the critical moment, being unable to go astern, and she drifted to the other side of the entrance, only just failing to block the channel. Four men had been killed, among them Commander Hirose; the rest were brought off safely, about a dozen men having been wounded.

Makarov had witnessed the attempted blocking operation from aboard the destroyer *Otvashni*. As the firing died down, he ordered his fleet to get steam up, and as dawn broke the Russian ships began to emerge from the harbour entrance. This told the Japanese that the blocking attempt had again failed, albeit narrowly, and Togo took his fleet back to Haeju. He left behind him an opponent who was in no doubt what would happen next:

> In Admiral Makarov's opinion the attempt had been so nearly successful that it would certainly be renewed. Had one more stone-laden vessel been sunk between the two most successfully placed he knew the port would have been sealed for an indefinite period. All his energy was, therefore, devoted to preventing the enemy from completing their work. The late attempt had shown that a block ship, even when entirely disabled by gunfire, might carry on with her own way straight into the Gut and there sink. To guard against this two more vessels were sunk directly opposite the entrance, so that the port could only be entered on a tortuous course that would demand an uninjured helm and nice steering.[6]

In addition a new boom was fixed, but was found to be ineffective, and a triple row of mines was placed to seaward of it eastwards to Lutin Rock. On the Tiger peninsula side a further minefield was laid about 1,000 yards to seaward.

Makarov was also exercised in his mind about the extent to which the Japanese might be assembling an advanced base in the Elliot Islands. He did not have enough cruisers to spare for a reconnaissance in force there, so he was obliged to use his destroyers for the purpose, as soon as the weather, which had for the moment seriously deteriorated, permitted the operation. In the meantime he was still concerned about the efficiency of his fleet. When the weather moderated, he took his battleships out to Talien Wan. Although they managed to avoid actually colliding, their performance left him extremely dissatisfied.

Togo, meanwhile, was himself subject to serious pressures. The success in getting the First Army ashore unscathed now gave the Army General Staff in Tokyo the opportunity to plan the next moves, which would be to put the Second Army ashore on the Liaotung Peninsula to cut off Port Arthur and seize the railway, while at the same time landing a connecting force between the other two, to support whichever the Russians attacked, and to take part in the concentric advance into Manchuria.

6 Ibid, p. 169.

This would impose on the navy a further huge responsibility, and Togo could see no way of discharging it other than effectively to block the entrance to Port Arthur. Accordingly, he called for a force of no less than twelve block ships to be prepared. Tokyo was flabbergasted by the request; the result of naval operations to date had given rise to a belief that the Russian fleet was no longer a serious threat. On March 29 two staff officers were dispatched to Haeju to discuss the situation with Togo.

It was his conviction that the changed situation since Makarov's arrival was not understood. The risk of offensive enemy action was in his view now very serious. He understood Makarov too well to accept the complacent view of the Naval Staff. Since his arrival Makarov had had the best of things, and Togo was fully aware of the improvement in the spirit and efficiency of the Russian fleet, and it was his expectation that Makarov would very soon launch an offensive. This, he thought, would take the form of a breakout from Port Arthur to join the squadron at Vladivostok.[7]

It was with this in his mind that he greeted the two staff officers from Tokyo aboard the *Mikasa* on April 3. He convened a council of all flag and commanding officers, including the commanders of destroyer flotilla divisions. Togo was in no doubt where he stood. He had, before his visitors arrived, received a telegram from the Naval Staff setting out the position as it was seen in Tokyo. This pointed out that all available merchant shipping was already committed to essential naval and transport service; to take any of them as block ships would reduce the number available for that service. What was more, if he did not completely succeed at the next attempt, he would probably want still further ships. The question of releasing those for which he had asked could not be decided at once; Commander Takarabe of the staff was on his way with dispatches. When he had read these, Togo was to think over the good of his country, and carefully consider the question as a whole before transmitting his wishes. The buck, in other words, would stop with him.

Neither this, nor another lengthy discussion on April 3, changed Togo's mind. Next day he responded to the Naval Staff; the twelve vessels were essential, but if all these could not be found, then he wanted as many as possible. On April 6 he got his way, though only four had been released by the army; the other eight would come from those supplying the fleet.[8]

Having got his way, Togo could turn to the question of the disembarkation of the Second Army on the Liaotung Peninsula. The point to be selected was left to the admiral and the Naval Staff. The key objective in the first instance was Dalny, which would serve as a base to supply not only the operations against Port Arthur but also the left wing of the rest of the army as it advanced into Manchuria. The chosen landing point was Yentoa Bay, opposite the Elliot Islands. This, unlike the nearer inlets, appeared not to have been mined, and which was in any case well known to the Japanese from their experience in the Sino-Japanese War. It was, of course, still

7 Ibid., p. 163.
8 Ibid., pp. 173-174

dangerously close to Port Arthur, and was certainly within range of a torpedo attack. The blocking operation was, therefore, absolutely essential.

It would be a month before the army was ready to move, and much the same time would be needed to prepare the block ships, so the conference of April 3 turned to the question of striking an offensive blow at the Russian fleet in the meantime. The efforts to damage it seriously by means of the bombardments had not so far proved effective, and it was plain that another means must be found.

Both the Russians and the Japanese were fully alive to the potential of the mine as a naval weapon. Indeed, it has been suggested that Russia was probably the world leader at this time in the design and manufacture of mines, having employed them successfully in the Crimean War of 1854-1856 and the Russo-Turkish War of 1877-1878.[9] Their first use of them in the present war had been unfortunate, as first the *Yenisei* and then the *Boyarin* had fallen victim to their own mines. The Russians had, however, laid a number of further minefields, both to protect vulnerable areas such as Talien Wan, and also to take account of the manoeuvring pattern of the Japanese ships bombarding Port Arthur. One such minefield was that laid off Liautishan, which had effectively precluded the use of this sector as a safe zone for the Japanese battleships.

Pakenham, in his report of April 13, carefully described the plans made by the Japanese to use mining offensively, which was to have a dramatic outcome:

> On April 11 a portion of the Japanese fleet left harbour. One division of the squadron was composed of all the battleships, and in a second were placed two armoured cruisers and two cruisers of the second class. The squadron comprised also one small cruiser, twelve destroyers, three torpedo boats, and a small mining vessel. In addition, the small craft towed two rough boats fitted as mining launches, and covered in with tarpaulins.... It had been decided that the small vessels should drop mines in the entrance to Port Arthur, and that, while engaged on this task, those of their number who were unencumbered by mines should deal with any opposing force. As soon as the mines were laid, the flotilla was to set out to join the battle fleet at a rendezvous a few miles from the port.

It was hoped that the Russians would be lured out by the small cruiser squadron and be drawn into the minefield. If the Russians safely negotiated this and pursued the cruisers, the Japanese battleships might be able to interpose between the Russians and their harbour. This scheme, as Pakenham went on to describe, met with success:

> On the side of the Japanese the scheme was carried out in every particular. The mines were laid and their daring layers returned unhurt. The light cruiser division did exactly as directed. They drew out a considerable part of the Russian fleet, and then fled towards the battleships which were encountered as prearranged.

9 John Crossley, *The Hidden Threat* (Barnsley, 2011), p. 19.

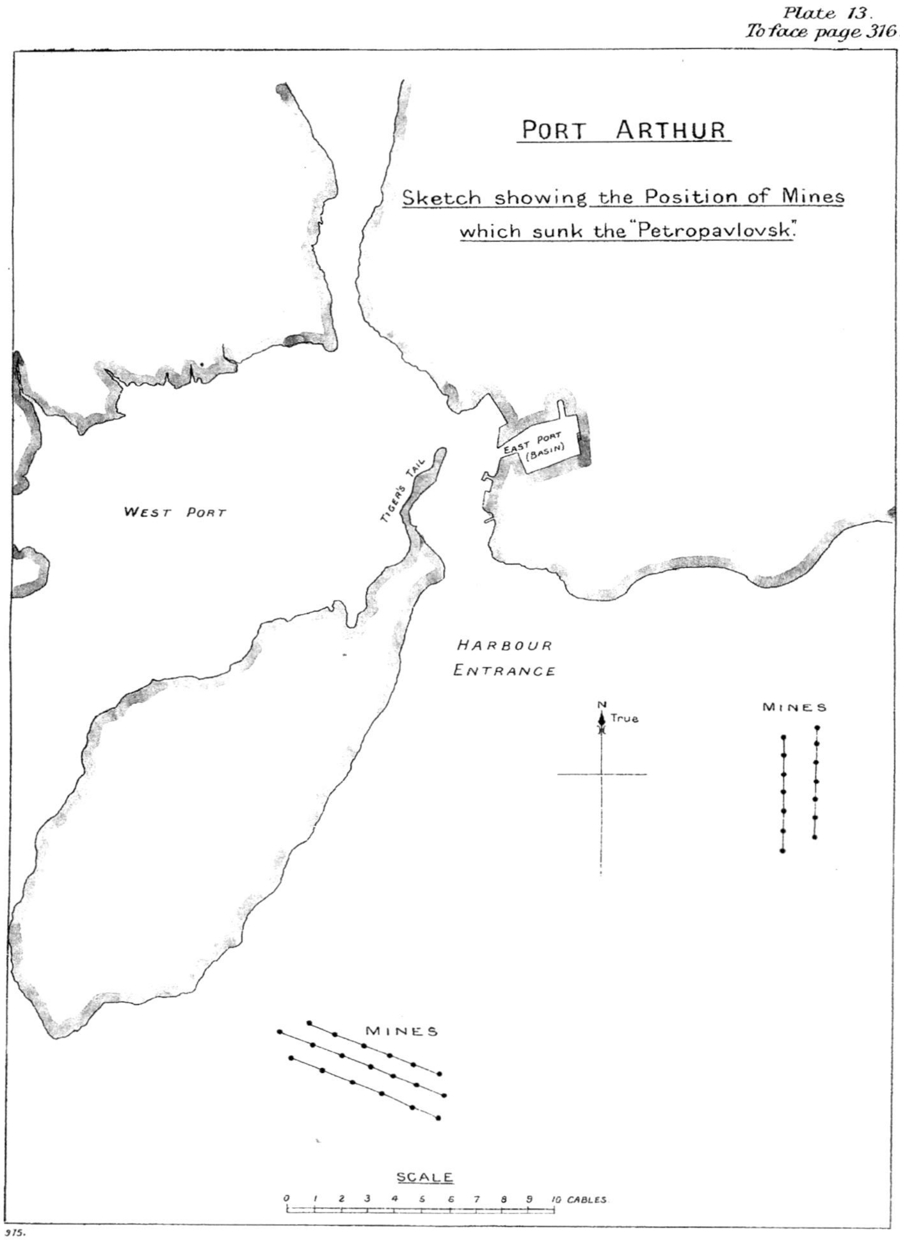

Sketch 3: Position of Minefields

> The Russians, however, after approaching the Japanese battle squadron until colours and outlines were becoming clearly visible, and a serious encounter seemed inevitable, changed their tactics, put their helms astarboard, and made for the entrance of Port Arthur, without undue haste, but in no distinguishable order. In the opposite quarter to that occupied by the Russians, and only very dimly distinguishable through the haze, it was now possible in the Japanese fleet to mark the neighbourhood of the armoured cruiser division. It seems probable that the hasty change of tactics by the Russians may have been caused by a warning from a hill signal station, from which this reinforcement, invisible to the fleet, may doubtless have been observed. By some inexplicable good fortune, the Russian ships seem to have escaped damage from the mines during their exit from the port, but their return was less fortunate. As the Japanese battleships were parading backwards and forwards before the port (going at a speed of 15 knots, each ship flying its two largest ensigns, not firing, although at quarters for action), attention was attracted by escape of steam through a funnel of one of the larger Russian ships. While speculating as to the cause of this, a pillar of blackish water and smoke suddenly rose at her side 200 feet into the air, sank a little, then spread by degrees, and concealed her from view. When the cloud had drifted away, the unfortunate vessel could no longer be seen, and the silence of the Japanese fleet was broken by an involuntary burst of cheering and handclapping, which was, in its turn, succeeded by sympathetic murmurs as the awful probable significance of such an event as that just witnessed, was realised. All agreed that one of the recently laid mines must been the cause of the explosion.[10]

What had happened was that after his short cruise with the fleet to Talien Wan, Makarov had dispatched two divisions of destroyers to reconnoitre the Elliot Islands. While awaiting their return on the night of April 12/13 he had gone on board the *Diana*, which was anchored in the Gut as guard cruiser for the night. He was very conscious of the risk of another Japanese attack, and wished to check that a proper lookout was being maintained. While aboard the cruiser, suspicious objects bearing south by east were illuminated by the searchlights, obviously quite close in. He refused permission for the *Diana* to open fire, thinking that it might be the destroyers returning. Semenov, serving aboard the cruiser at this time, described Makarov's conversation with her captain:

> 'Shall I open fire?' the captain asked. 'Oh, who can tell what it is,' the Admiral replied rather crossly: 'They are probably our own destroyers. They know nothing of night work. Some of them probably got separated from the rest and are now pottering about in front of Port Arthur. They can't find the others, and dare not return into harbour from fear of being taken for Japanese. Bad luck to it!'

10 Naval Attaché Reports, pp. 58-60.

> Makarov mastered his ill humour at once, and added in a calm voice: 'Note the bearing and distance very carefully. If these turn out not to be our boats, we must certainly search the place very carefully tomorrow. Possibly something unpleasant for us has been dropped there.'[11]

At 4:15am Makarov returned to the *Petropavlovsk*. Soon after this smoke was seen to the eastward; this was from two of the eight destroyers that had set out. As the whole group were heading towards the Elliot Islands, after narrowly missing the Japanese at Thornton Haven, three of them had got detached from the others in thick weather, and turned for home. Two of these were the vessels now sighted; the third, the *Strashni*, discerned in the darkness a Japanese destroyer division that had been covering the mining operation and, taking it to be the main body of Russian destroyers fell in behind. When dawn came, and the mistake was realised, the *Strashni* set off for Port Arthur at full speed, but escape was hopeless. After a brave resistance, in the course of which a shell struck an undischarged torpedo which exploded, she lay on fire dead in the water, about fifteen miles from Port Arthur. The Japanese tried to take her in tow, but by now the Russians were alive to the situation, and the *Bayan* was coming out of harbour. The Japanese destroyers fell back on Dewa's squadron that was coming up to carry out its decoy duty in accordance with the Japanese plan, and the *Bayan*, after picking up five survivors from the *Strashni*, retired to the outer roadstead. There she met the cruisers *Novik, Askold* and *Diana*, while the *Petropavlovsk* and *Poltava* were coming out. At this point the rest of the Russian destroyers returned from the Elliot Islands.

Heading for the point where the *Strashni* had been last seen, Makarov, now joined by the rest of the fleet, managed somehow to avoid the Japanese minefield. Visibility was poor. Dewa, having turned away from the Russian vessels, turned back, and suddenly found himself in range. He radioed Togo to inform him of the situation and turned away to meet him. Aboard the *Diana*, Semenov felt uneasy. When Togo appeared on the scene, at about 8:40pm, he was conscious that the Japanese force was nearly twice as strong as the Russian:

> We followed our admiral, who was turning towards Port Arthur and retiring. The Japanese followed us, with the evident attention of attacking. The *Novik* and the destroyers made good use of their speed. They steamed ahead and a little to port. The *Diana* became rear ship. I confess quite candidly that our position was causing me some anxiety. We were steaming as fast as we could, but the distance steadily decreased. By 9.00am we were only 7,500 yards from the hostile leader (apparently *Mikasa*).[12]

11 Semenov I, p. 97.
12 Ibid., p. 100.

To his surprise, no order to open fire came from the *Petropavlovsk*; nor did the Japanese fire. At 9.15 the Russian ships were within range of the forts, and 15 minutes later the Japanese turned away.

Makarov, having arrived abreast of the Lutin Rock, began to turn to the south-west. At that moment, disaster struck. A fearful explosion enveloped the *Petropavlovsk*, followed at once by two more. It was 9.43. Semenov watched in mute horror:

> White steam now began to mix with the brown cloud. The boilers had burst! Suddenly the stern of the battleship rose straight in the air. This happened so rapidly that it did not look as if the bow had gone down, but as if the ship had broken in half amidships. For a moment I saw the screws whirling round in the air. Was there a further explosion? I don't know. It appeared to me as if the after part of the *Petropavlovsk* (all that was visible of her) suddenly opened out and belched forth fire and flames, like a volcano. It seemed even as if flames came out of the sea, long after it had closed over the wreck.[13]

In the face of this shocking catastrophe, Rear Admiral Prince Ukhtomski, the second-in-command, kept his head, signalling to the fleet to follow him as he pursued the course which Makarov had intended to take, across the entrance towards White Wolf Hill, where lay the other minefield. As he completed his turn, another violent explosion engulfed the *Pobieda*, second in line:

> She did not sink, but it was more than the hardest nerves could endure. A wild panic ensued. Ships turned this way and that in complete confusion, threatening every moment to ram one another; there was a cry of submarines, the gun crews began firing at random into the water and the shore batteries followed suit. The danger and confusion were now redoubled. Shell splinters were flying everywhere; order after order to cease fire had no effect; nor was it till the officers by main force tore the men from their guns that they recovered their senses.[14]

Finally, the fleet regained the safety of the harbour, the *Pobieda* leading the way with a heavy list.

The *Petropavlovsk* had taken with her all save 89 members of her crew of 735; Makarov was among those lost. The *Pobieda* was lucky; the mine had exploded under her coal bunker, which deadened its force. The catastrophe had inflicted enormous damage on the Russian fleet in material terms, but much more than ships had been lost. As Corbett put it, the soul of the fleet was gone. Trying to put heart into the boatswain, Semenov told him that he must cheer up the men; war could not be made without losses. The boatswain looked down: 'It's not that at all, your honour. What

13 Ibid., pp. 101-102.
14 Corbett I, p. 183.

is a battleship? They're welcome to sink another one, and even a couple of cruisers. That's not it; but we have lost our head, oh, why had it to be just him and not any of the others?'[15] He spoke for every man in the fleet. Their spirit, which Makarov had so strikingly revived, was quite broken.

15 Semenov I, p. 105.

11

Loss of the *Hatsuse* and *Yashima*

Since learning from the experience of others is the best and most cost-effective form of education, the British Admiralty was determined to take the fullest advantage of the unique opportunity provided by the Japanese to gather crucially important information. The battle experience of the Japanese would have been valuable at any time, but just now it was particularly relevant; there were a number of extremely important design issues under consideration.

To supplement Pakenham's reports, therefore, Commander Thomas Jackson was dispatched to Japan as an assistant naval attaché. Born in 1868 into a naval family, he entered the *Britannia* as a cadet at the age of 13, doing so well that he gained a year, and was rated midshipman on leaving in July 1883. He served on the China Station and later in the East Indies before returning to take his lieutenancy examinations. He reached the rank of commander on December 31, 1899. It was soon decided to strengthen the British naval representation still further, Captain John Hutchison being sent out as an additional support to Pakenham. Somewhat senior to Jackson, he was born in 1862, joining as a cadet in 1876; he became a sub-lieutenant in 1882, and commander in 1897, reaching the rank of captain in 1903. It was clearly expected that most detailed information should be collected, and the reports that were sent back duly reflected this.

On April 13, following the sinking of the *Petropavlovsk* and the retreat of the Russian fleet, Togo did nothing to follow up the advantage he had gained by interfering with the retirement, a fact which Corbett calls 'noteworthy.' Although there was plenty of time in which to engage, all Togo did was to parade to and fro in front of the harbour entrance, albeit at a safe distance, until the Russian ships had all entered. Togo was sticking to his plan, retiring to Thornton Haven to prepare for a torpedo and mining demonstration, followed by bombardment by his two new armoured cruisers.[1]

The destroyer demonstration passed off uneventfully, some dummy mines being laid on the roadstead. On April 15 the *Kasuga* and *Nisshin* arrived to begin their

1 Corbett, I pp. 183-184.

bombardment at 10.00am at a range of ten miles; this was possible due to the improved mounting of their turret guns. It was something that Pakenham addressed in his report on the subject of the bombardment:

> When it becomes known, the range at which this bombardment has been carried out will afford matter for the most serious study to all those interested in the attack or defence of fortified places. Before the effect of this day's operations upon the course of the present war can be estimated, their objective or objectives must be known. The most direct and obvious one, of generally annoying and harming an enemy, has no doubt been attained, as it is improbable the well-directed fire could have been sustained without the infliction of damage at least commensurate with its cost to the assailant... The capacity for high angle fire seems a common feature in Italian ship designs. A person likely to be well-informed states he is confident it is to be found in all, or in almost all, Italian battleships. There has been at least one occasion in the present war where the low limit of elevation to be obtained from the heaviest guns has been much felt, namely, the day the *Petropavlovsk* was destroyed. During the confusion introduced into the Russian fleet by this terrible event, a long-range cannonade would almost certainly have precipitated further disasters. For bombardment purposes, also, greater elevation would be most useful.[2]

Pakenham thought it probable that the gun mountings of the recently ordered battleships would be redesigned with this in mind.

As it was, only the Italian built *Kasuga* and *Nisshin* had the necessary capability, though in fact their bombardment on April 15 was ineffectual. The *Kasuga* fired 15 rounds of 10-inch and the *Nisshin* 46 rounds of 8-inch in an operation that lasted about two hours before they withdrew. Little material damage was done, though it no doubt contributed to the general loss of Russian morale, particularly due to the unprecedented range of the bombardment. Togo, after his usual parade in front of the harbour entrance, sailed back to Haeju.

Another aspect of recent events which occupied Pakenham's attention was the subject of drifting mines. While approaching Port Arthur before the bombardment by the two armoured cruisers the *Mikasa* had twice to alter course sharply to avoid drifting mines; the *Hatsuse* and *Yashima* left the line and exploded three by gunfire. It was clear that the *Mikasa* had been in great danger, disaster being averted only by the sharp lookout kept by the Japanese. Pakenham observed that if the *Petropavlovsk* had been destroyed by a tethered mine laid by the Japanese, then this was 'a perfectly legitimate act of war.' If, on the other hand, the mine that sank her had drifted from elsewhere, 'an entirely new order of ideas is introduced:'

2 Naval Attaché Reports, p. 65.

> Drifting mines will not confine their wanderings to the territorial waters of the belligerents. Indeed, of the mines which the Russians laid in the coastal indentations around Liaotung, many have been seen drifting about Korea Bay, and others have been washed ashore at considerable distance from their original anchorages.... It is thus open to question whether the perils of their use upon navigation do not constitute such a menace to neutrals in the exercise of their right to navigate the high seas in safety (wherever the belligerent forces are not in immediate contact) as to call for an international agreement prohibiting the use of mechanical mines in future wars.[3]

In Port Arthur morale continued to be very low. After receiving news of Makarov's death, Alexeiev had resumed direct command of the fleet, hoisting his flag aboard the *Sevastopol.* For the moment little seemed to be happening, as Semenov recorded:

> Meanwhile, the squadron slumbered on in the basins of the inner harbour. Even the scheme of guard ships in the outer anchorage was abolished. In fact everything established by Makarov disappeared. Precisely the same glorious state of affairs as had obtained before the war reappeared. The flag at the *Sevastopol's* main top mast head seemed to possess the peculiar power of paralysing all initiative, and stifling every word except the well beloved 'very good, sir.'[4]

The announcement of Vice Admiral Nikolai Skrydlov as Makarov's successor appears to have come as a surprise to the fleet. It was estimated that he should arrive at Port Arthur by May 3; in the meantime Alexeiev remained in command. However, by May 5 Skrydlov had still not arrived, and on that day Alexeiev departed rather abruptly for Mukden, fearing to be cut off in Port Arthur, and conferred command of the fleet upon Rear Admiral Wilhelm Vitgeft, previously the Chief of Staff of the fleet.

For the Japanese main fleet, the period after April 16 provided a short break from active operations. Kamimura, however, was to undertake a demonstration against Vladivostok. Although this originated with the Naval Staff in Tokyo, Togo endorsed the operation, judging that in the light of recent events the Russians would not have the courage to come out at present, and he accordingly gave orders to Kamimura to proceed to Vladivostok as quickly as possible.[5] Kamimura was to take four of his own armoured cruisers (*Idzumo, Azuma, Tokiwa* and *Iwate*) together with the *Kasuga* and Uriu's division (*Naniwa, Niitaka, Takachiho* and *Tsushima*, with the *Idzumi* from the 6th Division), and to assemble his force by April 18 at Sylvia Basin at Masampo, before proceeding into the Sea of Japan.

3 Ibid., pp. 69-70.
4 Semenov I, pp. 110-111.
5 Corbett I, pp 188-189

Togo, meanwhile, received orders to initiate the operation to land the troops which were to serve as the connecting force between the First and Second Armies. The need to take the Russians by surprise with this movement meant that absolute secrecy was essential until the landing took place. It was also necessary to ensure that the islands which would thereafter serve as the fleet's advanced base were free from enemy activity, particularly minefields. Dewa, with one armoured and two protected cruisers, three torpedo boats and a dispatch vessel, was ordered to carry out the reconnaissance. He proceeded first to Thornton Haven to sweep it from mines, and then linked it by cable with Haeju, before sweeping the Elliot Islands. Thereafter he was to find a suitable landing place upon the coast between West Tunguz Cape and the Tayang Ho. His first efforts were disappointing; the only location found was barely suitable, since transports could only get to within four and a half miles of the shore. The work was hampered by thick fog, but eventually on April 25, after Dewa had gone in personally in a torpedo boat, he found what appeared to be a suitable beach at Houtushih in the West Bay of West Tunguz Cape.[6]

Kamimura left Masampo and sailed to Gensan, arriving on April 22. Next day he set off for Vladivostok, but almost at once ran into thick fog. The further he went, the thicker it got, and on April 24 he turned back south towards Gensan. As it happened, Kamimura's mission coincided with an operation by the Russian squadron in Vladivostok, which was now commanded by Rear Admiral Iessen. He had arrived there on March 16, hoisting his flag in the *Rossiya.* He was hampered at first by the ice in the harbour, but this had melted by April 8. Since his arrival he had taken his squadron out on three occasions, each time for one day only in order to exercise his ships and crews. By April 22 he felt able to make a more ambitious cruise, and at 9.00am on the following day he put to sea. Thick fog delayed him for several hours, and he also had to send back the *Rurik* because she could not develop full power. He finally sailed to Gensan at 6.00pm accompanied by two torpedo boats which were to attack Japanese shipping there. By 9.00pm the fog was so thick that Iessen reduced speed to 7 knots. Next morning, wireless traffic indicated that a Japanese squadron was nearby, as indeed it was, though Kamimura had no idea that he was close to the enemy. Iessen pressed on to Gensan, where one Japanese merchant vessel was found by the torpedo boats; after being searched, it was sunk by a torpedo. The torpedo boats rejoined Iessen who now made for Cape Chestakov; a small Japanese coaster was encountered, and duly sunk.

Kamimura had left the collier *Kinshu Maru* and four torpedo boats at Gensan. After he had gone, news was received there about a force of Russian soldiers, about 250 strong, marching to Pukcheng. On April 24 between 200 and 300 Japanese infantry were embarked on the *Kinshu Maru* which sailed early next day for Iwon in Pallada Bay under the escort of the torpedo boats. No enemy was found. On the way back to Gensan the torpedo boats stopped for the night at Chahopho. At about 11.00pm the

6 Ibid., pp. 190-191.

Kinshu Maru encountered Iessen's squadron, which was taken at first to be Japanese. The Russians gave all those on board an hour to leave the ship; some did, but many of the troops refused to surrender, replying with their rifles when the Russians opened fire after the hour's grace. The *Kinshu Maru*, hit by a torpedo boat from the *Rossiya*, began to sink; some of those aboard took to the boats, eventually reaching the shore. When Iessen heard from prisoners of Kamimura's presence, he abandoned his cruise, returning safely to Vladivostok at 8.00pm on April 27.[7]

Kamimura returned to Gensan at 1.00pm on April 26, where he learned of the Russian raid. He put to sea next day in the hope of locating the *Kinshu Maru*, but only wreckage was found. He then sailed north to Vladivostok, where he laid a total of 75 mines in three groups. He then returned to Gensan, and finally to Takeshiki. Apart from the mining his mission had been a failure; but Iessen had had a narrow escape:

> It had proved to be one of those incalculable games of blind man's buff which have been so marked a feature in the annals of naval warfare, and the luck had been heavily on the Russian side. With admirable judgment the Japanese had planned their movements at a time when, if ever, the situation must tempt the Vladivostok detachment to venture a counterstroke. But for a fog the two squadrons must have been in contact on the morning of April 24, and the escape of the Russians would have been almost impossible.[8]

On April 24 Togo met with General Oku, the commander of the Second Army, to concert the arrangements for the landing of the troops, which were arriving in transports at Chinampo. It had originally been intended to commence the disembarkation on May 1, but the situation was seen as still being too uncertain. Togo's next blocking operation was much in his mind, and on April 25 he called for volunteers to man the block ships, which had now arrived at Haeju; once again, he got an overwhelming response. An Imperial edict required him to select the crews from among those who had not taken part in previous attempts, which of course had the effect of depriving the venture of the experience gained by those who had gone before. In any event, the movement of the troop transports would not begin until after the blocking expedition had taken place.

The block ships would be escorted by the fleet, but would be accompanied only by a torpedo flotilla when going into action. They put to sea on May 1; the length of the line as it set out was very considerable. It was headed by four protected and two armoured cruisers, followed at a distance of over 4,000 yards by the battleships. Then came the block ships, with the torpedo flotilla on one flank and three gunboats on the other. At 7.00pm on May 2, the fleet dispersed, the crews cheering the block ships as they parted company. Stormy weather that night made station keeping extremely

7 *British Official History* I, p. 99.
8 Corbett I, p. 196.

difficult, while the intended speed of 6 knots was difficult to maintain. As a result, they lost touch during the night, while their immediate escort also became scattered. Pakenham commented on the reasons for this:

> According to British ideas, such a complete dispersion would demand a good deal of explanation. Even the bad weather and unequal steaming powers of the ships would hardly be considered an adequate excuse. But it must be remembered that any form of close order is still unfamiliar to the Japanese, as neither the pressure upon their harbour accommodation, nor the size of their seagoing fleets, has yet forced anything of the kind upon them. The consequent looseness of their formations should not be hastily condemned.[9]

Pakenham was, nonetheless, deeply impressed by the courage and determination shown by all the block ships. Those who had not seen the defences of Port Arthur might, he thought, find it hard to realise what they had achieved: 'In a total of 18, each has performed a feat of heroism which, by itself, would adorn the naval records of any country. Besides such actions, the exploit of the *Merrimac* seems an exhibition of childish folly.' [10]

It had been intended that the block ships, ranging in size from 2,000 to 4,000 tons and loaded as previously with stones and cement, should go in in four groups, with four ships in the first group, three in each of the next two, and finally two which would follow up to lay mines. However, these careful plans went completely awry. Of the first group, only the fourth ship got in, forcing its way through two booms before anchoring and being scuttled. The task this time was far greater than on previous occasions, due to the vastly improved Russian defences:

> Both the previous attempts had been child's play to this one. As each ship appeared she became the centre of a storm of fire that combined with the glare of the searchlights and the heavy seas made navigation impossible. Yet with extraordinary resolution nearly all staggered on through it. The leading ship cleared all obstacles and, torn to pieces, reached the western edge of the entrance. Anchoring deliberately she blew herself up, but she was too far out, and there an hour later she was joined by another.[11]

Casualties had been high. The torpedo boats did their best, but several of the block ships went down with all their crew. One of the two mining vessels, for instance, herself struck a mine, and sank so quickly that none of her crew survived. The Japanese Official Naval History later concluded that none of the block ships went down closer

9 Naval Attaché Reports, p. 77.
10 Ibid.
11 Corbett I, p. 210.

than 1,800 feet from the entrance, and not one had got right into the channel. The reports reaching Togo, however, led him to conclude that the operation had been a success. As the survivors came back they had no idea of how their ships had actually been placed when they went down. Their reports of success appeared to be confirmed by the fact that no Russian ships had appeared outside. Togo remained off the port for as long as he dared in the hope of finding more survivors; as still no enemy appeared his confidence of success grew almost to certainty. As a result he felt able to report that 'the harbour entrance appears to have been completely blocked to the passage of cruisers and larger vessels.' On the strength of this, the operation to land the Second Army could now go forward.

In a history of the war published in 1974, it was suggested that Togo must have been aware that in fact the entrance had not been blocked, and that 'by a deliberate falsehood, he risked not only his own reputation but the lives of the men of the Second Army.'[12] This was a view that was followed in a later history of the war published in 1988. The allegation is a serious one. Corbett, writing much earlier, although he had access to Pakenham's reports, reached no such conclusion; and it may more accord with the truth of the matter that Togo believed what he wanted to believe in announcing that the Russian fleet could not get out to interfere with the landing of the Second Army.

The task of escorting the troop transports fell to Vice Admiral Kataoka Shichiro, whose Third Squadron had previously been based at Takeshiki on Tsushima with the responsibility for covering any Russian attempt to force the straits. This, for the moment, was now Kamimura's task, and Kataoka would have the conduct of the operations to put Oku's army ashore. Rear Admiral Hosoya's 7th Division would cover the first wave of transports, consisting of 30 vessels carrying the main strength of the 1st and 3rd Divisions. In fact, the movement had been halted by an order from Togo on May 3, when he was unaware of the outcome of the blocking expedition. Next day, however, the order came to carry on, and the transports, escorted by Kataoka's squadron, followed the first wave led by Hosoya out of the anchorage at Chinampo.

Whatever Togo may have initially thought about the success of the blocking expedition, he had by May 4 reached the unpalatable conclusion that he must make his decision on the basis that it was still possible for the Russian fleet to proceed to sea. At the end of that day Dewa was ordered to take up his station off Port Arthur, where he appeared early on May 5. Togo, with the battle fleet, followed, arriving in the course of the morning to institute a close blockade of the entrance to Port Arthur.[13]

Before Alexeiev had prudently if somewhat hastily left Port Arthur on May 5 he had summoned the officers commanding the two destroyer flotillas to tell them that something must be done to interfere with the landing of Japanese troops. At this time there were twelve destroyers available; the distance to the expected landing place

12 Warner, p. 275.
13 Corbett I, p. 215.

was about 90 miles, and there were about eight and a half hours of darkness. The officers told him that it was unlikely that the Japanese transports would remain at their anchorage overnight, and they would in any case be heavily protected. They went on to point out the consequences of making such an attempt:

> Even if we were to succeed in cutting through this cordon and effecting anything, we should be on the further side of Dalny at daylight, and unless we were then supported by several of our larger ships, nothing would result except a morning action of the destroyers with the Japanese escorting vessels. Should we not encounter the transports, it was still desirable that destroyers should be protected by cruisers. 'Well,' said the Viceroy, 'talk it over with Admiral Vitgeft.' He then went off to his train.[14]

Alexeiev did not, however, leave the matter there. On his journey northward to Mukden, he next day sent a telegram to Vitgeft from Wafangou: 'Destroyer attacks against the enemy's transports very advisable, and very important for the defence of the fortress. The enemy's transports are all now within the radius of action of our destroyers.'[15] Vitgeft was disinclined to accept the responsibility for ordering such an operation, and called a meeting of all the flag officers and captains. This resulted in a decidedly feeble memorandum being drawn up, suggesting that in view of the limited number of ships available, and the risk from mines, the sortie might mean annihilation. Without support from the larger ships, the dispatch of destroyers alone was pointless and would probably be fatal. Vitgeft reported this to Alexeiev. The Viceroy authorised the preparation of a scheme for an operation involving both cruisers and destroyers; but on the two or three occasions on which it was contemplated putting this into effect, it was found that, for one reason or another, the cruisers could not go out.

The Japanese transports had sailed for Houtushih on May 3, arriving next day at dawn. For some unknown reason the Russians had not mined this part of the coast. When they arrived at their anchorage the transports were drawn up in three lines close inshore, protected by Hosoya's cruisers, and at 5:30am on May 5 a naval landing party went ashore, followed by two battalions of the 3rd Division. As the process of disembarkation continued, it was realised that Houtushih was not as suitable a landing place as had been thought, and on May 9 the transports were shifted some four miles further west to Samchiatzu. The landing of the 3rd Division was completed by May 10, and that of the 1st Division three days later. The army commander General Oku and his staff went ashore on May 8. Disembarkation of the 4th Division began on May 10. Throughout the operation the landing was unopposed.

In his report of May 12 Pakenham reflected on the current situation:

14 Captain Bubnov quoted *British Official History* I, p. 139.
15 Semenov I, p. 120.

> Japan has taken no unnecessary risks hitherto, but she is now playing a bold and dangerous game. Of men she has enough. The weak point of her armament lies in her inability to replace armoured ships as long as the war continues. As her antagonist does not suffer from this disability, it behoves Japan to husband her resources most carefully in this particular; unfortunately for her, in the present undertaking, these are the very ones most hazarded. The exact strength of the Russian fleet is uncertain; surmise would give it at least three battleships and an armoured cruiser with a very competent supplement of torpedo craft, numerous, and so far as is known, efficient. Though such a body could not sustain a daylight encounter with the Japanese battle squadron, it would be superior to any other single section of that fleet now in these waters, and possesses, besides, power and quality to make itself feared by all as the agent in possible raids.[16]

Pakenham, while feeling great confidence in the Japanese ability to protect the transports against a sudden attack, thought that if the Russian destroyer captains were as bold as their Japanese counterparts, any night could produce a tale of disaster: 'At any moment the occasion may produce the man.' The limp response in Port Arthur to the news of the landing of the Second Army shows that Pakenham's fears were in fact groundless.

An important aspect of the situation was, in his opinion, the move of the Japanese fleet's base to the advanced position in the Elliot Islands to cover the landing:

> In its effect this movement is twofold, and it amounts to a permanent change of naval front. Though Russian naval inertness may deprive it of much of the importance which, as a clever strategical device, is its due, it cannot lessen the interest attaching to an ingenious shuffle of the cards, more common in land than in sea warfare. In the latter, the front is always changing, and the position of the base not seldom; but a more complete instance of a sudden change of both, brought about by the seizure of a harbour on the coast of the enemy, is not to be readily found. The Japanese fleet will now derive all the advantages of having a base close to to the scene of active operations, with a line of communication protected by the whole fighting force, and an enemy constantly in front.[17]

The result of the recent operations meant that an effective blockade had been established, although this was not formally notified to the Powers until May 26. Meanwhile Port Arthur had been cut off by land, and it was subject to an unceasing watch by sea. Thus far, everything had gone remarkably well for the Japanese navy; very soon, however, the situation was to change dramatically.

16 Naval Attaché Reports, p. 74.
17 Ibid., p. 79.

The first of a series of setbacks for the Japanese navy came on May 13, when the dispatch vessel *Miyako*, operating close inshore in support of the army, and engaged in minesweeping operations in Kerr Bay, struck a mine, and sank at once. Next day a more serious incident occurred. Dewa had been on blockade duty since May 12. He had with him two cruisers of his own division, *Chitose* and *Yoshino*, but also had been given the battleship *Fuji* and the armoured cruisers *Yakumo* and *Kasuga*. On May 13 the visibility was sufficiently good for him to observe the entrance to Port Arthur, but on the following day the fog was so thick that he could see nothing, and he spent the day steaming slowly back and forth some twenty miles offshore. He withdrew in the evening, instructing the destroyer flotilla that would be watching the harbour that he would later that night return to the base in the Elliot Islands. The fog thickened again at 1.00am and the *Kasuga* lost touch with the rest of Dewa's force for a while. She found them again at about 1:30am, but, as luck would have it, it was just as they began to turn that the armoured cruiser rammed the *Yoshino*. Holed below the waterline, it was soon clear that the light cruiser was going down. The ceremonious delay caused by the removal of the Imperial portrait was disastrous; as the crew were beginning to abandon ship she heeled over and quickly sank taking with her all her boats except one cutter. Of her total complement of 419, all save 97 were lost. The *Kasuga* had also been badly damaged, her ram being bent 29° to port; she made her way back to the base, but the damage was found to be beyond the capacity of the repair ships there, and she had to be sent home.[18]

Makarov had instituted a policy of laying mines not just inside bays and inlets, but out to sea as well. This had, though, been confined to a limit of seven miles or so offshore, and it was not the practice of the Japanese battle fleet to approach as close as this. The movements of the blockading ships were, however, very regular, and Captain Fedor Ivanov of the mine layer *Amur* had for some time been pressing for the chance to lay a minefield further out to sea in the track usually followed by the enemy. Vitgeft had refused permission for some time, but finally gave in, and allowed the operation. On May 14 Ivanov got the weather he needed, and he took the *Amur* to sea, escorted by the *Novik*, unobserved in the low-lying fog. He proceeded to lay a line of mines, from fifty to a hundred feet apart for a mile across the Japanese track some ten miles south by east from the harbour entrance.[19]

The blockading duty on May 15 had been assigned to Rear Admiral Nashiba. Flying his flag in the battleship *Hatsuse*, and accompanied by the battleships *Shikishima* and *Yashima*, he also had with him the cruiser *Kasagi* and the dispatch vessel *Tatsuta*. He sent on the *Kasagi* to look into the entrance; she rejoined to report that all seemed quiet, and sending her inshore to watch the coast he began his patrol across the mouth of the harbour, steering a course slightly further north than usual as a result of the *Kasagi's* report that there was no sign of the enemy. This took the squadron into the middle

18 Corbett I, p. 233.
19 Ibid., p. 234.

of Ivanov's minefield, and at 10:50am, about ten miles south-east of Liautishan, the *Hatsuse* struck a mine with a loud explosion. She began heavily to list to port. Nashiba at once ordered the squadron to turn together eight points to starboard, but it was too late; a few minutes later the *Yashima* also struck a mine. In her case there were two explosions, but for the moment both battleships remained afloat. Nashiba signalled all ships to beware of submarines, and the *Shikishima* began firing into the water. He signalled to the cruiser *Takasago*, which was in the vicinity escorting a cable ship, and sent the *Tatsuta* to call back the *Kasagi* to take the *Hatsuse* in tow. The *Kasagi* arrived at 11.30, but just as a hawser was passed to the battleship she struck another mine which exploded her magazine:

> A deafening explosion was followed by a burst of yellow smoke. Both her funnels fell; her main mast broke off; her upper deck flew into the air, and in a minute and a half she had gone down with her ram high out of water. So sudden and complete was the catastrophe that the loss of life was appalling.[20]

Nashiba and the *Hatsuse's* captain were saved, with 334 of her crew, but 496 men had gone down with the ship.

Meanwhile strenuous efforts had been made to keep the *Yashima* afloat, with the use of a collision mat and constant pumping, and by 12.30 she began to make her way under her own steam towards Encounter Rock. Nashiba, now aboard the *Tatsuta*, had re-assumed command, and he ordered the *Kasagi* to assist the *Yashima*. Just then it was seen that Russian destroyers were coming out and the *Kasagi* took up a position to cover the stricken battleship. At this point Rear Admiral Togo Masaji, with the light cruisers *Akashi, Suma*, *Chiyoda* and *Akitsushima*, alerted by radio to the disaster, came up. He detached the *Suma* to assist the *Yashima*, and joined the *Kasagi* and *Tatsuta* in engaging the Russian destroyers, which turned for home, pursued by the Japanese cruisers until they reached the shelter of the shore batteries at about 3:50pm.

By 4. 20 the *Yashima* had got as far as Encounter Rock, but her situation was deteriorating. Captain Sakamoto set a course for the Elliot Islands, but by 5,00pm it was clear that she could not survive. She anchored about five miles ENE of Encounter Rock and after the Imperial portrait was duly taken aboard the *Suma*, the crew took to the boats. The cruiser then took them back to the base, while the *Kasagi* remained by the doomed ship until dark. During the night she went down. Nashiba's troubles were still not over; as the *Tatsuta* returned to the anchorage she ran aground, and was not refloated until June 12.

In Port Arthur the arrival of Nashiba's squadron off the port had been noted, but the appearance of blockading ships no longer occasioned much remark. Semenov was at breakfast, when he heard a commotion:

20 Ibid., p. 235.

> Suddenly we heard the sound of people running about on deck, some loud exclamations, and then what sounded like distant shouting, which penetrated to all decks below. 'The Japanese are on top of our mines!' the quartermaster shouted at me, instead of making a proper report. There was great excitement on deck. The men went aloft. Everyone tried to get up as high as possible, in hopes of getting a view of something over Golden Hill, Lighthouse Hill, and Tiger Hill. The gunnery lieutenant forgot his rheumatism and went into the fore top. The sub lieutenants climbed higher still. Loud cheering was suddenly heard from Golden Hill and the adjoining batteries. 'Another one! Another one! She has sunk!' shouted our people from aloft.[21]

Semenov concluded that the Russian fleet could have sortied, and if it had, the rest of the Japanese squadron could have been destroyed, arguing that 'the brilliant, the only favourable opportunity of the whole war was missed.' He rejected the official view that this would have been impossible, pointing out that the battleships *Peresviet, Poltava* and *Sevastopol* could have gone out, with the *Bayan* and the cruisers *Askold, Pallada, Diana* and *Novik*, as well as the destroyers. Unfortunately, these vessels were not ready for sea because, Semenov thought, 'those in command at Port Arthur had, however, already lost all faith in the possibility of such a success.'

Pakenham, aboard the battleship *Asahi* with the rest of the Combined Fleet, had not been present to witness the disaster. His report, dated May 19, was delayed at the request of the Japanese Naval Staff, who hoped to keep secret the loss of the *Yashima*, which had gone down out of sight of the enemy. In this, they were successful, as the result of taking immense pains to conceal the news from the public. Pakenham considered that the loss of the two battleships was of huge significance. It provided conclusive evidence 'of the preponderating influence certain weapons must be henceforth expected to exercise in the areas best adapted to the development of their powers.' He went on:

> At a single blow, and without corresponding loss to the enemy, Japan finds herself deprived of one third of her prime fighting force. Great as is the material loss, it cannot for a moment be compared with the possibilities of ultimate strategic injury it infers, and in its greatness are merged minor misfortunes, themselves sufficient in ordinary times to cause a general dissension and recrimination. The national mettle is about to be severely tested.[22]

Pakenham also devoted a lot of his report to the morality of minelaying as a weapon:

21 Semenov I, pp. 126-127.
22 Naval Attaché Reports, p. 325.

> Reference to the noxious character of the mechanical mine becomes wearisome, but in the present instance it should be remarked that the question appears under a new aspect. Hitherto, in blaming the Russians for filling these seas with drifting mines, their competence as miners has been impeached, but they have not been charged with the wilful commission of a crime against national comity. When, however, it comes to laying mines in a public fairway, on a vague chance of catching an enemy rather than a neutral, the action shows such cynical indifference to the general weal as to merit the severest condemnation … It is a pity that a bold and clever device, crowned with the success that may be properly described as appalling, should have contained in its execution an element so deserving of public reprobation.[23]

The British Admiralty had prior to the war become increasingly doubtful about the effectiveness of the mine as a weapon, and in 1903 took the decision to abandon the use of independent mines altogether. It was reckoned that they were ineffective in defending a fleet in harbour against torpedo attacks; the official position was that 'the increased range and accuracy of heavy guns made them unnecessary.'[24] The moral issues raised by Pakenham do not appear to have played any part in this decision which, following his reports, plainly must be revoked. Orders were soon placed for the construction of 1,000 'Naval Spherical Mines', although a penny-pinching attitude on the part of the Admiralty led to the design actually adopted proving extremely unsatisfactory.

The loss of the two battleships came as a fearful shock to the Naval Staff, whose Chief wrote to Togo to urge the most extreme caution upon him:

> The duties of the navy during the coming combined operations with the army are very heavy and dangerous, and the work of the squadron directly detached for it will be difficult. Moreover, though the accidents of the last few days could not have been prevented, they will give the enemy occasion for recovering their spirit and they will probably seize the opportunity for some definite course of action. I earnestly beg, therefore, that if as the result of the last blocking expedition there is no fear of the enemy's large ships coming out, you will watch the entrance of the port with light fast vessels capable of maintaining communications with the main fleet.[25]

Togo of course was perfectly aware of the heightened need to husband his remaining battleships, but he was also now aware that the entrance was not effectively blocked, at least to cruisers, the *Novik* having emerged in support of the Russian destroyers

23 Ibid., pp 328-329.
24 Crossley, p. 25.
25 Corbett I, p. 240.

on May 15. Safeguarding the battle fleet was his highest priority, and if this meant abandoning the close blockade of Port Arthur, then so be it. The battleships remained at anchor in the Elliot Islands, and Dewa assumed responsibility for watching the harbour entrance with his cruisers. Togo also ensured that the approaches to the port should be regularly mined, ensuring that sweeping would be necessary before the Russians came out, which would delay their exit long enough for the battle fleet to be ready to meet them.

Pondering the effect on his hosts of the disasters of May 15, Pakenham had something to say about the role of the Press in moulding public opinion in Japan, which he contrasted favourably with that in Western nations:

> In fact the plane of national thought has not yet been debased to the level it occupies in civilisations on the European model, and the fortunate consequences to the Japanese have been shown in almost every action of this war, where it has been made evident that the same standards of military honour prevail among the humblest of their troops as it is customary to suppose obtained in other countries in more heroic ages. It is this chivalrous conception of the insignificance of the unit that has enabled Japan to bear without a murmur, almost without a word, a blow that would have shaken any other country to its foundations and that would have caused the Western Press to exhaust itself in hysterical superlatives.[26]

Pakenham had a very low opinion of the fourth estate.

26 Naval Attaché Reports, p. 331.

12

Vitgeft

On land the campaign of the Japanese armies had been making good progress. The three divisions of the First Army, under General Kuroki, had moved up to the River Yalu. The operation to cross the river was timed to coincide with a landing of General Oku's Second Army. The crossing was opposed by the Eastern Force, commanded by General Zasulich, which had taken up an extended position covering a front of twenty miles, from a point four miles west of Antung to a bend in the Ai Ho, a tributary of the Yalu. Zasulich had a total force of about 16,000 infantry and 2,350 cavalry with 48 field guns, eight mountain guns and six horse artillery. Kuropatkin, who had by now assumed command of the Russian armies in Manchuria, reminded Zasulich that his position on the Yalu was not intended 'for a decisive action with the enemy in decisive numbers.' This injunction he repeated on April 25. However, while Kuropatkin required Zasulich to fight only a rearguard action, Alexeiev seems to have urged him to offer a vigorous resistance.[1]

Kuroki's attack went in at dawn on May 1. In spite of a determined resistance along part of the Russian front, Zasulich was compelled to retreat, having suffered a total of some 3,000 casualties compared to about 1,000 Japanese. 21 guns were captured by the First Army together with a large number of ammunition wagons. The moral effect of the Japanese victory was considerable, while it meant that the army's first objective, the occupation of Korea, was assured.

Once safely ashore, the Second Army made rapid progress towards the isolation of Port Arthur. By May 6 communications with the fortress were temporarily interrupted, though soon after re-established. The Japanese did not intend to destroy the railway, as they proposed to make use of it themselves in due course. At this time the difference of opinion between Kuropatkin and Alexeiev as to the correct strategic course to follow was especially pronounced. Kuropatkin's view was that he should concentrate his troops at Harbin until the organisation of his force was completed, which would involve the evacuation of Liaoyang. This seems to have begun, but was

1 *British Official History* I, p. 112.

then halted. Alexeiev's policy was to conduct a more aggressive campaign, and it was after his arrival on May 6 from Port Arthur that the evacuation was cancelled. On May 16 Oku's 1st Division and a part of his 4th Division defeated part of the 4th East Siberian Rifle Division at Shihsanlitai, as a result of which the Kwantung peninsula was isolated, and communications with Port Arthur had been finally severed.

It was the Russian intention to hold up any advance on Port Arthur by the defence of a position at Nan Shan on the isthmus separating the bay of Talien on the east from that of Chin-chou on the west. This position consisted of a roughly circular group of hills about a mile in diameter, and was in most respects extremely strong. The total width of the isthmus, depending on the tide, was from 4,500 to 6,000 yards. On May 26, supported by the gunfire of the gunboats *Tsukushi, Heiyen, Akagi* and *Chokai*, and a flotilla of torpedo boats, Oku launched his attack on the Nan Shan position. During the night of May 25/26 there was a heavy thunderstorm which, with high winds, made movement very difficult. Overall command of the Russian forces in Chinchou and on the Nan Shan heights was held by General Fock. The trenches and redoubts on the heights were held by the 5th East Siberian Rifle Regiment under Colonel Tretyakov. During the battle the Russian gunboat *Bobr* offered considerable support by harassing the left and rear of the Japanese advance. For a long time, in spite of repeated assaults, the Japanese made little progress, but Oku persevered, and after a turning movement by his 4th Division Tretyakov's men were forced back, and the Russian position began to crumble. The British Official History summed up the outcome:

> The battle had lasted 14 hours, and had been won by nothing but hard fighting. The ruthless determination of the Japanese commanders to carry out their task regardless of loss, the refusal of the infantry to admit the possibility of failure, and the boldness of the artillery support were characteristics of the Japanese fighting. Yet the sacrifice might perhaps have been unavailing had the Russian commander put his whole strength into the fight and employed, in a vigorous counterstroke, some of the four regiments which he kept at his disposal, and were never fully engaged.[2]

Casualties were extremely heavy on both sides; of the 3,000 odd Russian troops actually engaged, over 700 were buried on the field of battle; 23 prisoners were taken but the number of wounded is not recorded. The total Japanese losses amounted to 4,885 men killed and wounded.

Kuropatkin appears to have discouraged General Stoessel, the military commander at Port Arthur, from engaging in a prolonged action at Nan Shan, writing to him on May 17: 'It is most important to get Fock back within the Port Arthur garrison in good time.'[3] After the battle the Russians evacuated Dalny and fell back towards Port

2 Ibid., p. 167.
3 Quoted J.N. Westwood, *Russia Against Japan 1904-1905* (New York, 1986), p. 166.

1 William Pakenham, British Naval Attaché

2 Julian Corbett, naval historian

3 Ernest Troubridge, British Naval Attaché

4 Thomas Jackson, Assistant British Naval Attaché

5 Admiral Togo, Japanese Commander in Chief

6 Admiral Yamamoto, Japanese Minister of Marine

7 Admiral Kamimura, commander of Japanese armoured cruiser squadron

8 Admiral Ito, Chief of Japanese Naval Staff

9 Admiral Makarov, Commander in Chief of Russian Pacific Fleet

10 General Kuropatkin, Russian War Minister

11 Admiral Rozhestvenski, Commander in Chief of Russian Second Pacific Squadron

12 Japanese battleship *Mikasa*, flagship of Admiral Togo

13 Ill-fated Japanese battleship *Hatsuse*

14 Japanese battleship *Shikishima*

15 Japanese battleship *Fuji*

16 Japanese armoured cruiser *Nisshin*

17 Japanese armoured cruiser *Idzumo*

18 Japanese light cruiser *Yoshino*

19 Japanese battleships opening fire

20 Russian armoured cruiser *Varyag*

21 Russian battleship *Petropavlovsk*, flagship of Admiral Makarov

22 Russian battleship *Peresviet*

23 Russian battleship *Tsarevitch*, flagship of Admiral Vitgeft

24 Russian battleship *Oslyabya*

25 Russian armoured cruiser *Gromoboi*

26 Russian light cruiser *Askold*

27 Russian armoured cruiser *Rurik* sinking at battle of Ulsan

28 Russian armoured cruiser *Rossiya*, showing damage sustained at battle of Ulsan

29 The Second Pacific Squadron on May 26 1905, with *Suvorov* leading and *Oslyabya* in the foreground

Arthur, while Oku, with the bulk of his troops, moved northward to support Kuroki in the operations in Manchuria. For some time, although the Russians seem to have been unaware of this, there remained only Oku's 1st Division covering Port Arthur. The Japanese plan was for a new Third Army, under General Nogi, to undertake the siege of Port Arthur, while a Fourth Army was assembled under General Nodzu to join the campaign against Kuropatkin.

In Port Arthur it was expected that following the capture of Nan Shan, the Japanese would push forward an attempt to capture the fortress by assault. A naval council was convened on May 27 to consider what might be done to assist in meeting the threat. The majority of those present took the view that active operations would not be possible, as too many of the damaged ships were unfit for sea. Reporting this to Alexeiev, Vitgeft told the Viceroy that thirty 6-inch guns and a hundred smaller guns had been lent to the garrison, and to take them back at this stage might be fatal to the defence. Corbett concluded that in the particular circumstances it was possible to have some sympathy for this view:

> Our own traditional view, which forbids devoting a fleet to the defence of its base, rests, it must be remembered, in a confident hope that we have at least a fair chance, if not of a victory, yet certainly of dealing a blow that will seriously cripple the enemy and contribute substantially to the ultimate issue. In the Russian case, as in the similar cases of Louisburg and Sevastopol, there was no ground for such confidence.[4]

Inside Port Arthur the spirits of the fleet continued to decline. On May 29 Semenov wrote in his diary that he felt wretched:

> We ought to go out and fight, not sit here in idleness. A battle is said to be impossible because the forces are unequal: are they so in reality? And if they were? Then we must force our way through to Vladivostok. They say this would be like flight; that we must not desert our comrades here. All very fine – what heroes we are! Not in the least conceited?[5]

Semenov was not alone in having no confidence in the leadership of the fleet, which was, as he pointed out, in Vitgeft's hands as a matter of pure chance, 'in consequence of Admiral Alexeiev having fled and Admiral Skrydlov not having arrived.' He did not doubt Vitgeft's courage, remarking that he had proved it:

> For the rest, he had the reputation of being a scrupulously honest man and diligent worker, but he had almost the whole of his time on shore. A seaman he

4 Corbett I, p. 266.
5 Semenov I, p. 133.

> was not; he confessed it quite openly. When Vitgeft assumed command of the squadron, he said at the first meeting of flag officers and captains: 'Gentlemen, I expect you to assist me with words and deeds; I am no leader of the fleet.' Vitgeft said this quite honestly and openly. In my opinion he had better have held his tongue.[6]

Togo had issued on May 26 the formal announcement, in accordance with international law, of the blockade of Port Arthur. Thereafter it was, of course, essential to maintain constant vigilance to enforce the blockade. Hitherto a considerable number of neutral vessels had been able to make their way into Port Arthur, and even after May 26 a number of blockade runners got through; but, coupled with the taking of Nan Shan, it seemed clear that sooner or later Port Arthur must fall. The arrival on June 6 of General Nogi, the commander of the Third Army, to undertake the siege of the fortress coincided with Togo's well-deserved promotion to the rank of full admiral. For the moment the battle fleet was enjoying a quiet spell, but for Togo's fleet as a whole it was a busy time. Not only was it necessary to maintain the blockade; there was also a great deal of work involved in clearing the approaches to Dalny so that the port could be used to supply the army.

Pakenham, in his next report dated June 19, had some important comments to make on the subject of naval artillery:

> Every war brings with it new lessons, but it is not often these appear to be retrograde. In the Sino-Japanese War the quick firing gun made its debut, and ever since the most important part, numerically, of the armament of a man-of-war has been largely composed of such weapons of comparatively small calibre, thus in great measure superseding the system till then in vogue of arming a ship with heavy guns to the detriment of her lesser artillery. If night conflicts between torpedo craft are excluded, the quick-firer has had few opportunities of showing its capabilities, and if the actions of the larger primary ships are examined, it will be seen that guns of a calibre less than 8 inches have seldom or ever been usefully fired. So far it has been a heavy gun war.[7]

If high angle gun mountings had been fitted, he thought that 'the tendency to outdistance the power of medium artillery would have been even more marked, and any increase in the range of torpedoes must accentuate this difference.' In future ship design, he considered, it might be possible to build ships that though smaller might have the same value in battle as larger vessels; but such vessels 'must not have proportionately lighter artillery; for equality, they must carry the same guns as the larger ships.'

6 Ibid., p. 135.
7 Naval Attaché Reports, p. 86.

In this report Pakenham also addressed the question of defence against torpedoes for ships at anchor:

> Since the successful torpedo attack on the Russian fleet, the leading Japanese naval officers, headed by the commander-in-chief, have realised the inadequacy of the protection afforded by the present system of partial net defence, and the occupation of an anchorage so close to Port Arthur has drawn still greater attention to the matter. Through about 60° of arc, the nets in these battleships give no protection whatsoever; for another 100⁰ or so they only slightly reduce the size of the target, and should the broadside be turned to an attack, so as to get the benefit of the maximum length of net defence, the maximum of risk is thereby invited by the offer of the unprotected ends. The flagship has tried rigging an extempore defence for her bows, and various other plans have been suggested for counterbalancing present deficiencies, but so far all have been rejected; their common weak point has lain in an endeavour to contrive a symmetrical extension of the present system round the bow and stern. Besides being difficult, this arrangement is probably unnecessary, and, had the inventors been satisfied with hanging nets from the ends of the existing forward and aft booms to the extremities of the ship, they would have made a valuable and immediately practicable addition to efficiency, and would have closely approached ideal protection.[8]

It was understandable that the Japanese thought that their battleships, in their unprotected anchorage in the Elliot Islands, offered a tempting target to Russian destroyers and torpedo boats; but they need not have worried. The Russians displayed little ambition to make use of what opportunities presented themselves for torpedo attacks.

Pakenham had been considering what the Russians might now do:

> The fall of Port Arthur in a not remote future now seems assured, and the fate of the Russian fleet confined there must consequently soon be decided. In spite of the dangers attending a sortie, it is one of the solutions that must be contemplated as possible – indeed, probable. Should one be attempted, some, if not all, of the ships taking part could escape the dangers of the minefield, and supposing enough did so to enable the watch on the port to be defied, it would be interesting to know what course this force would take. The Japanese battleships are lying nearly 70 miles to the north-east of Port Arthur, and would therefore start at a great disadvantage in chase of a fleet breaking away to the south. Even allowing the Japanese a large superiority in steaming power, their fleet could not expect, in the most favourable conditions, to catch up with the Russians in less

8 Ibid., pp. 93-94.

> than thirty, and more probably in not less than forty eight hours. Vladivostok has been well mined at its entrance, a force of Japanese armoured cruisers lies in the way, and any portion of the Port Arthur squadron running the gauntlet of these, and getting in, would only find the conditions of Port Arthur repeated. Vladivostok, therefore, does not seem likely to attract the fugitives.[9]

Pakenham thought that rather than this risky course, the Russians would sail for a neutral port, which would give rise to serious international complications.

His analysis, however, took no account of the pressing Russian need to preserve as much of its fleet in Port Arthur as possible, so that it could be ready to join forces with the reinforcements from Europe which it had been announced would be sent. The Baltic Fleet was designated the Second Pacific Squadron, while that at Port Arthur would henceforth be known as the First Pacific Squadron. The command arrangements were announced on May 8. Vice Admiral Petr Alexeivitch Bezobrazov was appointed to command the First Pacific Squadron; unfortunately, by then it was no longer possible for him to reach Port Arthur, so he made his way to Vladivostok. There, he joined Skrydlov, who was appointed to overall command of all Russian naval forces in the Far East, but who had likewise not arrived in time to get to Port Arthur. Vitgeft, therefore, continued in command there. The Second Pacific Squadron would be commanded by Rear Admiral Zinovi Petrovitch Rozhestvenski. The overall strength of his squadron was not such that it could meet the Japanese fleet confident of success; cooperation with Vitgeft was therefore very desirable – if, that is, the First Pacific Squadron could survive long enough for this to be possible. If it was compelled to leave Port Arthur because of the imminent fall of the fortress, Vladivostok would be the only destination that would give it the chance to play any further part in the war.

It was a testament to the incompetence of the Russian Admiralty and government that an immediate decision to reinforce the Pacific Fleet was not taken immediately war broke out. Four months after this, discussions as to the composition of the fleet to reinforce that at Port Arthur were still continuing. It was only at the beginning of June that it was announced that Rozhestvenski's fleet would sail around Africa en route to the theatre of war, and there was still a great deal of work to be done to prepare it for combat. Togo could therefore be confident that in the immediate future it would only be the fleet in Port Arthur and the Vladivostok squadron with which he had to deal. In St Petersburg an over optimistic date of July 15 was set for the departure of the Second Pacific Squadron, but there was no way in which it could be ready to sail by then. In fact it was not be until October 16 that it was finally on its way.

For the moment, therefore, Vitgeft and his fleet were on their own. From the safety of Mukden, Alexeiev, while endorsing the support being given to the garrison, advised that the fleet should also put to sea to fight a decisive action. It was not a prescription

9 Ibid., p. 87.

which commended itself to Vitgeft and his staff; rather it was seen as merely a recipe for self-destruction. That a more active policy, short of a full-blown sortie, might have put Togo under pressure, was not appreciated. The Japanese commander was, in fact, already concerned about his situation, as his general orders of May 30 indicated:

> Our strategy is beginning to be more restricted. As the enemy now cooped up in Port Arthur will probably make desperate efforts to obstruct us, every section of the fleet must be strictly on the alert and be absolutely ready to start at a short notice in order to follow and destroy the enemy should he break out and go southward.[10]

The information reaching Togo from the Naval Staff was that Vitgeft's fleet was on the point of breaking out and would probably attempt to reach the German port of Tsingtao.

Within Port Arthur, the army command was dissatisfied with the naval inactivity. General Kondratenko, a key figure in the garrison, met with Vitgeft to try to arrive at an understanding, and as a result the admiral convened a joint meeting on June 2 of flag officers and generals to discuss the question of what could and should be done. The first issue was whether the fleet should put to sea in the immediate future; the second was whether it should conduct operations around the fortress to assist in its defence, or head for Vladivostok to concentrate all available naval forces. Stoessel and Kondratenko argued strongly for operations to interdict further Japanese reinforcements and support the advance of Russian forces to the relief of Port Arthur. Smirnov, however, the naval commandant of the fortress, took the view that the first priority was to achieve command of the sea, and that the fleet should go to Vladivostok. The general naval view was that at present the fleet was unfit to fight; 100 of its guns were ashore, with 600 men and 20 searchlights, and the fleet had had no recent gunnery practice.

The meeting ended without agreement. Two days later Stoessel sent Vitgeft a memorandum prepared by Kondratenko restating the army's position. Smirnov's opinion was discarded. Stoessel also sent a copy of a dispatch from Kuropatkin, outlining the steps being taken to relieve Port Arthur. The pressure on Vitgeft was becoming irresistible, and on June 5 he called together his flag officers and captains for a further discussion. They took Stoessel's paper to be a conclusive statement that unless the fleet acted to interfere with the Japanese operations, Port Arthur was doomed to fall very shortly. With it would go the fleet. The army, however, insisted on retaining the ships' guns which were being used to bolster weak points in the defence. Vitgeft and his officers had not changed their view of the unreadiness of the fleet for a sortie, which would face all the difficulties of the Japanese minefields and the block ships, while there were only half a dozen destroyers fit to sail with the fleet. Vitgeft

10 Corbett I, p. 268.

again made no secret of the fact that he did not consider himself capable of leading the operation. Nonetheless, in view of the army's position, it was reluctantly agreed to undertake a sortie as soon as all the necessary repairs had been completed and the men and guns that could be spared from the defences had been returned.[11] The earliest date for the sortie would be mid-June.

Vitgeft reported this decision next day to Alexeiev, explaining that it had been taken because Stoessel had said that the fortress was in a critical state, and insisted that the fleet should put to sea. He asked the Viceroy for instructions, and copied his telegram to Stoessel, who asked Vitgeft when he intended to sail. In reply, the admiral said that he would do so as soon as possible, without even waiting until the channel had been cleared of mines, but stressed that he would only be taking this course because of Stoessel's statement about the critical state of the defences. He asked if this was still the case, as he needed as much time as he could have for minesweeping. Stoessel backtracked, claiming never to have said that the fortress was in a critical state but rather that its situation was extremely difficult. On the following day, June 10, he reiterated his demand for support from the fleet for his most advanced positions; but priority was being given to the minesweeping, and no assistance could be given, although the request was repeated on June 13.

The arrival of two telegrams from Alexeiev, sent off on June 11, the day before Kuropatkin's move to relieve Port Arthur had begun, answered Vitgeft's request for authority. The sortie was duly authorised; in fact, Vitgeft was ordered to carry it out, while taking all precautions to ensure safe exit. Stoessel was ordered to stop persecuting the admiral who, Alexeiev reminded him, was solely responsible for the fleet. Nothing was said about breaking through to join the squadron in Vladivostok in these telegrams, but in an earlier telegram which had been delayed in transmission Alexeiev had written: 'I am taking all measures for the speedy raising of the investment of Port Arthur, but … it is necessary for the fleet, while protecting the fortress, to prepare to proceed to sea for a decisive action with the enemy, to defeat him, and to continue its course to Vladivostok.'[12] The combined effect of these telegrams was hardly such as to clarify the position in which Vitgeft found himself. If he broke out successfully, he was to go to Vladivostok, but not if Port Arthur was still holding out. Clearly, however, there must be a sortie, and he ordered the necessary preparations to be made. Repairs to the *Tsarevitch* had been completed by June 8, and Vitgeft had shifted his flag to her, appointing Rear Admiral Matusevitch as his Chief of Staff. By June 16 the *Pobieda's* repairs were also completed, although eight of her 6-inch guns were retained by the garrison, with sixteen of her 12-pounders.

McCully, noting this, saw that the fleet was now ready to go out:

11 Ibid., p. 277.
12 Ibid., p. 279.

> However, when I asked if, in case it did go out, I might accompany it, they seemed surprised that I had acquired the knowledge, and the Chief of Staff asked me who told me that the fleet was going, apparently thinking the fact could not be discovered from observation. He informed me that the fleet had no intention of going out. Still the intention was plain, though I barely thought it possible until *Pobieda* had all her guns.[13]

It was to the Viceroy to whom Vitgeft applied for instructions; although two admirals had come east to take command in succession to Makarov, and both were now in Vladivostok, it was still Alexeiev who was still giving orders to the fleet.

While Vitgeft was preparing for the sortie, the squadron at Vladivostok had been active, in an effort to create a diversion in support of Kuropatkin's advance and the impending sortie. Bezobrazov was ordered to sail with his three armoured cruisers and raid the Japanese communications of southern Korea. He was to proceed to the eastern channel of the Tsushima Straits, and after two days to double back by the western channel. If this proved impossible, he was to make for Port Arthur to join Vitgeft.

The operation which these naval activities were to support was not one which Kuropatkin would have chosen to undertake. If he had been given a free hand, he would have concentrated his army as far back as was necessary to enable it to be built up, undisturbed, until it was strong enough to overwhelm the Japanese armies opposed to him. If that meant abandoning large swathes of Manchuria to the enemy, so be it. As it was, he was obliged to hold Liaoyang as his concentration point; his strategy was nevertheless for his advanced units in touch with the Japanese to delay them as long as possible but not to get involved in pitched battles.

He was not, however, allowed to pursue this policy for long. The need to do something to relieve Port Arthur was becoming a mounting concern, both to Alexeiev and to St Petersburg. It was realised that if the fortress fell, it would be the end of the Pacific fleet. It would also be a public relations disaster. On May 19 Alexeiev gave Kuropatkin the choice of two alternative strategies. He could either block the advance of Oku's Second Army while he drove Kuroki's First Army back over the Yalu; or he could contain Kuroki while he drove Oku into the sea. Since transport problems would make an advance through the mountains against Kuroki wholly impracticable, Kuropatkin was obliged to opt for an attack upon Oku.

He discussed his choice at an extremely rancorous meeting with Alexeiev at Mukden on May 27. He pointed out to the Viceroy that both the alternatives carried with them grave dangers. It was Kuropatkin's view that Port Arthur was of little military significance, and should be left to defend itself, while the Russian army around Liaoyang prepared to resist what he saw as the inevitable Japanese assault. The discussion with Alexeiev was reported to St Petersburg where, unusually, the Tsar

13 McCully, p. 108.

convened a council of war to consider what should be done. The conclusion which this reached was to uphold Alexeiev's view that Port Arthur must be held at all costs, and immediate action taken for its relief.[14] Kuropatkin bitterly recorded this in his memoirs, observing that the decision had been taken 'in spite of my opinions as to our unreadiness for any forward movement; in spite of the fact that out of twelve divisions of reinforcements only one had arrived; in spite of the inefficiency of the railway.'[15]

Kuropatkin knew in his heart that this would be the decision in St Petersburg. He did not await confirmation of this, but on May 28 met with Lieutenant General Stakelberg, whose 1st Siberian Army Corps would be undertaking the operation, reinforced by additional infantry and a cavalry brigade; he had a total of about 35,000 men and 94 guns. It might well have been possible to commit a substantially larger force, but Kuropatkin was not prepared to endanger his positions elsewhere. In the orders he issued to Stakelberg on June 7 he outlined the immediate objective for his corps as being the weakening of the Japanese forces in the Kwantung peninsula by 'drawing upon itself the greatest possible number of the enemy's forces.' In the face of superior numbers, however, decisive action was to be avoided. The ultimate objective would be the recapture of Nan Shan, and an advance towards Port Arthur.[16]

It was not an exceptionally upbeat message to a commander whose advance was intended to reverse four months of military and naval setbacks. It was based on the incorrect assumption that the bulk of Oku's Second Army was committed to operations at Port Arthur, and that Stakelberg would therefore encounter the rear of that army. Stakelberg's method of carrying out his orders was to establish, and then advance through, a series of defensive positions on his way south, and he concentrated his forces astride the railway to the south of Telissu. His position there was attacked by Oku on June 15, who deployed all three of his divisions. An attempted Russian counter-attack failed, in part due to poor communications. Stakelberg's troops fell back in some disorder towards Kaiping; he was saved from a pursuit by the victorious Japanese, which would have led to complete disaster, by a torrential rainstorm which began at about 3.00pm. Total Japanese casualties were 1,064; the Russians lost more than three times as many. The attempt to relieve Port Arthur had completely failed. Nonetheless, the planned naval operations went ahead.

14 *British Official History* I, p. 173.
15 Quoted in Warner, p. 312.
16 *British Official History* I, p. 177.

13

The Sortie of June 23

The object of locating a squadron of armoured cruisers based on Vladivostok had been to weaken Togo's main battle fleet by compelling the detachment of substantial forces to meet the threat that it could pose. By the time the battle of Telissu was fought, this objective at least had been achieved. Responsibility for the defence of the Tsushima Straits was now assigned to Kamimura, who had a substantial force at his disposal. In addition to his own four armoured cruisers, he had Uriu's squadron of four light cruisers; he also had four divisions of torpedo boats. Kamimura posted Uriu, with in addition one division of torpedo boats, at Sylvia Basin, Masampo, with orders to guard the Western Strait, while his own squadron was at Osaki, at the mouth of the Takeshiki inlet. Corbett was extremely critical of this deployment:

> This distribution, we are told, remained materially unaltered till the middle of June; but seeing how fully alive was the Imperial Staff to the probability of some energetic action on the part of the enemy, the arrangement is difficult to understand, for apparently it left the Eastern Strait dangerously open. Nor does it seem to provide adequate security for the main transport route to and from the Straits of Shimonoseki. Yet transports were continuously passing both homeward and outward bound, and unless there was a group of them no escort was provided ... It was in the nature of an open blockade with no provision made for getting timely news of the hostile squadrons putting to sea.[1]

In accordance with his orders Bezobrazov had put to sea on June 12. Flying his flag in the *Rossiya*, he was accompanied by the *Gromoboi* and *Rurik*. The remaining vessel of the squadron, the cruiser *Bogatyr*, had suffered serious damage when on May 15 she had gone aground near Cape Brius, some 20 miles south-west of Vladivostok. Although repairs had been effected, she was not fit to go to sea with the rest of the

1 Corbett I, pp. 283-284.

squadron, and was not able to undertake any operations until almost the end of the war.[2]

Bezobrazov arrived off the island of Okinoshima, in the eastern channel of the Tsushima Straits, in the early hours of June 15. That morning two large transports had sailed from Shimonoseki, each carrying over 1,000 men. The *Hitachi Maru* was bound for Takushan with a battalion of the 1st Guards Reserve Regiment; Takushan had been established as a base for the 1st Guards Brigade of Kuroki's army. The *Sado Maru* was heading for Yentoa Bay with a railway battalion. Also at sea in the area was the *Izumi Maru*, returning homeward bound from Yentoa Bay. Kamimura's dispositions had meanwhile somewhat changed; Uriu, with two of his cruisers, had joined him at Osaki, while the *Takachiho* and *Niitaka* had gone to Takeshiki for repairs. On the morning of June 15, Uriu's smallest cruiser, the *Tsushima*, was on patrol off Okinoshima, while the dispatch vessel *Chihaya* was heading northward.

At about 7:15am the *Tsushima*, after reaching Okinoshima, had turned back to the south when she sighted smoke to the north east. Within minutes she had sighted the three Russian armoured cruisers, and at once radioed a report to Kamimura. Getting no response, she headed south at full speed towards the Tsutsu wireless station at the southern end of Tsushima Island. As she went, she repeatedly sent out a warning that the Vladivostok squadron was on the loose. Four merchant vessels were seen and warned to run for shelter. By 8.15 the *Tsushima* was aware that her warning message had been received, although in fact at first it was garbled in transmission, and it was some time before it was clear to Kamimura that the Russians were out. It was only at 9:45am that his armoured cruisers were clear to sea, but at 9.00 a message from the *Tsushima* was received that the Russians were firing on a merchant vessel south of Okinoshima.[33]

This was the *Izumi Maru*. Chased by the *Gromoboi*, which opened fire, it was not until some 30 men had been killed and wounded aboard the transport that she stopped and surrendered. About 100 men, including a number of sick being repatriated, were taken out of her. Others refused to leave and were sunk with the ship. Visibility, due to heavy rain, was poor; at about 10.00am the other two transports found themselves close to Bezobrazov's squadron. Both refused to stop, and tried to escape. After the *Sado Maru* was overhauled by the *Rurik*, she struck her flag; 40 minutes were given for the vessel to be abandoned. Before the time was up, the *Rurik* was recalled, and she put two torpedoes into her prize, which did not, however, sink. Meanwhile the *Gromoboi* had turned her attention to the *Hitachi Maru*, which endeavoured to escape despite being hit several times. Before long, the vessel was a wreck; the battalion commander destroyed the colours, and then committed suicide. The ship went down with all save 150 of her passengers and crew. The *Sado Maru,* which had still not sunk,

2 Piotr Olender, *Russo-Japanese Naval War 1904-1905* II (Sandomierz, Poland 2010), p. 164.
3 Corbett I, p. 286.

managed to save some of them, having lowered her boats when preparing to abandon ship; she survived, and was towed back into port.

Kamimura had been delayed by the bad weather, and it was after noon before he rounded the cape at the south end of Tsushima. He had been completely in the dark as to Bezobrazov's position and headed north at full speed for Okinoshima. Hutchison reported on what followed:

> About noon, however, he received information through the *Tsushima* that the Russians were steering to the north-west, and were then 15 miles south of Okinoshima; the *Tsushima* here lost sight of the enemy owing to a heavy rain squall, but at 1:30pm was lucky enough to sight them again 5 miles south of Okinoshima Island. The Admiral was at once informed, and shaped course for the position signalled; unfortunately, the fog growing thicker and thicker, the *Tsushima* here lost sight of the enemy, with the result that the Japanese squadron had a hopeless search. The *Tsushima* here joined the Admiral. Admiral Kamimura, thinking that the enemy would make for their home port, at once started in pursuit for a prearranged rendezvous, in order, if possible, to cut them off.[4]

Bezobrazov, having realised from wireless traffic that a Japanese squadron was in his vicinity, had indeed taken the decision to abandon any attempt to reach the western channel, and was making for home. He recognised, however, that Kamimura would try to cut him off from Vladivostok, 'and instead of taking the most natural course he took the most improbable one, that is up the coast of Japan, continuing his depredations as he went.'[5] Next day, the weather had cleared. The Russian squadron sank two schooners, and captured the British steamer *Allanton*, carrying coal to Singapore. Since her papers showed that she had previously carried contraband, a prize crew was put aboard her, and she was taken back with the squadron, which safely returned to Vladivostok.

Kamimura had been severely hampered by the heavy weather, which continued throughout the afternoon of June 15. He had to send his torpedo boats back for shelter, and it was not until dawn next day that Uriu joined him. He was heading for Matsushima, an island 200 miles north of Tsushima, on a direct line to Vladivostok, which he reached at about 8.00. The horizon was clear and there was no sign of the enemy. Kamimura concluded, quite wrongly, that Bezobrazov must be heading for home by way of Gensan, and he altered course accordingly. Next day he heard reports that the Russians had been seen off the Oki Islands, but it was only later that he heard the appalling news of the loss of the transports. Corbett was critical of Kamimura's

4 Naval Attaché Reports, pp. 96-97.
5 Corbett I, p. 288.

failure, though allowing that he might have been acting under definite orders from the Naval Staff:

> To a great measure it was certainly due to his not making the most of his force. He had sufficient strength to have detached some at least of his light cruisers to keep in touch with the Japanese signal stations, but not having done this he was drawn into the common error of acting on mere impressions which he could not verify. A central course between Okinoshima and Matsushima, with a cruiser off each island, should have given him contact, or if it did not he would have failed by bad luck rather than bad judgment.[6]

This is no doubt true; but in his ignorance of the actual position of Bezobrazov's squadron, he would have been exposing his isolated cruisers to the risk of meeting the Russians alone.

The loss of the transports was a serious setback for the Japanese. In addition to the troops who had died, three batteries of heavy guns had gone down with the *Hitachi Maru*. They had been intended for the siege operations at Port Arthur, and would have been invaluable in hastening the fall of the fortress. There was huge public indignation, and Kamimura was strongly criticised, particularly in Tokyo, where many of the troops lost had been recruited. Demonstrations took place outside his house, in which not only stones were thrown but also a short sword, with the suggestion that he should commit *hara-kiri*.[7]

Yamamoto, however, was not disposed to blame Kamimura, sending him on June 19 a reassuring telegram, as soon as he returned to his base at Osaki:

> Your arrangements and appreciations with regard to the recent sortie of the Vladivostok squadron are considered most appropriate by us in the Admiralty and by those outside who have any knowledge of naval affairs. But there are some who, knowing nothing of such matters, have blamed you, being influenced by misconceptions or by their connections with the men lost in the transports, and they have published criticisms in the newspapers and magazines. As we will here devise some method of letting these people know the real truth you should not look back at this affair but do your utmost to secure the original object. I hope you will achieve a splendid result.[8]

The disaster of June 15 meant that Yamamoto was obliged to explain himself publicly, since the continued exposure of transports and other merchant vessels to the risk of

6 Ibid., p. 290.
7 Warner, p. 285.
8 Quoted in Corbett I, p. 291.

enemy action remained a matter of considerable public concern in Japan, as Hutchison reported:

> The mind of the people, in thinking that the government had not taken the Vladivostok squadron seriously of late, was shown by a committee of the Progressive Party waiting on the Minister of Marine, from whom they received the following reply: The government perfectly understood the reason which had prompted the deputation, and assured them that everything was being done with the limited squadrons at their disposal to ensure the safety of transports, with the main objective of keeping the Vladivostok squadron from making any attempt, with success, of joining hands with the Port Arthur fleet, or a raid into the Gulf of Pechili.[9]

Yamamoto went on to explain to the anxious politicians that when any large number of troops and material were shipped, special convoy arrangements were made. On the basis of the information from the fleet, he was able to say that.the exit from Port Arthur had been effectively blocked to the ships larger than the cruiser *Novik*. This was very soon proved, though, not to be the case.

In Port Arthur, meanwhile, notwithstanding the denials by Matusevitch that any sortie was intended, preparations continued to be made. Exactly what Vitgeft had in mind is far from clear. He did not apparently have much faith in the assurances from Alexeiev's staff that the Japanese fleet was seriously weakened, but in his subsequent report to the Viceroy he suggested that on the basis of this, he intended to make for the Elliot Islands 'and seeking out the enemy to attack him as a whole or in detail.' Captain Bubnov recorded that 'after a long deliberation it was decided to put to sea for a three days' cruise, to examine the Elliot Islands, and to engage the enemy should he be met with in considerable force.' There was no suggestion that the object should be to break through the enemy and make for Vladivostok.[10]

The First Pacific Squadron, for that of course was the official designation now of the ships in Port Arthur, was in fact somewhat short of its apparent strength, because a large number of guns lent to the garrison had not been returned. In all, 18 6-inch guns and 23 12-pounders were missing, while the 600 men sent ashore to man the guns were still there, and had to be replaced from the smaller ships, the naval barracks and the reserve. In emerging for a sortie Vitgeft's squadron had also to negotiate a considerable number of Japanese mines recently laid off the port. On June 15, in a message carried by the destroyer *Lieutenant Burakov* to Newchwang for transmission to the Viceroy, Vitgeft had reported that while the need to put to sea was acknowledged, it must be delayed until further sweeping operations had been conducted. To this, Alexeiev replied on June 18 in familiar terms, ordering the fleet

9 Naval Attaché Reports, p. 95.
10 Corbett I, p. 299.

to put to sea and engage the enemy, choosing the most favourable opportunity while taking every precaution.[11]

Togo was convinced that a sortie was imminent, though uncertain in what strength it would be made. For him, the problem was to ensure that his fleet should be concentrated at the right time and place to meet the enemy fleet. On June 18 he issued a general order outlining the careful watch that was to be kept on the entrance to the port, and the steps that would be taken in the event of the enemy emerging. The concentration point would be Encounter Rock. The fleet was now organised in two squadrons. The first, under Togo's direct command, comprised the 1st Division of the four battleships, and Dewa's 3rd Division of five cruisers (*Yakumo, Asama, Chitose, Takasago* and *Kasagi*). The second squadron, under Kataoka, comprised the 5th Division and the 6th Division. The older vessels of the 5th Division, *Itsukushima*, *Matsushima*, *Hashidate* and *Chinyen*, under Rear Admiral Yamada, would constitute a standing force to guard the Elliot Islands base. This left Kataoka with the armoured cruisers *Nisshin* and *Kasuga* (now newly repaired) and a dispatch vessel, and Rear Admiral Togo Masaji's 6th Division (*Akashi, Suma, Akitsushima* and *Chiyoda*).

In making the necessary arrangements to intercept the Russians should they come out, Togo's principal concern was to block their path rather than to bring about a decisive action. He was ever mindful of the risk of losing any of his heavy ships, and wished his subordinates to be left in no doubt of what he wanted to achieve. He added a key paragraph to his general orders:

> The above orders explain what is intended to be done if the enemy come out. But the object of our strategy is to prevent them from escaping. Our blockading division should always bear this in mind and intimidate the enemy by letting them see our ships.[12]

Pakenham reflected on the options open to the Russian fleet, observing that any very definite reverse to the Vladivostok squadron would remove one of them. That, of course, had not happened; and he was in no doubt that a sortie was imminent, in which case he thought speed would be crucial:

> The persistency with which the Russians sweep the mines off Port Arthur favours the existence of a desire to resume activity, and the present position of the main body of the Japanese fleet is so disadvantageous for coping with any sally to the southward that the speeds the two fleets will be respectively able to command have been much discussed. The Russian engineers are not credited with being able to obtain the best speeds of which their ships were originally capable, but against this may be set the foul bottoms of the Japanese fleet, whereas the

11 *British Official History* I, p. 291.
12 Corbett I, p. 296.

> Russians would have it in their power to start clean. The chance of overtaking the Russians would be greatly improved by any attempt on their part to take lame ducks with them, and it is much to be hoped they may be tempted to make this mistake. A concentration off Port Arthur, followed by a bold endeavour to cut a way through the Japanese to Vladivostok, would furnish a solution of very general interest.[13]

On June 20 Vitgeft instructed his ships to raise steam, to be ready to sail by noon. He then issued the following order:

> By order of Admiral Alexeiev the squadron, having completed the repairs to the ships which were damaged by the enemy before war was declared, will now put to sea so as to afford assistance to our comrades on land in defence of Port Arthur. With the help of God and St Nicholas the wonder worker, who is the protector of mariners, we will endeavour to fulfil our duty loyally and conscientiously and to defeat the enemy, who have already lost some ships by striking our mines. The little gunboat *Bobr* has shown us what can be done in very difficult circumstances. May God be with us.[14]

At 10.00am, however, all the flag officers and captains were called to the flagship *Tsarevitch*, and 20 minutes later a general signal was hoisted: 'let the fires die out.' The sense of anti-climax was powerful; cynics remarked that it was no doubt due to the Japanese having had in advance a proof copy of the order. Semenov remarked: 'our spirits could not have been at a lower level than they were.'[15]

The reason for the last minute cancellation was the realisation that the state of the tide would not allow the fleet on that day to get out of the harbour soon enough to get beyond the range of torpedo attacks before nightfall. Vitgeft accordingly postponed the sailing of the fleet until 2.00am on the morning of June 22; another delay became necessary when it was realised that the Japanese had succeeded in laying more mines, and further sweeping operations would be necessary before the fleet could depart. It was finally settled that it should sail early on the morning of June 23; and this, in spite of further minelaying by the Japanese, was adhered to, and at 4.00am that morning the Russian ships began to move out of the harbour.

Unbeknown to the Russians, Togo's force had been further depleted by the need to support the military operations. Oku had asked for a naval escort to cover his store ships as they brought up supplies and ammunition required for the planned concentric advance towards Liaoyang. Togo acquiesced, although it would materially reduce the effectiveness of the screen that he wished to deploy to cover any move by the Russian

13 Naval Attaché Reports, p. 89.
14 *British Official History* I, p. 291.
15 Semenov I, p. 145.

fleet towards the Shantung peninsula. He agreed to detach Rear Admiral Togo's 6th Division of four light cruisers and a dispatch vessel. The Naval Staff in Tokyo found this extremely worrying; Admiral Ijuin telegraphed Togo:

> As the fate of Port Arthur is becoming exceedingly critical, their fleet will certainly make a desperate attempt to break out. Although I am sure that you have fully prepared a plan to meet such a move, I beg, as a matter of form, that you will not send ships too far away from you so that in emergencies you can concentrate and send them all against the enemy.[16]

Aboard the *Mikasa*, anchored with the rest of the battleships in the Elliot Islands, Togo received the news that the Russians were coming out at about 8:20am, and within minutes had ordered all the ships of his fleet to raise steam. It was, however, not until 10:45am that the battleships finally began to move out, and, preceded by Dewa's squadron about 10 miles ahead, steamed towards Port Arthur at 14 knots. Togo was expecting, when he got there, to encounter three Russian battleships, three cruisers, some gunboats and a large number of destroyers. The news reaching him was that the enemy fleet had left the harbour, but was not advancing. To Pakenham and his Japanese hosts, 'it seemed incredible that such a force should offer battle, unless the garrison of Port Arthur was in much greater straits than there had been any reason to suppose.'[17]

By 3:20pm the sound of gunfire could be heard, and it was supposed that this might be Dewa trying to cut off stragglers from the Russian fleet endeavouring to escape. It was in fact a brief action between destroyers, which ended after the *Novik* drove off the Japanese. At 3.45 the hills above the entrance to Port Arthur came in sight, although nothing could yet be seen of the Russian ships, and at 5.30 Togo ordered his fleet to clear for action. It was just at this moment that Vitgeft, still out of Togo's sight, was forming his battle line. Togo's own battle line had now been joined by Kataoka's two armoured cruisers *Nisshin* and *Kasuga*. Dewa was steaming on the fleet's starboard quarter, about a mile away. The prevailing opinion in the Japanese fleet had been that the Russian movement did not presage a sortie, but was merely intended to make the Japanese show their force, and would re-enter the harbour at 6:30pm when the tide would serve. This view was soon proved wrong, as Pakenham reported:

> About 7.00pm the leading Russians came in sight, and it was observed with some concern that, though the actual leader was the *Novik*, the fighting line was headed by the *Tsarevitch*, and, a few minutes later, six large ships could be made out in the Russian line, while several others were slowly emerging from the haze under the land. This was more than had been bargained for. It had been

16 Corbett I, p. 297.
17 Naval Attaché Reports, p. 102.

thought the *Pobieda* might come out, but no one had expected a resurrection of the *Tsarevitch*, and when in the second ship the *Retvizan* was recognised, with the *Pobieda* behind her, it was felt that the Japanese fleet had got into a very warm corner. The other Russian ships were the *Peresviet, Sevastopol, Poltava, Bayan,* and two or three cruisers of the *Diana* class. It was not possible to make out with certainty which ship was flying the Admiral's flag; some thought it was in the *Novik,* while others asserted it was in the fourth ship in the line, but the colours at the mastheads were confusing. Probably there was an admiral's flag flying in both the ships.

The signal to the Japanese fleet to hoist colours for battle was made at 7:12pm, and at 7:22pm was followed by the brief and inspiriting address: 'This battle will decide the fate of our country. Everyone will do his best.'

The situation was one to try the nerve of the strongest. Having anticipated an encounter with an inferior force at most, and latterly having ceased to expect action of any kind, the sudden discovery of the superior strength of the enemy and the need for instantly taking a resolution that must have the most momentous consequences, formed a juncture only a great man could deal with adequately.

At 7:15pm the Japanese turned to the same course as the Russians were on, and in another 10 minutes the Russian line was completely formed, with intervals of about four cables between the ships, but with the cruisers separated from the battleships by a distance of about 10 cables. The *Novik* was leading, and on her further side there were a few destroyers, and there may have been another small vessel on the far side of the cruisers.

The fleets were about 20,000 yards apart, and were steering parallel courses, with guns trained on one another. The distance sounds great, but the circumstances either improved visual power or stimulated imagination, as it seemed possible to see the whites of the eyes of the opposing guns' crews without the aid of a telescope. At such a time, a few guns, hard-hitting and of superior range, seem worth their weight in gold, and the fact that some ship in the enemy's line only carries 10-inch guns, or that the guns of another are of old pattern, is recalled with the keenest gratification.

The Japanese fleet had been steaming 14 knots, and was now drawing steadily ahead of the Russians, whose speed was variously estimated at from 10 to 12 knots. About 7:40pm, the *Mikasa* altered course two points to starboard, which soon brought the *Tsarevitch* on a bearing a little abaft the beam of the second ship in the Japanese line. Liautishan promontory was now abeam of the leaders. Though the hour was late there was still half an hour of good daylight, with the prospect of a long twilight, and a bright moon to follow; it was not too late to fight, and no one in the Japanese fleet thought for an instant that the Russians would allow such an opportunity to escape.

The fate of the day now trembled in the balance. The slightest thing would have rendered an engagement inevitable. The fleets were closing in, and the moment was at hand when Admiral Togo would probably decide to take

> advantage of his superiority of speed to cross ahead of his enemy and concentrate his fire on the leaders of the opposing line. The Japanese, and probably also the Russians, awaited orders in a thrilling and breathless silence; then, after a few anxious minutes, during which both fleets held steadily on their courses without either making an overture of any kind, the *Novik* was seen to turn to starboard and go behind the Russian line. This looked conclusive of an intention to fight, and when the *Tsarevitch* commenced to follow the *Novik* round, the Japanese could hardly believe their eyes were not deceiving them. The Russians were now heading for Port Arthur, the *Novik* made her turn at about 7:50pm, and the last ship in the Russian line did not turn till 8:18pm, so the line must have tailed out somewhat. The day was won! The retirement of the Russians left the victory to the Japanese. It was now too late for the Russian fleet to re-enter harbour, and they would have to pass the night outside, either at anchor or underway, it was immaterial which. It now only remained for the Japanese to convert a moral and bloodless triumph into a material one.[18]

Before the Russian turn had been completed, Togo turned his ships eight points to starboard together and, for a moment, it seemed that he intended to attack the Russian rear. But the risk of a confused action, with night coming on, and the consequent possibility of losing an armoured ship, led him to think better of it, and leave the rest of the action to his destroyers and torpedo boats. His principal object, to head off the Russian escape, had now been achieved, and he took the safest, and in Pakenham's view, the wisest course.

Try as they might, the Japanese torpedo craft failed to inflict any damage on the Russian fleet. They were taken by surprise by the reckless speed with which the Russian ships hastened towards Port Arthur through waters strewn with Japanese mines. In the bright moonlight the oncoming Japanese vessels were exposed to a concentrated fire not only from the Russians' secondary armament but from their main armament as well. In the face of this, it was impossible for the Japanese to judge distances or aim their torpedo tubes accurately. They launched torpedoes at ranges between 440 and 1600 yards, and scored no hits whatever. Four Japanese vessels were damaged, but all got away. The only damage sustained by the Russians was to the *Sevastopol,* last but one in the line. The Japanese torpedo attacks began while the Russian fleet was still under way, and when she edged away to port she struck a mine forward. The damage was not serious, and she got back into harbour under her own steam.

Thus the sortie ended in anti-climax. Vitgeft explained to Alexeiev the reasons behind his decision to abort the mission. These were, he said, first owing to the lateness of the sortie, secondly owing to what he described as the enemy's force being

18 Ibid., pp. 103-105.

far superior, but mainly owing to the large number of torpedo craft against which he could only oppose seven destroyers and two torpedo vessels.[19]

It may well have been encountering the Japanese fleet so close to Port Arthur that was decisive in Vitgeft's mind. It meant that any operation against the Elliot Islands would be hugely risky, while he most certainly would not have been able to get a sufficient start to have any chance of escaping to Vladivostok or anywhere else, even if that had been a course which he considered. The problem for the Russians was the time it took to get to sea, which made it possible for Togo to appear on the scene before significant progress could be made. The judgment of the Official History on Vitgeft was bleak:

> The skill of his mechanics, coupled with the disasters which had deprived the Japanese commander of two battleships, had given Admiral Vitgeft a splendid chance of retrieving all that had been lost in the early months of the war; but unfortunately for his country he was not the man either to conceive or to carry out a resolute policy. Of his personal courage there is no doubt; where he failed was in those moral qualities which enable the great commander to recognise and to seize the fleeting opportunities which fortune throws in his way.[20]

Predictably, Semenov was overcome with despair at the ending of the sortie; looking back, he believed that 'the fate of the Port Arthur squadron was finally sealed on that day.' Even during the night, after the Japanese torpedo attacks had died away, there was hope that the sortie might be resumed next day, but the general signal at 5.00am next day shattered all illusions:

> The shadow of death seemed to lie on our ship. Only a few minutes before the officers had looked almost cheerful, notwithstanding 30 hours without rest or peace, and had kept the men in good spirits with jokes and kindly words. Now, at one blow, all life seemed to have gone out of them; their faces all became dark and dejected.[21]

With the Japanese battle fleet at anchor again in the Elliot Islands, Pakenham reflected on what the day had meant:

> If a country were ever saved by the action of a single man, Japan was yesterday saved by Togo. Only his calm self-restraint at one period of the day, and his resolute and decisive action at another, extricated Japan from what in the hands of a smaller man might have been a most cruel reverse of fortune. Though the

19 Corbett I, p. 307.
20 *British Official History* I, p. 296.
21 Semenov I, p. 153.

> Japanese have had a wonderful escape from immediate danger their position is now critical. Evidently all assumptions and estimates based on the supposed weakness of the Russian fleet must be revised, but this cannot be done until better information as to the extent of their losses is available; if they should prove to be substantially the same as those that have been mentioned, the strength of the fleet in Port Arthur would not differ greatly from what it was just after the loss of the *Petropavlovsk*; but the present position of the Japanese is more open to attack than their then base was, and to this extent they are now at a disadvantage. When to this is added the losses the Japanese navy has since suffered, it will be seen that their enterprise is seriously menaced at its very root, and that only heroic measures, or a repetition of the good fortune that did not desert them yesterday, can save the situation.[22]

Presuming the continuing existence in superior strength of the Russian fleet, Pakenham concluded that a great and unforeseen complication had been introduced. As a result, he discerned a real tension and sense of anxiety among his Japanese hosts. One significant factor which he noted was the failure of the Japanese minefields to claim any victims:

> The double escape of the Russians from the dangers of the minefield reflects credit on their courage and dexterity, but is disheartening from the point of view of their opponents. Both sides had learned to fear the effects of mines, so this instance of their neutralisation may decrease the extreme caution with which mined ground has latterly been approached, and, if so, there may be a renewal of the serious losses that characterised one period of the war. At the same time, the Japanese must not conceal from themselves that mines alone have been insufficient to keep the enemy in his port, and it is to be hoped new measures may be devised that will be more successful.[23]

Describing the events of June 23 in a letter to his sister on July 6, Pakenham observed that a more vigorous confrontation had best been avoided: 'nationally, such a battle would have been most disastrous to Japan, even if she had won it, as she cannot replace lost or seriously damaged armoured ships, and the threat of the Baltic fleet is not to be ignored.' In the meantime, he added, 'the British Naval Attaché is thankful for a whole skin, which is more than he expected a few days ago.'[24]

Meanwhile Commander Jackson had an outing which marked a more open approach to public relations on the part of the Japanese. A liner, the *Manshu Maru*, had been fitted out to take foreign attachés and observers, as well as foreign and Japanese

22 Naval Attaché Reports, p. 108.
23 Ibid., p. 111.
24 Pakenham Papers, Caird Library, National Maritime Museum, PKM/2/5.

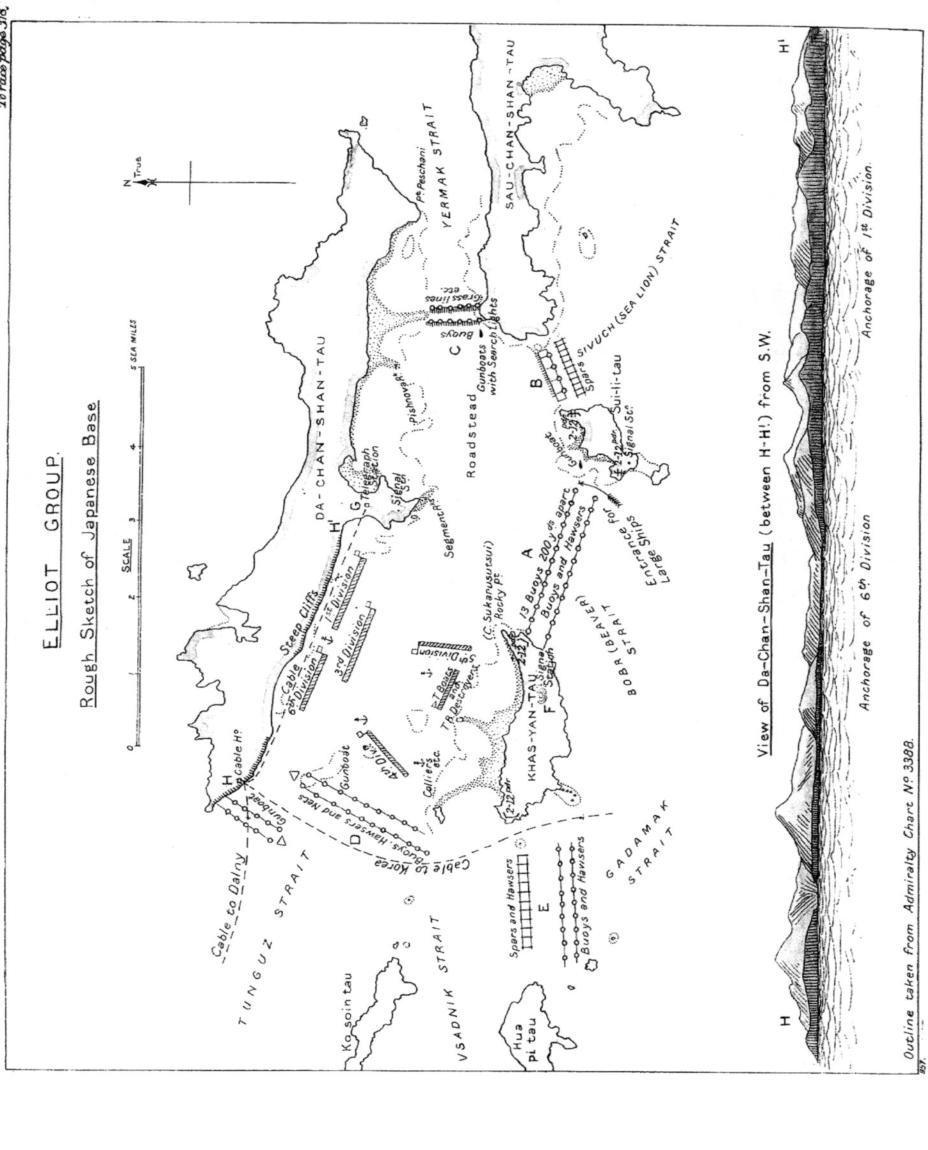

Sketch 4: Elliot Islands

journalists, to visit the Japanese fleet. Its base in the Elliot islands had hitherto been kept secret, and it was only as the vessel approached the anchorage that the captain informed his passengers what they were about to see. One of the journalists aboard, Frederick Villiers, described the experience:

> There was considerable excitement on board, especially among the correspondents. We were now nearing 'A Certain Place' – the mysterious naval base whence all those sharp and incisive attacks on Port Arthur by the Japanese came from. Soon the greyness passed away, and bright patches of blue sky gradually lit up the islands; but there was no sign as yet of any naval life in these waters, not even a scouting torpedo boat ...A wide bay suddenly opened out, a dense cloud of smoke hanging over it, and in the centre, near a lofty grey rock, with a crown of emerald grass on its summit, the victorious fleet lay at anchor. The sun was setting behind this rock, whose shape was as sheer as that of Gibraltar, turning everything into tones of sunset and molten gold; the black pall of smoke above looked like a curtain about to descend and shut out the picture.[25]

The visit had been carefully choreographed. The foreign attachés and the journalists were taken aboard the flagship *Mikasa*, which Villiers thought in a condition which rivalled a British ship; he had 'never seen a deck so trim.' The commander-in-chief, on the other hand, presented a much more low-key image than the journalists had been hoping to describe.

25 Quoted in Jonathan Clements, *Admiral Togo: Nelson of the East* (London, 2010), p. 176.

14

The Vladivostok Squadron

Togo was perfectly aware that the appearance of Vitgeft in such strength on June 23 meant a significant change in the perceived balance of advantage. The effect was as marked on the land campaign as much as on the naval. Although on the face of it the sortie had been an ignominious failure, the Japanese recognised that it was a strategic setback. Their plan had turned on an immediate concentric advance upon Liaoyang in the week or ten days that remained before the rains set in and orders for the advance had already been given. On June 24, the day after the sortie, the whole movement was stopped. Not only had the sortie made it impossible for Oku to advance because the intended establishment of his supply base could not be undertaken, but the comfortable assumption of the military that the fleet was now so dominant in the Yellow Sea that there was no danger of communications with the army being interrupted was now unsound.[1]

The Imperial Staff concluded that the fact that the Russian fleet was now able to come out of port, and that as a result the continued transport of supplies for the army fighting in Manchuria was at evident risk, meant that the battle for Liaoyang could now not take place until after the rains. With the example of the previous raid by the Vladivostok squadron fresh in mind, and the public reaction to the losses suffered, the government could take no risk of such a disaster being repeated. In any case, the delay in positioning Oku's army for the concentric advance meant that a postponement was unavoidable. Port Arthur was now, it was plain, the key to future operations, and it would be the navy's task to support General Nogi to the full in his advance on the fortress.

The raid of the Vladivostok squadron prompted Pakenham to make some further observations about the Japanese response. He had something to say about the remarks of Admiral Mahan on the subject, which he considered were misconceived:

1 Corbett I, p. 310.

> In his comments on the raids, Mahan seems not to have allowed due weight to the geographical difficulties in the way of the Japanese, nor to the necessary limitations of power and number of the force they can afford to depute for the observation of Vladivostok. He assumes a permanent watch is kept on this port, and is reported as having said 'the Japanese division in watch of the port should have been itself so posted as to be able quickly to get between the enemy and his return.' That is all very good, but with all the respect due to so high an authority, it must be admitted that this opinion shows no signs of having been founded on reflection, or of being anything but the enunciation of an ideal, which, in the present instance, is visionary and unpractical. From time to time the Japanese have visited Vladivostok, but they have been quite unable to establish themselves in such a position as to watch the port.[2]

Following the sortie of June 23, Togo was obliged to keep an especially close watch on Port Arthur, and a report of smoke rising on June 26 was enough to bring him out with his battleships, and that night the whole fleet remained at sea in position to intercept the Russians. The battleships, with a strong flotilla, were posted halfway between Port Arthur and the Korean coast in a position which was roughly at the centre of the Yellow Sea. Between it and Shantung Admiral Dewa's cruisers of the 3rd Division covered the more westerly section, while Rear Admiral Togo was some 25 miles north-east of Chefoo. At dawn next day the fleet converged on Round Island; nothing having been seen of the Russians, Togo withdrew to the Blonde Islands, where he remained fogbound until the end of June. He returned to the Elliot Islands on July 2, and published revised general orders for the conduct of any battle with the Russian fleet. In these, he stated that 'the tactics we must employ must be designed so that we may constantly take the offensive, utilising the superior speed of our battleships and the superior numbers of our destroyers and torpedo boats.'[3] The new instructions set out in detail the way in which the Japanese fleet would deploy as soon as a warning signal was received that the Russians were coming out. Togo proposed to spread the different units of his fleet on three diverging courses, with his fastest cruisers nearest the enemy and the battleships furthest away, occupying a line westward from Ross Island.

Before Togo could return to the Elliot Islands, the Vladivostok squadron caused a further alarm. In response to a suggestion from Alexeiev, Skrydlov ordered Bezobrazov to put to sea, to create a further diversion in support of Vitgeft's movements. At this time the Viceroy had not yet received news of the events of June 23. Bezobrazov, with his three armoured cruisers and eight torpedo boats, accompanied by the auxiliary cruiser *Lena*, was to take the flotilla to Gensan to make a night attack. After this, the flotilla, escorted by the *Lena*, would return to Vladivostok, while the cruisers steamed

2 Naval Attaché Reports, p. 119.
3 Corbett I, p. 314.

through the Straits in the direction of Quelpart. Bezobrazov sailed on June 28, and on the night of June 29/30 attacked Gensan, destroying two small merchant vessels and bombarding the settlement. Unfortunately one of the torpedo boats ran ashore, and had to be blown up, and the cruisers were not able to move off to the south until noon on June 30, giving Kamimura, who as before was at Osaki, plenty of warning. The *Lena* returned to the Vladivostok with the torpedo boats, and Bezobrazov headed for the Straits.

Kamimura had deployed Uriu's cruisers (except the *Naniwa*, which was escorting a transport) covering the line Fusan-Tsunoshima (on the Japanese coast) and at 8.00am he ordered his armoured cruisers to prepare to steam up the western channel. He put to sea at 8.35; soon, however, a developing anxiety that the *Naniwa* and her charge might be in danger led Kamimura to send off the *Chihaya*, his dispatch vessel, to try to overtake them and send the transport back to safety, while he also called the *Takachiho* and *Tsushima* to leave their patrol stations and join him at Cape Clonard. He heard at 3:40pm that the enemy had been seen at 9.30 heading south-east from Gensan, but that was all he knew, and he decided that for the night his squadron should take up a patrol position 30 miles off Matsushima, in order to cover the Straits. Next morning there was still no news of the enemy. At 11.00am he heard that the transport was safely on her way home. With no other information, he set off with the squadron to the point where the eastern channel met the transport route from Shimonoseki to Hakko.

By 6,00pm he had reached the southern end of the Straits with his four armoured cruisers and with the *Naniwa, Takachiho* and *Tsushima*. Only the *Chihaya* and *Niitaka* were out scouting for the enemy. Corbett found this concentration quite unjustified:

> In default of an explanation we can only put it down to bad leading and cramped handling of his force. Even on elementary principles to keep three of his five light cruisers tied to the tail of his battle division, which was superior to the enemy he was seeking, was an inexplicable mistake and in this case condemned him to failure. Had he made the most ordinary attempt to feel round him, he could scarcely have failed to get contact with the Russians in such a way as to force them to an action. For at this time he must have been steaming approximately on the same course as the enemy without seeing them.[4]

In fairness to Kamimura, it should be noted that visibility in the area was very limited, due to fog.

The Russian squadron had been steaming southwards at a low speed; it was not until 6:30pm that they were finally through the channel and turned westward in the direction of Quelpart. Kamimura received an indecipherable message from the *Naniwa* at 6:14pm, and continued to steam southwards; and then, at about 6.40 he

4 Ibid. I, pp. 322-323.

sighted smoke and soon after was able to see the Vladivostok cruisers about 15 miles away; they appeared to be coming south. Bezobrazov did not immediately sight the Japanese squadron, but as soon as he did he turned back to the north-east, increasing to full speed. Kamimura naturally swung round to follow them, working up to the maximum speed of his squadron. As the range began to shorten, it could be seen that the *Rurik* was falling behind her consorts, and it seemed that it would be possible to bring the enemy to action. Kamimura sent the *Tsushima* to bring up the torpedo boats, and held on at 19 knots, closing on the *Rurik*, which at this point could do only 15 knots. Soon, however, she began to pick up speed, and although Kamimura increased to 20 knots, the range ceased to diminish. By 8.00pm, when the sun had set, it was still 8 to 10 miles, and the Russians were almost lost to sight.

Just as Bezobrazov began to think that he had got clean away, however, the torpedo boats of the Okinoshima patrol appeared. Eight approached on his port bow and three to the starboard. When they were first sighted, at a distance of some two miles, the Russians, switching on their searchlights, opened such a heavy fire that the torpedo boats hauled off, to wait until it was quite dark. Kamimura, seeing the lights, switched on his own to ensure that the enemy did not double back. The torpedo boats chased the enemy, but could not regain touch; it had come on to blow with a rising sea, and the small torpedo boats could not reach their maximum speed. The Russians did not switch on their searchlights again, and altered course; Kamimura, inevitably, lost touch with them completely. Then, at about 10.00pm, he received a signal that the enemy had been sighted west of Okinoshima. This might mean that they had doubled back; but the moon was up, and there was no sight of them. Kamimura decided that his duty was to cover the Straits, and turned back to the south-west. All day on July 2 he continued to cruise near Shimonoseki. Togo sent a signal enquiring where Kamimura thought the enemy had gone, but it was not until next day that he was able to send a reply that they had last been seen heading north eastwards. There was a pronounced concern in Tokyo that Bezobrazov might still be on the loose, and Kamimura was directed not to move far away. It was only on the morning of July 4 that he finally concluded that he could safely return to Osaki.

Meanwhile at 9.00am on July 2 the Russian squadron, on its way home, encountered the British steamer *Cheltenham*, en route from Otaru to Fusan with railway material. She was stopped and boarded, and a prize crew took her to Vladivostok, where she was duly condemned by the prize court. Apart from this, Bezobrazov was able to make for home unobserved, and he finally returned to Vladivostok at about 5.00pm on July 3.[5] For the Japanese it had been another embarrassing failure, damaging to the navy's public reputation. Corbett reckoned that the outcome was due in part to bad luck and 'the incalculable chances of the sea,' but mainly due to Kamimura's neglect to adopt a sound system of covering the Straits. He had been given, in his four armoured

5 *British Official History* I, p. 377.

cruisers, a superior battle division, and he should have kept it where it could not fail to strike the enemy if they approached the sector which he was to defend:

> To this end it should have been rigidly confined, and all scouting that was needed to give it timely warning should have been performed entirely by his other cruisers and the flotilla. Yet we see a recurring tendency to confuse the functions of the two sections of his force, a restless anxiety to seek out the enemy's fleet with his battle division, or with his massed force, on any alarm and on quite inadequate information. The result was that not only did he miss decisive contact, but that he permitted the enemy to penetrate the vital area from which it was his primary duty to exclude them.[6]

Mahan, noting belatedly that the activities of the Vladivostok squadron had resulted in the transfer of Kamimura's squadron to the Tsushima Straits, recognised that this was a position which it was vital for the Japanese to occupy. He quoted with approval a report from a correspondent of The Times dated July 10:

> Kamimura's Squadron is not powerful enough to blockade the two entrances to Vladivostok. It has been compelled to adopt the minor role of sealing the Tsushima Straits, so as to cover the line of communication southward of that point. The naval people pray daily for freedom to wipe out the score Vladivostok has run up against them… The three big cruisers stationed in Vladivostok, and their accompanying swarm of torpedo craft, are so many thorns in the side of Japan. It irks her grievously that, while winning signal successes on the principal stage, there should be a by play of unpunished raids against her own merchantman, transports and peaceful settlers; that the sea which goes by her name should be an open field for her enemy's enterprises; that her shores should be open to attack by a comparatively petty force; and that, while she has swept the main body of the Russians out of Western Korea, marauding bands of Cossacks should defy her along the north-western shore of the peninsula. It is difficult to remedy this flagrant fault in the situation, until the fleet can be freed from its all absorbing duties at Port Arthur.[7]

It was no wonder, Mahan thought, that the same correspondent noted that it was rumoured in Tokyo that the Naval Staff were advocating the reduction of Port Arthur as the overwhelming priority. This, he considered, indicated the correctness of the Russian decision to retain the port.

There was mounting concern in Tokyo about the failure of the navy to regain the initiative. There was there an inability to grasp the reality of the situation, since it

6 Corbett I, p. 326.
7 Captain A.T. Mahan, *Naval Administration and Warfare* (London, 1908), pp. 101-103.

appeared that the Imperial Staff did not appreciate that the communications of the army had been left undisturbed due to the inaction of the Russians rather than to what their own fleet was able to do against a force that was equally strong. Now that the Russian fleet was recovering its activity the real situation 'was declaring itself with disturbing effect.'[8]

In a report of August 4, Pakenham commented on another aspect of the campaign which would have been considered highly relevant by the British Admiralty. This was the use of auxiliary cruisers, only one of which appeared to have done anything to earn her keep. Two of them had been used as part of the escort of the military transports, but apart from providing accommodation for the naval brigade which Togo had formed, they had remained idle. Pakenham described the subsequent employment of one of these vessels, which had been armed with two 6-inch guns and four smaller guns, and were equipped with searchlights. The cost of their hire was considerable:

> About 10 days ago, Shanghai reported loaded vessels were leaving for Newchwang, and the *Hongkong Maru* was sent to intercept them off the Shantung promontory. Two of the steamers were caught and sent to the prize court at Sasebo, but a later cruise, in company with the dispatch vessel, has been unrewarded. Though the auxiliaries are fine ships, of sufficient speed, and offering a good gun platform in ordinary weather, their armament is ill-disposed, and the broadside guns will only fire on very limited bearings, besides being both few in number and light. As the *Hongkong Maru*, acting apparently according to instructions, fled in daylight from what was thought to be a Russian destroyer, the opinion held by the Japanese of her fighting value cannot be high. This distrust seems to be fully merited. In fact, the auxiliary cruisers of this fleet have been very costly superfluities hitherto, and must catch several more cargo boats before they will have liquidated their cost to the country.[9]

Since 1901 the British Admiralty had been giving particular consideration to the possibility that the German navy was planning to launch an assault on Britain's seaborne trade by the use of armed merchant vessels. There was concern that German shipping lines received government subsidies, which had been vigorously denied by Albert Ballin, the head of the Hamburg-America line, in a letter to *The Times* of August 23, 1901, in which he wrote:

> We do not even receive the subsidy which the British Admiralty pays to the large British steamship companies for fitting and keeping certain specially suitable steamers at the disposal of the Admiralty in case of mobilisation. The

8 Corbett I, p. 327.
9 Naval Attaché Reports, pp. 134-135.

> large German steamship companies have hitherto agreed to render like services without demanding any payment.[10]

This was not reassuring, carrying as it did the apparent confirmation that the Germans might well make use of suitable armed merchant vessels, and the debate rumbled on. At the same time, of course, as Ballin's letter had pointed out, it was certainly the case that Britain would herself be considering the use of such vessels in wartime. Pakenham's report of their apparent ineffectiveness was something that the Admiralty would have to take into account.

At Vladivostok, the Russians were planning a more ambitious stroke than had previously been attempted. The plan was to launch a raid by the squadron to disrupt Japanese international communications, specifically those between the ports on Japan's eastern and southern coasts and the United States and Australia. It would mean a lengthy voyage, with the enhanced risk of being caught by superior force far from home, but it would have the advantage of surprise. With no apparent action contemplated by it or by the fleet in Port Arthur, Alexeiev was anxious to see something being done. It was decided that the operation should be led by Rear Admiral Iessen, with his flag in the *Rossiya*. Skrydlov authorised the operation on July 17, and later that day the squadron put to sea. Iessen's orders were to steam through the Tsugaru Strait, and then head southward to attack shipping off Tokyo.[11]

One key difficulty faced by Iessen was the problem of his coal supply. The need to conserve this as far as possible meant that the squadron was obliged to steam at its most economical speed. This, combined with the effect of fog which was encountered, meant that Iessen did not reach the entrance to the Tsugaru Strait until the evening of July 19. He had intended to pass through the Strait during the night, but in view of the fog waited until dawn. Then, steaming at 15 knots, he entered the Strait and was off Hakodate within two hours. To his surprise he encountered no opposition. The small, and old, warships that were available to watch the Strait were not on patrol; when Iessen reached Hakodate, where these vessels were concentrated, they made no attempt to bar his progress; they would not have stood much of a chance if they had. Nor did the coastal batteries open fire, and by 7.00pm Iessen was clear of the Strait. Almost at once he took a small steamer which, after allowing the crew to take to the boats, he sank. Next he took a British vessel, the *Samara*, but let her go as she was bound for Seattle. These activities had been observed from the coast, and he soon picked up a wireless message warning all ships to remain in port.

Heading south, he was by 7.00pm on July 20 some 60 miles east by south from Shiriya Zaki, where he took and sank a small schooner. He then captured a small steamer, but finding her full of women and children, he let her go. He was finding

10 Quoted Matthew S. Seligman, *The Royal Navy and the German Threat 1901-1914* (Oxford, 2012), p. 26.
11 Olender II, p. 168; Corbett I, p. 341.

it difficult to locate suitable targets, thanks to the prompt warnings which had been issued, and he pressed on southward during the night. Next day he continued on this course, steaming slowly to conserve fuel. By 7.00am on July 21 he had made only 100 miles towards his real objective, which was the area off Tokyo. It was on that morning that the Naval Staff got a report of Iessen's movements from fishermen who sighted the squadron off Yamada. Next day the squadron made a prize of the German steamer *Arabia*, and sent her to Vladivostok, but pickings continued to be small. Nothing came his way next day, but on July 24 he took the *Knight Commander*, a large British vessel carrying railway material; her crew was taken off, and she was sunk by shell fire. By now Iessen had reached his target area but he was already experiencing practical difficulties. He had not been able to spare a prize crew for the *Knight Commander*, while his coal supply was causing great anxiety. For some reason the *Gromoboi* had been burning fuel at a high rate, and Iessen was seriously concerned about the risk that he might not be able to get back safely to Vladivostok. He decided, however, that he should continue his cruise, and return via Sakhalin, where he could take on coal.[12]

The squadron had been sighted by a Japanese lookout station at 8:30am on July 24, and was reported half an hour later to have turned west. The Naval Staff in Tokyo had, thus far, not felt able to order any substantial movement to intercept Iessen, either from Togo's fleet or Kamimura in the Tsushima Straits. Now, however, orders were sent to the latter: 'The Vladivostok squadron of three ships are steaming slowly off Idzu and threatening merchant ships. You must leave at once, bringing with you the vessels of your command which are near you. Proceed to Toi-Misaki and await orders.'[13] This was a surprising decision, prompted by a panic response to the probable reaction of the Japanese public to the news that the Russians could attack the coast adjacent to the capital with impunity. Dismissing the explanation given in the Japanese Official History that the move was intended to meet the possibility that Iessen was heading for Port Arthur, Corbett pointed out that this had already been provided for:

> The inference is that the true cause of the change was the irresistible moral pressure of the threat to the coasts which everyone but the men on the spot well knew could never be anything more than a threat. The fowler had spread a net in sight of the bird and in spite of the best resolutions the destruction of a single ship had been enough to make the bird walk into it.[14]

The decision of the Naval Staff meant, of course, that the door to the Tsushima Straits had been left open to whatever other raids, such as by torpedo boats, that the Russians might choose to mount. Only small torpedo boats remained at Takeshiki.

12 *British Official History* I, p. 379: Corbett I, p. 341.
13 Corbett I, p. 342.
14 Ibid., p. 343.

The Naval Staff's order overrode an instruction which Togo had given to Kamimura, as soon as news came in of Iessen's appearance off Tokyo. The commander-in-chief's immediate response had been to take steps to ensure that Iessen did not get back safely to Vladivostok:

> You must leave at once with the 2nd Division (the four armoured cruisers) the *Chihaya* (dispatch vessel) and two divisions of first-class torpedo boats for the west side of Oshima (off the Tsugaru Strait) and Shirakami Zaki to bar the return of the Vladivostok squadron which you will attack with your utmost strength ... you must guard the Tsushima Straits with the 4th Division (Admiral Uriu's cruisers) and the rest of your flotilla.[15]

Unfortunately, Kamimura did not receive this instruction until after he had the order from the Naval Staff, with which he felt bound to comply.

Meanwhile Iessen had continued to steam westward in July 24 after sinking the *Knight Commander*. Two schooners with fish and rice were sunk. The British steamer *Tsinan* was stopped, but being solely a passenger vessel she was released. By now Iessen's anxiety about his coal supply was mounting, and during the night of July 24 /25 he turned back to the east. He picked up the German ship *Thea*, and next morning decided to sink her as she appeared to be carrying contraband. The boarding party had misread the bill of lading as suggesting that her cargo was fish and oil, rather than fish oil and meal as was in fact the case.[16] Sinking her proved not to be as easy as might have been expected; it took the *Rurik* 200 rounds and four hours to accomplish the task. Later that morning Iessen captured the British steamer *Calchas,* a 6,000 ton vessel which was carrying a cargo of which about half could be considered contraband, and he decided that he could spare a prize crew for such a valuable prize, sending her back to Vladivostok by way of Korsakovsk.

Next day the Naval Staff, doing their best to make sense of the various reports reaching them of Iessen's movements, began making Kamimura's life difficult by bombarding him with instructions. The information reaching him suggested that the Russians had either entered the Inland Sea or were still heading westwards, presumably towards Port Arthur. Kamimura headed south so that he could head them off if the latter was the course, but of course found nothing. The confusion continued. Another report seemed to indicate that the Russians had taken a collier, and might be amongst the Dzunan Islands in order to coal their squadron, and Kamimura was ordered to investigate this. He was becoming extremely frustrated at the torrent of instructions reaching him fromTokyo, and in the end sent a respectful protest:

15 Ibid., p. 332.
16 Olender II, p. 168.

> What I most fear is that the enemy have gone back northward, or are steaming south-west for some purpose of their own. I am therefore uneasy at the idea of keeping the squadron in a position from which it cannot readily cooperate with the main fleet. I accordingly submit that we be given directions to withdraw.[17]

At 3.00am on July 30, Kamimura was finally ordered to return to his post in the Tsushima Straits.

In all this time he had never been near to Iessen's squadron. After the capture of the *Calchas* on July 25, the Russian commander had reviewed his position. His coal supply was dangerously low, and if he was to get back unmolested to Vladivostok it seemed to him that it would be safer to go north and instead of risking the Tsugaru Strait to proceed beyond Hokkaido and make use of the La Perouse Strait before heading home. Early on July 27, steaming northwards at 10 knots, he passed the Tsugaru Strait well to the east, but then began to run into thick fog, as he headed towards the easternmost cape of Hokkaido. This gave him a serious problem. The *Gromoboi* was down to eight days' coal. The fog continued to blind him; in an unsuccessful endeavour to ascertain where he actually was, he turned south, and all through July 29 continued to feel his way cautiously. It was only on the morning of the next day he was able to sight land and he turned into the Tsugaru Strait, fully expecting to find the enemy in strength when he emerged from the other end. Iessen's ships made their way through the Strait, unmolested by the coast defence ships there or by the batteries, and by sunset were clear, to find no enemy awaiting them. At 3.00pm on August 1 the squadron returned safely to Vladivostok, having sailed 3100 sea miles.[18]

Iessen's raid had yielded relatively little in terms of shipping captured or destroyed, principally due to the prudent warning to merchantmen to stay in port until the danger had passed. It had, however, created enormous confusion, resulting in a substantial increase in freight prices and a reduction of 20% in deliveries to Japanese ports during the month of August. It was an episode which illustrated the danger of interference by the central authorities in the arrangements made by the commander-in-chief at sea, not least by the taking of important decisions without any consultation with him. Togo's advice had been ignored; the government had effectively lost its head. Had his advice been taken, 'annihilation would have been as certain as anything in war can be. As it was the Japanese paid the price and bought nothing but a demoralising sense of failure.'[19]

Admiral Ballard took a much more charitable view of the Japanese government's response to Iessen's raid, suggesting that 'these depredations on shipping represented a subsidiary reverse of the kind absolutely unavoidable in maritime war, never justifying any reduction of the force at the main points of contact with the enemy.' Comparing

17 Corbett I, p. 349.
18 Olender II, p. 168.
19 Corbett I, p. 351.

this with Corbett's view quoted above, it must be concluded that Ballard was simply wrong in his assessment of the government's actions; and that Corbett was right to conclude that the pretence that the orders to Kamimura were to prevent Iessen getting into the Yellow Sea 'was obviously only a cloak for a desire to have a squadron near the threatened capital.' Ballard, writing in 1921, did go on to comment on the problems which commerce raiding could cause, observing of Iessen's movements:

> Although its direct fruits were unimportant, his cruise has a somewhat special historical interest, as the first example anywhere of the immense difficulties of dealing with an elusive raider under modern conditions, when the whole seas lie before him; a difficulty illustrated on a still wider scale ten years later by the performances of German cruisers.[20]

20 Ballard, p. 247.

15

Councils of War

Pakenham was very conscious of the limitations of the reports that he sent, as he explained in his report of August 3:

> A single observer can see but a small part of the field, and for the rest must depend on what people, frequently officially reminded to be on their guard, choose to tell him. Even of what he can see, he may not always be at liberty to tell the whole. If he should be a guest, and also an officer in the employment of his government, he would be far from carrying out the wishes of the latter if he did not exercise discretion in withholding anything whose divulgation could be construed as a disloyalty to his hosts.[1]

His holding back of his report of the loss of the *Hatsuse* and the *Yashima* was of course an example of his discretion.

One influential aspect of modern naval warfare, to which he naturally devoted a good deal of attention, was that of communications, as he explained on August 3:

> In an area of limited size, such as that in which the present war is being waged, wireless telegraphy entirely supersedes the despatch vessels (the Japanese bases have always been in direct cable communication with home), and does away with a good deal of ordinary signalling also. Despatch boats are attached to the squadrons, but have been employed for almost every purpose except that of carrying messages. With greater experience, it has been evident that the estimation in which this form of telegraphy is held by the Japanese has been constantly increasing, and hardly a week passes without witnessing the introduction of the wireless apparatus to ships hitherto without it. Although a very few of the oldest small craft have not yet got it, it would be practically correct to say it is fitted in every ship in the Japanese navy above the size of a destroyer, as well as in the

1 Naval Attaché Reports, p. 126.

> principal vessels of the supply fleet. Though no destroyers carrying it have come under observation, it is said to have been installed in several, and to be effective up to 35 or 40 miles. Recognising that every ship may have to act independently at some time, and that the value of single ships or small squadrons is enhanced, and their safety increased, by the possession of a ready means of communication, the Japanese have been lavish in its supply to everything into which a tall enough mast could be put. Certainly, the small detached forces that have done all the lookout work in this war could not have been thrust forward, as they have been, if they had not been enabled to keep touch with their reserves.

The system in use, he reported, was the Marconi, to which apparently the Japanese had made some modifications. Pakenham went on to point out one key development which would in the future come to be of crucial significance: 'What seems very much wanted is an indicator that would show the direction whence came enemy signals. It is a poor satisfaction to a lookout to know an enemy is within wireless range, but to be unable to determine his bearing.'[2]

In the period following the sortie of June 23 there was not a great deal to report in the way of fleet operations, save the activites of the Vladivostok squadron and the steps taken to meet them. These, however, Pakenham and his colleagues did not cover, and the reports sent in July and early August were largely concerned with the operations of the navy in support of the army. Pakenham did though find space to address the question of the efficiency of the Japanese torpedo flotilla, which he described as 'a subject of great interest to the naval service, as is evidenced by the letters received, asking the reason.' It was not due to the design of the vessels, he considered; they had been built variously in Great Britain, France, Germany and Japan. The fuel used had been usually Welsh coal. The comparison with the Russian performance was, however, striking:

> Comparing the duties upon which the boats have been employed, up to the time of the sealing of Port Arthur there was little to choose between the flotillas of Russia and Japan – both scouted or raided, patrolled harbours and accompanied fleets; yet the one was never able to show in numerical strength, while every unit of the other, although with no dockyard to fall back on, throughout the whole period of the war has never failed to respond to the most sudden calls.[3]

It was a question which was certainly relevant to the British navy. Pakenham concluded that it was the Japanese method of carrying out normal practice that was the explanation, and which offered useful lessons:

2 Ibid, pp. 127-128.
3 Ibid., p. 121.

> There will be found the utmost regularity possible in alternating work with suitable periods of repose, slow speeds except when in action, tactics reduced to their simplest form, great latitude for the exercise of common sense, definite responsibility accompanied by freedom from close supervision, unpretentious repair and depot ships that do not ape men of war, single-minded attention to duty undisturbed by fashionable distractions. In short, the needs of a flotilla are understood and supplied, the officers work hard and are held responsible for efficiency.[4]

In spite of this, and the courage and skill of the crews of the destroyers and torpedo boats, it must be observed that their effectiveness throughout the war, on both sides, fell far short of the dominant role envisaged by the *Jeune École*.

Meanwhile Jackson, aboard the *Manshu Maru*, had been taken on a tour of the Japanese fleet bases. This trip was rather disparagingly described by Pakenham as a 'government picnic party,' but it did enable Jackson to describe the arrangements for telegraphic communication, as well as the facilities that had been erected at Haeju and the various landing points at which the armies had been disembarked. For his part, Hutchison sent a detailed account of the preparations for battle aboard the *Asama*, to which he had been assigned. He found it 'extraordinary how little is done in the way of preparation.' In the accommodation, both for officers and crew, nothing was removed, with the exception of a number of the boats which were left behind; 'it really seems as if the responsible people had thought that they were simply going out for target practice.' Hutchison learned that the captain intended fighting the ship from the foretop, and would control the whole of the fire, passing messages as to the course to be steered to the conning tower.[5]

The attack by General Nogi on the 'Position of the Passes', a hugely important move against the defences of Port Arthur, was scheduled for July 26. It was preceded by a period of appalling weather at sea, commencing with a storm of wind and rain on July 19, followed by dense fog which set in until the evening of July 25. A brief clearance enabled Togo's battle fleet to move out of its anchorage into open water, where it then had to anchor. Next day the fog persisted, but since the Third Army would have begun its advance, the fleet weighed and moved to its support. It soon encountered better weather. Togo had in the meantime sent the shallow draught ships of the 7th Division (*Seiyen, Tsukushi, Fuso, Akagi, Chokai, Maya* and *Uji*) with some torpedo boats to the west coast of the peninsula, while the 3rd Division (*Kasagi, Chitose* and *Takasago*) strengthened by the addition of the *Asama* and *Yakumo* kept a lookout about 12 miles of Liautishan, in case the Russians came out to interfere. The rest of the fleet was to be stationed off the east coast; the 5th Division, comprising the *Itsukushima, Matsushima, Hashidate* and *Chinyen* went inshore to support the left flank of Nogi's army.

4 Ibid., p. 122.
5 Ibid., p. 143.

The cooperation of the fleet on July 26, was however, severely restricted by the weather, which prevented the warships from getting close inshore, and disturbing the minesweeping operations which were essential for this. Corbett commented on the additional problems presented by the extensive Russian mining operations:

> Tactical cooperation of a fleet with an army has always been one of the most precarious elements in warfare owing to the difficulties of coastal work in unfavourable weather, and now the new element of minefields proved to have increased the uncertainty. In this case the Russians had the initiative in the mining operations, and the Japanese naval officers found that, work as they would, they could not dominate them. Minefields still obstructed their inshore operations, and until they could clear the ground it was impossible to give the army the assistance which it had a right to expect.[6]

In the event, the attempted cooperation was a complete failure. To make matters worse, the light cruiser *Chiyoda*, which with the rest of Rear Admiral Togo's division had moved closer inshore during the late afternoon, struck a mine; seriously damaged, and in a sinking condition, she managed to stagger into the harbour at Dalny, where she was at once moved into the dockyard. Efforts to deploy the ships of the 7th Division on the following day were abandoned when a message came from the army that no further assistance from them was required; they were redeployed further up the coast in support of General Oku's Second Army. Meanwhile Vitgeft sent out his cruisers, which drove back the Japanese minesweepers and then, for three hours, bombarded the Japanese positions in support of the counter-attack which Stoessel had ordered.

Next day Nogi resumed his attack, and Vitgeft was again asked for naval support for the troops fighting on the Russian right. On this occasion the armoured cruiser *Bayan*, and the light cruisers *Askold, Pallada* and *Novik* were accompanied by the battleship *Retvizan*, as well as three gunboats, a torpedo gunboat and 13 destroyers. Throughout the afternoon of July 27 these ships poured a heavy fire on Japanese positions. Togo, in response to a suggestion from his destroyer commander, sent forward the *Nisshin* and *Kasuga* from the main fleet, which at this time was standing on and off Round Island. The two armoured cruisers were in range by 2.45pm, and opened a steady fire from their 8-inch and 10-inch guns at a range of over 16,000 yards, to which the Russians were able to make no effective reply. Pakenham reported that they had between them fired some 20 rounds.[7]

The Russians now suffered a serious setback. As the *Bayan*, returning to harbour, was about to enter the Gut, she struck a mine, and was seriously damaged. She was, however, able to return to her berth in the West Basin, though well down by the bow. Her watertight bulkheads had stood, and only the foremost stokehold was flooded.

6 Corbett I, pp. 354-355.
7 Naval Attaché Reports, p. 131.

She would, however, be out of action for a considerable time. This deeply affected the already despondent Vitgeft, who was obliged to tell Stoessel that he could provide no further support for the army on either the east or west side of the peninsula. It was at about this time that Nogi's sustained assault finally succeeded in taking key positions in the Russian front line, which two counter-attacks failed to recover, and the whole Russian army fell back to the Wolf Hills, the last position in front of the permanent defences of the fortress.

Vitgeft's pessimism was accentuated by what Pakenham described as 'a very brilliant little destroyer action' which was fought off Port Arthur on August 5, when three Japanese destroyers effectively put to flight a flotilla of 14 Russian destroyers. Togo, in his next fleet orders, observed that their gallantry had 'deserved the admiration of the whole fleet.' Pakenham considered that the action was remarkable 'as being the first practical indication of the acknowledgement by the Russians of Japanese superiority in this kind of fighting.'[8] A somewhat different view of the engagement was taken by the Official History, based on Russian accounts. According to these, three of the Russian destroyers had steamed towards Dalny with the object of drawing off the Japanese destroyers, while the rest engaged in mining operations off Port Arthur. These were successful, as the Japanese were lured away, and after an hour all the Russian destroyers were able to return unscathed to port.[9]

Ever since the abortive operation of June 23, Vitgeft's belief that the right course was for the fleet remain in Port Arthur had been hardening into absolute conviction. His report of June 27, describing the sortie and the reasons for his retirement, had not reached Alexeiev until June 30. The Viceroy was appalled, and next day sent a dispatch making clear his extreme dissatisfaction:

> On careful consideration I do not find sufficient grounds to justify you, instead of carrying out my directions to steam out to sea and attack and defeat the enemy, in returning to the roadstead in spite of the obvious danger from the enemy's minefields and night torpedo attacks… As I have repeatedly pointed out to you, the whole importance of a sortie consisted in inflicting a defeat on the enemy.[10]

All that Vitgeft had achieved, in Alexeiev's mind, was to reveal to the enemy that the entrance to Port Arthur was free and that the damaged ships had been repaired. While some of Alexeiev's previous pronouncements appear self-serving, it is difficult not to have some sympathy with a commander whose subordinate so flagrantly ignored a direct order. The Viceroy reinforced his dispatch with an Imperial command which he had just received from St Petersburg; this was an order to put to sea as soon as the

8 Ibid., p. 145.
9 *British Official History* I, p. 328.
10 Corbett I, p. 334.

Sevastopol had been repaired, and the necessary stores completed. The objective would be to get to Vladivostok, avoiding action if possible.

Alexeiev's express instructions to Vitgeft were slightly different, but couched in terms which ought to have been sufficiently explicit. These were that the ships should be immediately prepared for sea and kept in constant readiness; that Vitgeft should so far as he could assist the defence of Port Arthur by means of active operations; that the fleet was to remain at Port Arthur only as long as it could safely do so; and that in the event of Port Arthur no longer being a safe refuge for the fleet, it was, notwithstanding that the *Sevastopo*l was under repair, to put to sea in good time and head for Vladivostok.[11]

Vitgeft was told that he must convene a conference of his flag officers and captains to consider these orders and settle the plan of operations. With the benefit of hindsight, it is clear that repeated discussions of the explicit orders given would not be helpful, and insisting that a conference be held was a mistake. Before convening it, Vitgeft sent a reply on July 5 restating his position. A sortie was, he said, out of the question. The previous operation had shown that there was no such thing as a favourable moment. The Viceroy's staff had underestimated the strength of the enemy. Nor did he consider himself capable of succeeding in such a venture: 'I do not think myself a capable fleet leader. I am only commanding by force of circumstances till a commander-in-chief can arrive.'[12] This confession of his incapacity should have been enough for Alexeiev to relieve him of command at once, as should his repeated expression of opinions directly in conflict with those of the Viceroy. The Admiral plaintively repeated these:

> I did not go out for display, but in accordance with orders. Change of circumstances required my return in order to avoid useless loss. After the departure of the squadron to Vladivostok, the enemy would clear a channel and capture Port Arthur with his fleet and troops in a very short time; moreover he would not permit our squadron, weakened by nightly attacks and with its ships damaged, to proceed forward or backward without an action. For the squadron there are only two decisions. Either it is necessary for it to defend Port Arthur in conjunction with the troops until reinforced, or to perish; the moment for a sortie to Vladivostok can only arise when death faces us simultaneously in front and rear.[13]

Although he added that the will of the Tsar was of course sacred, it was plain that he did not intend to carry it out.

This reply, not surprisingly, enraged Alexeiev, who apparently considered the possibility of relieving Vitgeft by Skrydlov or Bezobrazov, but he was evidently

11 *British Official History* I, p. 301.
12 Corbett I, p. 336.
13 *British Official History* I, pp. 301-302.

dissuaded from taking this step. Instead, on July 9, he insisted again on a conference of senior officers being held:

> I have received your dispatch of July 5. Your opinion expressed in it, that there are only two methods of procedure for the squadron, to defend Port Arthur or perish with the fortress, so little corresponds with the Imperial commands and the function of the forces entrusted to you, that I must lay the question of the squadron making a sortie and breaking through to Vladivostok before a Council of flag officers and captains, in which the commandant of the port, Rear Admiral Grigorovitch, is to take part. A brief summary of the decision of the Council is immediately to be forwarded to me by every possible means of communication.[14]

Alexeiev accompanied this by a second message setting out how the operation was to be conducted. The squadron must leave the port as early as possible, and not anchor outside. An overcast morning, or fresh weather, should be chosen to limit the effectiveness of the enemy's flotilla; and if the squadron had to fight, it should do so boldly.[15]

These messages arrived on July 15 and 16, and next day the Council was held. Its conclusions, signed by all those present, were entirely predictable; they were sent off on July 18. The Russian official account of this meeting recorded these in the following terms:

> A favourable and safe moment was out of the question, as the danger of mines was always present. A sortie in fresh weather was impossible owing to the continual mining and the pilotage difficulties caused by the sunken block ships. Having inferior speed they could not get to Vladivostok without an action. Since the enemy had an overwhelming flotilla he could use it to cripple the fleet and then choose his own moment for action. Consequently nothing could justify the event unless and until the fortress was *in extremis* and it was no longer possible for the fleet to assist in the defence, as it was then doing by annoying the enemy's flanks[16]

These conclusions had not reached Alexeiev by the time he next wrote to Vitgeft in a letter dated July 18, which the admiral received on July 23. This was a long and urgent appeal expressing the grave anxiety felt by himself and the Tsar, who considered it of the last importance that the fleet should get to Vladivostok, and whatever the risk nothing could justify the identification of its fate with that of the fortress, unless the

14 Ibid., p. 302.
15 Corbett I, p. 336.
16 Ibid., pp. 336-337.

place was certain to hold out until relieved.[17] The historical parallel with the case of Sevastopol was, wrote Alexeiev, inappropriate, since in the Crimean War, the sailing fleet was sunk because it was opposed by a steam fleet. No such inequality obtained in the present case; indeed, the reverse was true. Alexeiev was clearly aware that both the Japanese battleships that were mined had sunk, and that Togo now had only four. This evoked yet another protest from Vitgeft on the following day; he told the Viceroy that in any case the earliest date for a sortie would be August 8, but that at the same time he had not altered his opinion; nothing could justify a sortie unless Kuropatkin was driven north.

On July 28, aware that the garrison of Port Arthur had been driven back to its final position outside the fortress, Vitgeft despondently convened yet another council of war. 11 officers were present; only two, Matusevitch and von Essen, the captain of the *Sevastopol*, favoured an attempt to break through to Vladivostok. All the rest voted for staying put. One of these was Captain Virens, who was soon to be promoted over everyone's head to the command of the squadron; he recorded the majority decision with which of course Vitgeft readily agreed:'The fleet to remain at Port Arthur and form with the place an undivided organisation. The vessels to be divided into those which go out into the roadstead and those which will remain in the harbour, the latter to pay off and land their crews in defence of the fortress.'[18]

Vitgeft, who did not accept the reports that the Japanese were down to four battleships, sent this off to Alexeiev on July 30 with news of the loss of the *Bayan*. This showed more clearly than ever the impracticability of a sortie. He followed this up with a further despairing telegram to Alexeiev in Mukden:

> The squadron cannot go out; the roadstead has been sown nightly, during fogs, by numerous torpedo craft and mine layers, with mines and especially drifting ones… After praying and considering the situation we have decided finally that the squadron must withstand the siege or perish in defence of Port Arthur. The enemy have drawn near and our forces have retired to the forts. There are continual fogs. I have begun indirect firing on the Japanese troops.[19]

This correspondence was getting Alexeiev nowhere. He appealed to the Tsar, from whom he got a reply which he at once sent on to Vitgeft: 'I fully share your opinion concerning the importance of the squadron making a speedy sortie and breaking through to Vladivostok.'[20] The Viceroy followed this with a final blunt and unmistakable order to Vitgeft. He told him that he could not accept Vitgeft's decision to remain at Port Arthur. The fleet, he said, had a special function and should not in

17 Ibid., p. 359.
18 Ibid., p. 360.
19 *British Official History* I, pp. 302-303.
20 Ibid I, p. 302.

any circumstances share the fate of the fortress, nor could he permit it to fall into the enemy's hands. Port Arthur could not be relieved before September, while the Baltic squadron could not arrive before December. Vitgeft was therefore expressly ordered to carry out Alexeiev's instructions exactly; he concluded by spelling out clearly the consequence of any further disobedience:

> I again reiterate my inflexible determination that you are to take the squadron out of Port Arthur. I must recall to you and all senior officers the exploit of the *Varyag*. The failure of the squadron to proceed to sea regardless of the Imperial will and my command, and its extinction in the harbour in the event of the fall of the fortress will, in addition to the heavy legal responsibility, leave an indelible spot on the flag of Saint Andrew and on the honour of the fleet. You are to make known this telegram to all admirals and commanding officers and are to report its receipt.[21]

In the face of this, not even Vitgeft could fail to act, and he despondently began to prepare. For the moment, the projected sortie remained confidential, but in the fleet there was a sense that something was about to happen, as Semenov recorded:

> No more grandiloquent orders were issued announcing the resumption of the offensive with simultaneous appeals to the heavenly hosts. No sensational rumours were spread in the town. The clerks who were sent to the Admiral's office did not bring back bits of news confided to them by some'very reliable people; yet there was something in the air.[22]

21 Ibid, p. 303.
22 Semenov I, p. 176.

16

Battle of the Yellow Sea

On August 7 the Japanese artillery began to bombard the Port Arthur basin, as well as on the old town and as much of the harbour as could be observed. It was a clear warning that the fleet could no longer be regarded as safe there. Several ships were damaged, and the *Retvizan* seriously enough for her to take on several hundred tons of water. The flagship was also hit twice, and Vitgeft himself was slightly wounded. The Japanese were threatening the heights of Taku and Hsiaoku, and Rear Admiral Loshchinski took the *Novik*, with two gunboats and eight destroyers, into Takhe Bay to enfilade the Japanese advance and halt it. When Togo, with the main fleet at Round Island, heard of this, he sent the *Nisshin* and *Kasuga* to deal with the situation; when they appeared, Loshchinski withdrew, and after this the Japanese infantry pressed forward again, taking both heights after nightfall. Time was running out for the squadron.

Vitgeft's reluctant decision to obey Alexeiev's demand for a sortie had not been readily accepted by all his colleagues. Grigorovitch, for example, urged that the slower *Poltava* and *Sevastopol* should be left behind, to give the squadron a better chance of escape. Loshchinski was of the same opinion, offering to take these two ships and all the flotilla to attack Dalny as a diversion to assist the squadron's getaway. Vitgeft would have none of it. His view of the correct strategy had been rejected by Alexeiev; he had been told to take out the squadron and that was what he was going to do.[1]

Semenov conveyed the frame of mind in which the squadron received the news of the intended sortie:

> Our people, who had long since received their baptism of fire, and who had now so often looked death in the face, prepared for this battle as for a serious task, full of responsibility. 'The thing is settled. Tomorrow morning we go out into the deadly fight. Thank God! Apparently no one is thinking of himself. One's duty has to be carried out.' These few lines I scribbled in my diary, as I was going to

1 Corbett I, p. 369.

> bed on the eve of sailing. There was yet something in the minds of all which I should not like to pass over in silence. There was a certain sense of satisfaction. We felt that at last there was an end to the divergence between the intentions of the leaders and the hopes and aspirations of the masses … The news that our sailing was imminent did not produce any enthusiasm, but only a general sense of relief.[2]

The *Diana*, which had been acting as guard ship, would be the last to leave port.

McCully, who had not received permission to sail with the fleet, watched the scene as it left Port Arthur:

> Wednesday, August 10, was fair and warm, with light south-easterly breezes, horizon hazy with occasional wisps of fog in the morning. At 5.00am fleet began to move, all being out at 8.00am, and anchored off the entrance. *Tsarevitch* (flag) then got under way preceded by trawlers and accompanied by 16 torpedo boats, and steered to south-westward along shore as far as large rock three and one half miles south-west of entrance, then turned to south-eastward followed in order by *Retvizan*, with a slight list to port from injury of previous day, *Pobieda*, *Peresviet* (flag), *Poltava* and *Sevastopol*. Next came cruiser division *Askold* (flag), *Pallada, Diana*, with *Novik* detached on left flank and hospital ship *Mongolia* in the rear. Gunboats *Gremintschny Otvajny*, and *Bobr* followed to mark the turn and cover retirement of trawlers. All ships had battle flags up, and went out quickly and in excellent order, acting as a fleet with a purpose. Ships kept 400 yards apart, and made a very handsome show.[3]

That morning Togo, with his four battleships and the dispatch vessel *Yaeyama*, was in his usual position off Round Island. He sent in the *Nisshin* and *Kasuga* again to prevent any further interference by the Russian fleet with the Japanese advance, while Dewa, with the *Yakumo* and three protected cruisers (*Kasagi, Chitose* and *Takasago*) was 15 miles south of Liautishan covering the vessels cooperating with the Second Army at Newchwang. Rear Admiral Togo, with the 6th Division (*Akashi*, *Suma* and *Akitsushima*) was 2 miles west of Encounter Rock; his fourth ship, the *Idzumi*, had gone back to base to coal, as had Dewa's second armoured cruiser *Asama*, aboard which was Captain Hutchison. Pakenham, as usual, was aboard the *Asahi*.

At 6.30pm it was seen from the Japanese siege lines that there was movement outside the harbour. The *Novik*, accompanied as usual by the minesweepers and their gunboat escort, was emerging from the Gut. A message to this effect was sent by the new Japanese signal station ashore and passed on by the *Fuso*, in Dalny harbour. For the moment, nothing particularly serious seemed to be happening, but then Russian

2 Semenov I, p. 183.
3 McCully, p. 138.

battleships began to follow, assembling on the west side of the roadstead. It was unclear to Togo whether this meant that the entire Russian fleet was putting to sea, and, if so, whether it was an operation to attack the left flank of Nogi's army, or a sortie into the Gulf of Pechili. By 8:50am, however, so many ships had emerged from Port Arthur, that Togo decided to close in nearer to them. Pakenham produced a very detailed account of what followed in his report of August 17:

> At 12:40pm the Russians loomed suddenly through the haze; apparently they were in two divisions, in line abreast, with the battleships in front, and were steering straight for the Japanese fleet.
>
> The Japanese battle line, accordingly, turned four points to port, together, and increased speed to 14 knots. At first the line was very irregular, the *Shikishima* dropping astern until she must have been at least half a mile astern of station, so speed was reduced to the former 12 knots, to allow errors of position to be rectified; and it may be noted that from this time forward, throughout the remainder of the action, the station kept in the Japanese line was nearer perfection than had been remarked on any previous occasion.
>
> The Japanese soon (12:50pm) turned back into line ahead on the same course as before. The Russian fleet was now more clearly visible, and was at a distance of perhaps 12 miles from the Japanese, whom it appeared fully determined to fight….
>
> The Japanese held their present course only until it was certain that they had crossed the line of Russian advance; course was then (12:59pm) altered eight points to port together. Sections of the torpedo flotilla were now joining their respective squadrons, taking post on their off sides.
>
> It was now 1.00pm. In both fleets national colours were hoisted at the peak and main, except in the *Peresviet* and *Pobieda*, which appeared to have no gaffs. The Russians were seen to be unmistakably in line ahead, and the *Nisshin* (1:05pm) fired two shots to test the range; both fell close to the *Tsarevitch*, which replied almost at once by throwing a heavy shot which, passing between the *Mikasa* and *Asahi* fell 200 metres beyond. As the range, though great, was practicable the Japanese turned eight points to port together which brought them into line ahead, but in inverted order, and both the *Tsarevitch* and *Retvizan* opened a slow fire (1.13) from their bow guns at the *Mikasa*, several very good shots being made before that ship fired her first gun (1.16). The range, which had been 18,000 metres, may now have been about 15,000, and the firing of the Russian leaders was becoming more frequent, though the only reply elicited as yet was an occasional shot from the *Mikasa*, round whom the Russian shell continued to fall with considerable accuracy.
>
> Before long the Japanese altered course in succession four points to port, and the Russians soon after changed direction to starboard, so that the fleets were standing opposite ways. The *Asahi* then fired her first shot, at a range of 14,000 metres, and as they approached their new course the Russian ships that had not

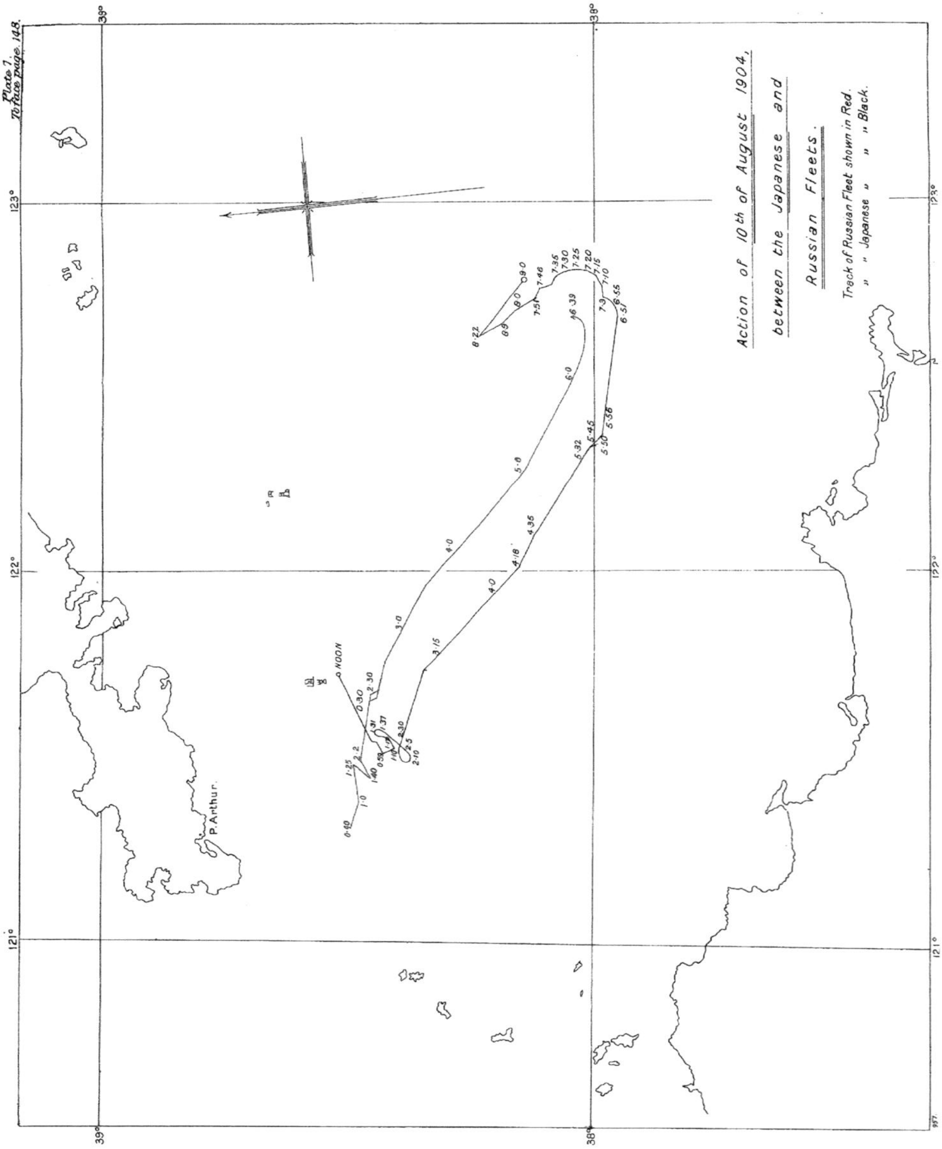

Sketch 5: Battle of the Yellow Sea

yet fired joined their leaders in firing chiefly at the two rear ships of the Japanese line. Though very slow, the fire now became general in both lines, each attacking the leaders of the other. The Russian shooting looked so accurate, it seemed impossible the *Mikasa* and *Asahi* could escape severe punishment, while that of the Japanese was disappointing, as their guns were apparently out of range.

At 1:31pm the Japanese turned together 16 points to starboard, which restored the natural order and this movement was met by the Russians with a large turn to port, so that the fleets were again defiling past one another, but this time on more nearly parallel, though still opposite, courses. The speed of the Japanese had been 12 knots but was now increased to 14, the distance of the *Tsarevitch* being about 13,000 metres. The distance apart of the ships in line in both fleets appeared to be 400 metres. The last turn of the Russians was remarkable as being the last time they acted offensively; after that their only effort was to escape.

Hitherto only primary guns had been used, but now medium artillery began to take a part, and the fire became warmer. It must have been at about this time that the *Mikasa* was hit by a 12-inch projectile, just above the heel of the second torpedo boom from forward, where there is said to be 7 inches of armour, of which an irregular piece about 3 feet in diameter was knocked out, making a hole extending down to the wooden ledge. Fortunately the sea was smooth and no water entered; but had it done so, this wound might have been attended with serious consequences to the Japanese.

It was not until 1:45pm that the Japanese got in their first blow, when a shell, fired, perhaps, from the foremost barbette of the *Asahi*, struck the *Tsarevitch* close, apparently, to her foremost 6-inch gun turret, but as these guns fired almost before the smoke cleared away, they must be well protected from the effects of the explosion. It being the first effective shell, the sight offered was felt to be most impressive. The whole ship seemed to reel. Smoke rushed in great quantities from her funnels, and clouds of steam from the forward steam pipe. From the foremast aft, the whole of the upper part of the ship was enveloped in a parti-coloured cloud of such volume and upward velocity, it looked as though the explosion of a boiler or magazine must have contributed to its formation. There was an appearance of manifold disaster that was most sensational, but which became more familiar later in the day, when it was understood it did not necessarily imply vital injury. When the *Tsarevitch* again became fully visible, she had apparently altered course a little outwards to give time for recovery.

In a few minutes the Russian cruisers, in line astern of the battleships, began to come gallantly into the fire zone, and peppered away bravely with their 6-inch guns. Their leader, the *Askold*, seemed to be struck in her fore upperworks almost immediately, but she courageously held on her way. Even the *Novik* passed, and though, it may be, no other hit was made, the firmness with which these unarmoured ships complied with orders dictated by no obvious necessity commanded the respect of a generous foe.

To close with the cruisers, the Japanese made a successive turn (2:05pm) of about two points to starboard and soon after the Russian fleet having then passed, another turn was begun to starboard, which was continued gradually through about 24 points of the compass, in conformity with the somewhat similar movements of the Russians who also turning to the south-eastward, though on a circle of larger diameter. The effect of these alterations of course was to place the Japanese on the starboard quarter of the Russian fleet, whose last cruiser bore about two points before the beam of the Japanese leaders, the *Tsarevitch* being almost out of sight. A slight continuation of the turn, and the interior position of the Japanese enabled the latter to recover their distance so quickly that there was little or no intermission in the firing of the Russian battleships, the last of which now dropped a shell almost on the quarterdeck of the *Asahi*. The approach of the Japanese was facilitated by a manoeuvre of the Russian Admiral, who appeared to have recognised the mistake of exposing his cruisers to the fire of more powerful ships, and who, therefore, turned his battleships to starboard together about four points, turning back when he had made room for his cruisers on his far side. The Russian destroyers now began to move from the rear to the head of the line. The Japanese flotilla had aligned itself along the starboard side of the fleet, but at some distance from it; the *Izumi* squadron was on the starboard bow about 7 miles off, and the smoke of the *Yakumo* squadron could just be seen on the port quarter.

The Japanese fire now ceased for a short time, though the Russians continued able to plant shells just over or just short of the leaders. At 2:48pm two projectiles from the after turret of the *Tsarevitch* fell within a few yards of the bows of the *Asahi,* and this was followed by another which was thought, though wrongly, to have exploded against the armour under the fore barbette. A fountain of water arose which wetted the ship from end to end, and many large fragments of steel fell about the upper deck. As the *Mikasa* was being equally threatened, and such warnings could not be neglected with prudence, fire was reopened. The *Sevastopol* was then nearly abeam of the Japanese leaders, and while the *Mikasa*, supported by the fore barbette of the *Asahi*, fired at the *Tsarevitch*, almost all other guns were directed at the rear ship of the Russian line, and the *Sevastopol* was hit for the first time very shortly after.

The Japanese flagship, from her position, was now exposed to a very heavy fire, to which her natural supporters, tempted apparently by the greater proximity of other ships, and with guns almost, if not quite, out of range of the Russian leaders, made no determined effort to reply. To this extent, then, the position was distinctly unfavourable to the Japanese, the composition of whose fleet made it a singularly difficult one to dispose in line of battle. There can be no doubt that the intention and desire of Admiral Togo was to place his line before the beam of the Russians, as he did later in the day, and as he had done on June 23. If he could at once have had his way in this respect, his armoured cruisers would have found themselves opposed to several unbeaten battleships, with but one probable result. Both positions had their special dangers for such a line as Togo's. In the one case his most important ship ran heavy risk of disablement, and in the other, a useful tail would have been almost certainly destroyed. Had Togo himself been in the centre, the fate of his leading ship would have been less important; but it must be conceded that his decision was beset with difficulties.

At 2:55pm the range to the *Sevastopol* was about 10,000 metres, having been reduced to this figure rather by the continued turn of the Russians towards the Japanese than by any difference in their speed, and the tendency was still to turn south. The Russian hospital ship was steaming along between the lines, though astern of the line of fire, and from her an excellent view of the battle must have been obtained. The *Sevastopol* was now being subjected to a severe concentration of fire from the heavy and medium artillery of the rear Japanese ships, but it was not apparent that she was being much damaged, while it was becoming more and more evident that any attempt to crawl along the whole length of the Russian line would be a hazardous and prolonged operation. It was at about this time (3.25) that the Japanese at last, and unwillingly, recognised their present speed was inadequate, and put on their last knot, bringing their speed thus to 15 knots, beyond which the *Fuji* could not be much trusted. The courses were about south-east, the distance between the fleets had again increased, no hits were being made, and the Japanese gradually ceased to fire.

The shortest range up till now had been 8,000 metres. At 3:10pm the Russians appeared to alter course a little outwards, and by 3.40 all firing had ceased. The Russian cruisers and destroyers were now observed to be going ahead of the battleships, though still on their port side. The Japanese were about to make an effort to gain a more relatively advanced position. The men fell out from their guns, and weary and parched by the great heat, the excitement and the smoke, most of them lay down at their stations and felt the respite most welcome.

The resumption of action depended now upon whether the Japanese did or did not possess a real superiority of speed. A boom, coming from the port quarter, now drew attention to the *Yakumo* which was firing at the *Sevastopol* from a great distance. The shots felt so short that they drew no reply, and were only intended, probably, as an assertion of a share in an action which seemed to have reached its termination. The Japanese flotillas began to close in on the starboard side, one division leading at some distance on the bow. The Russians again commenced a dropping fire, and one of their shots (3.55) fell just in front of a junk, which philosophically continued its course, without taking the least notice.

The sea was calm, a light breeze blew from the north-west, the Japanese had begun to creep ahead, and course was altered toward the Russian line. It became evident the Russians were trying to extract every fraction of a knot of speed from their ships that was consistent with remaining in company, and this was telling upon the *Sevastopol*, which had commenced to show signs of falling astern of her station. By 5:10pm the distance separating the fleets had manifestly much decreased, and the Russians had shown their first indication of irresolution by appearing to be edging to the northward.

The men were again sent to their guns. The Russian hospital ship had moved over in rear of the cruiser line, and the *Yakumo* and her consorts had begun to come up towards their place at the rear end of the line. A new cloud of smoke was also seen on the port quarter, showing the approach of three more ships. Owing to slight alterations of course, the position of the Japanese relative to the Russian line did not greatly differ now from what it had been when firing ceased, but the *Asahi* was abeam of the *Poltava,* or rather before it, and all ships were within range. The *Sevastopol* was the first to resume firing, and this gave the signal for a simultaneous outburst of fire from all ships on both sides. The last named ship, which had already withstood a long spell of heavy fire, must now have been at least a mile astern of the *Poltava,* and the three rear ships of the Japanese line devoted themselves entirely to her. Leaders fired at one another, and the *Retvizan* also joined in the attack on the *Mikasa*, which, as before, was only supported by the forward guns of the *Asahi*, whose after guns, and all those of the *Fuji*, fired at the *Poltava*. The *Pobieda* and *Peresviet* were thus free to fire at the *Asahi*, which they did unanswered until a sudden change left ships at liberty to attend to them.

The scene was now one of greater vivacity than it had been earlier in the day. The decreased light of late afternoon permitted the gun flashes to be seen more distinctly, while the greater rapidity of fire, and the growing frequency of hits, contributed to the spectacular effect. Firing had hardly recommenced before the *Tsarevitch* was hit (5:40pm) in the same place, apparently, as in the morning. Again she seemed to reel under the blow, but experience did not allow such great hopes to be founded upon its effects as on the former occasion. It was at this time, perhaps, that the *Yakumo* first took an effective part in the battle. She appeared to have come up to her place astern of the *Nisshin*, but on account of the less range of her guns, to have moved about 500 yards nearer the Russian line, and she continued to occupy this position until she was sent on other duty. The first outward signs that the Japanese guns were making an impression were visible when the after mast of the *Peresviet* was shot away just above the military top, but when, five minutes after, the foremast also fell, cut off at the electric light platform, the Russian line seemed to be assuming the ragged appearance appropriate to naval battle, and it was felt that at last the fleets were really in action. Several guns had now got the range of the *Peresviet* very exactly, and she was struck time after time. After her masts had fallen, both turrets of the *Peresviet* were put out of action, but it could not be seen whether this had been done by wreckage or by any more permanent defect. Though these turrets could be seen to train at intervals, it is believed they may be considered to have taken no further part in the events of the day.

Owing to further alterations of course, which, though slight, produced a change of bearing between lines going at nearly equal speeds, the *Sevastopol* again came abreast of the *Asahi*.

The *Sevastopol,* as well as the *Poltava*, was receiving a heavy fire, but both were carrying themselves nobly, and were doing all in their power to preserve their places in the line. Again (6:37pm) the *Tsarevitch* was hit well forward, but when she turned abruptly to port her movement was attributed to a gallant intention of proceeding to the assistance of her distressed sisters in rear. As she turned, she appeared to be listed to port, to the joy of many, who saw in this sign that the famous patch had at last given out. Although, on the helm being righted, she resumed an upright position, a belief in her disablement had gained ground, and this served to cheer on the Japanese to greater efforts. Reports from Kiaochow explain the sudden movement by saying the conning tower had that moment been knocked away, killing Vitgeft and most of his staff.

It is probable that the *Retvizan* marked her leader's turn, without guessing the cause; she therefore followed suit under the impression she was complying with the intentions of her Admiral. However, this may have been, the temporary duplication of the Russian line gave the Japanese an opportunity, which they instantly seized, by closing and increasing their rate of fire. The range was reduced to about 6,000 metres, the fire became exceedingly brisk, and every moment contributed to the establishment of the definite superiority of the Japanese fire.

Those with leisure to look could now see the *Tsarevitch* was moving uncertainly. After appearing to try to re-enter the line astern of the *Pobieda*, she eventually came in behind the *Poltava*. The Russian line was now under the leadership of the *Pobieda*, who, until now, had fared better than her companions. This was more than compensated for by the heavy fire of which, as leader, she became the object, and she had no relief from this until the *Retvizan* returned to her place at the head of the line (7.00pm). On first turning, the *Retvizan* had almost immediately discovered her mistake and had come round as short as possible; but her brief absence from her post had made great differences, as her next astern had, in that brief interval of time, received nearly all the beating she wanted. Hitherto, the *Retvizan* had had less than her share of the knocks, but this was now to be reversed. The Japanese had been gradually closing, and the *Tsarevitch* was now at about 8,000 metres from the *Asahi*, and the *Peresviet* was at 6,000. Steam was escaping from one of the steam pipes of the *Poltava*, which was wheeling to port. The *Retvizan*, finding what a very exposed position hers was, had hardly got back to the head of the line before she made a slight deviation to port, followed by the *Pobieda*. When it was time for the *Peresviet* to make her turn, she went a little beyond the wheeling point, and this, together with the failure of the *Poltava*, gave her temporarily a very conspicuous position, in which she seemed to lie helpless under a storm of fire; eventually managing to complete her turn, she passed out of the line astern of her next ahead.

Now the Russian line was in complete confusion. The two rear ships, *Sevastopol* and *Tsarevitch*, had also wheeled to port and the *Retvizan* was for a moment the only ship broadside on to the Japanese; but the *Pobieda* returned, and pluckily stationed herself under her stern. This caused the *Mikasa* to sheer off momentarily, but on the *Retvizan* definitely turning away, the Japanese resumed their wheel, and were then steering almost at right angles to their afternoon courses. The distance to the *Retvizan* was now about 4,900 metres, and she was at the centre of the circle on whose arc the Japanese fleet was formed. Every gun was trained on her, and was being fired with the greatest rapidity, even the 12-pounders joining in. Imaginative artists have often been derided for the number and size of the splashes with which they indicate the fall of projectiles in battle, but, however inclined they may have been to exaggerate, their wildest conceptions have fallen far short of reality. A big shell often throws water and spray to a height greater than twice that of a tall ship's masthead, and these, and smaller splashes, were now so numerous, and the smoke from explosions so dense, that the *Retvizan* was frequently concealed from view in a mountain of smoke and spray for appreciable periods of time. The excitement of the moment and the indistinctness of the object caused many projectiles to fall very wide of their mark, and it is probable a great deal of ammunition was wasted. Though not the most important, this was the most dramatic event of the day.

The time during which the *Retvizan* was exposed to this withering fire was not really long, and her slowly continued turn finally enabled her to increase the distance to 7,000 metres, when fire was relaxed, chiefly on account of the heating of the guns. Every ship in the Russian line had now been battered, and their fire overcome. The advance of the line had been definitely abandoned; all the Russians were heading in different directions, and the *Tsarevitch* was heeling to starboard and appeared to have lost a mast. The *Retvizan* could expect no support. The Japanese were still closing in, and their victim looked to be at their mercy. Her doom seemed certain. But the *Retvizan* was not to perish now; she was saved by what was probably an accident.

When the Russian battle line had been headed off, the sweeping movement of the Japanese had not embraced the Russian cruisers nor their destroyers, and these were now making off in a north-westerly direction. Just then (7:25pm) distant guns were heard, fired from some point beyond the *Askold,* which at once headed back towards her main fleet, accompanied by her companion cruisers. The destroyers, however, did not turn. It was soon seen that the firing had come from the *Asama,* which had hurried from the base, whither she had been sent to coal, and whose captain, guided by the sounds of battle and his own good sense, had arrived on the scene in the only position where it was still possible for him to be of any use. To the right of the *Asama*, and also firing at everything that presented itself, was the *Hashidate* and her consorts, and the united fire of these four ships had been sufficiently effective to cause the reversal of course of the Russian cruisers.

Togo and Yamada were now approaching one another at an acute angle, through whose apex the Russian destroyers would pass rather in advance of either Japanese line. It could not be judged from appearances whether the destroyers were manoeuvring for a position from which to attack, or if escape was their only object, but it was evident that the Japanese battleships would run great risk of being torpedoed, if they either continued their turn to port or merely held on a straight course. Every instant was now of immense importance, if fatal damage was to be done to the Russians. Here was an opportunity for the Japanese destroyer flotilla, that had been on the bow so long; but, alas! These boats, not having conformed to the turning movement of the fleet (on account, doubtless, of the close range at which the fleets had begun to fight), were now lying miles astern. There was no choice; the battleships had to turn away.

Yamada was quickly to see his chief's need, and without false regard for the safety of his own comparatively unimportant ships, he steered for the Russian destroyers, and scattered them with gunfire, compelling them to a disordered retreat on their main body. It is probable that they discharged some torpedoes at both Japanese squadrons during their retirement.

Valuable time had been lost, but the *Mikasa* at once (7:46pm) ordered a simultaneous turn of the ships in her line to port. A heavy pall of black smoke hovered over the Russian fleet, obscuring the sunset and curtailing the usually prolonged twilight. The range had increased to 8,200 metres, and as soon as the Japanese had got back into line ahead, there was a short recrudescence of fire in the quickly fading light; but it was too late to think of trying to deliver a final and crushing blow.

The *Asama* was firing away merrily, if not very effectively, but fire from other ships had become desultory, and the Russians seemed to be re-forming line with heads to the north-west, being then on the same ground they had traversed between 4.00 and 5.00pm. The *Retvizan* or *Pobieda* appeared to be leading, followed in order by the *Pobieda* (or *Retvizan*), *Peresviet*,*Tsarevitch*, and the other two battleships. The cruisers were heading the same way but at greater speed.

The gathered smoke was now descending and mingling with the mists of evening; thus the Russian fleet, though at no great distance, was gradually passing out of view. When last seen, the *Tsarevitch* had fallen out of line, and seemed to be going in a northerly direction by herself, and the remainder were heading to the north-west, the *Sevastopol* and *Poltava* jogging along together, a long way behind the others of their line. The *Askold*, *Novik*, and some destroyers were trying to break away to the southward, with the *Izumi* squadron in pursuit, and the sound of a rapid succession of shots (8:15pm), followed for half an hour by the flashes of guns and searchlights, gave hope that the Russians would not escape scatheless. The main body of the Russian fleet had now been brought nearly ahead, but the brilliant yellow afterglow that suddenly lit sea and sky only served to show the scene of the recent battle, abandoned by every trace of the combatants.

As for the lighter part of the Japanese fleet, some of the cruisers were following the *Askold* and others were now sent out on either side to guard against an unnoticed escape of the Russians to the southward during the night. It was presumed that the flotilla, if this had not been done already, would be immediately launched after the shaken Russian battleships, but the orders given to these small craft have not transpired. The numerous Russian flotilla had probably been dispersed and might be prowling at random. It was therefore time the Japanese should take measures for the safety of their own main fleet.

Togo may have felt a choice between the two principal courses of action now open to him somewhat difficult. If he should go southward and the Russians should go to the north, his base might be attacked and destroyed in the morning, before he could intervene; while, if he should decide to protect his base, the fleet of his enemy might escape without another battle. He did not hesitate an instant. The Russians were hardly out of sight when speed, which had been reduced during the latter part of the turning movement, was again set at 15 knots, and the Japanese battle line, changing course through east, dashed off to the southward, determined, at all hazards, to bring the Russians to action once more, if possible.

Though worthy of the Japanese leader, the resolution just mentioned was not destined to hasten matters to their final issue. The Japanese fleet anchored near its base on the night of August 11, moving in on the following morning, and at once commencing to replenish and refit.

The very natural desire of the Japanese that certain matters should not be discussed until they shall have ceased to have any possible effect on the situation must explain the postponement of all reference to them.

Not only on August 10, but throughout the war, the Japanese Admiral has been fighting with a rope round his neck and the scope of his activities has been limited by a stringent necessity from which he could not escape. On Togo's shoulders rested a weight far greater than that imposed on those of Villeneuve at the battle of Trafalgar. What Villeneuve so conspicuously failed to do then, the Japanese Admiral now had to endeavour to accomplish. The same law bound them both. The main force of the enemy had to be met and beaten. Here, however, the resemblance ended. Neither Nelson nor his antagonist were expected to win victories without loss of ships, but this was the task set the latest comer among maritime celebrities.

The Japanese have met and fought a superior force, which has been routed and scattered. This in itself constitutes a victory, though not as yet one of those whose immediate decisiveness mark epochs in the life histories of nations. Whether or not the battle will prove indirectly conclusive still remains to be seen, and as any moment during the next few days may bring with it a pronouncement for or against the Japanese, the precariousness of their future would not repay a reference, if it might not enable those not on the spot to understand what seems to be the balance of probabilities as seen during this time of suspense.

There is an old proverb about fighting and running away that may be singularly applicable to the present situation. Every day that passes increases the probability of the reappearance of the Russian fleet as an efficient fighting force. When the opening lines of this report were penned it was believed that the army besieging Port Arthur both could and would advance its date of attack so as to prevent the restoration of the hostile fleet, but a week has been allowed to go by, and in that time much may be done to render ships, not vitally injured, again fit for their places in line. Though the resources of Port Arthur are not known, they may be adequate.

After the action, and the fleet had anchored at the base, all captains assembled in the flagship. An officer who was one of the last to arrive stated he had fully expected everyone would at once acknowledge the great services his ship had rendered. No one referring to them, however, he modestly drew the attention of the commander-in-chief to the fact that his ship had fired the shots that had struck the *Tsarevitch* the first and last times, and that she had also been responsible for cutting away the masts of the *Peresviet*. To his surprise a chorus of indignant protest was at once raised, and he then found each arriving captain had made the same claim, only to find it warmly rebutted by the commander-in-chief, his chief staff officer, and the captain of his flagship, all of whom had combined to attribute every shot that had been attended with any conspicuous result to the prowess of the *Mikasa*. The discussion seems to have been conducted with excellent temper, but it may be considered to furnish additional evidence of the thoroughness with which the Japanese have impregnated themselves with the spirit of older navies.

When war arrangements were being settled, the captains implored Admiral Togo to occupy a central position in the line, but he absolutely declined. Both he and the Russian commander-in-chief led their respective fleets, and no stronger argument than the damage inflicted on the two leading ships can be advanced to illustrate the dangers of such a course if an accident should happen.

The Japanese commander-in-chief, and as many of his staff as could find standing room, were on the pilothouse, the remainder being on the fore bridge, and a shell, which had struck the semaphore, burst and killed four of the Admiral's *entourage*.

When the after bridge of the *Nisshin* was struck, also by a shell, Admiral Kataoka and his chief of staff had only just left in order to go forward. The remaining four staff officers, with the inspector of machinery at their head, were all killed. So far as is known, the captains and navigating officers throughout the Japanese fleet also occupied their usual navigational stations on the pilothouses.

Although, curiously enough, the Japanese suffered little by it, this self-exposure of principal officers must be held to carry with it great danger to the organisation of the fleet. It is not clear where the Russian officers stood, but as the commander-in-chief, his chief staff officer, and his captain were all killed, while the navigating officer was not, it seems probable they were not all in the same place.[4]

4 Naval Attaché Reports, pp. 147-162.

17

Aftermath

Pakenham's battle report was written only seven days after it had taken place, based on his own observations and those of the Japanese officers he was able to consult. He could not, of course, be aware of all that had taken place outside his immediate view. It was, nonetheless, a remarkably comprehensive eyewitness account of the battle. In addition, he made a number of important observations with regard to the conduct of a modern naval battle.

Chief among these arose from the range at which the battle was fought. He observed that although ranges of over 13,000 yards sounded preposterous when compared with peacetime target practice, they were not really so. Experience of the battle suggested to him that firing began to look possible at about 22,000 yards, and reasonable at 15,000 yards, while close range might be regarded as setting in at about 11,000 yards. At a range of 5,500 yards, he thought that 'ships might as well be alongside one another so far as appearances and sensation of proximity go.'

He went on to review the performance of the Japanese gunners at long range:

> While the big guns only were firing, and distances were still great, results were so unsatisfactory that the after rangefinder (that had been stowed below for safety) was substituted for the one in use, but without producing any improvement … When it is considered the Japanese fired over 400 rounds of 12-inch, and about half as many 10-inch and 8-inch at long ranges, for a number of hits that probably did not exceed 10, and that during the greater part of this firing the distances were only changing slowly, it must be admitted that the large proportion of lost shots requires more accounting for than an occasional and temporary outranging of the guns alone could supply.[1]

1 Naval Attaché Reports, p. 162.

Whilst editing his reports for publication, the Naval Intelligence Department noted that Pakenham's estimate of not more than 10 hits was a considerable underestimate; nevertheless, his continued observations were still very relevant.

It seemed to him that the usefulness of an accurate estimate of the range needed some qualification:

> When first made no two guns shoot exactly alike, but each has an error whose effect increases with every increase of range. This initial error soon becomes absorbed in another, which arises from the wear of the bore and which every shot fired tends to accentuate. Then again, in practice, charges may be drawn from magazines kept at different temperatures, but what is of more importance is that these charges may be put into guns of very different degrees of heating.
>
> Whatever the source of error or combination of errors, their effect increases with the range, and a gun is considered efficient only so long as the total effect of the error remains negligible at short ranges. With guns of all ages this error becomes appreciable at longer ranges, and at the longest assumes such importance as to give each gun a very strongly marked individuality, which requires special consideration when adjusting its sights, and which tends to throw it back, more and more, with every increase of range, upon itself as the only range indicator whose showings have the least applicability to its peculiar needs.
>
> At short range, say 4,000 metres, it may be useful to have an instrument that will show the range accurately, because if, at such a distance, every gun would have been laid for the central point of the target, every shot would hit the target somewhere, the error of none of the guns being sufficient to carry a projectile altogether clear. But suppose the range to be increased, say to 12,000 metres. Should an instrument exist that would give such a distance correctly, and should every gun be laid by it, it is possible not a single shot so directed might hit the target.
>
> Should this be true, it follows that it would be of little use to know the exact range at great distances. When word had been passed to a captain of gun that the range was 12,000 metres, his mental attitude towards the information should not be that it was a heaven sent revelation of the adjustment necessary for his sight, but that it was an approximation, probably closer than any he could have made with his unaided eye, and that he still had to apply his knowledge of the peculiarities of shooting of his gun, to watch the fall of his first and succeeding shots, and to continue to move his elevation and deflection scales in accordance with their teaching.[2]

Pakenham's conclusion was that 'under present conditions of ship construction and disposition of guns,' it was wrong for a single rangefinder to serve more than one

2 Ibid., p. 163.

group of guns. Since most ships were equipped with two rangefinders, each should be worked solely in connection with the nearest group of the heaviest guns. There should be a strict understanding that at long ranges only a rough approximation could be given.

Another crucially important issue was that of fire control. Pakenham found that at no time in the action was this very rigidly enforced, while after rapid fire had once started 'central authority was quite unable to exercise any control except over the foremost guns.' Although every gun was bound to lay for a certain point on the target, it seemed that a good deal of latitude was taken or allowed in the selection of an object. He had been unable to find out if there were any general rules for this, but it obviously did nothing to increase the accuracy of the firing. Captains, he thought, should not attempt the impossible task of detailed supervision when all guns were firing that they might have applied to a single gun in peacetime target practice.

It was Pakenham's view that, in a modern engagement between battleships, the guns of a lesser calibre such as 6-inch were of extremely limited value:

> By the time the 6-inch guns really came into play, the action was already going against Russia, but it is believed an inspection of the ships would show that the fate of the day had lain with, and had been entirely decided by, heavy guns, if not by the heaviest only. The Japanese expressed regret that their new cruisers do not each carry a pair of 10-inch guns, and everything in this war has tended to emphasise the vast importance to a ship, in every stage of her career, of carrying some of the heaviest and furthest shooting guns that can be got into her.[3]

He had a conversation with 'a very prominent official of the construction and ordnance branch,' which confirmed his opinion.

Pakenham reported that total Japanese casualties during the battle had amounted to 70 killed and 146 wounded. On the Russian side 74 had been killed and 394 wounded. Togo's flagship, the *Mikasa*, had suffered by far the greatest number of casualties, with 125 killed and wounded. Russian losses were more evenly divided, the *Peresviet* suffering a total of 90, while the *Retvizan* lost only 49 and the *Tsarevitch* 63.

Pakenham was unaware of the fate of those Russian ships that did not return to Port Arthur. Of these, much the most important was the *Tsarevitch*. She had, like the other battleships, endured the attacks of the Japanese torpedo boats, after which she became separated from the battle fleet. As dawn broke next day she was close to the Shantung promontory. She had suffered considerable damage in the battle; in particular her funnels had been damaged, causing a sharp increase in her coal consumption, and it was decided to head for the German port of Kiaochow. She arrived there at about

3 Ibid., p. 167.

9.00pm on August 11. A few days later, as she was in her damaged state unable to put to sea, she was formally interned for the remainder of the war.[4]

The Russian fleet had put to sea with a force of eight destroyers. Three of these had returned with the fleet to Port Arthur, while the rest scattered to various destinations. One, the *Grozovoi,* reached Shanghai, and was duly interned there. Three more, the *Bezshumni, Bezstrashni* and *Bezposhchadni,* all made it to Kiaochow and were interned there. The fifth, the *Burni,* was not so lucky. After being chased by Japanese destroyers, she ran ashore at 2.00am on August 11 on the northern coast of Shantung; her captain landed the crew, and then destroyed the vessel, before marching to the British territory of Weihaiwei.[5]

The *Askold,* carrying the flag of Rear Admiral Reitzenstein, had shaken off the Japanese cruisers in the darkness. He authorised the *Novik* to act independently, and then steamed slowly towards the Shantung promontory. His intention was to make his way to Vladivostok, but found that the damage to the *Askold's* funnels meant that her consumption of coal was too high to get there. He headed for Shanghai, where the cruiser was docked. Japanese cruisers then appeared off the mouth of the river Yangtze to prevent her escape, and on August 25 she was interned, with the consent of the Russian government.[6]

The *Diana,* meanwhile, had been having an adventurous time. Lacking the speed to follow the *Askold,* she had fallen in behind the cruiser *Pallada,* but her captain decided to try to carry out the fleet's original instructions and head for Vladivostok, a decision that was endorsed by his officers. They then discussed what to do if they encountered Japanese torpedo boats; Semenov had a suggestion to make:

> I made a proposal, which at first met with general opposition, and nearly raised the suspicion that I was not in my right mind. I proposed simply to do nothing. If, for instance, we were to light up any destroyer with our searchlights and fire at her, we should bring the entire flotilla down on us. Against an attack in numbers we were powerless.[7]

He pointed out that a lone destroyer, meeting the *Diana,* would speed past her, and without searchlights to locate her, would not find her again. The captain, remarking that it was quite a new method of repelling a torpedo attack, agreed, and gave orders accordingly. Between 9.00pm and 10:15pm a large number of Japanese destroyers were sighted, but only on a few occasions was the *Diana* attacked, and none of the torpedoes fired at her hit their target. However, it was clear that there was a pressing need for more coal. If the cruiser went to Kiaochow she would be interned. The officers

4 *British Official History* I, p. 350.
5 Ibid.
6 Ibid., p. 347.
7 Semenov I, p. 200.

were still keen to attempt the voyage to Vladivostok, but the captain decided to head for Saigon. After picking up small quantities of coal at two ports en route, she finally reached the French port on August 25, where she was disarmed. Semenov then made his way on a French steamer to Marseilles and from thence to Paris, where he caught a train back to Russia, in time, he hoped, to join the Second Pacific Squadron.

The cruiser *Novik*, when she left the *Askold*, set off to Kiaochow in order to take on sufficient coal to enable her to reach Vladivostok. She reached the German port on August 11 and remained there for only ten hours before setting off, intending to steam around the east of Japan. She was, however, sighted by a Japanese merchant vessel after passing through the Osumi Strait, and the cruisers *Tsushima* and *Chitose* were sent north to cut her off. These reached Hakodate on August 17, and the question now was whether the *Novik* would use the Tsugaru or La Perouse Strait. The Japanese cruisers opted to cover the former, but when by August 19 the *Novik* had not appeared, they set off northward. Nothing was seen of her, and the *Tsushima* headed for Korsakovsk Bay, where on August 20 she found her quarry. The *Novik* had kept well out in the Pacific, but headed for Korsakovsk to take on coal and water. When the *Tsushima* appeared, the *Novik* steamed out, opening fire at 6,000 yards. For an hour there was a brisk action, in which both cruisers were damaged, and both drew off to make repairs.

Just before night fell, the *Tsushima* was joined by the *Chitose*, and they kept watch over the entrance to the bay in case the *Novik* should try to escape. However, she was found to have suffered irreparable damage to her steering, and her captain, sending the crew ashore, scuttled her in shallow water. When the *Chitose* arrived in harbour next morning, she found the *Novik* partially submerged, and shelled her for an hour before withdrawing.[8]

Reviewing the battle, Corbett considered the effect of the shell which had hit the flagship *Tsarevitch*:

> Admiral Vitgeft was dead. A 12-inch shell had struck the foot of the mainmast, and in bursting had killed him and one of his staff, as they stood near the conning tower, as well as 13 men. To make matters worse, it severely wounded the Chief of the Staff and the Flag Captain, both being rendered senseless. Then another struck under the roof of the conning tower, broke into two parts, and the base portion breaking up inside, killed or stunned every officer and man stationed there. At the same time, for some undetermined reason, the helm was forced hard astarboard, where it remained fixed. It was this that caused her to break through her own line, and being quite out of control, she had to stop.[9]

The effect of the *Tsarevitch*'s turn had been to cause immediate confusion. The *Sevastopol* and *Peresviet* passed in front of her, receiving the concentrated fire of

8 *British Official History* I, p. 349.
9 Corbett I, p. 393.

the whole Japanese battle line. The *Retvizan* turned towards the enemy ships in an attempt to draw their fire, heading for the *Mikasa* with the intention of ramming. As she approached, however, she was struck by a 12-inch shell, which seriously wounded her captain, and he ordered that she rejoin the squadron. Ukhtomski, as second-in-command aboard the *Peresviet*, made the signal 'Follow me' as soon as he saw the signal from the flagship 'Admiral transfers command,' but both his top masts were down, and his signal, made from the bridge rails, was not clearly seen, which was the reason it took so long for the Russian line to be re-formed.

Corbett had the benefit of access to a considerable volume of material, both Russian and Japanese. In his analysis of Togo's movements as soon as the Russian fleet was sighted, he found it difficult to accept the official Japanese explanation that Togo's turn away at 12.55 was to lure the enemy out to sea. He deduced that in fact there was a Japanese minefield near Encounter Rock, as Dewa had actually suggested in his report, and that Togo's tactics were not to attack until the Russians had got into the minefield; and then, since they had escaped unscathed, Togo realised that he must fight, clear of his own mines. This also, Corbett thought, contributed to his decision to fight at extreme range. Subsequently, when the Russian line seemed to be pulling away to the north-east would, Corbett criticised Togo's response:

> In order to carry out the principles of his Tactical Memorandum by 'pressing the van' and maintaining a position between the Russians and their destination he should have turned back at once while there was yet time for another pass ahead of them. But this for some reason he did not do. As the Russian line came round and steadied on its new course, the cruisers in its rear became dangerously exposed, and the chance of dealing them a rapid blow, which would compel Admiral Vitgeft to cover them, was perhaps too tempting to lose.[10]

It should, Corbett considered, have been Dewa's task to deal with the Russian cruisers; the reason that he failed to do so was the problem of mutual interference caused by Togo's system of using cruiser squadrons as battle units.

Before the first stage of the battle came to an end, at the time when Togo's position in relation to the enemy was no longer between the Russian fleet and its destination, he contemplated closing the range and bringing about a decisive action. He was dissuaded by Shimamura, his Chief of Staff, who pointed out that it would be better to open the range, and use the speed of the Japanese fleet to get ahead again. This advice was obviously sound:

> Accordingly, at 3:30 Admiral Togo signalled for the last knot, and 20 minutes later he inclined inwards again about parallel with the enemy. The situation was far from promising. A wholly indecisive action had degenerated into a chase, and

10 Ibid., p. 382.

> it was a chase that might well last till nearly nightfall unless something could be done to check the Russian speed. For this he could only look to his cruiser squadrons.[11]

In the event neither of his cruiser squadrons was in a position to do anything to slow down the Russian fleet; Rear Admiral Togo was well to the rear of Togo's battle line, while Dewa, on the far side of the Russian fleet, was exposed to the fire of Vitgeft's battleships, and was obliged to break off and get out of range.

Even after the balance of advantage had so decisively changed with the death of Vitgeft, and the ensuing confusion of the Russian battle line, Togo still erred on the side of caution, opening the range by steering approximately north-north-west while the Russians were heading north-west. As Corbett remarked, 'instead of pressing to the utmost the advantage he had gained he was content to continue the action under conditions which constantly decreased the chance of a decisive victory.'[12]

Togo's caution, and his willingness to pass up the opportunity for a crushing victory, was of course principally due to his need carefully to husband his battleships. Beyond this, however, he had a clearly defined intention with regard to the Russian fleet, as the Official History noted:

> There is no doubt that the underlying idea of Admiral Togo's strategy at this period was to confine the Russian fleet to Port Arthur, where its fate would be sealed with that of the garrison, and to preserve his own ships for the inevitable battle with the Baltic Fleet … It was far more to the advantage of Japan to force Admiral Vitgeft back to his original base, than to destroy some of his ships and allow the remainder to escape.[13]

Pakenham had not been able to find out what had happened to the Japanese destroyers at the end of the battle, noting only that it was presumed that they would be launched after the retreating Russian battleships. That, indeed, had been Togo's order at 7:55pm, at which point he had decided that, in the gathering gloom, there was no more that his battle fleet could do. He wrote in his report of the battle: 'Most unfortunately the sun set completely before the battle was over, preventing us distinguishing friend from foe and from destroying the enemy as we could have done in the daylight. We abandoned the battle to the flotilla and followed the courses laid down in the programme.'[14]

When he made his signal for the torpedo attack, Togo had 18 destroyers and 29 torpedo boats. They were, however, not all well placed at that moment; only one division of destroyers was with the battle fleet, the rest being some way astern.

11 Ibid., p. 387.
12 Ibid, p. 396.
13 *British Official History* I, p. 340.
14 Corbett I, p. 401.

Conditions were, however, not unfavourable, and a number of uncoordinated attacks were launched. They were hampered by the disorganised line of the Russian fleet, enabling the individual ships to turn to avoid torpedoes. The Japanese destroyers and torpedo boats did their best, closing into short range, and attacking under heavy fire. Either because of battle damage or out of a prudent desire to avoid becoming a target, the Russian ships did not use their searchlights, and manoeuvred skilfully as the Japanese torpedoes were launched. Not one of these hit their target, and as dawn broke on August 11 the battered Russian fleet was once more safely anchored under the guns of the fortress.

None of their attackers had been sunk during these engagements, which had continued throughout the night. A total of 74 torpedoes had been launched; Corbett reflected on the reasons for the lack of success:

> If the failure of the prolonged attack is to be attributed to any one cause beyond the defensive tactics of the enemy, it is to lack of combination that it must be set down. The Japanese practice of acting independently was as well marked as ever. Even where a division came across a group of the enemy, it would break up, each boat attacking a different ship. Not once was there an attempt to push home in a bewildering mass, nor was there any case of two divisions combining to attack from opposite sides as the Tactical Instructions had provided. Every commanding officer seemed to play for his own hand, and when the day broke every hand was empty.[15]

During the course of the battle, almost 1,200 rounds had been fired from the primary armament of the Japanese fleet, and over 6,000 rounds from the secondary armament (6 inch to 12 pounders). In the light of this, there was a feeling of dissatisfaction in the Japanese fleet, especially among the rearmost ships, which had not felt the full effect of the Russian fire:

> To them it seemed that the Admiral had shown excessive caution in his conduct of the action. It was complained that he should have pressed in to decisive range, but at what point of the engagement is not clear. There was, however, a definite idea that he might at least have cut off the two rear ships, presumably about 4 o'clock, when they had fallen astern. Half an hour it was urged would have sufficed to destroy them, and that would have left time enough to pursue and beat the remaining four – even if Admiral Vitgeft had left them to their fate.[16]

Corbett rejected this criticism as 'a vicious sentiment which spoiled so many of our own actions – the tendency to rank trophies above the strategical object of the battle.'

15 Ibid., p. 412.
16 Ibid, p. 404.

Had Togo pursued such a policy, it would have gravely risked his strategical objective, and might have allowed the four most powerful Russian ships to get through to Vladivostok.

Lacking reserves, Togo had no alternative but to follow the path of caution. And it was not just a naval question:

> Quite as disturbing was the moral factor of public opinion at home. Dominating his every action there was the spirit of an impressionable and over sanguine people that was not to be trusted if any substantial part of the enemy's fleet was permitted to escape into the Sea of Japan. Throughout the war it had been a cause of deflection and since the last Vladivostok raid it had become a consideration of the most serious kind.[17]

In Port Arthur Lieutenant McCully had, even before the squadron put to sea on August 10, made up his mind to leave, as a protest against the way in which he had been treated by the authorities there. He had been subjected to sustained discourtesy, amounting to harassment, even to the point of being arrested when observing Russian military movements from an authorised observation point. He had enjoyed a good relationship with some of his fellow attachés, and particularly with the German Captain Albert Hopman; he wrote in his diary that in the isolated position of an American in Russia, 'when friends have been so few, it is most pleasant to meet so good a one as he, and [it] makes one feel more amiable to the whole German nation.' A number of senior Russian officers had, though, also been very kind to McCully.[18]

In his report, McCully reviewed the performance of the Russian naval and military leaders in Port Arthur. He was particularly critical of Vitgeft:

> The great misfortune of the Russians was in their commander-in-chief, Rear Admiral Vitgeft. The Russians themselves said that on account of his mediocrity he had been chosen for chief of staff by the Viceroy, who did not wish to have clever or energetic men about him, as being likely to be disturbers. Their idea of the Viceroy himself was that he was an able man, very sympathetic and tactful, but first of all a courtier. He always wished everything to go smoothly and without friction, and if there should happen to be any of either, he did not wish to know of it, or if he was compelled to know it himself, he would not inform the Emperor of it, for fear of disturbing the Imperial serenity. As commander of a ship or in command of the fleet, Russian officers nevertheless had a high opinion of him. Admiral Vitgeft was a typical bureaucrat of very limited intelligence, and an intense dislike to action. He was obstinate, superstitious, and fearful of

17 Ibid., p. 405.
18 Charles J. Weeks Jr, *An American Naval Diplomat in Revolutionary Russia* (Annapolis, Maryland, 1993), p. 51.

> responsibility, being always oppressed by the idea that he was only temporarily commander-in-chief and lacked full power.
>
> After the isolation of Port Arthur it is hard to understand how the fiction was still retained. He was exceedingly affable to his inferiors, and looked on the enlisted men as his children. Disliking energy or action in both theory and practice, he spent the entire time in the cabin of his flagship, reported to be fondest of lying in his bunk and reading Zola. In personal appearance he looked older than his age of 57, appearing more like a slow thinking benevolent old professor, with long grey uncombed hair. In 1899 he was promoted to rear admiral, but the first time he ever commanded a squadron under way was on June 23, 1904 in the first sortie. Obtuse, purblind to actual conditions, hating activity and fearful of responsibility, yet when once forced to a decision his obstinacy would have impelled him to persist in its execution and, had he lived, he would probably have brought some of the ships into Vladivostok.
>
> The second-in-command, Rear Admiral Prince Ukhtomski, was not esteemed as particularly able, but was considered a Russian patriot, and had the credit with the fleet of having forced Admiral Vitgeft to make the sortie of June 23.[19]

Now, once again, a decision would have to be made as to the future command of what remained of the fleet in Port Arthur.

19 McCully, pp. 164-165.

18

The Battle of Ulsan

News that the fleet had left Port Arthur, and had been in action, did not reach Vladivostok until 4.00pm on August 11. There had been no attempt to coordinate any movement by Iessen's squadron with Vitgeft's sortie, and it was not until 5.00am next day that he sailed with the *Rossiya*, *Gromoboi*, and *Rurik*. Iessen's intention was to sail southward in the hope of being able to reinforce the main fleet, but since it was calculated that Vitgeft would reach the Tsushima Straits no later than early on the morning of August 13, it was unlikely that the Vladivostok squadron would join him in time to take part in the crucial battle.

Meanwhile Admiral Kamimura was in a state of extreme uncertainty as to what was required of him. At 5.00pm on August 10 he was informed by the Naval Staff at Tokyo that the Russian fleet had come out of Port Arthur that morning. As the night wore on, rumours reached him that a battle was in progress, and he put his squadron on standby to raise steam. At 8:15am on the following morning he got a telegram from Tokyo to tell him that some Russian cruisers might have got through after the battle and made for Vladivostok, and the guard on the Straits must be strictly kept. Half an hour later he heard from Togo that there had been 'a fierce engagement;' telling him the position as it had been at sunset. The message went on: 'The enemy remained near the north of Shantung promontory and were attacked by our destroyers. We are making for position 475 [the mid-sea rendezvous] and will turn back tomorrow. The Second Squadron must come at once.'[1] Togo's record of the message included an order that Kamimura should go to Ross Island, where he could still cover the Straits; but as received by him, this was not mentioned, and it appeared that he was expected to reinforce the fleet at or near Shantung, which meant giving up his watch on the Straits.

Kamimura's view accorded with that of the Naval Staff, and notwithstanding Togo's message he was not prepared to leave the Straits unguarded; he was painfully aware of popular feeling, as Pakenham later observed in his report of August 31:

1 Corbett I, p. 421.

> The whole navy sympathised with Kamimura, who had been made the object of strictures and acrimonious criticisms among the uninformed, and whose private residence even is said to have been attacked, and its windows broken. The Minister of Marine himself had received formal expostulations that meant more than they expressed in words, and a general state of moral tension had been produced, much greater than the real damage done by these raids warranted.[2]

Accordingly Kamimura left Uriu's division (consisting of the *Naniwa, Takachiho, Niitaka* and *Tsushima*), and the torpedo boat flotilla, to cover the Straits, and at 10:40am on August 11 set off intending to meet Togo and the main fleet at the mid-sea rendezvous at 10.00am on the following day. He had his four armoured cruisers (*Idzumo, Azuma, Tokiwa* and *Iwate* and the dispatch vessel *Chihaya*). So far as he could tell from messages he picked up en route, four of the Russian battleships had returned to Port Arthur, but the *Retvizan* and *Pallada* were unlocated, while the cruisers *Askold* and *Novik* had escaped to the south.

At 10.00pm he made wireless contact with Rear Admiral Togo's cruiser squadron. Togo could give him little information, save that he had chased and lost the *Askold* northwest of Ross Island, and Kamimura headed for a position west of there. At 4:30am next day he received a message from the commander-in-chief telling him, incorrectly, that the *Bayan* and several destroyers had got away to the south, as well as the *Pallada*. In fact the *Bayan* had never left Port Arthur, to which the *Pallada* had returned; the reference to the latter was a mistake for the *Diana*. This left Kamimura even more in doubt as to what he should do, and he resolved to pursue his junction with the main fleet. In fact, Togo's message had included an order to return to the Straits, but this part of it did not get through, and it was not until 9.30, just after Rear Admiral Togo's division joined him off Ross Island, that Kamimura received the full text of the commander-in-chief's message. He at once set off for the Straits at 15 knots, and by the morning of August 13 was back on his station to cover the Straits, patrolling between the northern end of Tsushima and the coast of Japan.[3]

His principal purpose at this time was to look out for the *Askold* and *Novik*, which it was assumed would be heading through the Straits en route for Vladivostok. These vessels were not, of course, pursuing that course, but at 8:30am on August 13 Kamimura heard directly from Togo, who was with the main fleet in the Elliot Islands, of the arrival of the *Tsarevitch* at Kiaochow. This message was already 24 hours old when Kamimura received it. It read:

> You must do your utmost to attack in the Straits the enemy's cruisers from Kiaochow Bay and at the same time be on your guard against a descent of the Vladivostok squadron. Part of the 3rd Division is leaving this afternoon to act

2 Naval Attaché Reports, pp. 189-190.
3 *British Official History* I, p. 385.

> against the Kiaochow enemy. The Port Arthur enemy need not be taken into consideration.[4]

This, out of date though it was, at least left Kamimura in no doubt that it would only be cruisers that he had to face, and he issued orders deploying his armoured cruisers, Uriu's light cruisers, and the six divisions of the torpedo boat flotilla accordingly. The order to the flotilla, however, did not reach its destination, due apparently to the congestion of messages passing through the wireless station at Takeshiki.

On the morning of August 14, however, all doubts regarding the Vladivostok squadron were resolved when at 4:50am, when Kamimura was just abreast of Ulsan, he sighted Iessen's three cruisers on his port bow. Before the squadron had got very far from Vladivostok after it sailed on August 12, news had reached there of the fate of the sortie, and a torpedo boat was hastily sent off to recall Iessen, but she failed to catch him, and he proceeded on his way. By the night of August 13/14 he had reached a position due east of Fusan, and at that moment Kamimura was well out of the way, and had he wished to do so, Iessen could have made his way through the Tsushima Straits unobserved. However, his intention was to wait for the Port Arthur squadron, presumed to be coming north, at the northern end of the Straits, so he turned west towards the Korean coast, and then to the southward. As he did so, Kamimura came up behind him, also heading southwards.

What followed was known only to Pakenham from newspaper accounts, so in his next report of August 31 he made only a passing reference to it. Jackson, in a report dated September 28, briefly mentioned it, but was more concerned to record the damage sustained in the action by the *Iwate*.[5]

It was Kamimura's opportunity to put paid once and for all to his old adversary, but even now he was not disposed to take any risks. He turned to port and steered eastwards in an effort to ensure that Iessen should this time not be able to escape. As the two squadrons converged, at 5.00am Kamimura opened fire at 9,000 yards with his 8-inch guns; the Russians replied at once, but although they worked up to 17 knots, they soon found that the Japanese were showing better speed. Kamimura had a total broadside of twelve 8-inch and twenty-seven 6-inch guns; Iessen had only six 8-inch and twenty one 6-inch. The Japanese also had the advantage of position, with the rising sun behind them making it difficult for the Russians to mark the fall of shot. The range gradually came down; by 5.30 it was about 5,000 yards, and all three Russian cruisers had been hit several times. Fires in both the *Rossiya* and *Gromoboi* were put out quickly, but the *Rurik* had suffered more serious damage. When Iessen turned to starboard at this time to open the range again, it left the *Rurik* in an exposed position, and the Japanese scored further hits.

4 Corbett I, p. 426.
5 Naval Attaché Reports, pp. 179-180.

Iessen now made a move intended to take him around the Japanese to the west, hoping then to be able to head north. He turned 16 points in succession, which gave the *Rurik* a chance to make up some of the ground which she had been losing. Kamimura, however, responded quickly, turning 16 points to port in succession, and heading north-west by west to cut them off. The Russian move had, however, opened the range to just under 10,000 yards, and the Japanese ceased fire. The Russians continued to fire, though, and an 8-inch shell hit the forward turret of the *Idzumo*.

Still cautious, Kamimura made no effort for the moment to close the range. It was Iessen who, edging to starboard in an attempt to get away north-westward, began to shorten the range. By 6.00am, when the Japanese again opened fire, the *Rossiya* had had three of her 6-inch guns disabled, while the *Rurik*, now some way behind her consorts, signalled that her steering gear was disabled, and began to turn towards the Japanese squadron. Iessen ordered her to steer with her engines, and for a while this was effective. She had, however, sustained serious damage, suffering three hits on her port side, and she continued to drop further behind the other two Russian cruisers. As a result she came in for a further battering from all the Japanese cruisers as they pursued the *Rossiya* and *Gromoboi*, passing her at about 6,000 yards.

Another shell hit the *Rurik's* steerage area at about 6.40, and she turned helplessly towards the enemy. Seeing this, Iessen gave up for the moment his attempt to escape, and turned to port in succession to try to give some protection to the stricken *Rurik*. The move, however, exposed both the other cruisers to a raking fire as they turned. Unluckily, at this moment the *Rurik*, which had turned south away from the enemy and was almost stopped, forged ahead again, swinging around so far to starboard that the other two cruisers passed to the south of her and not between her and the enemy. The Japanese Confidential History described what followed:

> The enemy came up on the disengaged side of the *Rurik* and turned to starboard, thereby getting their three ships in a line on our starboard side. We poured upon them a very effective fire from which the *Rurik*, whose range was less than 5,500 yards, suffered more severely than the others.[6]

Kamimura took full advantage of this fortunate position, and maintained his course until the Russian turn was completed, so that for a short while the adversaries were on opposite courses. During this time the Russians scored a very effective hit on the *Iwate* with an 8-inch shell which exploded in her foremost upper deck casemate, putting out of action that 6-inch gun and also that in the casemate below, as well as a 12-pounder. This cost the Japanese 41 killed and 43 wounded. Soon after this Kamimura made his own 16 point turn so that his course conformed to that of the enemy, but his continued caution was shown by his choosing to turn to port, rather than towards the Russian cruisers. In thus abandoning the chance of using his torpedoes, he was apparently

6 Corbett I, p. 489.

motivated by the fear that he would be vulnerable to those of the Russians. The range was, however, now 6,500 yards as the two squadrons steamed in parallel before Iessen, in another attempt to aid the *Rurik* by interposing his other cruisers between her and the enemy, turned to starboard. Once again he was thwarted by the *Rurik's* erratic movements, and turned back to the north, while Kamimura fired on him at ranges between 6,000 and 7,000 yards. The Japanese admiral did not, however, immediately follow Iessen, evidently concerned to finish off the *Rurik* if he could. A few minutes later Iessen turned back yet again to try to get on the *Rurik's* engaged side in an effort to shield her from the Japanese fire. Kamimura responded by closing on the *Rurik*, heading to cross Iessen's course, and the latter had no choice but to turn south so that once again the squadrons were on parallel courses, at a range of about 8,000 yards.

Gradually the *Rurik's* course fell away to port, bringing her between the other two Russian cruisers and the Japanese squadron, from which she suffered a further battering. At about 7:40am, seeing Iessen's cruisers drawing clear, Kamimura altered course and opened fire on them at about 9,000 yards. The Russian commander now made yet another attempt to ease the pressure on the *Rurik* by turning back towards her. Again, briefly, the squadrons were on opposite courses, as Kamimura did not make a corresponding turn, upon which Corbett commented:

> His motive is not clear. The course he chose to keep obviously permitted the Russians to get to the northward of him and deprive him of the dominating position he had hitherto maintained on their line of retreat. He may have been influenced by the fact that Admiral Iessen now turned to the eastward and was passing again on the far side of the *Rurik*, so that once more he could keep her between him and her consorts. This, in fact, is what he did. As Admiral Iessen passed within hail of the *Rurik* he called to her: 'full speed to Vladivostok,' and then turned northward. Admiral Kamimura responded by altering to the north-westward across his wake.[7]

Corbett suggests that Kamimura may have overestimated the damage he had done to the *Rurik*, reckoning that he could finish her off and still be able to catch Iessen's other two ships. Certainly the *Rossiya* had been seriously damaged by a fire on her upper deck and forecastle, and Kamimura may have supposed that her speed would have been reduced so much that he could easily catch her after dealing with the *Rurik*. As a result, he left Iessen with the initiative to make his getaway if that was what he decided to do; Corbett remarks that Kamimura may have been conscious of the mistake which he thus made, 'for his narrative at this period of the action is so vague and obscure that it is only from the track chart that we can learn what he did.'[8]

7 Ibid., p. 441.
8 Ibid., p. 442.

Iessen's final attempt to assist the *Rurik* was made at 8.08; having got the fire on the *Rossiya* under control, he turned south. Kamimura inclined away to starboard, evidently in an attempt to bring the guns of his whole line to bear on the Russians as they came on. Having ordered the *Rurik* to proceed to Vladivostok, Iessen himself turned north, under the concentrated fire of all four Japanese cruisers at a range of 6,500 yards. An officer on board the *Rossiya* described the damage suffered by the flagship:

> The remaining guns were put out of action one after the other; casings and funnels were shot through; we had holes on the waterline and a list; all five torpedo tubes were disabled; a torpedo had burst in one of them; two masts were riddled; shells flew continuously; small fires broke out which we could not get under; two boilers were damaged.[9]

Kamimura's decisions had left Iessen with an excellent chance of escape. As his cruisers headed north by east towards safety, the Japanese were on their starboard quarter, some 8,000 to 9,000 yards away. Behind them, the crippled *Rurik* was falling far astern. Kamimura had summoned the light cruisers *Naniwa* and *Takachiho* to join him, which they now did and he ordered them to deal with the *Rurik*, while he continued his pursuit of the *Rossiya* and *Gromoboi*. They were far enough ahead to render the Japanese fire ineffective, and Kamimura, to conserve ammunition, ordered that such fire as was maintained should be slow and deliberate. At 8.30 Iessen turned eastward, perhaps in an attempt to draw Kamimura further away from the *Rurik*; the Japanese admiral did not attempt to close the range, which he might have done, but merely altered course to conform to the Russian movements. After about 15 minutes Iessen turned north-northwest, which brought him to a heading directly for Vladivostok, with the Japanese some 4 miles on his starboard quarter. A long stern chase was now in prospect.

As it continued, the range gradually diminished, and hits on the two Russian cruisers were still being scored. By 9.45 the range was down to 5,000 yards, but Kamimura then began to edge away to starboard and it increased to over 7,000 yards. Why he did so is unknown, but he was certainly uneasy about being drawn far away to the north of the position which his squadron was charged to protect. At about 10.00 he received a report, apparently incorrect, that the *Idzumo's* ammunition was down to 25%. This seems to have decided him, and 10.05 he abandoned his pursuit of Iessen and turned back to the south.

By the time Kamimura reached the scene of the action between the *Naniwa* and *Takachiho* and the crippled *Rurik*, he found that the Russian cruiser had sunk. She fought to the end; all her senior officers were dead or seriously wounded, only the junior gunnery officer Lieutenant Ivanov remaining. He himself was wounded by a

9 Ibid., p. 443.

6-inch shell which burst in the conning tower; he ordered the cruiser's last torpedo to be fired, but it was clear to him that further resistance was hopeless. He gave orders that the wounded be brought on deck, and that the torpedo magazine be blown up. When this was found to be impossible, he ordered the engine room to open the Kingston valves to flood the ship, and she began to sink by the stern. Rear Admiral Uriu, commanding the Japanese cruisers, ordered as many boats as possible to be lowered to pick up survivors, as did Kamimura's armoured cruisers when they reappeared, with the result that 625 members of the *Rurik's* crew were saved before, stern first. she sank at 10:20am.

Ivanov's dedication was recognised three years later, when an official announcement was published:

> Lieutenant Ivanov, to whom the command of the *Rurik* reverted after the captain and commander had been killed in the action of Ulsan on August 14, 1904, and who behaved gallantly on the occasion, is for the rest of his service to be known as 'Ivanov trinadtzati' or Ivanov the thirteenth, in commemoration of this notable event.[10]

This number reflected the fact that Ivanov was the thirteenth officer of that name on the Navy List.

During the battle the Japanese had fired 958 8-inch shells and 4,528 6-inch shells (761 of the latter had been fired by the *Naniwa* and *Takachiho* at the crippled *Rurik*). A total of over 200 hits scored, but between 100 and 150 of these were on the unfortunate *Rurik*, which could defend itself to only a limited extent against what was, at the end, very close range. In the rest of the battle the percentage of hits was extremely low, amounting to no more than 1.5% of all the shells fired. The Russians actually did somewhat better; it has been suggested that they achieved hits from between 200 and 230 8-inch and 6-inch shells; but the better armour of the Japanese cruisers meant that they suffered less damage.[11]

Kamimura's decision to break off the action when he did has been justly criticised. The British Official History suggests as possible explanations either that he was not confident that Uriu's cruisers could deal with the *Rurik*, or that his coal or ammunition was running short:

> It is possible that, as the speed of his opponents had not been greatly reduced, he failed to realise their almost hopeless condition; and his ignorance of the fate of the ships which had escaped from Port Arthur may have influenced the decision to turn back. But in any case it can hardly be denied that Admiral Kamimura's

10 *British Official History* I, p. 389 n.
11 Olender II, pp. 172-173.

> judgment was at fault, for had the engagement been continued for a short time longer it is most improbable that either vessel would have reached port.[12]

The Japanese Confidential History gave an explanation which Corbett found neither adequate or convincing:

> The action had been a long one (nearly 5 hours). During the chase all the guns' crews were warned to fire slowly and make certain of their aim. But at 10.00am it was reported to Admiral Kamimura that the *Idzumo's* ammunition was running short. Seeing that the enemy's speed had not slackened in the slightest in spite of the waning of their gunfire he considered it better to use his remaining ammunition in sinking the *Rurik*, and making certain that she at least did not escape.[13]

As Corbett pointed out, if this was the true reason for letting Iessen escape, it was a bad one. The tactics which Kamimura applied throughout the battle were entirely consistent with the cautious policy pursued by the Japanese navy since the start of the war. His conduct of the battle at long ranges for most of the time, and his failure to maintain his position on Iessen's line of retreat meant that Kamimura had not achieved a decisive result.

He had, though, effectively put the Vladivostok squadron out of action for the time being. It took over two months for the *Rossiya* and *Gromoboi* to be repaired. When these were completed, the latter damaged her hull when running acceptance tests on October 13, which meant a further long delay before she would be battleworthy. Then, in December, orders were sent from St Petersburg that no operations should be undertaken which involved any risk, pending the arrival in the Far East of the Second Pacific Squadron.[14]

Alfred Mahan, writing in 1906, looked back at the operations of the Vladivostok squadron and found in them confirmation of his strongly held opinion of the uselessness of armoured cruisers:

> Such result as was open to the Vladivostok squadron to produce was further limited by the fact that it was composed of armoured cruisers, a compromise double-faced type of vessel, the advisability of which has long been questioned by respectable professional opinion, and now and more loudly than ever … If instead of being ships built with one eye on fighting and one on speed, the Vladivostok ships had been fairly and frankly cruisers, pure and simple, unarmoured, and gunned only so as to meet their like, and if the tonnage thus economised had

12 *British Official History* I, p. 389.
13 Corbett I, p. 447.
14 Olender II, p. 174.

> been devoted to speed and coal endurance, their fitness for the work of molesting commerce and transportation would have been distinctly increased.[15]

He was, of course, writing before the advent of the battle cruiser, which immediately rendered the armoured cruiser obsolete, though itself in some respects an anomalous design.

15 Mahan, p. 154.

19

Port Arthur: The Siege Continued

Following the battle of the Yellow Sea, Togo expected daily that the Russians would make another sortie, and an even closer watch was kept on Port Arthur. Reconnaissance both by day and at night was maintained hard by the harbour entrance. In the battle squadron steam was always kept in readiness. On August 16 the Japanese put to sea to beat back and forth, cruising to the south-east during the night and returning towards Port Arthur and Round Island at daybreak. While conducting these manoeuvres, Togo kept in touch with his cruiser squadrons; Dewa's 3rd Division was stationed south of Liautishan and Rear Admiral Togo's 6th Division, close in to the port in daytime, retired at night to a position south of Encounter Rock. Kataoka, with the 5th Division, was off Cap Island during the day and Round Island at night. Hosoya's 7th Division was engaged in direct support of the army.[1]

Togo's concern about the threat still posed by the Russian fleet was sufficiently strong for him to protest vigorously when the Naval Staff authorised Kamimura to bring his ships into dock at Sasebo. In the face of this, the Naval Staff yielded, and revoked the order. Tension was high among the Japanese leaders on both land and sea, Nogi was preparing his assault on the fortress, and his summons to the garrison to surrender was curtly rejected by the Russians.

The Japanese attack went in on August 18, and was maintained through seven days of fierce fighting, which cost Nogi over 10,000 casualties. During this period, a coded signal was received aboard the *Mikasa* that the enemy ships were coming out, and Togo at once issued orders for a concentration near Encounter Rock. It proved, though, to be a false alarm, and the fleet returned to its blockading stations. However, it was no longer felt safe for it to return to base, and the 1st and 3rd Divisions coaled at sea.

Pakenham shared Togo's concern about the likelihood of a sortie. He considered that the possibility that one of the five remaining Russian battleships had been seriously damaged would, if true, be a piece of singular good fortune: 'Otherwise, the

1 Corbett I, p. 458.

relative strengths of the two fleets is such that the result of the next engagement is far from being a foregone conclusion in favour of the Japanese.'[2] The Russians, however, were faced by a ring of mines; if they were less careful than on the previous occasions when they left port, they might not be so successful in avoiding them. Nevertheless, in Pakenham's opinion the Japanese naval supremacy was now far from being secure.

Neither he nor Togo knew, of course, what had gone on inside Port Arthur. Stoessel, with the commencement of the Japanese assault, had called on Prince Ukhtomski for direct assistance; to defend the fortress he needed all the resources of the fleet, particularly for the supply of 10-inch and 6-inch guns and ammunition. Ukhtomski called a Council of War on August 19. It concluded that even after the ships were repaired, it would be impossible to break out and sail to Vladivostok; even single ships would not succeed. It went on to accept that the fleet should assist the defence directly with all of the available guns and men that could be spared, retaining only enough in the ships to fight an action at anchor.[3]

As a result Pakenham's next report, dated September 17, spoke of there having been an 'extremely quiet' period. Both sides had been actively mining; it was suspected that the Russians might have been using Chinese junks to lay mines about 5 miles offshore. Pakenham observed that 'if Port Arthur should eventually fall, it will be through no fault of the Chinese, who have allowed no opportunity of aiding the Russians to pass if money could be made from it.' [4] Meanwhile, news of the fall of Liaoyang lifted Japanese spirits, although Pakenham hoped that the failure to strike an annihilating blow at Kuropatkin's army had been allowed for in Japanese strategic planning.

The pause in active naval operations gave him the opportunity to speculate about Japanese plans to build two new armoured cruisers. It was rumoured, he wrote, that these would 'far excel anything hitherto built, possibly even proposed.' They would be of 12,000 tons, with a speed of 21 knots, carrying an armament similar to the latest Japanese battleships, but with lighter armour. Although they were to be built at Kure, the design had probably been made in England:

> It will be interesting to see what modifications the experience of this war causes to be introduced. This experience has hitherto been all in one direction, which is that the first necessity for heavy fighting ships is heavy gunfire power, while, from the destroyer upwards, no vessel can be considered useful that does not possess one or more guns, heavy and of long-range, in proportion to her size. Unless the next battle should reverse the lessons of former fighting, it may be ventured that the Japanese will regret putting 10-inch guns into their battleships instead of 12-inch. In Kamimura's action, the effect of 6-inch and 8-inch gunfire

2 Naval Attaché Reports, p. 194.
3 Corbett I, p. 462.
4 Naval Attaché Reports, p. 197.

> upon armoured cruisers, when it is compared with the vast expenditure of ammunition, may truly be called insignificant.[5]

What was also vitally important, in Pakenham's opinion, was that the design speed of 21 knots should actually be achievable, and not be a repetition of the 'old story' whereby vessels were produced that were unable to do more than 17 or 18 knots under service conditions. If the boiler capacity as built was capable of the higher speed, the new vessels would not only be a match for most battleships, but would also be able 'to run down in a long chase any warship now afloat.' Most of the elements of future battlecruiser design were here to be seen, as was another issue which would prove significant. This was the work being done to improve the safety of the magazines 'by removing them from the influence of mine and torpedo explosions, or by protecting them against these, as no ship has yet been sunk unless her magazines were affected.'[6]

News of a change in the command of the Russian fleet had however reached Pakenham. For the moment he treated as an unconfirmed rumour the information that Captain Robert Viren of the *Bayan* had been promoted over the heads of senior officers to take command in succession to the ineffectual Ukhtomski. Pakenham was in fact rather sceptical about the report, suggesting that it had been spread 'as a species of Voltairean encouragement to Ukhtomski to harden his heart against his next encounter with the Japanese, and that the man from the *Bayan* will be second-in-command.' If the rumour turned out to be true, however, it might be of great importance to the Japanese, 'who feel that they can rely upon finding a rival of very moderate ability in Ukhtomski.'[7] The news was indeed accurate, and it represented one of the more sensible decisions of the Russian naval leadership, though in the event it was not to make much difference.

Togo, meanwhile, had done what he could to support Nogi's army in its operations against the fortress, ordering Kataoka to take the *Nisshin* and *Kasuga* close inshore to create a diversion from a point out of range of the Russian coastal batteries which were causing Nogi a good deal of difficulty. This was on August 23, and the diversion appeared to have succeeded in its object, so Togo ordered that it be repeated next day. This prompted an urgent message from the Naval Staff in Tokyo:

> For the present, when the heavy guns of the fleet have already fired half the rounds which their lives will endure, and several of them are so badly damaged as to be unserviceable, everything must be done to husband them for action with the Port Arthur and Vladivostok squadrons and with the Baltic Fleet, which will sooner or later arrive. The thought of wearing them out in minor engagements with parts of the fortress cannot be tolerated. I therefore request that no ships of

5 Ibid., p. 201.
6 Ibid., p. 202.
7 Ibid., p. 203.

> higher value than the 7th Division be employed for the present in bombarding the fortress.[8]

It was a wise admonition, but Togo seems not to have regarded it as an explicit order, merely instructing Kataoka to avoid firing unless it was absolutely necessary. Nogi, meanwhile, had reached the conclusion that his offensive against the fortress had failed. Not only had his casualties exceeded 10,000 men; he had expended nearly all the ammunition for his artillery. This news dismayed Togo; his crews were exhausted, and his ships in dire need of refitting, and the spectre of the Baltic Fleet that was preparing to sail was constantly in his mind. However, when a staff officer brought him the news that the attempt to storm Port Arthur had for the moment been given up, he replied only: 'What will be, will be.'[9]

Thus Pakenham must, like his Japanese hosts, await further action at Port Arthur in the hope that it might lead to the early destruction of the Russian fleet. The expectation was that the dispatch of the Second Pacific Squadron could not be long delayed; in the meantime Pakenham was able to observe in his report of September 28 that 'local dearth of incident seems to make the present a favourable time for a few remarks on various naval subjects that either have not found a place, or that have not been fully dealt with in previous reports.' Since there would, in due course, be another battle, and since, as he wryly observed, 'neither the Geneva Conference nor the Hague Conference appears to have made any provision for the safety of onlookers,' he thought it best to pass on such further information that he had.[10]

One rather unexpected issue which he raised was the possible use of the ram in the next battle. This he thought would occasion no surprise:

> The Japanese might certainly expect to derive whatever benefit could be obtained from this method of attack, now so unfashionable among theorists, whether it were directed against themselves, or whether they were the aggressor, because they have adopted the principle of gun attack that offers the greatest probability of either deflecting an approaching enemy from his course, or of confusing one whom it is proposed to ram; but with their well-grounded fear of the torpedo, it can hardly be supposed that they would permit the hostile fleet to come within torpedo range except in case of extremity. The Russian position may be somewhat different, and may have the effect of hastening the adoption of desperate measures before circumstances really call for them. For one thing, there is reason to think the Russians take a much more despairing view of their chances of success than they ought to do; and for another, their fleet is almost

8 Corbett I, p. 463.
9 Ogasawara, p. 307.
10 Naval Attaché Reports, p. 206.

> certain to be manoeuvred into such a position that its only road to safety will be through the ranks of the Japanese.[11]

Pakenham thought that any attempt at ramming in the next battle would be particularly instructive, 'as both ram and torpedo, as adjuncts to the offensive of big ships, are now trembling on the brink of abolition.' The new Japanese cruisers, he noted, would have no rams, while the trend of opinion seemed to be turning against the fitting of torpedo tubes to such vessels.

Pakenham also drew attention to the reluctance of commanders to make use of conning towers:

> So far as the late action is concerned, the only light it shed on the suitability of the present form of conning tower for the purpose for which it is intended is to be judged from the apparently universal avoidance of these structures by all who were supposed to make use of them. No instance is known of anyone in this fleet having sought the shelter of his conning tower, and it is gathered that Vitgeft himself abandoned his for the bridge, so it is likely that Russian and Japanese practices coincided in this respect. All who have spoken about it say they cannot stand being in a place from which everything looks so different, and that they are unable to command their ships from inside the tower. There is nothing new in that; the same cry has probably been heard in every navy, and is now nonetheless plaintive because stale from age and repetition.[12]

There had, Pakenham noted, been no suggestion for the improvement of the conning tower in the Japanese fleet. He thought it might be a good idea to insist that the navigating officer occupy the conning tower, as a temporary expedient, separating the command function from that of steering, which would be linked by voice tube. He also suggested that future design should reduce the area of target, whether or not strongly armoured, adding: 'How little it takes to burst a shell was shown in the *Mikasa*, where one burst against the fore-bridge semaphore, killing or wounding four of the Admiral 's staff.[13]

In his report of September 28, Pakenham returned again to the subject of long-range fire, to which he had throughout the campaign devoted particular attention. He had been examining its effectiveness, and the extent to which a fleet might be obliged to open fire at a range longer than was desirable by the action of the enemy:

> In reading the account of the large amount of ammunition fired at long ranges in the late action, and in comparing the number of hits probably made with the

11 Ibid., pp. 206-207.
12 Ibid., p. 207.
13 Ibid., p. 208.

> number of rounds fired, some may be inclined to feel that, if they had commanded either fleet, they would have reserved their fire until the distance separating the lines had been reduced by one half. This is a point on which theory is apt to be misleading, and the more so as it is recorded that successful commanders in the past occasionally ordered their guns not to return the fire of the enemy until within 'a half pistol shot' or 'the throw of a biscuit.' The vastly increased power of the heavy gun has changed all that. However great the protection afforded by armour in the present day, a single well-placed shot of large calibre can produce effects so very much more serious than its corresponding shot of 100 years ago, that an Admiral no longer has it in his own absolute discretion whether to withhold his fire or not. Fire must be begun, as a measure of the most elementary self-protection, as soon as the opposite side opens with his artillery, provided always that the ships are within range.

This, he pointed out, was what had happened to the Japanese in the battle of August 10. He went on to point out the design consequences of the increased range:

> Long range fire has come to stay for the present, and, in the disposition of armour, steeper angles of descent must be considered, and blows of great force must no longer be expected to come wholly in the horizontal. The 7-inch armour on the starboard bow of the *Mikasa* was shattered, on August 10, at a range of probably not less than 13,000 or 14,000 yards, a triangular hole (3.5 x 3.5 x 4', about) being made just above the heel of the second torpedo defence boom from forward. The perforated or barred tops to hoods of barbette guns should now give place to some other device for ventilating the interior of the turret, and for permitting the removal of the guns.[14]

Pakenham had also devoted a lot of time to thinking about the relative ineffectiveness of the torpedo attacks launched by the Japanese since the start of the war. Partly this was due to the torpedoes being set to run maximum ranges, with a consequent reduction in speed, which reduced the chance of hitting the target. This caution mirrored that of the Japanese admirals in relation to their heavy ships; the Japanese fleet was a finite resource, and tactical decisions flowed from this. The Japanese had a great number of torpedo boats, but not so many destroyers; it was the gun armament of the latter which was, to Pakenham's mind, of particular importance:

> A destroyer with an artillery feeble in proportion to her size is an hermaphrodite sort of vessel, very different for an Admiral to class, and in action against an enemy strong in real destroyers, she will have to be ranked with the torpedo boats, but with all the disadvantages of increased size and cost … It should be

14 Ibid., pp 209-210.

> remembered, however, that no vessel can justly be called useless in the strictest sense of the term ... When the word useless is applied to a ship it should be translated as 'bad value for the money.' Destroyers cannot go on any longer with only one 12-pounder gun.[15]

He advocated the fitting of a second 12-pounder, even if this meant removing some of the 6-pounders presently carried. Of course, strengthening the armament of the destroyer in this way would in due course lead to significant increases in the size of such vessels.

In his next report, on October 20, Pakenham described the disappointing results so far achieved by the naval guns landed in support of the Japanese army. A daily bombardment by 4.7-inch and 6-inch guns had achieved a considerable number of hits on the Russian ships in the harbour, but had failed to result in their being driven to put to sea. It was, of course, not yet fully realised by Pakenham and his Japanese hosts that the firm decision had been taken by the Russians to operate in support of the garrison rather than to prepare for another sortie. In its present position, the Russian fleet was fairly safe, for the Japanese had not taken any position from which they could observe the fall of shot. On the other hand, the Russian ships had been effective in their fire on the Japanese positions:

> The fire of the Russian ships has greatly impeded the advance of the Japanese army, and there is no denying that their apparent determination to remain in Port Arthur to the last is far more embarrassing to the Japanese then the alternative course of coming out and fighting to a finish, although a pitched battle might not be the object of a sortie; supposing when they came out the battleships were to steam at full speed for their destinations without waiting for the laggards, the Japanese would be much puzzled how to deal with them, as a ship for ship pursuit is almost out of the question.[16]

The length of time it was taking to reduce the fortress was having a considerable effect, not only tying up a large Japanese army that was needed elsewhere, but also delaying the refitting of the Japanese fleet in readiness to face the Second Pacific Squadron.

An interesting light was shed on Russian thinking when a steamer bound for Port Arthur with supplies of ammunition was captured. On board was an army captain of engineers named Eggard, from whom some information was gleaned with regard to the opinions held at Kuropatkin's headquarters. Pakenham reproduced the notes taken by the interpreter who conversed with the officer:

15 Ibid., pp. 211-212.
16 Ibid., pp. 217-218.

> Russian government relies on the Baltic fleet to redress previous misfortunes; strongly urged by Kuropatkin to hasten it; expects it will be joined by heavy ships from other parts of the world, including sister ships of *Nisshin* and *Kasuga*; it is intended to make it up to seven battleships and fifteen powerful cruisers. The Russians think that if Port Arthur can hold out the war will not last much longer. Large reinforcements are coming to Kuropatkin from Vladivostok. If on August 10, the remainder of the Russian fleet had persisted in trying to make its way to Vladivostok, the Russians would have thought it a great victory, in spite of the loss of the *Tsarevitch*; Vitgeft a coward; regret return of the fleet to Port Arthur.[17]

Eggard apparently went on to offer some extravagantly critical comments about the generals in command in Port Arthur. It is doubtful whether the Japanese paid much regard to this intelligence; almost certainly their own intelligence network would be seen as producing more authentic information.

The failure of Nogi's latest advance on Port Arthur, which had prompted Togo's great concern that the attack by land should be vigorously resumed as soon as possible, had led the Imperial Headquarters to consider the question of the refitting of the Japanese fleet. It was suggested to Togo, who it will be recalled had protested about the proposal that Kamimura's squadron should go into dock, that he might send his ships in one or two at a time. Togo would have none of it, insisting that all the ships on station outside Port Arthur must remain until the fortress was taken. Another proposal that caused the admiral disquiet was to transfer troops from the siege of Port Arthur to the Japanese army which was at this time preparing for the assault on Liaoyang. An enquiry from Oyama as to the current strength of the Russian fleet brought a firm reply from Togo:

> The main force of the Russian fleet at present remaining in Port Arthur consists of five battleships ... Two second-class cruisers *Bayan* and *Pallada,* three gunboats and ten destroyers. The *Sevastopol* will not be able to fight for a fortnight at least, but the four other battleships have made temporary repairs and have recovered most of their fighting power, so that they are considered already able to steam. The *Pallada* and *Bayan* are expected to finish their temporary repairs in the course of the present month.[18]

It would therefore be unsafe to reduce the strength of the blockading fleet at all until the fortress fell. Togo was, however, persuaded to allow Kamimura to send his cruisers in to Sasebo two at a time for refitting.

17 Ibid., pp. 218-219.
18 Corbett I, p. 466.

The battle of Liaoyang, although resulting in a victory for the Japanese, had proved indecisive. Kuropatkin was able to withdraw his army in the face of Oyama's concentric advance, and get it back safely beyond the Taitzu Ho, and by September 9 was taking up a strong position around Mukden, having been driven back only about twenty miles. At the same time the continued failure of Nogi's army in front of Port Arthur left the Japanese Imperial Headquarters feeling distinctly uneasy about the overall position of the war. While Port Arthur continued to hold out the effect on the fleet was corrosive, as Corbett observed:

> It prolonged their exhausting defensive at sea, and week by week the wear and tear of maintaining their position tended to diminish the power of the blow which sooner or later they would have to strike for the permanent command ... The most general comment on the war, as a whole, is that it exhibits the great advantage possessed in a maritime theatre by the belligerent that has the command of the sea. But there is a lesson less trite and of a deeper significance. In a sense, as we know now, the Japanese had the command; they had at least as large a degree of command as is to be expected between two nearly equal belligerents. From the outset the Russian fleet, if boldly faced, would have had little power to interfere with the free movement of the Japanese troops. But this they did not know with sufficient certainty. Clearly what is needed in such cases is not mere physical preponderance – it is the sense of security.[19]

Accordingly, the invariable caution which the Japanese naval leaders displayed continued to be applied to every situation faced by the fleet all the time that Port Arthur remained untaken, and the Russian fleet thereby continued to be a potential threat. The insecurity which was growing was increased, of course, by the as yet unrealised threat presented by the potential dispatch of the Second Pacific Squadron. Aboard the fleet, there was profound disappointment that a further assault on Port Arthur which began on October 30 was again unsuccessful. Pakenham, in a report of November 11, looked ahead with concern to the effect on Togo's ships of the approaching winter weather, as well as the minor actions continually being undertaken in support of Nogi's army. He noted that the battleships had been a year out of dock, and that minor defects had been accumulating in that time, while the main armament of three of the four battleships had suffered serious injury. Pakenham considered that Togo's position was unenviable: 'It was essential that his deficiencies in heavy guns should be made good before the strategic situation became more delicate.' The expedient, now finally adopted, of sending the battleships one at a time to Japan to be repaired and refitted meant a significant reduction in the strength of the blockading fleet, which

19 Ibid., pp. 468-470.

at any time would have to give battle to the Russian fleet if it emerged from Port Arthur.[20]

The first to leave the fleet was the *Asahi*, which needed to replace two of her 12-inch guns. She had suffered damage from a floating mine in October 26, which exploded on her port side, abreast of her rear turret. The battle fleet was about 70 miles from Port Arthur at the time. She escaped without serious damage, the force of the explosion having gone upwards. A total of four mines close together had been sighted, and it was particularly fortunate that the *Asahi's* port propeller had not caught one of them. The *Mikasa* and the other battleships passed the mines within four feet; as Pakenham observed, the good luck was phenomenal.

Within the fortress there had continued to be discussion among the naval leaders. On November 13 Rear Admiral Viren convened a conference to discuss the options available. He announced that he had decided to commit all the fleet's resources to the defence of the fortress, observing that even if the battleships and cruisers were seaworthy, they would be unable to leave port because of the lack of personnel. The conference decided that all 6-inch shells should be landed, except the remaining armour piercing shell, and that the batteries covering the Gut should be strengthened. A further conference a week later discussed the policy of completing the *Bayan* for sea, which was agreed in principle. The 6-inch ammunition from all the other ships was to be landed. Captains von Essen of the *Sevastopol* and Sarnavski of the *Pallada* protested, arguing that the ships should remain armed and be kept ready to go to sea when the Baltic Fleet approached. They argued that without them, the newly arrived squadron would have no chance. Their views received no support, however, and except for a handful of officers, all the ships' crews went ashore.[21]

20 Naval Attaché Reports, p. 223.
21 *British Official History* II, pp. 584-585.

20

Capitulation

Out at sea, Togo continued to be profoundly anxious about the potential threat still posed by the Russian fleet in Port Arthur, particularly in the light of the dispatch from Europe of the Second Pacific Squadron. Since the ships in Port Arthur showed no immediate signs of coming out, thus denying him the opportunity to get at them, it must now be the army that took the necessary action to destroy them. Despite the repeated attacks by Nogi's troops, and the fearful casualties which they had suffered, the position of the Japanese front line was not such as to permit observation of the fall of shot into the harbour. Togo concluded that this situation could be rectified if 203 Metre Hill could be taken, and he sent one of his staff ashore to explain to Nogi the pressing need for the army to gain possession of this crucial point.

The British Official History observed that here was a concrete demonstration of the fact that the Japanese operations around Port Arthur were directed to obtaining and maintaining effective command of the sea:

> It also illustrates the interdependence of naval strategy and land tactics, and throws light on the intimate relations and cooperation between the Japanese navy and army. Indeed in this case the threat contained in the movement of a fleet some thousands of miles away was the ultimate cause of the further prosecution by the land forces of a definite tactical operation which resulted in one of the most desperate struggles and some of the bloodiest fighting in the whole war.[1]

For the Imperial Headquarters, it had become a question of prioritising the use of the limited resources available. The main force of the enemy was to be found in front of the Japanese armies advancing in Manchuria. Basic military principles called for a concentration of force there. However, the army in the Kwantung peninsula was conducting an operation of vital importance to the navy, upon which lay the responsibility for maintaining the security on which the army ultimately depended.

1 *British Official History* II, p. 586.

Moreover Togo saw the overall situation as being a lot less favourable than was supposed in Tokyo:

> Being in close contact with the army, he could realise more vividly than his superiors at Headquarters how much the pure considerations of naval strategy were restricted by the practical need of adjusting it to the plans and needs of the army. In his eyes, therefore, his task in the Yellow Sea was far from done, and as he was able to appreciate the situation he had work enough and more than enough for everything he could lay hands on. It was not only that he believed he had inflicted a merely temporary check on the Port Arthur squadron and that sooner or later it must make another dash for Vladivostok, but it is clear that a loyal anxiety to assist his military colleague in doing for the fleet what it could not do for itself had taken possession of him.[2]

It was his desire to support Nogi that had led him to use his ships in a manner that had so disturbed the Naval Staff. Now, as the reality of the dispatch of the Second Pacific Squadron made itself felt, Togo was anxious to see direct action being taken against the Russian ships in Port Arthur.

Previous attempts to storm 203 Metre Hill had failed with heavy loss, and in reviewing his plans for the next assault on the fortress Nogi reached the conclusion that it would be impossible to take the position before seizing the other key points of the northern defences from Sungshu Shan eastwards to Chikuan Shan. A general attack on these positions was planned for November 26. This was heralded in the two days beforehand by a number of probing attacks along the whole front, which were repulsed by the Russians with heavy losses. When the main attack went in it was preceded by a heavy bombardment, which increased in intensity as the morning progressed. By 11.00am the Chinese Wall, as this line of fortifications was called, had been damaged in several places, and a mine had been exploded under the parapet of Fort Chikuan. The Japanese infantry stormed forward, to be received with a murderous fire. Although temporary footholds were obtained in some places, it was clear as night fell that the general attack had again failed and it was resolved to try a night assault in a final attempt to break through at Sungshu Shan. Led by General Nakamura, 2,600 volunteers were launched on the position; but after several hours of hand-to-hand fighting, in which Nakamura was seriously wounded and 1,000 men died, the Japanese fell back defeated. Many of those lying wounded on the battlefield froze to death in the bitter cold.

General Kondratenko, commanding the Russian defenders in the front line, grasped the fact that the Japanese would next make a fresh assault on 203 Metre Hill, and began to move his reserves to the threatened point. This part of the position was held by a force led by the able Colonel Tretyakov. The garrison there had, however, been

2 Corbett II, pp. 43-44.

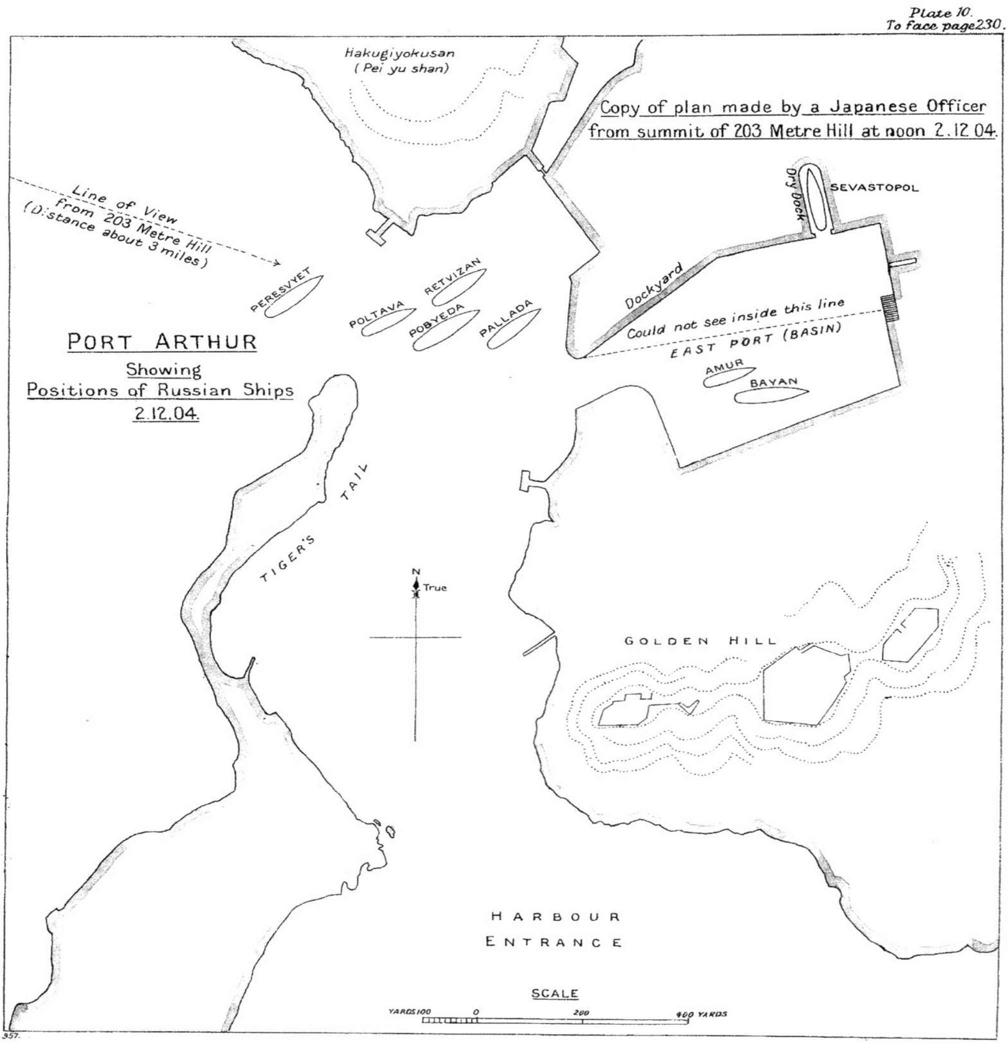

Sketch 6: Port Arthur December 2 1904

greatly reduced, not only by casualties but also by disease; and although the assault of November 26 had been successfully repulsed, there was a growing despondency among the Russian troops as to how long the fortress could hold out.

During the night of December 1/2, the Russians undertook a number of minor sorties to probe the Japanese intentions. These found that all along the front the Japanese trenches were strongly held. The Japanese now made a series of demonstrations to retard the Russian ability to concentrate at the decisive point, which Nogi now accepted should be 203 Metre Hill. This was going to be a tough proposition; the hill was almost solid rock, making it difficult for sappers to push forward saps approaching the Russian lines.

The assault was to be carried out by the 1st Division. In the early evening of November 27 an attack was made on both 203 Metre Hill and the adjoining position on Akasaka Yama. Over the course of the next two days the two hills changed hands several times. By November 30 it seemed that the attack had failed, again with fearful loss; but on the following day a further assault left the Japanese in possession of a key part of 203 Metre Hill, and by December 5 the whole of it was in Japanese hands. Some 14,000 Japanese soldiers and over 5,000 Russians had died in the course of the struggle for this one small position. On December 6 an observation post was established on the hill, and a ferocious and accurate bombardment rained down on the Russian fleet.[3]

In the end it was the powerful siege guns of the Japanese, rather than their courageous and long-suffering infantry, which broke down the Russian defence. One observer, Colonel von Schwartz, wrote that it was 'the accurate and destructive fire of the Japanese siege guns which converted all the works into shapeless heaps of rubbish.'[4]

Once 203 Metre Hill had fallen there was no longer any hope for the remains of the Russian Pacific Fleet; its ships were abandoned to be destroyed at their moorings by the Japanese artillery. There was, however, one exception, as Pakenham explained in his report of December 13. After listing the destruction, one by one, of the rest of the Russian fleet, he described what had happened to the *Sevastopol.* She had been in dock, and it was believed that she was unseaworthy, so had been spared the attentions of Nogi's artillery:

> So far all had gone well with the Japanese; but trouble was in store for them. Soon after dawn on December 9 it was signalled that the *Sevastopol* had left the dock, and was then lying, the last active remains of the Port Arthur battle squadron, at anchor outside the port. To her, all attention has been devoted ever since to prevent her escape, and to put her out of her misery, by sending her to

3 Warner, p. 436.
4 Quoted *British Official History* II, p. 624 n.

> join her fellows at the bottom of the sea. With care, she will lead the Japanese a fine dance, and may then escape after all.[5]

In the position which she had taken up, the *Sevastopol* was not an easy target for the Japanese torpedo boats, protected as she was by the shore searchlights and batteries and her net protection. Essen, who had been determined to make an attempt to break out, had managed to withhold about 25 rounds per gun, and got 700 tons of coal aboard. When he asked Viren for permission to take his ship outside, he was at first allowed to do so; but after further discussion Viren changed his mind, and refused the request. Essen was not prepared to take no for an answer, and after a prolonged debate Viren said that he could do what he thought best. Essen had managed to collect 60 more men to add to the 40 he already had on board, and succeeded, not without difficulty, in getting his ship out of the harbour and safely moored. Once there, more ammunition was brought out in lighters, and Viren sent out 200 more men. This brought his crew up to less than half the ship's complement, but Essen was determined to make a break for it. Viren, however, now sent him an order expressly forbidding it.[6]

For the Japanese navy, the final destruction of this last survivor of the Russian fleet now became an issue of the greatest importance, and Togo was firmly enjoined to do all that was necessary to prevent the *Sevastopol's* escape. Pakenham noted that this was more than just an operational necessity:

> It is evident how strategically desirable the destruction of the ship must be. So long as she remains active the Japanese battleships must keep the sea; whereas, if she were to be made an end of today, the armoured fleet would probably be broken up at once. There is, however, another reason, which the Japanese navy feels keenly. This has so far been a military victory, bought with the blood, courage and skill of the army; and the sailors realise that if they allow the *Sevastopol* to escape them, the mass of their friends will consider it a slur on the navy, not to be easily wiped out.[7]

During the week that followed a number of attacks by Togo's torpedo boats were launched against the *Sevastopol*, though it was unclear whether they had inflicted any serious damage. While these continued, the Japanese suffered a major casualty when the cruiser *Takasago* struck a mine just after midnight on December 13. Within twenty minutes she was listing heavily, and in spite of all that could be done, she sank at 1:10am. Only three boats had been launched, and most of her crew, clinging to floating spars and wreckage, succumbed in the bitterly cold sea.

5 Naval Attaché Reports, p. 231.
6 Corbett II, p. 106.
7 Naval Attaché Reports, p. 232.

Further torpedo attacks on the *Sevastopol* continued, without achieving much success, and in spite of the torpedo boats closing in to suicidally short range. Essen calculated that 60 torpedoes were fired on the night of December 14/15 alone. This attack had cost the Japanese one torpedo boat sunk, three more permanently disabled and many others damaged. On the night of December 16/17, however, a further attack achieved greater success. Two torpedoes had got through the gaps that had been blown in the boom which protected the *Sevastopol*, and damaged her side, while another blew a huge hole in her unprotected stern. She took a list of 10°; although Essen managed to right the ship, she had taken on so much water that her stern now touched bottom every tide. Although Togo had contemplated a further attack, he cancelled it, finally satisfied that the battleship was going nowhere. The *Sevastopol* was, therefore, left where she was with her flag still flying defiantly, as though to proclaim to the world that the spirit of the fortress whose name she bore was still alive.[8]

On December 16 Nogi sent one of his staff to Togo, expressing condolences for the loss of the *Takasago*, and saying that to avoid the risk of further disasters to the fleet blockading Port Arthur, the admiral should now withdraw the bulk of his fleet and not worry further about the Third Army. It was a generous message, typical of the good relations that existed between the two commanders. Making the necessary arrangements to ensure that blockade runners should not get through to Port Arthur, Togo sailed for his deserted base in the Elliot Islands, which he reached that night.

With the fall of 203 Metre Hill, and the destruction of the Russian fleet, it was not long before the fortress itself must succumb. While the Japanese infantry and artillery had concentrated their attention on the crucial heights, it was the engineers who were now principally responsible for the operations to reduce the major permanent works of the fortress which had held out for so long. Their endeavours particularly caught the attention of the British Official History:

> Much of their work is from its very nature obscure, for it chiefly lay underground in narrow tunnels in which there was hardly room to stand upright. Yet enough is known to give some conception of the desperate nature of the struggle round these three forts, which is almost without parallel in the history of warfare. From a purely military point of view the operations possess a peculiar interest in view of the fact that they are the only instances of mining on a grand scale under modern conditions.[9]

The first of these forts to fall was Fort Chikuan, which was mined and successfully assaulted on December 19. Togo learned of this when, at the request of the Naval Staff, he paid a visit to Dalny to verify as far as possible the situation with regard to

8 Corbett II, p. 126.
9 *British Official History* II, p. 660.

the ships that had composed the Russian Pacific Fleet. His visit confirmed that all had now been disposed of with the exception of the *Sevastopol* and six destroyers, and he was able to send a confident report that the Port Arthur squadron had been completely destroyed for all practical purposes. He went on:

> Throughout this long blockade, under war conditions, with ever present danger from mines either placed or drifting, and in frequent stress of weather and fog, we have lost two battleships, two cruisers, one dispatch vessel, four of the 7th Division and two destroyers. Moreover, a large number of officers and men have laid down their lives for the country. But we have succeeded in maintaining the blockade and have crushed the enemy's schemes every time he made a sortie, till with the very great help of the besieging army, we at last see the almost total destruction of the enemy's fleet in this part of the world.[10]

The next fort to fall was Fort Ehrlung, mined and then stormed on December 28, and on the December 31 the Third Army successfully assaulted Fort Sungshu Shan. With these works in Japanese hands there was no longer any hope of prolonging the defence of Port Arthur, and on the afternoon of January 1, General Stoessel sent a flag of truce into the Japanese lines to begin negotiations for a capitulation. In the harbour, meanwhile, the navy had begun the mournful task of ensuring that each of the ships were destroyed where they lay. Even in this task, the Russians were unable to achieve a complete result; some of the vessels, already resting on the bottom, were not totally destroyed, as Viren had intended. Aboard the *Sevastopol*, though, Essen was determined to make absolutely sure that his ship could not fall into the hands of the Japanese by being scuttled in shallow water, and he had her towed out into deep water, where he took off his remaining officers and crew, and had the Kingston valves and watertight doors opened. The battleship sank in about a quarter of an hour, going down in 30 fathoms. The six remaining Russian destroyers got away, four reaching Chefoo and the other two Kiaochow, where they were all interned.[11]

With the effective destruction of the Russian Pacific Fleet, there was no compelling reason for Pakenham to remain with Togo's fleet, and in his report of December 18 he paid a gracious compliment to his hosts:

> After so long a stay in the Japanese fleet, it would be impossible to leave it without placing on record an expression of the gratitude felt for the consistent courtesy and kindness, for the friendliness and generosity of the hospitality shown to their guest by all, who throughout a time of much national and frequent personal strain, never forgot the consideration due to the stranger within their gates.[12]

10 Corbett II, p. 129.
11 Ibid., pp. 133-134.
12 Naval Attaché Reports, p. 238.

Pakenham had not been long back in Tokyo, however, when the Japanese surprised the foreign naval attachés there by inviting them to visit the headquarters of General Nogi. The invitation was made before the assault on the key forts been launched, and the *Manshu Maru* was put at the disposal of the naval attachés, who accepted the offer with alacrity. By the time the vessel reached Dalny on January 1, its passengers arrived in time only to witness the last hours of the siege; when on the evening of the next day they heard news that terms had been agreed for the capitulation of the fortress, the attachés were gloomily reflecting that 'it was only too probable that in the sudden rush of work consequent upon the capitulation, the interests of the visitors would suffer.'[13]

They were, however, by no means idle, visiting a number of interesting locations in and around Port Arthur, upon which Pakenham made extensive reports. Because they would not be there long, the naval attachés decided to devote an entire day to Fort Ehrlung, another to 203 Metre Hill, and the last to Port Arthur itself. Pakenham remarked that notwithstanding the high price paid for the capture of 203 Metre Hill, the Japanese had never expected that its capture would be so significant:

> Questioned as to this, the Chief of General Nogi's Staff said the surrender had come upon him as a surprise, that the further proceedings of his army had been mapped out, and, at the moment of capitulation, were in progress ... General Ijichi said also that he was quite at a loss to explain the surrender, which, though inevitable, a proper utilisation of the remaining defences might have considerably postponed.[14]

On January 7 Pakenham and the other naval attachés were taken on a tour of the harbour in a large steamboat captured from the Russians. Unfortunately it ran aground on the falling tide, and the visitors had to embark in a rowing boat, which, heavily laden, made only slow progress. The larger warships, except the *Bayan*, had been collected close in under the hill dividing the old town from the new. Even at high tide, they were only partially submerged, and 'presented a striking and pitiful sight.' Although time was short, Pakenham was able to note the damage sustained by each of the larger ships. He was interested to note that their hulls had been painted black, while the topsides 'were of a grey or reddish drab, the latter hitting off with remarkable accuracy the shade of the surrounding hills.' He observed that during the course of the war it had often been remarked how little the colour of the paintwork mattered, provided that there were no strong contrasts and white was avoided. The visit had not, in fact, told the naval attachés very much:

> So far the view had been cursory, external and un-informing. The Japanese said that mines had been exploded under the ships; they were, however, not

13 Ibid., p. 277.
14 Ibid., p. 289.

> only ignorant of the damage these might have inflicted but did not themselves yet know to what to attribute the sinking of the Russian fleet, whether to the opening of valves, to mines, or to shell injuries. The ships had not been boarded since the capitulation. To foreigners, there were two main points of interest demanding settlement. Had sinking been directly caused by shell fire; and would it be possible to separate injuries inflicted on August 10 from those more recent? Much importance attaches to the establishment, if possible, of such a distinction. Medium artillery is being tried for its life, and evidence of its value must be anxiously awaited in all quarters responsible for the design of warships.[15]

Not surprisingly, the Japanese officers to whom Pakenham spoke were rather more interested in the possibility of raising and refitting the ships.

The attachés were, however, able to board the *Pobieda*, which was aground with a list to starboard that was not so great as to prevent them walking on parts of her decks. According to the Japanese, she had been hit only 15 times. In spite of the difficulty in making their way through some parts of the ship, the attachés were able to examine a large number of the injuries which the ship had suffered, and concluded that she had sunk as a result of action on the part of the Russians rather than as a result of Japanese shellfire. Pakenham thought that if the *Pobieda* was a fair example of the damage that could be inflicted by 11-inch shells, the Russians might have protected their ships efficiently, and that as it was, the ships had not been so damaged by the Japanese as to justify further destruction by their crews: 'Though sea fights had left such scanty traces of their material effects, the disappearance of this fine force is witness that they were not fruitless, but caused deterioration of power more influential than any that could follow the mere wreck of guns and armour.'[16]

After returning from Port Arthur Pakenham remained ashore, staying at a number of different hotels in Tokyo. There was not a great deal to report during this period. The Japanese fleet was undergoing an urgent refit at various dockyards. Priority was given to the battleships and armoured cruisers, which underwent the overhaul and replacement of guns, repairs to armour, cleaning and painting underwater parts of hull and important repairs to machinery and boilers. Captain Hutchison, in a report of March 1905, noted that it was only when these works had been carried out that 'the naval dockyards were entirely given up to unarmoured cruisers, destroyers, and torpedo boats, a certain number being sent to private yards for general overhaul and repairs.' It was soon found that the smaller vessels required much more attention than had been expected; all the boilers of destroyers and torpedo boats needed re-tubing, and all condensers required lifting out and re-tubing, and working parts of machinery replaced. Once all these vessels had been completely refitted, the battleships and

15 Ibid., p. 293.
16 Ibid., p. 298.

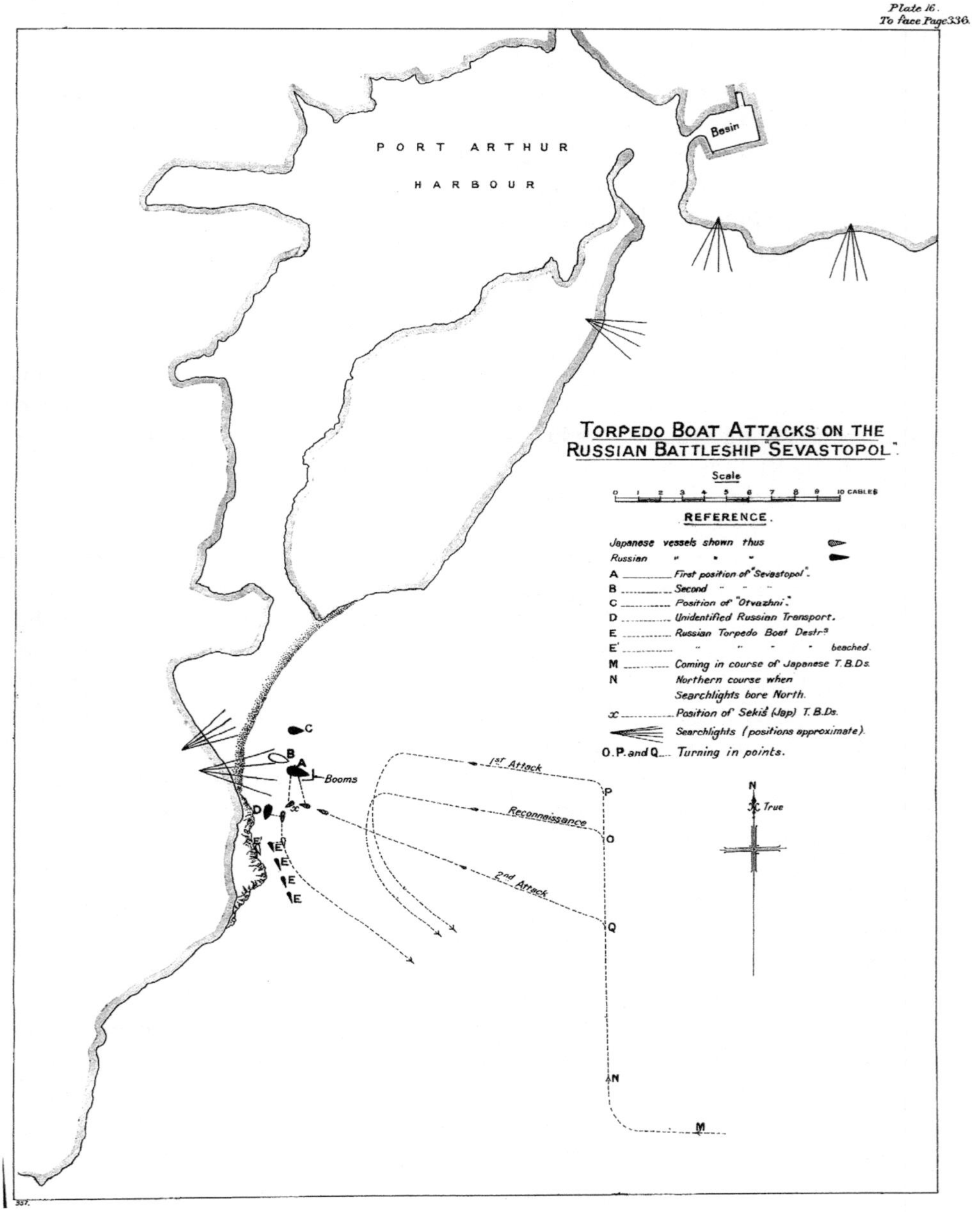

Sketch 7: Attacks on the Sevastopol

armoured cruisers would go back into dock for a final refit and examination of underwater fittings.[17]

While ashore, Pakenham had been reflecting on the operations launched in December in an attempt to destroy the *Sevastopol* while she was moored outside the entrance to Port Arthur. In a report dated April 19 he described the series of attacks on the battleship made by groups of torpedo boats. There were up to twenty in each attack, led by Lieutenant Commander Seki, who was the leader of a division of first-class torpedo boats. These attacks were hampered by extensive minefields, both Russian and Japanese, and Seki's problem was to thread a course between them. After there had been an initial attack on the night of December 10/11, which had been unsuccessful, Seki laid on a reconnaissance by twelve torpedo boats on the following night, in order to try to establish the exact position of the *Sevastopol* and the coast defence vessel *Otvazhni*, which was also moored outside. His aim was to locate the booms protecting these vessels and also the Russian destroyers which were also outside the harbour. On the following night Seki took in a force of twenty torpedo boats each of which, under heavy fire, launched two or three torpedoes at the *Sevastopol* and *Otvazhni*. One torpedo boat was lost in the attack, but it appeared that no hits had been scored on the Russian ships.

Two days later a fresh attack was made, in the course of which a Russian destroyer was badly damaged. Five other torpedoes were observed to hit a target, but it was unclear whether these were the booms or the *Sevastopol* herself. In organising the torpedo fire of his flotilla, Seki intended that the first torpedoes launched should clear the way for the succeeding shots, and he had set his own torpedoes to run close to the surface. The attackers suffered no casualties in what Pakenham described as a 'well-conceived and courageously executed little exploit.'[18]

The subject of the *Sevastopol* was one which interested Pakenham particularly, since he had formed a distinctly unfavourable view of her captain, whom he thought had been considerably overrated in the Press. This first arose from Essen's previous exploits as commander of the light cruiser *Novik*; in his report of these, Pakenham wrote sarcastically that it had become 'evident to the trained intelligences of the strategic writers in the Press that she was commanded by a man of more than average capacity, and that if the Russians had possessed more officers of equal calibre the Japanese navy would have suffered more severely.' When Essen, who prior to the sortie of August 10 had been transferred to the command of the *Sevastopol*, was 'complimented on the skilful way in which his ship had been handled,' Pakenham was moved to observe:

> Those who consider rapid and frequent turns conducive to good shooting, who believe the main object of a sea fight has been attained when damage from the

17 Ibid., pp. 343-344.
18 Ibid., p. 388.

> projectiles of the enemy has been avoided, will see in this alleged conduct ship strategy of a high order.[19]

Noting that Essen therefore had a reputation to maintain, he went on to review his handling of the defence of the *Sevastopol* during the last few days of her career. In particular, he was highly critical of the fact that the battleship made no attempt to escape. Pakenham concluded, in a strikingly pompous passage:

> Armchair criticism should be lenient to the actions of men of ability, as these get nothing they have not fought for. Not so mediocrities, who, arousing no jealousy, make no enemies, but glide forward on a wave of prosperity which nothing short of death seems to arrest. More copiously endowed in this respect than often falls to the common lot, von Essen need not be pitied, as his failures have probably been sufficiently marked to secure his professional future.[20]

Pakenham may not have been aware that Essen had only a skeleton crew, with which escape would not have been possible; the Naval Intelligence Department, in publishing his reports, evidently considered that he was being unfair, and added a footnote to the effect that the *Sevastopol* lacked the majority of her crew and a number of her guns.

In his report Pakenham did suggest, rather more usefully, that consideration of the way in which the *Sevastopol* had been defended might lead to a general examination of 'how, in anchorages without efficient permanent defence, net defended ships should be used to shield from torpedo injury ships without this protection; also to those other occasions when the situation might be reversed; and to the manner in which both operations should be conducted.'[21]

By the time he wrote this report, Pakenham had rejoined the Japanese fleet. Dramatic events were about to unfold in the Sea of Japan.

19 Ibid., p. 339.
20 Ibid., p. 342.
21 Ibid.

21

The Baltic Fleet

The likelihood that the Russian Pacific Fleet would sooner or later be reinforced from Europe was perfectly apparent to all who had considered the balance of naval power in the Far East. As early as his report to the Admiralty of February 28 1904 Troubridge had recalled that in the summer of 1903 a Russian naval officer had told a British colleague who was visiting Vladivostok 'that Japan could never defeat Russia at sea, for if their fleet in the Far East were defeated, Russia would send another as strong as the Japanese fleet.'[1]

Within three weeks, the British Naval Attaché in St Petersburg, evidently well informed about Russia's naval planning, was reporting that a Baltic squadron was to be formed to sail to the Far East during the summer, and that Rear Admiral Zinovy Rozhestvenski, the Chief of the Naval Headquarters Staff, had been chosen to command it. At that time, though, there had been no planning for the operation, and the ships to take part had not been decided, and doubt was expressed not only as to whether it could sail before the autumn, but even whether it would sail at all.[2]

The genesis of the decision lay in the Tsar's order that Virenius, en route to the Far East with reinforcements for the Pacific Fleet, should be recalled. He had got as far as Djibouti, when he was instructed to return home. His recall was in spite of the emphatic advice from Makarov, the newly appointed commander of the Pacific Fleet, that Virenius should be allowed to complete his journey and that he, Makarov, would accept the responsibility of ensuring the safety of the detachment's junction with the fleet at Port Arthur. Rozhestvenski strongly endorsed Makarov's opinion. His view was that to win the war all that was needed was to achieve and maintain naval equality in the Far East, enabling the Russian fleet to dispute command of the Yellow Sea. Above all, he argued, under no circumstances must the strength of the Russian Pacific Fleet fall below that of the Japanese. His urgent request to be allowed to take out the

1 Naval Attaché Reports, p. 38.
2 Corbett II, p. 8.

rest of Virenius's squadron was, however, denied, apparently because he had already been chosen to command the Baltic Fleet that was to be sent out.

Thus it was that the naval high command in St Petersburg disregarded the strongly held opinions of both the new commander of the Pacific Fleet and the Chief of the Naval Headquarters Staff:

> Lacking their finer strategical insight, they were dominated by certain crude and elementary maxims which took no account of the possibilities of a naval situation in which no decision is immediately possible. In the most exalted quarters the prevailing view was that nothing would serve short of a decisive action against the Japanese at sea.[3]

The decision, which could only be implemented after a delay of perhaps half a year, was based on the premise that the army, acting on the defensive, could effectively hold up the Japanese on land; and it could only be justified if such a delay could ensure such a preponderance of naval force that the result of a decision at sea was beyond a reasonable doubt.

The British Official History set out the powerful arguments in favour of letting Virenius continue to make his way to the Far East:

> Had the *Oslyabya* and her consorts continued their voyage, they might have reached eastern waters at a time when the Russian ships in Port Arthur had once again become capable of assuming the offensive. In that case it seems probable that their proximity to the theatre of operations might have created a very useful diversion and have caused grave anxiety to the Japanese strategists, even if the detachment had been unable to join the First Pacific Squadron in time to take part in the impending battle. It is obvious that to despatch reinforcements to the theatre of war in driblets was to risk defeat in detail. But the Russian naval force was divided and exposed to this danger from the outset; and there was less to be gained by waiting for a few more ships than by sending in good time even a small force which might reach eastern waters while the fleet in Port Arthur was still effective.[4]

And any additions to the relieving force gained by a delay might simply be counterbalanced by the attrition of the force at Port Arthur. One other aspect of the matter, which seems not to have been properly examined, was the potential difficulty of coordinating the operations of the outgoing force with the fleet in Port Arthur; good communication would in all circumstances have been essential.

3 Ibid., p. 9.
4 *British Official History* II, p. 644.

Rozhestvenski enjoyed a high reputation in Russia. Born in October 1848, he was nine months younger than Togo, but unlike his future adversary he did not come from an aristocratic background. His father was a military doctor; his status was sufficient, though, for his son to enter the Naval Academy, where he did very well. In 1877, with the outbreak of the Russo-Turkish war, Rozhestvenski was appointed to the Black Sea, where he was posted as supervisor of the naval artillery of the vestigial Black Sea fleet. He went to sea aboard the armed steamer *Vesta*, which became engaged with a Turkish battleship. He took command of the steamer's guns when several officers were injured, and succeeded in scoring a hit on the enemy; Captain Baranov, the commander of the *Vesta*, managed to avoid further damage before the Turkish vessel withdrew. Rozhestvenski was promoted, and decorated. When the exploits of the *Vesta* were talked up as a great triumph, he felt obliged in a newspaper article to point out that all she had done was to flee for five and half hours from the Turkish battleship. His article attracted violent criticism as denigrating Baranov, a war hero.

He was next posted to Bulgaria, as commander of the incipient Bulgarian navy, and not without difficulty succeeded in establishing it as an effective force. He was recalled in 1885, and resumed his career in the Russian navy, before in 1892 being posted to London as the naval attaché there, where he served until 1894. He left to take command of a cruiser, and aboard her he served in a squadron commanded by Makarov in the Far East. The two men disliked each other, but each came to respect the other's professional competence.

Promoted to rear admiral in 1898, Rozhestvenski finally made his mark when his unit of the Baltic Fleet was chosen to perform for the visit of Kaiser Wilhelm II to Russia in July 1902. Rozhestvenski was a man prone to violent rage; famously, during this exercise, he lost his temper when one of the Russian ships made a mistake, and threw his binoculars into the sea. Overall, however, the artillery practice which he staged for his Imperial audience went extremely well, and Tsar Nicholas II was greatly impressed, and in March 1903 appointed him to the position of Chief of the Naval Headquarters Staff. Reporting to the Minister of Marine, Rozhestvenski had become the effective leader of the Russian Navy.[5]

Now, in 1904, the steps to make the fleet that was to sail to the Far East a reality were, at first, of little effect; but the death of Makarov on April 14 lent the project a new urgency. His successor as commander of the Pacific Fleet was Vice Admiral Nikolai Skrydlov, who in his first report set out firmly the objective of the dispatch of the Baltic Fleet to the Far East:

> Our victory at sea depends mainly on the squadron which will come from the Baltic, and which consequently ought to be stronger than the part of the Japanese fleet which may be opposed to it. What above all must be considered is not the composition of the squadron at its departure, but its condition when it reaches

5 Constantine Pleshakov, *The Tsar's Last Armada* (Oxford, 2002), p. 38.

> the theatre of war as well as the date of its arrival, which, according to whether that happens before or after the fall of Port Arthur, will have results altogether different … The squadron which is sent from the Baltic will have for its task to assist the naval forces which still remain to us in the Far East, to recover the command of the sea ... The Port Arthur squadron and the Vladivostok division are much weaker than the Japanese fleet, and for this reason would probably not be able to pursue the Japanese if the latter sailed south to meet the Baltic fleet. The latter should for this reason be of sufficient strength to be able to inflict, single-handed, a severe blow on the main Japanese fleet.[6]

This extract from Skrydlov's clear-sighted report comes from one of the books on the Russo-Japanese war written by the officer appointed as his Chief of Staff, Capt Nicholas Klado, who journeyed with him as he made his way across Siberia to take up his command. By the time they reached the Far East, however, Port Arthur had been cut off and Skrydlov and Klado made their way to Vladivostok where they were joined by Vice Admiral Peter Bezobrazov, who had been appointed as commander of the fleet in Port Arthur, now redesignated the First Pacific Squadron. The Baltic Fleet was designated as the Second Pacific Squadron, and Skrydlov was to be the overall commander of the fleet. For the moment, however, there was not much he could do apart from supervising the operations of the Vladivostok squadron.

Lieutenant McCully, when he came to write his report after the war, observed that Skrydlov had, previous to the war, 'an excellent reputation as disciplinarian, was an able courtier, and was considered a very fair officer.' Noting that he was too slow in starting from St Petersburg to reach Port Arthur before it was invested, McCully reckoned that he had several opportunities to get in by sea, the implication being that he had not tried hard enough. McCully also reported that he appeared not to get on well with others of high rank in the Far East, particularly the Viceroy and also, at Vladivostok, Iessen, whom he was said to have described as '*cet animal*.' Iessen was not backward in responding to the insult, referring to Skrydlov as 'sitting in a girls school entrenched behind his icons.'[7]

As it was, the Vladivostok squadron of four cruisers was now presided over by three admirals, prompting one army officer to remark that in time of war there were two admirals necessary for a fleet, one to command it and the other to live onshore and send it to sea. This was something of an understatement; Skrydlov never went to sea, and generally neither did Bezobrazov, leaving it to Iessen to command the squadron. In January Skrydlov's rather pointless stay in the Far East ended when he was recalled to St Petersburg. He had been preceded by Captain Klado; as Skrydlov's Chief of Staff Klado had drawn up the plans for the sorties of the Vladivostok squadron, but

6 Quoted Nicolas Klado, *The Russian Navy in the Russo-Japanese War and the Battle of the Sea of Japan* (London, 2014), pp. 123-124.
7 McCully, p. 202.

in August was sent back to St Petersburg to report on the commander-in-chief's plans. The 44-year-old Klado had a high reputation as an intellectual, and was the author of a number of important books on naval matters whilst serving as professor of mathematics at the Naval Academy. He was well known for a series of public lectures on the development of the navy and the need to create powerful squadrons. After his return to Europe he was appointed as flag captain to Rozhestvenski.[8]

In the report previously quoted, Skrydlov went on to point out the huge difficulties which the Baltic Fleet must overcome to reach the Far East. In particular, the international laws of neutrality meant that it would have to rely on its own colliers and repair ships. The need for repair ships was especially great, and he urged that several of these accompany the fleet. He went on to list the vessels that should be sent. This list was in part determined by selecting only those ships that could be made ready in time to reach Port Arthur before it was too late. There should be six battleships; four of these had been laid down as part of the 1898 programme. These were the *Suvorov, Alexander III, Borodino* and *Orel*, relatively fast and reasonably well armoured, and mounting four 12-inch and twelve 6-inch guns. They displaced some 15,000 tons. These were nearly ready for sea. In addition Skrydlov specified the older and much slower battleships *Sisoi Veliki* and *Navarin,* which were really scarcely fit to lie in the line of battle. There were nine cruisers listed, of which five were new ships. Four of these (*Zhemchug, Izumrud, Almaz* and *Oleg)* were capable of 23 knots; the fifth, the *Svetlana*, could do 20 knots. There were three elderly armoured cruisers, the *Nakhimov*, *Vladimir Monomakh* and *Dmitri Donskoi*. Finally there was the *Aurora*, a new first class cruiser. There were also to be twenty destroyers, with two repair ships, coal, water and provisions transports, together with hospital ships and parent ships for the destroyers. Skrydlov had in mind also sending a supporting squadron, which would comprise the as yet unfinished battleship S*lava*, the elderly battleship *Nikolai I*, dating from 1887, four old coast defence ships, three torpedo cruisers, the old cruiser *Admiral Kornilov* and the icebreaker *Ermak*.[9]

The inclusion of elderly ships, of little fighting value, was with a view to conducting operations in support of the army, in much the same way as the Japanese had done. Skrydlov's plan was to exercise the command of the sea, once it had been gained by the destruction of the Japanese fleet, by conferring on the Russian army the mobility enjoyed by the Japanese. Whether encumbering the Second Pacific Squadron with these aged vessels was wise became a subject of spirited debate at St Petersburg. Rozhestvenski thought not, and objected strongly; the Minister of Marine, Avelan, took the opposite view. In the end Rozhestvenski's view prevailed, and most of the ships of the follow-up squadron which Skrydlov had identified were discarded. Rozhestvenski retained his post as Chief of the Naval Headquarters Staff, but his work in this position was taken over by Virenius, his deputy. Squadron commanders

8 Klado, pp. 151-152.
9 Corbett II, p. 12.

in the newly assembling force were to be Rear Admirals Felkerzam and Enqvist, while the Chief of Staff was to be Captain Clapier de Colongue. It was upon Rozhestvenski that fell the huge burden of preparing the fleet for its journey to the Far East, and the work involved was colossal. One aspect of this was supervising the completion and fitting out of several of the newer ships. Two of the cruisers would not be ready in time; the *Izumrud* and *Oleg* would leave after the rest of the squadron, and catch up en route.

Although he threw himself into the task that he had been set, Rozhestvenski had from the start serious doubts about the wisdom of the enterprise. As early as April 11, when interviewed for the French magazine *Petit Parisien*, he was reported as becoming heated when the question of sending out the Second Pacific Squadron was raised with him. He suggested that it was already too late for such a venture and went on to say: 'We are now doing what remains to be done, we are defending the honour of the flag. It was at a previous stage that another course ought to have been taken. Attack should have been met by attack. Sacrifice the fleet if need be, but at the same time deliver a fatal blow to Japanese naval power.'[10]

A number of other observers recorded that Rozhestvenski was at the least extremely doubtful of the squadron's chances of success. According to one of his staff who was working with him to get the squadron ready, Rozhestvenski said that he 'had neither supported nor opposed' the plan to send it to the Far East, and that he had not tried to convince anyone of the unwisdom of the project 'because they would merely have concluded that he was afraid of the difficulties.'[11]

As the summer went by Rozhestvenski worked tirelessly to prepare a squadron that was more or less homogeneous. It was to consist of the four *Suvorov* class battleships, together with the *Oslyabya*, together with six of the most modern cruisers. It would appear that it was the fall of Nan Shan at the end of May which changed that; it was now considered necessary to supplement the force that Rozhestvenski was preparing by the addition of some of the older vessels, notwithstanding their limited fighting value. This was in part due to the fact that it was also now realised that the squadron would not in any case be ready to leave before the autumn. The likelihood that the Second Pacific Squadron would encounter at least the bulk of the Japanese fleet rather than a detachment lent further weight to the argument that it should be quantitatively strengthened. One recent historian has described the squadron as it was now constituted as 'a weird collection of ships,' although this is perhaps something of an overstatement.[12] The five modern battleships certainly gave Rozhestvenski a force to be reckoned with.

By the time he hoisted his flag aboard the *Suvorov* on August 14 the battle of the Yellow Sea had been fought. Its disastrous outcome gave rise to doubts as to whether

10 Quoted J.N. Westwood, *Witnesses of Tsushima* (Tokyo, 1970) pp. 52-53
11 Ibid., p. 53.
12 Pleshakov, p. 64.

it still made sense to send out the Second Pacific Squadron at all, and a meeting was convened on September 15 to discuss the issue. Three unpalatable truths were accepted; first, that Port Arthur's fall and the loss of the First Pacific Squadron was probable; secondly, that the Second Pacific Squadron was inferior to the Japanese fleet; and thirdly, that it would be impossible to establish a base on Chinese territory, and almost impossible to capture a Japanese island for that purpose. The conference then proceeded to debate what should be done:

> There was no lack of opinion, we are told, against allowing it to proceed, but Admiral Rozhestvenski, according to the same authority, would listen to no such fainthearted counsel. Insisting that the power of the Japanese was overrated, he demanded to be allowed to sail at once with the ships that were ready, and it would seem that for a time his opinion prevailed.[13]

Given his serious doubts about the prospect of success, it seems surprising that Rozhestvenski argued in the way that he did. There is no reason to suppose that his views had changed, but apparently he considered it necessary, as the commander-in-chief, to suppress them, and to express publicly an opposite view.

As usual, however, the Russian government vacillated. Information that Togo's fleet had suffered little damage in the fighting thus far created fresh doubts, and it was decided that the squadron's departure should be postponed for a further month. The opinion of Viren, the new commander of the First Pacific Squadron, reinforced the concerns in St Petersburg; in his report to the Viceroy of September 15 he had observed that without the reinforcement of the ships in Port Arthur, the Second Pacific Squadron 'would be powerless to contend with the Japanese fleet and should therefore not be permitted to leave for the Far East.'[14] Klado, on the other hand, who had been dispatched from Vladivostok to St Petersburg to join Rozhestvenski's staff, apparently at the admiral's request, brought with him a very different opinion; he was instructed to insist, in the names of Skrydlov and Alexeiev, on the expediency of immediately reinforcing the Second Squadron.[15]

Rozhestvenski was under no illusion about the extent of the logistical problem posed by the dispatch of such a large force from the Baltic to the Far East, which had been identified by Skrydlov. The difficulties attendant upon such a long voyage were aggravated by the laws of neutrality that would regulate the squadron's relationship with the ports at which it would touch on its journey. The most important issue was access to a reliable supply of coal. It was estimated that at their most economical cruising speed the ships of the squadron would consume 3,000 tons of coal per day and at full speed this could rise to as much as 10,000 tons. As Richard Hough wrote, 'for

13 Corbett II, p. 28.
14 *British Official History* II, p. 521
15 Klado, p. 128.

months this dirty, black mineral was to govern the Admiral's thoughts, calculations and strategy.'[16] The solution to the problem was the negotiation of a contract with the German Hamburg Amerika line for the delivery of nearly 340,000 tons of coal at various agreed points between Denmark and Chusan. Welsh coal was specified, producing greater energy per ton and less smoke. When rumours of this plan began to circulate, protests were made both by Britain and Japan, but the German government declined to intervene in what was a purely commercial arrangement.

Another major problem was that of repairs to ships during the voyage. The squadron was to be accompanied by the repair ship *Kamchatka*. An important member of Rozhestvenski's staff was the 30-year-old Eugene Politovski, a senior constructor at the Russian Admiralty, upon whom fell the principal task of overseeing the repairs to ships with the limited means available. He kept a detailed diary of the voyage out to the Far East, which revealed the extent to which his professional skill was constantly required. His diary disclosed his extreme pessimism as to the squadron's prospects; written in the form of letters to his wife, he did not conceal his belief that he would not survive.[17]

As was to be dramatically demonstrated in due course, early in the voyage to the Far East, there was a pronounced anxiety among the senior Russian commanders that the Japanese were preparing to take action against the squadron once it was on its way. It was feared, on the basis of reports from Russian consuls in the Far East, that the enemy would launch an ambush by torpedo boats, possibly with the connivance of the British government. This would necessitate a high state of alertness on the part of the ships of the squadron. However, their crews were a long way short of being fully trained to deal with such an event; following an exercise in the Baltic, Rozhestvenski was obliged to issue an order to the flagship *Suvorov*:

> Today at 2.00am I ordered the officer of the watch to sound the alarm for a torpedo attack. Eight minutes after the order was given there was still no sign of any preparations for repelling the attack; the crew and its officers were still sleeping; only a few men of the watch were, with difficulty, extricated from their resting places, but in any case they did not know where to go; not one searchlight was ready to illuminate the target; the torpedo specialists of the watch were absent; nobody even thought of the deck lighting, essential for operating the guns.[18]

Incidents like this tested the Admiral's temper severely.

16 Richard Hough, *The Fleet That Had to Die* (London, 1958), p. 34.

17 Eugene S. Politovski, *From Libau to Tsushima,* translated by Major F.R. Godfrey (London, n.d.), p. viii.

18 Quoted in Westwood, *Witnesses*, p. 77.

He used the postponement of the squadron's sailing to continue the programme of exercises which he began after hoisting his flag. On September 8 the Tsar paid a visit of inspection to the fleet at Kronstadt, and three days later Rozhestvenski took his ships to Reval to make the final preparations for the voyage. On October 9 and 10 there was a final inspection by the Tsar, and next day the squadron moved to Libau. There, the *Suvorov* was joined by Semenov, who arrived after his long journey from the Far East just in time. He recalled all the incidents of the day, and the 'general nervousness and irritability – be it in consequence of the weather, or of annoyance at all the small mishaps or … from anxiety due to ill omens.'[19]

On October 15 the squadron finally set off from Libau, and by October 20 was off the Skaw in thick whether. Left behind, under Captain Dobrotrovski, were the cruisers *Izumrud* and *Oleg*, the auxiliary cruisers *Dnepr* and *Rion*, and four destroyers. This detachment was intended to set off after completion of the fitting out. The repair ship *Kamchatka*, destined to prove the least competently manned ship in the squadron, succeeded in falling some 40 miles astern of her consorts. At 8:45pm on October 21 she sent a wireless message to say that she was under attack from torpedo boats. She opened fire at what she supposed to be an enemy vessel – it was the Swedish steamer *Aldebaran* – and for the next two hours sent a stream of messages in response to Rozhestvenski's urgent enquiries. By 11:20pm, however, the *Kamchatka* reported that she could no longer see the alleged torpedo boats. This, naturally, had put the whole of the squadron on the alert as it headed into the North Sea.

It was led by Felkerzam's division of battleships, consisting of the *Oslyabya*, *Sisoi Veliki* and *Navarin*; these, between 12 midnight and 1.00am sighted the Hull fishing fleet of between 30 and 40 steam trawlers, and having identified these as innocuous passed to the northward, making no report to the flagship. What happened next was the subject of much dispute, but it appears that an hour or so later a brief sighting of the cruiser *Aurora* was taken to be a torpedo boat, and first the *Suvorov*, and then others of the squadron opened fire, at the same moment that the fishing fleet was encountered. One of the trawlers was sunk, and several others damaged, two fishermen being killed and six wounded, as firing became general. The *Aurora* was hit five times, her chaplain being fatally wounded, and another crewman was wounded, before the squadron ceased fire, after about eight or ten minutes, and held on its way; Rozhestvenski was convinced that torpedo boats had indeed been on the scene.

The squadron continued its course across the North Sea, and entered the English Channel; on October 23. Felkerzam anchored off Brighton, where he took on coal, while Rozhestvenski's division held on to Brest, arriving there in thick fog on October 24. Judging it too dangerous in these conditions to enter the harbour, he steamed on to Vigo. The flotilla had coaled at Cherbourg and gone on ahead. In Britain, the news of the incident in the North Sea created a violent public outrage, and the government ordered a number of vessels to proceed to sea; six battleships and a cruiser

19 Semenov II, p. 225.

of the Mediterranean Fleet sailed from Venice for Gibraltar, and others received sailing orders, while the Home Fleet moved to the Firth of Forth. By the evening of October 25 it was known that the Russian squadron had put into Vigo; the rest of the Mediterranean Fleet sailed to Malta, and the Home Fleet proceeded to Portsmouth, the intention being that the Russian warships should be detained until matters were settled, by force if need be.

The diplomatic crisis was eased slightly when the Russian government proposed an international court of enquiry into the incident; but tension rose again when Rozhestvenski, understanding that this had resolved the issue, set sail from Vigo. This was seen in London as a breach of the understanding with Russia, and when Rozhestvenski reached Tangier, all British units were on full alert. There, he divided his force into two squadrons; one, under Felkerzam, would proceed to Suda Bay. Consisting of the *Sisoi Veliki, Navarin, Svetlana, Zhemchug* and *Almaz*, it would be joined there by the seven destroyers as well as five volunteer ships and five transports from the Black Sea, and would proceed through the Suez Canal. The rest of the Second Pacific Squadron would go by the Cape, apparently because the draught of the new battleships might be too great to pass the canal.[20] By November 4, however, the terms of the draft convention regulating the enquiry had been practically agreed, and Rozhestvenski was free to put to sea from Tangier.

One of the terms of the convention was that Rozhestvenski was to send home officers to give evidence. These were led by Klado, who was accompanied by an officer from each of the other ships in the first division, together with one from the *Kamchatka*. The choice of Klado amazed Semenov, who observed that when the first gun was fired by the *Suvorov* the flag captain was in his cabin about to turn in and his evidence could not be particularly valuable. Semenov disliked Klado extremely, a feeling which was intensified when the latter had returned to Russia, and Semenov heard what he had been doing.

Corbett described Klado's activities that had so seriously annoyed Semenov:

> Since November Captain Klado had been employing the enforced leisure of his attendance on the Dogger Bank arbitration in writing a series of vigorous articles in the Russian press inculcating with much plausible and well-informed argument an entirely new plan of campaign. His general line was that the war plan then in operation could not possibly result in success. For the final triumph of the Russian arms everyone was looking to the army – to General Kuropatkin's expected offensive return which was to relieve or recover Port Arthur and drive the Japanese from Korea. Fortified as he was with local knowledge and the plain strategical condition of the theatre of war he could point out that such a hope without command of the sea was chimerical. It was a simple question of communications.

20 Corbett II, p. 39.

Large armies in this area could not advance without being supplied by coastwise and riverine lines; the Japanese had only been able to advance with the assistance of the fleet, and Kuropatkin would be in the same position. Corbett went on:

> His case, in fact, came to this. Having been in touch with the staff on the spot he realised that Russia, for all her vast military power, was caught in the toils of a war based on limited territorial objects, which the enemy had practically isolated by sea and occupied in strength, and that only in breaking down that isolation by naval effort lay the way to getting possession of the objects.[21]

Klado argued that Togo had thirteen battleships and armoured cruisers to Rozhestvenski's seven. In addition, he pointed out that Russia could not rely on the bad condition of the Japanese boilers, or to look upon the Japanese fleet as having been materially weakened, or to count on the bad condition of the Japanese guns. The enemy had had sufficient time to make all necessary repairs. He urged the absolute necessity of reinforcing Admiral Rozhestvenski's squadron, identifying the as yet incomplete *Slava*, and the older battleships *Nikolai I* and *Alexander II* as being suitable, together with the three coast defence vessels *General-Admiral Apraxin*, *Admiral Senyavin* and *Admiral Ushakov*. He also proposed the two old armoured cruisers *Pamyat Azova* and *Vladimir Monomakh*, and the old protected cruiser *Admiral Kornilov*.[22]

Klado's articles were widely read and had an immediate and significant effect. Within a matter of days the Admiralty gave orders for the formation of a Third Pacific Squadron, composed of several of the vessels which Klado had identified, though in particular the *Slava* and the *Alexander II* were not included. In spite of the arguments put forward by Klado for their fighting value, the fact was that this force did not add substantially to the strength of Rozhestvenski's squadron, as he must have known. He next agitated for the Black Sea Fleet to be sent out. This fleet was not, by international treaty, permitted to leave the Black Sea, and the government drew the line at such a breach of its obligations, and the diplomatic problems that must ensue. For the moment, therefore, all possible efforts were devoted to readying the Third Pacific Squadron for sea; its commander was to be Rear Admiral Nicholas Nebogatov. It finally left for the Far East on February 18, after a hasty and perfunctory preparation, taking the Mediterranean route.

Rozhestvenski reached St Marie, in Madagascar, on December 18; Felkerzam had arrived before him, at Nossi Bé, where Rozhestvenski joined him on December 25, having now learned of the surrender of Port Arthur and the destruction of the fleet there. He was ordered to await the arrival not only of Dobrotrovski's overtaking squadron, but also the Third Pacific Squadron. His own conviction was that he should

21 Ibid., pp. 146-147.
22 Klado, pp. 91-96.

press on as fast as possible, and these orders seem to have led to either a stroke or a nervous breakdown. Semenov wrote:

> On February 4 the Admiral became so ill that he took to his bunk. Rumours floated around the squadron that this was as a result of his receiving news that Nebogatov's division had left Libau. It seemed that the Admiral had had some kind of stroke. After a couple of days he reappeared on deck, even thinner and hollow cheeked, slightly dragging his right foot.[23]

Rozhestvenski made plain to the Admiralty his view of the position. He had, he wrote, no chance of obtaining command of the sea with his existing force; Nebogatov's force would not strengthen him, but rather would hamper his force; and the only effective course to follow would be to press on with the best ships to Vladivostok, and operate against Japan's communications from there. The upshot of his exchange with St Petersburg was that he was ordered to wait for Dobrotrovski's arrival; he would rendezvous with Nebogatov later. After two and a half months in the humid and enervating climate of Nossi Bé, Rozhestvenski's fleet finally sailed on March 15, and for the next three weeks its whereabouts was unknown to the world at large. Its commander was under no illusion as to his situation, as Lieutenant Sventorzhetski wrote sadly in his diary:

> I am quite convinced that we will never in any circumstances gain command of the sea in this war. That is, we are not going to succeed in the task which has been given us. I think the Admiral thinks the same, but, of course, he is silent and does not tell anybody his own burdensome and soul destroying thoughts. He doesn't give the slightest thought to returning home with the squadron. He knows quite well that Russia expects something extraordinary from him – a victory and the destruction of the Japanese fleet. But this is something which only Russian society would expect, a society quite unacquainted with the situation of our navy and of the situation which will soon face our squadron when it leaves Nossi Bé.[24]

Sventorzhetski thought it shameful to acknowledge it, but looking at the situation dispassionately was in no doubt that an end should be put to the naval operations. The moral courage to take such a decision was, however, not to be found in St Petersburg.

23 Semenov II, p. 40.
24 Quoted in Westwood, *Witnesses*, p. 124.

22

Preparing for the endgame

Following his tour of inspection at Port Arthur, Pakenham gave a dinner party for Togo on January 7. The admiral had, with Kamimura, come ashore for consultations with the Naval Staff, particularly to discuss what should be done in respect of the anticipated arrival of Rozhestvenski's squadron. Pakenham's own view of the situation was expressed in a letter to his aunt on February 6. He considered that if the Japanese could beat the Baltic Fleet, their cause would be safe, adding that no victories that the Russians might gain on land could possibly make good the loss of command of the sea. On the other hand, he observed that 'looking at ships and guns, only, the Baltic Fleet should have an excellent chance.'[1]

It was evident to the Japanese that they at least had plenty of time to plan for the arrival of Rozhestvenski, but it was far from clear what would be the route that he would take. The assumption was, of course, that with the fall of Port Arthur, the Russian objective would be to make for Vladivostok. Several reconnaissances were undertaken to find out if there were any preparations on the part of the enemy to establish a base in Southeast Asia, but by January 11 these had found no evidence at all of this. The strategic question for the Naval Staff was therefore to settle upon the point of concentration for the Japanese fleet. This question was soon answered. The fleet would be concentrated in the Straits of Korea. The First and Second Squadrons would be based at Masampo in Sylvia Basin, while the Third Squadron, consisting of the 5th, 6th and 7th divisions and Admiral Kataoka, would provide the immediate guard for the Straits, based at Takeshiki.

There was to be some reorganisation of the tactical units of the fleet. The *Nisshin* and *Kasuga* were now assigned to the 1st Division in place of the battleships that had been lost. This division, together with the 3rd Division, constituted the First Squadron. The Second Squadron, led by Kamimura, consisted of his 2nd Division of six armoured cruisers and Uriu's 4th Division, together with three destroyer divisions

1 Pakenham Archive, PKM/2/6.

and one of first class torpedo boats. The Third Squadron at Takeshiki had attached to it five divisions of torpedo boats.[2]

There were, however, some naval operations to be undertaken in the period before the arrival of Rozhestvenski. The most important of these was the escorting of transports carrying infantry to Gensan and Songjin. Between February 10 and March 6 a substantial squadron, including the battleship *Fuji*, the armoured cruisers *Idzumo* and *Kasuga*, and the cruisers *Otowa, Akitsushima, Chiyoda, Suma* and *Chihaya*, with eight destroyers, was engaged on this work. The concern was that Iessen's cruisers in Vladivostok might attempt to disrupt these troop movements. He had, however, been ordered not to engage in active operations, but to remain concentrated in readiness for the arrival of the Second Pacific Squadron. In addition to covering these convoys, a force under Togo's former Chief of Staff, Rear Admiral Shimamura (now promoted to flag rank) maintained a watch on Vladivostok. This was reinforced by the laying of mines at the entrance to Peter the Great Bay between Askold and Korsakov Islands over a distance of 35 miles, a total of 715 mines being laid.

Meanwhile the Naval Staff continued to address what for them was the puzzling lack of information as to the intentions of the Second Pacific Squadron, still immobile at this time at Nossi Bé. Dobrotrovski had reached the rendezvous on February 15. Nebogatov, with the Third Pacific Squadron, had left Libau on the following day, although this was not immediately known. In a further effort to clear up the situation, Dewa was sent with the cruisers *Chitose* and *Kasagi* and two armed merchant cruisers to scout in the seas around Singapore. Leaving Sasebo on February 27, he was to proceed, via Hong Kong and Hainan, to Saigon and Singapore, returning via Borneo and Luzon to Sasebo; he was expected back on April 5. At the last minute it was decided that in addition to all these places, Dewa should also visit Camranh Bay in French Indochina, because it was 'the most suitable harbour north of Singapore large enough to take a Russian fleet of some score or so of ships.'[3] Dewa completed his cruise without finding any indication of preparations to receive Rozhestvenski, and concluded that he was waiting at Nossi Bé for the arrival of Nebogatov. Such was not the case, however; the Russian admiral, far from welcoming the arrival of the Third Pacific Squadron, had been awaiting the effect of his pessimistic advice to St Petersburg in the hope that the mission might not proceed. Finding that this was not so, he had ordered an abrupt departure from Nossi Bé in order to avoid being encumbered with the elderly vessels of Nebogatov's squadron.

Meanwhile Pakenham, after spending practically all his time at sea since he joined the Japanese fleet at the beginning of April 1904, found himself in the early part of 1905 in Tokyo with not a great deal to do. He had a number of reports to complete, but in general his situation was no different from the officers of Togo's fleet and the Naval Staff. It was simply a matter of awaiting the arrival of the Second Pacific Squadron.

2 Corbett II, pp. 153-154.
3 Ibid., p. 170.

Pakenham had by now almost completely identified himself with his Japanese hosts and their cause; it had become his practice to use the word 'we' when describing the activities of the Japanese fleet and its officers and men.

As spring approached, it was apparent that Rozhestvenski's arrival must be imminent, and on April 5 Pakenham had a meeting with Jackson to discuss arrangements for covering the forthcoming engagement. He would himself be with Togo's battleships as before, rejoining the *Asahi*, which was the last to complete her refitting and repairs, while Jackson would be assigned to the cruisers; he would be aboard the *Azuma*. Jackson had been compiling a day-to-day report of the activities of the Japanese fleet, and for this purpose during the latter part of April had served aboard the battleship *Fuji*. While with the battleships, he paid a visit to the flagship *Mikasa* on April 18 to call on Togo, reporting: 'He is looking infinitely better than he did in Tokyo in January, and is now the picture of health. He said that now the fleet had been refitted the ships were as good as new.'[4] On April 25 Jackson reported in detail on the target practice conducted by the battleships and *Nisshin* and *Kasuga*. The target range for heavy guns at the end of the harbour was an island about 80 to 100 feet long and 35 to 40 feet high. Each of the four battleships fired eight rounds from their 12-inch guns, the *Shikishima* scoring six hits, the *Mikasa* five, the *Asahi* three and the *Fuji* none. It was suggested that the *Mikasa* and *Fuji* were using old ammunition which might have deteriorated.

Pakenham himself rejoined the fleet on April 17, going aboard the *Asahi*, where he was pleased to return to his former cabin which he described as fitting him like a glove. This was in a letter written on the same day to his sister Margaret. He observed cheerfully that the Russian fleet might appear at very short notice: 'In the ensuing struggle, a good many of us will visit kingdom come. I must therefore write off my unanswered correspondence, while yet I may.' He continued his letter with a description of his life for the last few months in Tokyo, which he said his return to the ship had almost wiped out of his memory. He had evidently made the most of his period of enforced idleness:

> I had got the best rooms in the chief hotel, and was living in great comfort, including much dining out, and playing bridge up to 3.00am usually. And I had taken to dancing again too, not so much to the enjoyment of my partners as to my own … Even several love affairs have been suspended or ended by my departure – all, I am glad to say, with young married women, as there are no others apparently in Tokyo, and all conducted on the highest principles of Platonism. I gave a big dinner party shortly before leaving – 62 people, juggling and dancing afterwards. Rather well run by contract in the hotel, with plenty of good rooms. Food, drink, five floors: expense £90, and cheap at the price.[5]

4 Naval Attaché Reports, p. 346.
5 Pakenham Archive, PKM/2/19.

Meanwhile Rozhestvenski, having left Nossi Bé in haste in the hope of avoiding the junction with Nebogatov's ancient vessels, had made his way, unseen by the world, across the Indian Ocean, and successfully negotiated the Malacca Straits. Passing Singapore, the fleet got confirmation of the army's defeat at Mukden, which somewhat dampened spirits which had been raised by the successful passage of the Straits. News that Nebogatov had sailed from Djibouti in accordance with orders to catch up with the Second Pacific Squadron did nothing to improve morale. Semenov, who had an interview with Rozhestvenski on April 10, speculated as to what should now be done about Nebogatov's force:

> We had succeeded in eluding the watchful enemy. One move in the game we had won, but we dared not hope to win the next one. Moreover, we were still a respectable force: five good battleships, one armoured and three light cruisers, if the old vessels were not counted. What were we to do? Wait? Impossible! To go on, leaving him to his fate, to the attempt at getting through as best he could?[6]

Rozhestvenski steamed on to Camranh Bay, reaching there on April 14, where he would await the arrival of the Third Pacific Squadron. In spite of all the setbacks and difficulties, his achievement in bringing his force from Kronstadt to this point, a total of 16,628 miles, was considerable. It was marred, of course, by the disastrous incident on the Dogger Bank, but even more so by the lengthy pause at Nossi Bé, imposed on him by St Petersburg. This had ensured that the Japanese would have ample time to complete the refitting of their fleet. Once at Camranh Bay, the process of coaling the squadron got under way at once. News of the Russian arrival there prompted a firm protest from the Japanese to the French government, which was energetically supported by the British government.

Although he completed his coaling by April 18, Rozhestvenski lingered on at Camranh Bay, until the sympathetic local French commander, Admiral de Jonquières, had been obliged by orders from Paris to require him to leave. On April 26 Rozhestvenski did so; but he took the squadron only 40 miles up the coast to Van Fong Bay, where he dropped anchor, and awaited Nebogatov's arrival. On May 3 he put to sea with his larger ships; De Jonquiéres arrived in Van Fong Bay in his flagship the *Guichen* to find only Russian destroyers and transports there, and when these left, he departed. Once he was out of the way the Russian squadron returned to the anchorage. Rozhestvenski remained there for several days, claiming that an imminent typhoon precluded his putting to sea, until the *Guichen* returned on May 9. By now contact had been made with Nebogatov, and the two Russian squadrons met later that day in the open sea. Rozhestvenski, who was pleased to see that at least the refitting of Nebogatov's ships appeared to have increased their fighting value, would have liked to push on at once to the north, but a further delay was necessary to coal the new

6 Semenov II, p. 68.

arrivals. This necessitated a further violation of French territorial waters, before the concentrated fleet was able at last to sail on May 14.[77]

In the meantime Rear Admiral Felkerzam, who had been ill for some time, died aboard the *Oslyabya*. News of his death was not, however, made known to the fleet, which meant that Nebogatov was unaware that in the event of Rozhestvenski being disabled he would be in command.

News that the junction of the Second and Third Pacific squadrons had taken place, or was about to, was almost at once known in Japan. Aboard the *Asahi*, Pakenham had time to reflect on the prospects of the forthcoming encounter. The view which he held, that on paper at any rate there was not much between the rival fleets, was not by any means unique to him. The American Rear Admiral Bradley A Fiske, writing later in 1905, observed that the two forces were so nearly equal in materiel, that whatever difference there was might be ignored.[8]

Pakenham made a careful calculation of the relative strengths for his report of May 6, in which he reviewed the overall situation:

> Although tables of equivalents, and all similar ways of empirically assessing relative strengths of fleets of heterogeneous composition, have shown themselves absolutely unreliable as guides, yet people about to engage scrutinise gun powers closely, as it is in these the power of an adversary is most easily recognised. Thus, in estimating the comparative forces of the rival fleets, the numbers and calibres of the guns in each receive most attention.
>
> Nebogatov has brought with him two 12-inch guns, eleven 10-inch and four 9-inch, all carried in ships with considerable armour protection, one of them even having a complete belt. Given Japanese poverty in battleships of the first class and the weakness in primary gun power of their armoured cruisers, it must be admitted Rozhestvenski has thus received an important accession of strength. With the most recent addition he will have twenty six 12-inch guns, fifteen 10-inch, four 9-inch, and perhaps the eight 8-inch guns of the Vladivostok cruisers, all carried in from 11 to 13 ships, wherewith to meet 12 Japanese ships armed with sixteen 12-inch guns, eleven 10-inch, and three 8-inch.
>
> In the naval operations of last year, the Russian primary ships were held in check by their Japanese similars, and the Japanese fleet of secondary vessels was thus seldom menaced with the irruption into their field of activity of much more powerful ships. The question is whether the Japanese will be able to repeat this feat. Looking at the Russian dominance of heavy gun power, it will be a very remarkable achievement if they are able to do so.
>
> If the *Donskoi*, *Nakhimov* and *Monomakh* be omitted, all the Russian armoured ships may be classed as primaries with reference to the primary ships

7 Corbett II, pp. 197-200.
8 Quoted in Edwin A. Falk, *Togo and the Rise of Japanese Sea Power* (London, 1936), p. 380.

> of Japan. The battleships of the best class of both sides are held to be equally matched. The minor Russian battleships have thick belts, their armour area is small, their ends are mainly unprotected and their secondary armaments numerically weak. These ships are thus good targets for the Japanese high explosive projectile, fired also from the better furnished batteries of their armoured cruisers. The difference in fighting power in these two classes of vessel, the Russian minor battleship and the Japanese armoured cruiser, may thus be less than that shown by the disparity of their primary armaments alone.[9]

Tactically, Pakenham noted that the true objectives of each fleet were the first class battleships of the other, which must influence the disposition of the fleets:

> Whatever the formations or the orders of battle, the heads of lines will probably suffer, and it concerns all navies to study how these vulnerable points may best be reinforced. Perhaps the answer will be found in 'concentration.' It is thought the distance apart of ships in the line, 400 metres, is too great for this form of fighting, and that part of the manoeuvre of joining action should consist of a reduction of this interval, so as to bring closer together the fire from principal guns, thus strengthening the gun effort for attack or defence. This would be the natural way of adhering to a rule of warfare well tried by land and sea, namely, the concentration of all possible force in an attack on one point of the defences of the enemy. The Japanese maintain that too good a target would thus be offered to the fire of the enemy, and also that many of their ships would thus be left unattacked.
>
> However arranged, it looks as though this fight would resemble most others, in that its fortunes will be decided by the fate of very few ships. Togo seems to intend to lead again, and all his chief officers will doubtless expose themselves as before. Though it may be too much to hope that they will suffer as little by this as they did in the last action, if Togo can get a good lead before closing, the punishment that fell so heavily on the *Mikasa* on a previous occasion, this time may be more equally distributed. This will be even more important than before, as if anything should happen to Togo, the next admiral would only be found in the sixth ship of the line, a cruiser, and the rear is a disadvantageous position from which to command a fleet.[10]

Pakenham did not neglect to consider the possibility that the Russians might launch a fleet ramming attack, from which the Japanese might not escape without disorder:

9 Naval Attaché Reports, pp. 358-359.
10 Ibid., pp. 359-360.

> Ramming is now, perhaps, too much esteemed the last resort of the desperate. When postponed until then, it may justly be condemned as holding out small chance of a successful issue. Also, ramming in line ahead ('breaking the line'), or even in two or three lines ahead, may be considered no longer practicable. But if one fleet has been headed by another, the position of the inner fleet calls for bold remedy, and it may well be questioned whether of the alternatives that now present themselves, that which promises extrication soonest is not by a prompt attack with the ram. Of course it should be preceded by the simultaneous turn of all ships, so that contact with the enemy will be simultaneous down the part of his line aimed at. The enemy in the outer fleet has little choice in an emergency of this kind. He can try to defeat the attack by gunfire, while keeping his course; he can turn away and retire; or he can counter by essaying similar tactics against the inner fleet. In any case, the outer fleet will be called upon to take a vigorous defensive, and will almost certainly lose the regularity of its formation, and such advantage of position as it may have gained.
>
> The inner fleet must either ram or turn away. Ramming promises loss to both fleets and certain disorder to the enemy; turning away means loss, accompanied possibly by disorder, only to the inner fleet. If war vessels were built to steam equally in either direction, not only would the greater part of the tactical value of relatively superior speed disappear from fleet actions, but the position of an inner fleet might even become preferable to that of an outer one in an attempted turning movement. However, sailing ships always had a bow and stern, so steamships must have the same. The contention is too convincing to be arguable.[11]

Pakenham ended his report with a strongly upbeat assessment of the Japanese navy and its ships:

> Nothing could be better than the temper of the personnel of the Japanese navy, or than the condition of their fleet. All seems to have been done to bring both to a high state of efficiency, and though individual organisations may be open to criticism in some particulars, the chief essentials for success, well merited confidence in leaders and courage to fight are there, and are of a kind that makes small account of odds.[12]

11 Ibid., p. 360.
12 Ibid.

23

The Battle of Tsushima

As Rozhestvenski continued his progress north towards the inevitable battle that in his heart he knew he must lose, Togo, in his anchorage at Masampo, calmly awaited confirmation of his enemy's arrival. There was no question in his mind about the route that the Russian fleet would take; plainly bound for Vladivostok, it must pass through the Tsushima Straits, since the alternative routes around the east of Japan and through the La Perouse or Tsugaru Straits were quite simply too hazardous. The only issue was whether Rozhestvenski would take the eastern or western channel; whichever was chosen, Togo's fleet was well placed to intercept.

It was the auxiliary merchant cruiser *Shinano Maru* which at about 4:30am on May 27 located the Russian fleet, and reported that it appeared to be taking the eastern passage. In giving the position of the enemy, the *Shinano Maru* was in error; the bulk of the Russian fleet was between 10 and 20 miles ahead of that given, and as it happened was heading for a gap in the guard line of Japanese ships strung out across the Straits. Togo, aboard the *Mikasa* in Sylvia Basin, was anxiously monitoring the telegraph wires, and it was Kamimura who ordered the Japanese fleet to prepare for sea; and by 6.00am it was ready to weigh anchor. The *Mikasa* came down to join the rest of the fleet in Douglas Inlet at 6.30, and led out intending to pass around the north of Tsushima.[1] He was, though, still not entirely certain that Rozhestvenski was taking the eastern channel. Observation was difficult; the wind was blowing from west south-west, force 5 to 7, and the reports from the *Idzumi,* which had relieved the *Shinano Maru*, left the matter still in doubt.

Aboard the *Asahi,* Pakenham took up his station on the after bridge. Immaculate in his white uniform, monocle firmly in place, he stood there throughout the day until later, when tiring, he was provided with a cane chair. As the battle proceeded, he calmly took copious notes, 'like an official at a yacht race.' Based on these, he was able to produce a lengthy and detailed account, which he wrote up as soon as he could

1 Corbett II, pp. 226-228.

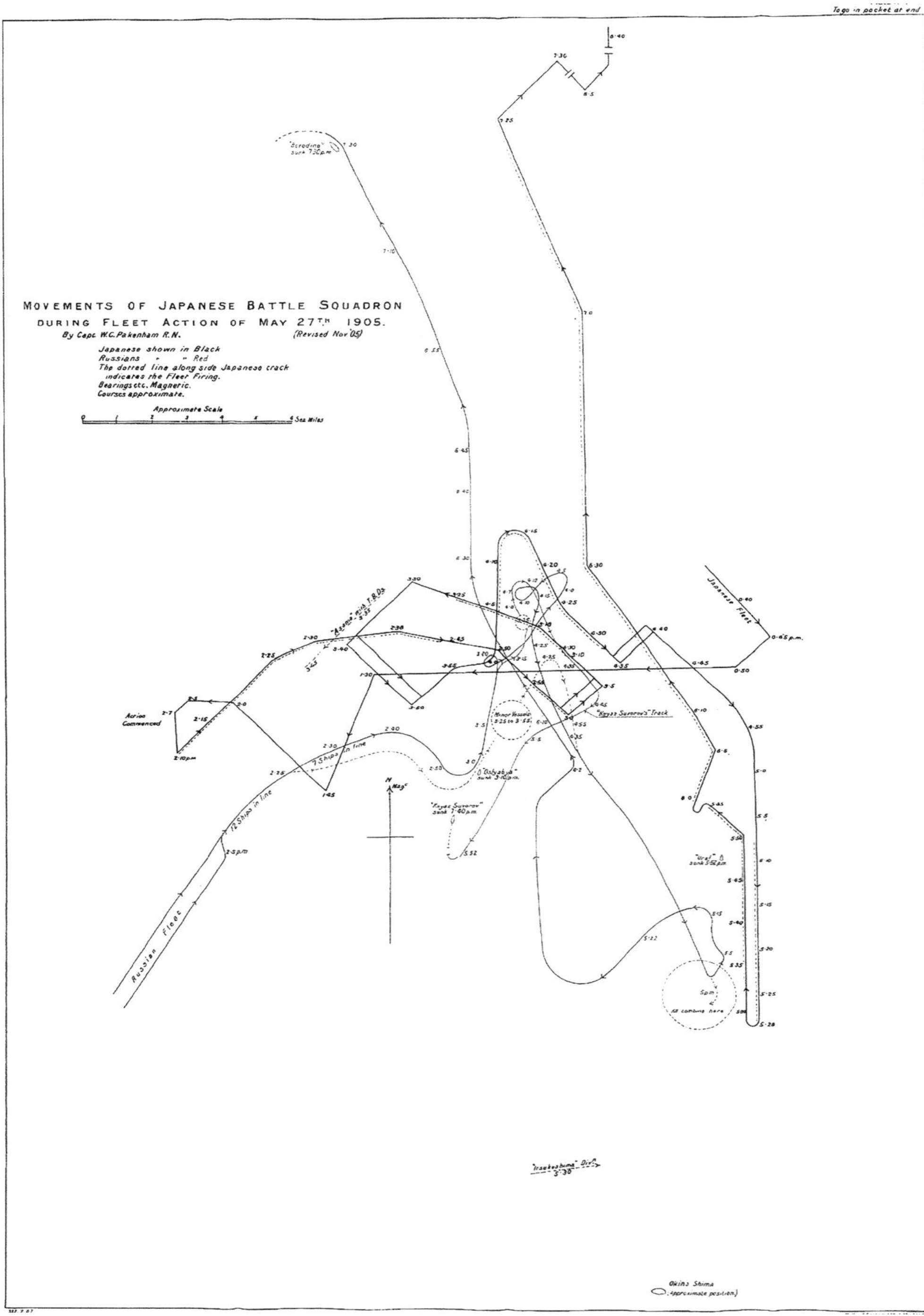

Sketch 8: Battle of Tsushima

after going ashore. Jackson, too, wrote a report of the battle from his position aboard the *Azuma*, though a good deal shorter.

Pakenham began with a description of the weather as the Japanese fleet put to sea:

> Preparation for battle was made (8.00am), and speed was set for 14 knots. A very stiff breeze was blowing from the south and west, and though, owing to the proximity of land, no heavy sea was able to rise, great inconvenience was suffered throughout the day from the water dashed through turret and casemate ports, and from the spray that constantly wetted the object glasses of the sighting telescopes. This observation will not be repeated, but it should be understood the same causes of annoyance endured until late afternoon, whenever the wind was either from ahead or on the bow. Of course, these drawbacks must also have been felt by the Russians. The chief disadvantage to the Japanese was that, at the early hour when the fleet put to sea, the smaller torpedo craft were unable to keep up, and had to be sent to Takeshiki for shelter and to await instructions.
>
> Another common inconvenience was that a rather thick haze, which a bright sun overhead seemed quite unable to dispel, hung over the sea, making objects indistinct outside distances of about 5,000 metres. Thus, though everyone rejoiced at the approach of the long deferred meeting, unfavourable weather was a source of anxiety.
>
> The *Idzumi* reported from her lookout station at 10.00am that she could distinguish, of the Russian fleet, five battleships, three cruisers and five other vessels all led by a cruiser of the *Zhemchug* type; but it was not assumed that these were all that were advancing. As a final preparation the Japanese wetted decks and boat covers, and the men were then (11.00am) sent to dinner.[2]

Togo led the Japanese line in the *Mikasa*, followed by the *Shikishima, Fuji, Asahi, Kasuga* and *Nisshin*. This was the 1st Division. Kamimura's Second Squadron consisted of the 2nd Division (*Idzumo, Tokiwa, Azuma, Yakumo* and *Iwate*; the *Asama* had been detached to shepherd several divisions of destroyers); Uriu's 4th Division came next, consisting of the *Naniwa, Takachiho, Akashi* and *Tsushima*. Dewa, upon whom the task of picking up the Russian fleet devolved, had in his 3rd Division the *Kasagi, Chitose, Niitaka* and *Otawa*. In addition Kataoka's 3rd Squadron, comprising his 5th, 6th (Togo Masaji.) and 7th (Yamada) Divisions, was close at hand. The information which Dewa was able to give about the Russian movements was however far from complete.

Rozhestvenski was proceeding northwards in his original steaming order, save that when he became aware from Japanese wireless signals of the proximity of the enemy he pulled back the 2nd Cruiser Squadron (*Almaz, Svetlana* and *Ural*) which had been leading, with orders to cover the transports, and sent on the *Izumrud* and *Zhemchug* to take station ahead of the battle squadrons. These were in two columns;

2 Naval Attaché Reports, p. 363.

the port column consisted of the *Oslyabya, Navarin, Sisoi Veliki* and *Nakhimov*, while the starboard column was split into two divisions. The first, comprising the foremost modern battleships, contained the *Suvorov, Borodino, Alexander III* and *Orel*; the second consisted of the *Nikolai I* (flying Nebogatov's flag), *Apraxin*, *Ushakov* and *Senyavin*. The remaining cruisers were to the rear. By about 10.00am Rozhestvenski became aware that Kataoka's squadron was closing on his port quarter, and prepared to form a single line ahead.

Togo was himself by now closing on the enemy, as Pakenham described:

> At 12:40pm the Japanese were a few miles north of Okinoshima; though there is uncertainty as to the exact position, this will be roughly taken as that where the more serious work of the day began. Having been steering south-east by a half east, direction was altered (12.45) to south-west by a half west, a course which, if pursued, would have led the respective fleets past one another with starboard guns bearing. However, partly perhaps because it was found difficult to stand against the wind in exposed places, but chiefly in the hope that change in their order of sailing forced upon them at the last moment might confuse the Russians, Admiral Togo decided to cross ahead of them, thus threatening the weaker line with the weight of the first attack. He accordingly led his own fleet round until it headed west. The haze continuing, ships in rear could hardly be distinguished.
>
> Before long, smoke was observed (1:20pm) on the port bow, and though at first believed to arise from Russian scouts, it was soon seen to indicate the approach of Dewa, who, with his squadron, was advancing ahead of the enemy, whom he reported to be about 5 miles behind, though only occasionally visible. Judging, presumably, from this information that he had crossed the bows of the Russian fleet, the Japanese commander-in-chief turned (1.30) to south south-west, but had not gone far on this course when the Russians suddenly hove in sight, a little on his starboard instead of on his port bow.
>
> The moment was one calling for prompt and decided action. In the then state of the atmosphere distances could not be accurately estimated. The enemy looked so close that the Japanese must have felt that they could only persist in the execution of their plan at the risk of yielding the power of initiative to those who, for all that was then known of them, might be capable of utilising their advantage to the utmost. In the relative positions of the fleets, the Japanese must therefore have been tempted to postpone the attempt to profit by manoeuvre until after the first shock, and to accept the simplest and most obvious way of opening the action, namely by a broadside to broadside rush past the foe on parallel, but opposite, course. Though deficient in character, such an opening might have been preferred to the missed chances miscalculation of speeds or distances would have entailed; and adherence to his intention in the face of weighty inducements to vary it, is evidence Togo promised himself great benefit from the method of engaging which he had selected. At any rate, the original

plan was not altered, but, hoisting battle flags, the Japanese turned in succession to NW, altering again to port (2.00pm) when directly ahead of the Russian fleet

It was then possible to see down the length of the Russian lines. In the right column, the four biggest battleships loomed enormous, dwarfing all others into insignificance. It was not easy to realise that the battleships of Japan were probably producing at least equal effect on the minds of the Russians. As Rozhestvenski made no attempt to defeat Japanese designs, the *Mikasa* shortly turned to SW, and then to south. The Russian right column was then observed to be heading to port, with the apparent object of leading the column of light vessels.

The *Mikasa* was now steering almost directly for the leading ship of the former Russian starboard wing, whose first few ships, still engaged in executing the evolution just mentioned, were heading several points to port of their original course. As soon as that was regained, the Russian leader opened fire (2.07pm), the first shot dropping only 20 metres astern of the *Mikasa*, and being rapidly succeeded by others that fell almost as close. The old port wing of the Russian fleet seemed to intend to remain in the line and also joined in the fire.

Few of those watching can have failed to recognise that the Japanese position was critical. Minutes passed slowly. While still approaching the Russian line of advance at a large angle, the Japanese leader had come under fire that grew hotter with each successive arrival in line of another Russian ship. Deterred by no answering fire, the Russian shot were being well aimed, and anyone of them might place the *Mikasa* out of action for the remainder of the day. The fact that the Russians would now be furnished with telescopic sights, and reports of the severe schooling their gunners had recently undergone were recalled, and many must have felt misgivings as to what might not be the result of the battle begun so unpromisingly.

Though the sole object of Russian fire, the *Mikasa* continued to advance without returning a shot. It was not obvious what Togo meant to do. Again, it would not have been very surprising if he had succumbed to an inclination to get out of a disagreeable predicament as quickly as might be, and had withdrawn from a very exposed situation by turning to starboard, thus leading his fleet past the Russians on an opposite course, and looking to the infliction of punishment on the weak rear of the enemy for compensation for the loss of advantage that had eluded him.

Not so Togo. Threatened with hardly less danger in his battle with Vitgeft, he had refused to accept the *Sevastopol* and *Poltava* in exchange for the abandonment of his greatest task. Already on this day he had preferred the greater to the less, and he now had another opportunity for the display of characteristic magnanimity and personal fearlessness. Recognising in the largest Russian battleships his proper objective, and thoroughly comprehending the importance of developing his whole gun effort against them early, he resolved

> to run all risks rather than be guilty of a defection from the path judgement had already marked out.
>
> Befriended by fortune, the *Mikasa* was able to run on unhurt until 2.10pm, when, turning eastward to the same course as the Russian Admiral, she opened fire as soon as steadied in a new direction. In both fleets, ships were now coming successively into line, but the Russian formation of heavy ships was, perhaps, two or three ships ahead of that of the Japanese. Part of the Russian fire followed the *Mikasa*, but the gradually increasing remainder continued to be converged on the Japanese turning point, and it was interesting to watch each ship approach and run through this warm spot, a feat all were lucky enough to accomplish without receiving serious injury. This commencement was made notable by the close shooting of the Russians, who, however, were unfortunate, as though they threw shell of all dimensions close alongside the Japanese ships, often dashing heavy bodies of water onto their decks, no projectile of calibre larger than 6-inch appeared to get home, though some of this size splashed on armour belts or plunged into upper works.[3]

Aboard the *Asahi*, Pakenham noted the difficulty which he was experiencing of appreciating exactly what was occurring:

> The limitations of a single observer should be understood. With no compass nearer than that in a director tower, he may not enter while others are exposed, he is dependent for his courses on the goodwill of any bystander whose possibly inexpert services he can enlist to read off a compass that is probably unsteady. If not in one of the leading ships, the most constant vigilance may miss the exact moment at which turns are made. Wherever he may be, he can only be in one place at a time, can only surmise the meaning of signals, and his imputation of motives to admirals can rest on little more solid than the hazard of a guess.
>
> When the lines had deployed there were 12 ships in each, though more may have entered the Russian lines subsequently. The heaviest vessels of either side were mutually engaged, and the *Suvorov* had been hit several times at short intervals, as also had the *Alexander III*. The Russian leader then seeming disposed to close, by a slight turn to port (2:20pm) the *Mikasa* increased to a distance, thus bringing the head of the Russian line abeam of the *Asahi*, at a range of about 5,000 metres, and under a good concentration of well-directed fire. In rear, the action was being warmly contested, the smaller Russians firing briskly, and seeming to have begun the business of the day as resolutely as their leaders had done.[4]

3 Ibid., pp. 364-366.
4 Ibid., pp. 366-367.

Pakenham's comments on the problems faced by an observer were no understatement. The ensuing movements as the battle developed were immensely complex; Corbett pointed out that 'no great naval battle since the prolonged and loosely handled actions of our own Dutch wars is probably so difficult to reconstruct as that of Tsushima ... After the first hour it degenerated into a game of blind man's bluff.'[5]

Pakenham continued his description of the fighting:

> This was the scenic part of the battle. Two long lines of ships were attacking one another vigorously; formations were as yet unbroken; damages were still conjectural, and the fate of the day seemed to hang on every shot. Kamimura was about 500 metres to port of the main Japanese line, but had not permitted the longitudinal interval between himself and the *Nisshin* to increase. The *Suvorov* (2:25pm) was hit again, and this may have induced her to break off a little, as range was observed to have become 6,000 metres. Russian fire was still well sustained. With the object, perhaps, of varying the range, the *Mikasa* was zigzagging in her course, and the ships in her immediate neighbourhood were attentively following her slightest turn.
>
> The wind was fair. Russian speed was estimated at from 12 to 14 knots, while that of the Japanese, which had originally been 14 knots, was increased to 15, and was maintained at that figure until the following morning. This superiority asserted itself from the first, though the Russians may have tried a higher speed, as two of their small vessels seemed unable to keep up. The Japanese battleships had begun to edge to the eastward, keeping the leading Russian abreast of the *Asahi*, and by 2:30pm the lines were heading nearly east. Shortly after, the *Suvorov* had been dropped a little, but her range was still about 6,000 metres. Fire had broken out in the *Oslyabya*, and the *Borodino* had recently been badly hit, though the principal attack of the Japanese battleships was being more and more directed at the head of the Russian line. An explosion under the after bridge of the *Asahi* filled the air with flying fragments. Of these, one fell underfoot. It was the right half of a man's lower jaw, with teeth missing. Everything and everybody for 20 yards round was bespattered with tiny drops of blood and minute particles of flesh that adhered to whatever they struck. A 6-inch shell had exploded against a 12-pounder gun, killing the officer and crew and some of the bystanders. In spite of the quantity scattered, the amount of blood left on the deck looked sufficient to fill a big cask.[6]

Pakenham was covered with blood. Without a word he left the after bridge and went below, leading his hosts to suppose that the experience was too much even for the imperturbable attaché. Not so, however; within a few minutes he reappeared to take

5 Corbett II, p. 240.
6 Naval Attaché Reports, pp. 367-368.

up his former station, having changed into a new and immaculate white uniform, and continued his observations:

> Only seven Russians could now be distinguished in the line. Either the turn had masked the others from view, or, and what is more probable, they had formed a second line to starboard. Russian fire, which had begun with an accuracy boding ill for the Japanese, already showed signs of receding from its high level. The *Mikasa* continued to turn gradually to starboard, but although the leaders were separated by only 5,000 metres, smoke and mist allowed little of the enemy, except the flash of his guns, to be seen. At 2:40pm the *Suvorov* had entirely disappeared, while of her next in the line only the after extremity was distinguishable. When range had been reduced to 4,600 m, it became obscured to such an extent that the Japanese discontinued their fire. By concealing disruption, a murky atmosphere thus deprived them of the keen gratification of witnessing the disorder of the foe. Although later in the day the enemy regained some regularity of formation, the Russian fleet had made its last appearance as an effective fighting force.
>
> By successive small turns, Togo had attained a direction almost athwart the former Russian course. When last seen, the *Suvorov* had been on the starboard quarter of the *Asahi*; and as it was now suspected that her disappearance had been caused as much by change of direction as by obscuration, the *Mikasa* began turning south-eastward, and very shortly discovered the Russian flagship on a parallel course. Though the distance between the lines was given as only 5,600 metres, the nearest of the enemy looked 10 miles away. The *Suvorov*, having been brought nearly abeam, fire was reopened; and when range had increased to 6,500 metres, it could be seen that the Russians were again turning. Though executed with an air of indecision (it has since been stated that the *Alexander III's* steering gear had been disabled), this turn seemed to be towards the Japanese, and was countered (3.00pm) in the Japanese battle line by a swing of eight points to port together.
>
> The Russian manoeuvre was now defining itself as a half-hearted dash for the north on the part of the larger battleships, the smaller either not participating or lingering behind. Fire had obtained a hold in the *Suvorov*, and probably also in another of the largest Russian vessels. A third, with a heavy heel, and also burning furiously, had fallen out of line. This was thought to be the *Oslyabya*, and it has since transpired that she sank (3:10pm) soon after. Even if they did not witness the final tragedy, the distress of this and other ships, combined with the disorganisation that could be seen to have overtaken the Russians, were welcomed by the Japanese as first signs of disintegration, though it may have taken the whole of the rest of the afternoon to impress upon most of them how successful their first attack had been, and how unexpectedly destructive their projectiles had proved. No exact estimate of damage could be formed, but on

> looking up and down the Japanese line it could be seen that none of its ships had suffered seriously, and this also helped to increase confidence.
>
> As soon as it had cleared Kamimura, Togo turned the battle line 8 points to port together, the *Nisshin* thus leading an inverted order with port broadsides presented. A small cruiser, probably a Russian, showed itself between the fleets, but ran through without effecting anything. The Japanese had not fired for some time, but, though the haze was still too dense to allow much to be seen, a heavy cannonade from within it persistently sent projectiles flying in from the port beam.[7]

In the course of the battering which the *Suvorov* had sustained, Rozhestvenski had suffered a number of injuries. His Chief of Staff, Clapier de Colongue, was determined to get him off the vessel. The flagship was plainly out of control, and in accordance with the instructions issued by Rozhestvenski four days earlier the *Alexander III* was bound to take the lead of the battle line, which she did. Subsequently the destroyer *Buini* came alongside the burning flagship and, with immense difficulty, the injured admiral was transferred. Semenov went with him. Pakenham thought that this occurred soon after 3.00pm, but in fact it was a good deal later. Pakenham could not of course have been aware of what was going on, still less of the command structure, or lack of it, of the Russian fleet. He noted that at this time the *Alexander III*, with the *Borodino* and *Orel* turned and headed straight for the Japanese line:

> The range having been reduced (3:18pm) to 2,500 m, the Russian leader, being then about a point abaft the beam of the Japanese, was subjected to a terrific attack that must have aggravated a situation which fire on board had already rendered uncomfortable. For a brief space those in the Japanese fleet who had witnessed the somewhat similarly rash effort of the *Retvizan,* thought they saw repeated an attempt that must always be dangerous, but which is desperate indeed when made without properly disposed support. Whether or no the *Alexander III,* if that ship it were, had entertained any other idea than that of rejoining her leader by the shortest route, she continued her turn to starboard until on the same course as the *Suvorov.* The punishment received must have been very severe, and if the hero of this rash adventure were in truth the *Alexander III,* it may be that here will be found an explanation of her cession of the leadership that had devolved upon her in the absence of the *Suvorov.* Except that in the engagement of the evening the *Borodino* almost certainly led, and the *Alexander III* occupied third place, no evidence is yet available by which this point can be determined.
>
> Less resolute or more prudent, the companions of the *Alexander III* (in one of whom a severe explosion had occurred) swung to port and gained the same course by passing through west and south.

7 Ibid II, pp. 368-369.

The Russians had formed the pivot of a small alteration to port on the part of the Japanese, who were thus steering about WNW. A small fire, quickly got under, appeared in the *Fuji*. The whole Russian fleet was on the port quarter, the biggest battleships heading toward the NE, while the smaller were further away and to their starboard. At 3.25, the *Suvorov*, still firing, was crossing the Japanese wake. A mast had fallen, and of her funnels only a stump of the foremost remained. Her companions had drawn to starboard, and were almost out of sight. Yet more to starboard, lesser vessels could be distinguished on bearings of from 2 to 5 points abaft the Japanese beam. When fire ceased at 3:27pm the shortest range was about 5,400 metres.

Soon, only two Russians could be seen, though the fall of projectiles told of the maintenance of an ill directed fire in the SE. Under the unresented splash of these, the Japanese battleships turned to SW. Two three-funnelled cruisers became visible to port; shot continued to drop in. On the starboard hand and steering a parallel course lay the *Asama*, attended by one or two divisions of destroyers. She had been originally detailed to conduct a similar force, whose duty it would have been to hamper the movements of the enemy by strewing in his way dummy and explosive obstructions; but weather and other conditions not having been propitious, it is believed the scheme was not executed, though circumstances are conceivable in which such a device might be by no means unpractical. When the torpedo boats were sent to Takeshiki, the *Asama* had rejoined her squadron. The time of her again quitting it had not been observed, so it could not be inferred whether her present position was due to having fallen out for repairs, or merely to have received new orders. (It is now known that the former was the correct explanation). Kamimura could be seen approaching, and is it is understood that the *Asama* took post henceforward in his rear, though frequently at some distance astern.

The Japanese turned at 3:40pm eight points to port simultaneously. The high land of Okinoshima could be made out a little to starboard of right ahead. The Second Squadron, following Togo's old course, was thus brought on the port bow, while the *Asama* and her destroyers in their advance had crossed to the starboard quarter. Another turn together to port gave the lead back to the *Mikasa*, and restored the natural order. The rear ships of Kamimura's squadron were then just crossing ahead. In making this turn the *Fuji* threatened the safety of the ships near her. Starboard broadsides were again presented, but only from a blur here and there in the haze, or from the fall of shot, could the positions of the Russians be judged. The course was now about NW, and Okinoshima bore on the starboard beam.

Thick smoke appearing on the starboard bow, course was altered four points southward, while Kamimura also turned and steered approximately parallel, his squadron being still to port. Russian fire from the starboard bow became stronger, but it was thought to proceed from the smaller vessels, and that the larger were ahead.

A northerly turn at 4.00pm brought the four bigger Russians once more into view, and it could then be seen that the Japanese line of advance would take them to port of all, but much closer to the *Suvorov* than to the other heavy battleships. When last mentioned, this vessel was crossing the Japanese rear at 3.25, when the damage suffered by her masts and funnels was commented on. She was still on fire amidships, and from this cause and from the absence of uptakes was not only perpetually enveloped in smoke herself, but was originating the greater density that reigned in her neighbourhood. Although heeling heavily, her fire was steadily maintained. When reports were collected on the following morning, it was learned that, since her last engagement with the battle squadron, she had sustained the united attack of Kamimura's five armoured cruisers. Now, however, she was steaming unmolested towards the north, though at a comparatively low speed.

Correct identification is here of special importance, as the unexampled lengths to which bravery and fortitude were carried in defence of this unhappy ship reflect underlying glory not only on her gallant crew, but on their navy and on their country. As there can be no reasonable doubt that this was the *Suvorov*, it will be assumed that hers it was to shed additional lustre on a name already synonymous with inflexible courage.

Coming within range, the *Mikasa* recommenced fire at about 4:05pm, other ships joining in in quick succession. Aim was divided between the *Suvorov* and her companions, who were steaming towards her, and whose endeavour it was expected it would be to attract Japanese fire to themselves. Here was an opportunity for one of those deeds that cloak all shortcomings. But no; opportunity was not seized, possibly was not even perceived. The advancing ships remained on the far side of their unfortunate comrade, and thus derived from him much of the protection which they should have bestowed.

From the standpoint of the mere observer, much sympathy is felt for the commander of the group formed, perhaps in the order given, by the battleships *Borodino*, *Orel*, and *Alexander III*. He seems to have been only of captain's rank, and at least one of his ships, the *Alexander III*, had probably received such punishment as had impaired her seaworthiness, and hence her speed. This officer had not only to arrive at a decision the most momentous, but he might have to enforce it upon squadrons commanded by those superior to him in rank, if his inferiors in competence.

His normal leader was little more than a wreck; but it was his duty to protect her, and this could be done either by imposing bodily between her and the Japanese, or, and far more effectively, by collecting the Russian fleet, and by hastening it north-eastward, thus compelling the attention of the Japanese main force in that quarter.

By 4:10pm, the *Suvorov* had been passed at a distance little outside 1,000 metres. Engaged in a slow wheel to starboard, the Russian battleships, as seen from the Japanese fleet, seemed to be in line abreast, with the Japanese on their port quarter. Their evolution was soon better understood. The *Suvorov* herself was slowly turning to starboard, and the other three were doing the same on her further side, in line ahead but independently of her, retiring afterwards towards the south. In that direction probably turned also about the same time the smaller vessels that had been unceasingly firing at the Japanese battle squadron. The Japanese themselves began to turn through east, thus keeping guns bearing on the *Suvorov*, though range had been allowed to increase considerably. At about 4.12, also, Kamimura, who had gained a position on the port bow and who was still drawing ahead, began to come into line ahead of the *Mikasa*.

Though slow, the retreat of the companions of the *Suvorov* caused whatever fire had hitherto been directed at them to dwindle away, until almost the whole gun effort was converged on her. When first seen in this phase of the battle, her condition had seemed sufficiently deplorable. Smoke, curling round the stern, was rolling horizontally away in the wind. If the absence of funnels contributed much to her air of distress, the now extensive conflagration raging amidships showed its reality. Less than half the ship can have been habitable; yet she fought on; from at least one of her heavy turrets was maintained a steady and frequent fire. When passed on a northerly course, she had been the object of an attack that short range must have rendered most severe, though little of its effect could be observed, save that heel had increased and that her already low speed had been correspondingly reduced. On their present southerly course, the Japanese had to pass to leeward, and the smoke surrounding her was then so thick that bow could not be distinguished from stern. At about 4.30, when she was being struck repeatedly, a 12-inch shell burst in the between decks, close to the after turret for 6-inch guns. Explosion was accompanied by a backrush of flame that must have been projected 50 feet from her side, and then through the enormous rent thus made could be seen the glow of the newly ignited interior, an appearance that the immediate aggravation of the fire on board amply corroborated. The foremast had long been down. Now fell the main topmast also, and, at the same instant, a considerable explosion occurred. Projectiles continued their rain, and it was thought the end must at last have come; but though only the tip of the stern and the raggedy end of a stunted mast protruded from the enveloping cloud, the *Suvorov* still maintained the unequal contest.

Passed again at about 4:30pm at a distance of 1,800 metres, when she again sustained the greater weight of Japanese fire without relaxing her defence, it seemed to be at last realised that it was a waste of time to try to sink by gun power a ship otherwise doomed, and attention was gradually transferred elsewhere. Torpedoes may have been fired, but, if so, they were ineffective.

It has been said that the retirement of the companions of the *Suvorov* was slow and towards the south. The big battleships had never really passed out of range, which had reached its maximum of 7,400 metres soon after 4.25, when they could be distinguished with difficulty on the distant side of their more resolute friend. Though they had probably unintermittently received some portion of the Japanese fire, and had returned it, they had taken little practical share since their southerly turn at about 4.15. At 4.35 the Japanese, who had been steering south-easterly, turned together to NE; and the Second Squadron, which had been ahead, preceded by itself on the course the battleships had just quitted.

The inducement to make this turn is not plain. The Russian ships thus left astern passed out of sight, but shots from the quarter in which they had been last seen told of the continued presence there of vessels of some kind. Probably Togo had already observed or divined the numerous assembly in the SE, which others less favourably placed only saw later; also he may have desired bodily transfer to port for tactical purposes. Anyhow, after advancing for a few minutes, he again turned to starboard and resumed his former direction deflecting further to starboard at 4.45, when Kamimura was once more ahead. The alteration to starboard was continued, and soon after 4.55 the *Mikasa* was heading south.

The *Suvorov*, which had last been seen abeam, now lay broad on the quarter, smoking from one end to the other, and heading in a south-westerly direction. With unconscionable audacity, solitary but indomitable, she occasionally fired unaccepted challenge to the renewal of an unprofitable combat. Indistinctly outlined in the misty air, and seeming to mingle with the waves that washed over them, one or two divisions of destroyers were making their stealthy way towards her.

At 4:58pm the Second Squadron was swinging through 16 points to a course parallel to that of the *Mikasa*. Within another minute or two, Okinoshima was again sighted about a point on the starboard bow, and a disordered agglomeration of ships came into view on a broader bearing. Most seem to be standing about SSW. The larger Russian battleships could only just have caught up the remainder, and the smaller had not been much in advance, so it is probable that the Russians should be credited at this time with an attempt to evolve order out of chaos with the intention of again confronting their foe. At any rate, the Russian leaders were apparently to the northward of lesser vessels, and must have turned immediately to encounter the Japanese, as when the Russian leader was first singled out he was turning to port, apparently from a north-easterly course, and then steadied in a direction the opposite of that of the Japanese. The men had been supping, but were recalled at 5:05pm to their quarters. The enemy opened fire at 8,000 metres, and the Japanese replied when the range been reduced to 6,500 metres.

The three bigger Russians were now clear of the other ships and were leading to the north. By 5.10, the distance separating the leaders was 5,700 metres, and then after falling to 5,200 metres, it had again increased to 5,700 metres when, though almost concealed by smoke, the Russians were observed to be deflecting about eight points to port. The foretopmast of the leader had been cut away. The Second Squadron had gained a position on the port bow of the *Mikasa* but at some distance from her.

Smaller Russians then came within range, and from their number and confusion it seemed as though all the ships of the Baltic Fleet had got into a sort of pool, from which they were now successively emerging to string away after their leaders. Here was every description of vessel, from minor battleship to *ci-devant* merchantman. The filing off of the heaviest left a miscellaneous collection of weaklings at the mercy of the Japanese, and it says much for the intelligence of the cooperation of the Japanese light divisions that, though many of these vessels were possessed of good steaming capacity, the shelter of a scattered and hunted fleet was found preferable to a dash for freedom through the ranks of the enveloping enemy. An approach to order was accepted by the Russians but slowly. A three-funnelled cruiser, listed to starboard, and with half her after chimney gone, headed south. Nearby lay a similar vessel, with centre funnel missing. At 5:22pm the heavier Russian battleships appeared to be beyond the miscellaneous group, so it is probable that many of the latter had been standing to the eastward of the course of their leaders. At 5.25, the most conspicuous were a vessel with a single chimney making for the north; one of the *Apraxin* class (apparently), which came under a beam fire at 5,000 metres; and a cruiser with a heavy list, which lay on the Japanese quarter heading parallel.

The main part of Kamimura's fire was still masked by the battle squadron, but at the last mentioned time he had got such a lead that his rear ship was abreast the *Fuji*. The whole Russian fleet having been passed, the *Mikasa* turned 16 points to starboard, which brought her head round from N to NW. The sea was thus dashing against the port bow, breaking heavily over the ships, and evidently causing great inconvenience in the *Kasuga* and *Nisshin*. On this course the *Ural* was passed and destroyed. The Second Squadron pursued its way towards the SW, in which quarter the *Itsukushima* division could be perceived, and was not again seen until it rejoined the flag after dark.

Darkness to the westward showed that the ever contumacious *Suvorov* had survived the attack of the Japanese destroyers. It is said that she had only two 12-pounders available to repel the small craft, and that one of their torpedoes took effect. Her plight must have been pitiable. Even so, shattered, mutilated, halting, and with her name already indelibly inscribed in the pages of history, it is possible that this intrepid spirit was aspiring to the greater immortality of a deathbed surrounded by the battleships of the enemy.

But this was not to be. Though defiance ended only with life, towards nightfall another torpedo from a destroyer put an end to the struggle, and unconquerable as the *Suvorov* had fought, unconquered she died. But if at last she perished, at last she won; and in the apparent misfortunes of the last few hours of her brief career may be seen promise that in the future the Russian navy will redeem the reputation lost on this day. Honour to the brave! [8]

8 Ibid., pp. 370-375.

By about 6.00pm it was apparent to the Japanese that the Russians had to some extent been able to re-form. The *Borodino* was now leading, followed by the *Orel.* Some way astern came Nebogatov in the *Nikolai I* leading the rest of his division, *Apraxin, Senyavin* and *Ushakov.* The badly damaged *Alexander III* had fallen out of line, and was struggling on abreast of the *Senyavin*. Behind these came the remaining ships of the Second Division, the *Sisoi Veliki, Navarin* and *Nakhimov.* The day was drawing on; as the sun began to go down it combined with the haze to reduce visibility. Pakenham tried to make out exactly what the Russians were doing:

> At 6:08pm the three big Russians were in sight, with a long interval between the second and third. Then, range being 7,900 metres, a fourth became visible, with smaller vessels astern, prolonging the line until it could be seen extending over 2 miles. Shortly after, their general direction appeared to be towards NNW. There was still a long interval between the two leading ships and their next astern, and the range had been reduced to 6,700 metres. Appearances indicated the possible formation of the second line to port, headed by a big vessel, perhaps the *Nikolai I.* Firing was brisk. Frequently the flash of guns could be seen, when ships themselves were indistinguishable. It was doubtful whether Japanese fire was making much impression. There was an uncheerful feeling that it was not getting home on the enemy with the same accuracy as earlier in the day. Some Japanese destroyers were on the off-side of the Japanese battle line. By 6.30, battle was general, and had resolved itself into a broadside action in which the Russian leaders were a little before the beam of the *Mikasa*. The range was 6,600 metres. The *Alexander III* was still lagging, but, on the whole, the Russian order looked fairly regular, though it might have consisted either of one line, or of two.
>
> The Russian leaders, who had been keeping pace with the Japanese, may have found they were going too fast for those in rear. At any rate, the Japanese began to draw ahead, and by 6.40 the second Russian was only just before the beam of the A*sahi*. The third, the *Alexander III*, was a little abaft the beam, but seemed very far away. Little of smaller vessels, save gun flashes, could be seen, but there were indications that an engagement might be in progress on their reverse flank. At 6:40pm, the range of the Russian leaders was being steadily maintained at 6,800 metres, though their leader, the *Borodino*, was soon brought abeam of the *Asahi*. The *Mikasa* began to alter course a little to port. Wind was less strong, but the enemy, and particularly his leaders, could only be indistinctly seen. It is believed that the ship which now seemed to be fourth in the Russian line, as seen from the Japanese side, was the *Alexander III.* At 6.52, she was still visible a little abaft the beam. The three leaders, one of whom may have been the *Nikolai I*, were on a more advanced bearing.
>
> As the sun sank, fire effects became more visible, cheering the Japanese, as, with increased visibility, accuracy seemed to improve. Range had lengthened to 7,700 metres, when at 6:57pm a very conspicuous hit was marked on the

Borodino, which, with the two next astern, were the only vessels then in sight. Russian projectiles were falling short, but occasionally one hurtled over.

At 7.00pm the course was a little to eastward of north, and the distance between the lines was 7,900 metres. Small craft could be distinguished on the port bow of the Russian leader, whose loss of the foretopmast (interesting only as connecting her with the leader previously mentioned as minus the spar) could be clearly seen. For a few minutes the *Asahi* had to cease fire on account of the disappearance of the enemy; but at 7.05 fire was resumed, and the *Borodino* was again hit, the brilliant rosy glow of explosion showing up against her smoke. Both fleets had been steering practically parallel courses, though the Japanese had been zigzagging a good deal. When still ten degrees above the horizon, the sun disappeared. In its descent it had been in the eyes of the Japanese gunners, so when fog first dimmed and then hid it prematurely, its absence was not regretted.

Two divisions of Japanese destroyers had forged ahead, and were standing across the head of the line towards the Russians. The steady, undeviating advance of these small craft looked very threatening in the quickly waning light. The Russian battleships were irregularly disposed abeam, but only enough of their other vessels could be seen to make it certain that they still followed. The cannonade on the further side continued, without its having become apparent by whom it was being maintained.

The long-running fight had hitherto been tedious and indecisive, but the climax was fast approaching. At 7:18pm the Japanese was standing about NNW, the *Borodino* being distant 8,200 metres, when flames burst from her after battery, and, leaping to a height of at least 30 feet, at once gained possession of the whole breadth of the ship, and seen to be working forward rapidly. The silence of the after turret was thought to show that the crew had been driven from their guns.

It was already twilight, and the progress of destruction in the *Borodino* could be watched without the aid of glasses. After a few more shots, the *Mikasa* turned to about NE and ceased to fire. As the *Fuji* reached the wheeling point, her last 12-inch shot produced the sensation of the day. Entering the upper part of the *Borodino* near the foremost broadside turret, it burst, and an immense column of smoke, ruddied on its underside by the glare from the explosion and from the fire abaft, spurted to the height of her funnel tops. From every opening in engine rooms and stokeholds steam rushed, and in two or three minutes the ship from foremast to stern was wrapped in fiercely whirling spirals of smoke and vapour, gaily illumined by frequent tall shafts of flame. It was evident that the conflagration had reached a stage where it could defy control, and that the vessel's fighting days were numbered, though even so it was not realised how near was the end.

Though sudden, this was not dramatic. While all watched, the unfortunate ship disappeared at 7:30pm, her departure only marked by a roar not greatly louder than that of one of her own bursting shell, and, until dispersed by the

> wind, by a great increase in volume of the dense cloud that brooded over the place she had occupied. It is doubtful whether any in the Japanese fleet saw her go, as little but the outline of her stem had been visible for some minutes.
>
> Even if it should have been the *Borodino* that failed to rise to the heights required for the relief of the *Suvorov*; if more recently she had not displayed the qualities that either rescue from desperate situations or shed round failure a halo criticism shrinks from dissipating, her sullen perseverance and the punishment showed the possession of attributes which, though possibly not those most conducive to success, were of the nobility that must compel the seamen of every nation to follow her fight to its fatal conclusion with a respectful sympathy, from sharing which cannot be excluded her steadfast companion, the *Alexander III.*
>
> The repeated chronicle of Russian bravery should not be allowed to detract from the tribute due to the Japanese. If the fortune of war had been reversed, no one who has been intimately associated with those from whom the blockaders of Port Arthur were drawn almost at random, can doubt that if for them the sun had set, for each and all it would have sunk in splendour.
>
> With the catastrophe just related, fire ceased in the Japanese battle line, though an exchange continued a little longer in other parts of the field. Important vessels had been missed before, but now, by an accident and in sight of everyone, one of the most powerful had gone whence there was no return. To most of the Japanese this was the moment of victory, though, as Russian losses were still greatly underestimated and no great confidence was felt in the results of night attacks by torpedo boats, a renewal of fight on the following day was thought probable. The men were dismissed from their stations, and under a thinning hail of projectiles Togo turned SE, his squadron having been under an incessant, if latterly inaccurate, fire since the first shot of the engagement.
>
> Thus ended the principal function of the battle squadron in one of the most decisive of naval battles. Fought in obscurity, terminated in uncertainty, the damage suffered by the Japanese from an imperfectly seen enemy had been hardly sufficient to dispel a sense of unreality that might entitle this epoch making combat to the alternative name, 'A Battle of Shadows.'[9]

As night fell, and the Japanese battle line turned away, Togo's destroyers had their chance to harry the defeated enemy. Their most notable victim so far had been the *Suvorov.* As they closed on the Russian ships Nebogatov turned away to the south to avoid the attack of the flotillas, though the movement was executed in a disorderly fashion. By 8.00pm it had become quite dark, and the destroyers lost sight of their target until the Russians switched on their searchlights. Nebogatov, leading the line in the *Nikolai I,* turned to starboard with the object of resuming a northerly course, when the Japanese destroyers closed in on him again. In line, the destroyers fired their

9 Ibid., pp. 376-379.

torpedoes in succession, in the face of a heavy and accurate fire from the Russians, which inflicted a good deal of superficial damage; none of the torpedoes scored a hit. Immediately after this abortive attack Nebogatov, who had resumed his course for Vladivostok, ordered his heavy ships to switch off their searchlights.

The destroyers had been joined by several divisions of torpedo boats, and the attacks on the main body of the Russians, and on and Enkvist's cruisers, continued. A number of hits were recorded, but the Japanese lost three torpedo boats sunk as well as a number of others seriously damaged. During the night the *Navarin*, which had been badly damaged, had had to slow down, and had lost touch with the rest of what remained of the Russian fleet, when she encountered a division of destroyers equipped for minelaying; getting ahead of her, they dropped their mines and one at least proved fatal. A huge explosion rent the battleship's stern, and another explosion amidships caused her to capsize; she took with her all but three of her complement of 674.[10]

As the night wore on Togo was unaware of the extent of his victory, not realising that he had practically wiped out Rozhestvenski's 1st Division. It was his intention to get ahead of the enemy and fall upon them as they made their way north. As dawn broke, he was accompanied only by Kamimura's division; but at 5:20am the signal came in from the 5th Division that smoke had been seen, and further reports confirmed that the Russian fleet had been sighted. Togo, who had been well to the north, turned back southwards at 13 knots. Nebogatov, by now in sight of the 4th, 5th and 6th Divisions, resolved to force his way through them and make for Vladivostok.

There was in fact no chance that he could achieve this. Togo, steaming south, increased speed, and sent on Kamimura's cruisers. By 9.18 Togo came in sight of ships of Kataoka's squadron, and before 10.00am could make out the Russian ships apparently steaming on a north-easterly course. The Japanese battle squadron went to action stations, and hoisted battle flags, closing to within 12,000 yards 10.15. At 10.34 the *Kasuga* fired the first shot; the range was soon down to 8,000 yards, and all the Japanese ships were in action. Nebogatov, at that range, was with his obsolete guns able to make no reply, and 'he judged the resistance was out of his power, and that it was therefore his duty to surrender without further useless sacrifice of life.'[11]

Pakenham briefly described what followed:

> At 10.48, a rumour that the enemy had surrendered was circulated, and fire was accordingly interrupted; but as no confirmation was received, action was again begun, though in a half-hearted way, and a few more shots were thus fired. Still from the Russians came no reply. Their colours were flying, but battle flags had not been hoisted, and a signal was at last discerned at the forepart of each triatic stay, where, screened by smoke, it could not be easily seen. This signal may have been displayed from the first; but when entering action, leisure for scrutinising

10 Corbett II, p. 304.
11 Ibid. II, p. 320.

signals made by the enemy is wanting, so it is not surprising if this one had not been perceived and its purpose understood sooner.

In the Japanese fleet there was much self-congratulation. Battle flags were hauled down and the prizes were directed to hoist their new colours. It was still believed by most that the two leading battleships were of the *Borodino* class; the absence of an after turret in one of them was attributed to some accident of battle. When it had been ascertained beyond doubt that the leader was only the *Nikolai I*, the capture in her of Nebogatov was thought poor compensation for the disappointment. Besides this ship, the prizes were the *Orel*, *Senyavin* and *Apraxin*. The propriety of the surrender of the ships has been much debated, and Japanese feeling undoubtedly condemns it, though when judged by other standards it does not seem to have been dishonourable.

The remainder of the day was spent in sending prize crews and in distributing prisoners. The armoured cruisers were detached to the south in advance, and the *Yakumo* and *Iwate*, having perceived the *Ushakov*, engaged and sank her. Later in the afternoon, the battle squadron also started southward, escorting the prizes. The fate of the *Suvorov* and *Alexander III* became known, and reports as to the success of the night actions of the torpedo flotilla began to come in, though it may have been several days before all statements had been sifted and collated and their evidence examined.[12]

12 Ibid., pp. 381-382.

24

Conclusion

Corbett described the battle of Tsushima as 'perhaps the most decisive and complete naval battle in history.' The Japanese lost 117 officers and men killed and 583 wounded. Three torpedo boats had been sunk and several others seriously damaged. The losses of the Russians amounted to 4,830 officers and men killed or drowned; 5,913, many of them wounded, were taken prisoner and 1,862 were interned by neutral countries. Among the prisoners was the seriously injured Rozhestvenski. Taken first off the *Suvorov* by the destroyer *Buini* during the battle, he was transferred to the destroyer *Bedovi* on the following day. In company with the *Grozni*, she was making her way north when they were intercepted by Japanese destroyers. The *Grozni* made her escape, but the *Bedovi* surrendered rather than running the risk of exacerbating the admiral's injuries. He was taken to hospital, where he was later visited by Togo, who on taking his leave said to him: 'You performed your great task heroically until you were incapacitated. I pay you my highest respects.'[1]

Of the twelve vessels comprising the Russian battle line, eight were sunk and four were captured. Of the cruisers, four were sunk, one ran ashore and three (*Aurora*, *Oleg* and *Zhemchug*) were interned at Manila. Only one cruiser, the *Almaz*, made it to Vladivostok, together with two destroyers, the *Grozni* and *Bravyi*.[2]

In his final report, Pakenham reviewed some of the factors that contributed to the Japanese success. The first of these was the superiority of the Japanese gunners. Unlike the battle of the Yellow Sea, Tsushima was fought at close range from the outset, and accordingly gunners were not already fatigued, and the greater skill of the Japanese enabled them at once to establish fire superiority. Pakenham went on to consider this in detail, beginning with the effectiveness of the Japanese ammunition:

1 Richard Connaughton, *The War of the Rising Sun and the Tumbling Bear* (London, 1988), p. 270.

2 Corbet II, p. 333; *British Official History* II, p. 758.

Last year, the high explosive charges with which Japanese shell were loaded disappointed those who had expected them to work great havoc upon the enemy, who, in fact, suffered far less serious damage from their destructive effects than did their own ships, an important fraction of whose armaments were disabled by premature explosions. But the deception had not ended even here. It had been anticipated that the incendiary effect of the explosive would be enormous, but in no instance that can be recalled did it originate a fire of importance.

In the last battle, however, the achievements of the same explosive exceeded all that its fondest admirers had formerly predicted. By rejecting projectiles of inferior manufacture, by better protection of base fuses, and by stricter precautions against overheating and prematures were reduced. Thus, one very grave factor, that of self-damage, had been diminished.

Incendiary effect, that had not been satisfactory before, was this time tremendous. So great was it, indeed, that the whole battle hinged upon it. The modern ships were of similar construction on both occasions; why, then, should there have been this remarkable difference?

There seem to have been two reasons for this. The fuse had been rendered much less sensitive. Even now a considerable part of the force of explosion is lost outside a quarter inch plate. Before modification of the fuse, a much greater waste must have occurred. Both the former Port Arthur fleet and the *Orel* have been inspected, and it is evident that none of the ships in the former suffered, from individual projectiles, damages comparable with those inflicted on the *Orel*. A suitable fuse had therefore rendered the effect of each projectile that penetrated greater than it had formerly been.

In the later battle hits were more frequent, and it is to this, coupled with a greater individual destructiveness of each shell, that the greater degree of incendiarism observed on this occasion must be attributed. Where they receive immediate attention, fires in modern ships can be easily quenched; but if projectiles fall with such rapidity as to scare away the men whose duty it is to extinguish the flames, these will increase, and will gain a hold impossible to realise until it has been seen. In the former battle rapid hitting lasted but a short time for each ship, and came but once during the day, while in the latter it came earlier, lasted longer, and was more often repeated.

It might be asked, what caused the finest Russian battleships' eventual disappearance; was it the torpedo or the gun, and, if the latter, were shell able to perforate the thick armour belts with which the Russian ships were provided, or how did they bring the final catastrophe about?

It is not yet known what actually caused these new ships to vanish, but it is apparent that the gun may have been the agent. Formidable as they look on paper, and threatening as was their towering height when afloat, these ships proved admirable targets for the projectile opposed to them. Hitherto all estimates formed of the power of ships of the *Orel* type have been based on the assumption that they were as designed, that is to say that they were ships with thick and fairly high armoured protection at the waterline. Unless the *Orel* be exceptional, this is far from representing their nature under conditions of service. In the *Orel,* at the time of her entry into action, no more than from 2 to 3 feet of even her upper belt can have showed above water, and she might, therefore, almost be considered as a ship without waterline protection. At any rate, projectiles had been free to rend her sides, and had done so right down to the top of her belt, and a good deal of water had obtained admission through such apertures. It is thus easy to understand how a little more admitted might have produced a list such as that observed in the *Oslyabya* and *Suvorov*; and how, when that had once been done, water would be enabled to run in and out freely, thus reducing the water-plane area, and hence impairing stability. As they seem to have been when they came into action, the largest Russian battleships were defensively no match for those of Japan.

Another circumstance obviously likely to have been influential on the course and result of the late action is the relative accuracy of fire of the gunners of the two fleets. Was this more in favour of the Japanese in the late than in the former battle, and, if so, how should the difference be accounted for?

Fatigue is an element of enormous influence on accuracy. In the first battle, close action found the gunners of both sides already weary, while in the late one it found them fresh. After the first battle the Japanese understood the advantage derivable from an economy of the eyesight and nervous energy of their gun pointers; and the foregoing account will show how carefully they husbanded both on the later day. The same reference will lead to the conclusion that the Russians had failed to realise that a certain loss of power must accompany a too profuse expenditure of ammunition, as their projectiles never ceased to fall, whatever the range, and however unmolested they were by the Japanese at the time.

This factor alone is insufficient to account for the difference between the damage received and inflicted. The men of the Port Arthur fleet were war-seasoned veterans, while, in the main those of Rozhestvenski were receiving their baptism of fire. The Japanese had shown better marksmanship than the men of the Port Arthur fleet. Since then the former had been constantly practised in shooting, chiefly with aiming rifles, but sometimes also with heavy guns. But the improvement in training had not ended with an amelioration of the dexterity of the gun pointers. Among both officers and men shooting had formed the principal topic of thought and conversation for months. Thus not only was technical proficiency greater, but an all-round knowledge, which among the majority had last year existed only in embryo, had been diffused and matured.

With better sighting appliances than Vitgeft had possessed, at the outset the men of the Baltic Fleet showed that their training had been considerable, even if it had not brought them up to the level of the Japanese. In the Russian battleships the gunners were behind armour, which there is reason to think was never pierced. If their hearts had been kept up they could have fired thence with

> tolerable safety, and with every prospect of fair success. But it seems as though the demoralisation that early overtook the more exposed had communicated itself to the men at the guns, that accuracy had then fallen off rapidly, and that the external disorder of the Russian fleet finally became only a feeble reflection of the internal chaos of its units.
>
> Japanese shooting has produced an astounding effect, and the excellence of their marksmanship is likely to be overestimated in consequence. However, whatever figure of merit that fancy may attach to the marksmanship of the Japanese, and whatever share in the victory may hereafter be attributed to scientific manoeuvring of the Japanese fleet, or to any other contributory factor, the victory was in the first place a triumph of the gunner and the gun.[3]

As Pakenham observed, the best weapon may be misused: 'that of the Japanese was their fleet; Togo was the man to display its power.' He went on to examine the admiral's conduct which brought about such an astounding success. While the battle continued, he thought, 'few can have felt absolutely confident that the day had been lost and won in the first hour after the fleets came into contact.' But this was the case, and it was Togo's strategy that had produced this result. It was in this that was to be found the principle, and its application, that brought victory:

> As seen, this principle is as old as war itself; as true in conflicts on land as in sea fights. Already in these reports it has been discussed more than once. Superior forces must be thrown on the weak point of the enemy, and he must be crushed there. But the point selected must not be in some insignificant outwork; it must be so situated that its fall undermines the main position; otherwise, to attack it would only be to fritter away strength.
>
> At first sight, it may look as though the weakest point of the Russian fleet had lain in its tail, and that this should have been the part first attacked. For Togo to dash his battleships against those of the enemy may be thought to have been attacking him in his strongest, and not in his weakest, part. In a fleet with head and tail of more equal power, this might be true; but in the Baltic Fleet the disparity was so great, and the rear ships were so entirely dependent for existence on those at the head, that to attack them would have been to waste time and strength.
>
> Naval weakness may be of different kinds. It may consist in the inferiority of the unit, or in the exposure of its position. (This is not exhaustive, but is enough for the present purpose). Rightly rejecting the weakness resulting from individual inferiority, Togo assailed that caused by exposure. With fleets in line such positions must always exist at their extremities. Togo, then, cast his whole strength against the main defences of the Russians, but chose for his attack

3 Naval Attaché Reports, pp. 384-386.

> – what would correspond to an ill supported outwork on shore – the head of their line.
>
> It is probable Togo sought to confuse the Russians by forcing on them a change in their order at the moment of engaging, and that this was his chief motive in crossing ahead of them. Fog may have caused the mis-judgment of distance, but from the moment in which the Russians were sighted the risks of such an attempt were obvious. During the few minutes of the approach, the fate of Japan depended upon what happened to her leading ships. Persevering audaciously, Togo was happy in being confronted with an enemy as greatly his inferior in strategy as in marksmanship.
>
> This dangerous movement at length completed, Togo found himself at a range about half that at which it had been understood he had intended that action should be begun. However, superior speed soon gave him the coveted lead, and he was able to concentrate a heavy fire on the head of the opposite line. No retaliatory measure against the Japanese rear was attempted, and Russian numerical strength was thus not utilised. Nor was their shooting sufficiently good to compensate for this inertia, and for the sullen submission to the will of the Japanese admiral which it entailed. Togo, therefore, having hazarded much, stood possessed of all that heart of admiral could desire. In Japan the 'T' formation will henceforward be more highly esteemed than ever.[4]

In conclusion, Pakenham reflected that neither Togo, nor the Japanese navy, had been 'subjected to the ordeal of playing a losing game.' They had, from the outset, had the upper hand; when facing setbacks such as the loss of the *Hatsuse* and *Yashima*, their adversary had given them time to recover. Pakenham had formed the highest opinion of his hosts, observing that 'having controlled the situation from the first with strong and self-sacrificing determination, they have averted many of the evils incidental to the wars of the perfunctory and irresolute.' He ended the last of his reports with a glowing eulogy for the Japanese nation as a whole:'Showing great aptitude for complemental action, country and navy, national strategy and execution in the field, chief and subordinate, have showed themselves worthy of one another, and, thus united, have crushingly defeated an enemy of enormously greater potentiality.'[5]

Pakenham's work was done. He wasted no time in applying for leave, which was granted on June 9. Before leaving he sent a cheque to Rear Admiral Kato, Togo's Chief of Staff, as a personal donation to the charitable fund for the relief of the wounded and the relations of those killed at Tsushima, just as he had done after the battle of the Yellow Sea. Two days later he embarked on a steamer for San Francisco, where he arrived on June 27. Then, taking the train across the United States, he embarked at New York on July 6 on a steamer for Liverpool, arriving there on July 14. Next day he

4 Ibid., pp. 387-388.
5 Ibid., p. 391.

was in London, where he called at the Admiralty, bringing to an end an eventful and remarkably successful posting, in the course of which he had made a deep impression on his Japanese hosts. He was awarded the Order of the Rising Sun (second-class). Legend has it that when the Emperor asked Togo to name the bravest man in his fleet, the admiral astonished him by naming Pakenham.

Pakenham was based at the Admiralty for the next twelve months, by the end of which he was writing to his sister to say that he had had his fill of London. His letter was in reply to her congratulations on his being appointed to command the armoured cruiser *Antrim*. Showing a nice sense of his priorities, he told her that he was off to Goodwood before taking up the command:

> I shall be delighted to get back to work and to the only life that I really care for, though my affection for it may sometimes wane for a time. The *Antrim* is a very good ship, and it will suit me better in every way to have my base in England rather than abroad, fond though I am of foreign parts which always seem to be very interesting.[6]

He commanded the *Antrim* until September 1908. While serving aboard her, he was extremely put out to hear it suggested that it had been Troubridge who had been with the Japanese fleet during the battle of the Yellow Sea on August 10, 1904, and that the length of Jackson's service in Japan was about the same as his. He was sufficiently annoyed by this to write to the naval journalist Arnold White on May 10, 1907 with a detailed record of the relevant dates, showing that Troubridge's term as naval attaché had ended on March 29, 1904, while he himself had first embarked on March 31 and had finally disembarked at Maizuru on June 1, 1905, after 14 months spent largely at sea. He commented that it was 'difficult to refrain from the conclusion that not only was my good fortune greater than that of any other individual, but that it exceeded the aggregate of theirs.' He concluded his record:

> As Saito, the Minister of Marine, said at our last interview, 'you are the only foreigner who has seen a battleship action right through, and you have seen two.' He was full of envy, but it came about through poor Hutchison's ship, the *Asama*, not coming up until the close of August 10, and through Kamimura's want of appreciation (as I consider it) on May 27 of the proper function of his squadron in relation to the battle division of his chief.[7]

When Pakenham left the *Antrim*, he was next posted to the command of the pre-dreadnought battleship *Glory*, in the Mediterranean Fleet. This proved to be only a short command; six months later he took command of the battleship *Triumph*,

6 Pakenham Archive, PKM/2/19/3.
7 Ibid., PKM/2/19/5.

in which he served until December 1909. Next month came a plum appointment; Pakenham was appointed to command a brand new dreadnought, the *Collingwood,* which he commissioned in April 19, 1910.

Pakenham had become a good friend and great admirer of Jackie Fisher, with whom he conducted a regular correspondence. The First Sea Lord's resignation became effective on January 25, 1910, but the two men remained in close touch. Fisher was a vigorous and outspoken correspondent, frequently urging the recipients of his more indiscreet letters to burn them, and remained deeply involved with almost every issue affecting the navy. Not much of his correspondence with Pakenham has survived, but the latter wrote to him on April 26, 1911 in response to a request for confirmation about Togo's relationship with his Admiralty. This went back to a statement which Fisher had personally received from Yamamoto in 1907, and which was contrary to opinions that were now being expressed. Fisher had recorded Yamamoto's remarks in a letter of September 22, 1907 to John Leyland, the editor of the *Army and Navy Gazette:*

> We had three long private interviews of three hours each, we two alone. I said to him: 'Admiral! Tell me, is it true that you made Togo commander-in-chief only a few weeks before war broke out, superseding the man of your own choice and who had done excellently as commander-in-chief, and why did you do it? – Swapping horses while crossing the river (he understood and knew Lincoln's famous saying!) He replied: 'Because at the last moment I felt Togo was a little bit better than my friend, and when a fleet is worked up as our fleet was and yours is, the change of commander-in-chief is not what it was in Nelson's day.' Then I said, 'Did Togo act on his own initiative?' He replied, 'Never. I gave him orders for every movement that occurred; everything was directed from the Admiralty, but, of course, the final issue rested with him in bringing on the battle and fighting it out. Superior speed gave him his victory.[8]

Fisher was of course not always a reliable source, recollecting only what suited his own argument; but Pakenham confirmed that what he reported was also his understanding. In his reply he went on:

> I certainly think in looking back, when you see that all who have tried, you and you alone were successful in infusing life into all branches of that inert body, the navy. You have the justest cause for pride, and for confidently anticipating that such work cannot fail to obtain national recognition. Unfortunately the greater the work, the greater the opposition, and the longer before history can adjust its scales.[9]

8 Arthur J. Marder (ed.), *Fear God and Dread Nought* (London, 1956), p. 137.
9 *Pakenham Archive*, PKM/2/19/5

This may sound like sycophancy, but it was undoubtedly sincere. Admirers of Fisher were unswerving in their belief in the admiral's greatness.

The particular issue of Togo's relationship with the Japanese Admiralty was one which Fisher regarded as extremely important on the question of war planning. Pakenham had written a 'Memorandum on the War Direction of the Japanese Navy' in January 1908, in which he remarked that 'there can be no doubt that before the war began its proposed strategy was exhaustively discussed with Admiral Togo.' Fisher's reaction to this was prompted by his ongoing feud with Lord Charles Beresford, and he noted on Pakenham's paper: 'Impossible to tell Lord C. Beresford anything as he talks at random about the most secret matters to any and every listener (ladies included).'[10]

After leaving the *Collingwood* Pakenham served a term of two years as Fourth Sea Lord and then, by now a rear admiral, took command of the 3rd Cruiser Squadron on December 19, 1913. He continued in this post until appointed to command the 2nd Battle Cruiser Squadron, which he led at Jutland. When Beatty became commander-in-chief of the Grand Fleet, Pakenham succeeded him in command of the Battle Cruiser Force in November 1916. Unfortunately Beatty, who had been one of Pakenham's admirers, began to feel some dissatisfaction with his performance, writing to his wife on February 1 1917 to complain that 'it is his administration work which is badly done and things are forgotten, which means bad staff work.' Beatty remarked that he had continually to point out Pakenham's mistakes; 'still, he is such a gentleman that he (like many others would) never takes offence or tries to shirk the question.'[11] Beatty repeated his complaints in October 1917 about Pakenham's poor administration, observing that 'after all, he must remember that I had a devil of a fight to get him the appointment at all.' Evidently things did not improve; his wife had told Beatty about the opinions of Pakenham held by other officers, and Beatty replied on February 12 1918:

> Yes, I'm afraid old Packs is soft or weak or something, which prevents him making firm decisions. For instance, he wrote to me that the disaster to the K's had had a very shaking effect on the officers and men in the other submarines, and suggested that they should all be given leave! They want to be hardened, not softened, so I have sent one lot to sea and another shall follow at the earliest opportunity.[12]

Pakenham also got into a certain amount of hot water over his handling of the forces under his command at the second battle of Heligoland Bight in November 1917. The acerbic Captain Herbert Richmond wrote in his diary of this that 'Pakenham

10 Ruddock F Mackay, *Fisher of Kilverstone* (Oxford 1973) pp 365-366
11 B McL Ranft, ed, *The Beatty Papers* (London 1989) I p 397
12 Ibid, I p 512

ought to have been court-martialled and put ashore for his bungling on November 17.[13] Incidents of this kind, however, did not prevent Pakenham's promotion to vice admiral in September 1918.

After the war ended, he became president of the Royal Naval College, Greenwich and then, in October 1920, was appointed commander-in-chief on the North America and West Indies station, where he served until January 1923. In 1926 he retired from the navy at his own request, with the rank of admiral. He died, still unmarried, in San Sebastian, Spain, on July 28, 1933.

The other naval attachés to Japan also had their problems during the First World War. Jackson was serving as Director of the Operations Division in the Admiralty in 1916, and has attracted ferocious criticism from historians over a notorious incident on May 31, 1916. Intelligence had indicated that the High Seas Fleet was planning an operation, and the Grand Fleet had been ordered to sea. At about noon on that day Jackson visited Room 40 to ask the location of the call sign of the *Friedrich der Grosse*, the German flagship, and was told, correctly, that direction finding showed that it was still in Wilhelmshaven. In fact, Room 40 was perfectly aware that this call sign was routinely transferred from the flagship to the Wilhelmshaven W/T station when the High Seas Fleet put to sea, in an effort to mislead British direction finding stations. One officer serving in Room 40 wrote subsequently that 'without further ado and without asking for an explanation or comment, the insufferable Jackson turned on his heel and left the room.' Andrew Gordon, who quoted this, described Jackson as 'a ridiculous angry blundering officer,' suggesting that he 'disliked the miscellany of gifted amateurs who comprised the Room's crew, and resented the notion that such people could contribute anything of use to naval affairs.'[14] On the other hand, Nicolas Black, in his history of the British naval staff during the war, has more recently come to Jackson's defence, calling him 'perhaps the most vilified staff officer of the First World War.'[15] Jackson, who was soon after promoted to rear admiral, later served as senior naval officer in the eastern Mediterranean. After the war he was promoted to vice admiral, and retired in June 1923, subsequently being promoted to full admiral. He died in London on July 7, 1945.

Troubridge, who had held a series of senior appointments after returning from Japan, was serving in command of the 1st Cruiser Squadron in the Mediterranean on the outbreak of the First World War. His squadron stood in the path of the German battlecruiser *Goeben* and the light cruiser *Breslau*; Troubridge, who had been ordered not to be brought to action against superior forces, concluded that on a day of perfect visibility a battlecruiser was a superior force to a whole cruiser squadron, and turned away, and the German ships proceeded on their way, arriving in due course in Constantinople. Troubridge faced a court martial, charged with failing 'to pursue

13 Arthur J. Marder (ed.), *Portrait of an Admiral* (London, 1952), p. 315.
14 Andrew Gordon, *The Rules of the Game* (London, 2005), pp. 72-73.
15 Nicholas Black, *The British Naval Staff During the First World War* (London, 2009), p. 162.

the chase of his Imperial German Majesty's ship *Goeben*, being an enemy then flying.' He was acquitted, but his reputation was seriously damaged. He later did good service in the Balkans; was promoted to vice admiral on June 9, 1916, and full admiral on January 9, 1919 retiring on July 1, 1921. He died on January 28, 1926.

Pakenham's reports, supplemented by those of Jackson and Hutchison, were of the first importance. One historian has remarked that his 'observations as to the employment of battleships and suitability of tactics and equipment removed much of the guesswork from the research and development of a new generation of battleships.'[16] They contained much food for thought. The war had been fought at a time when warship design was at a crossroads, and in the British Admiralty as elsewhere there was a recognition that the navies of the world were about to undergo huge technical change. That process had already begun; indeed it has been suggested that there was in the Admiralty 'a tendency to regard the war as old-fashioned, fought between ships of an earlier generation, using obsolete tactics.'[17] Certainly the ships involved could be seen to belong to a class of battleship that was about to be rendered out of date; but their experiences were nonetheless highly relevant to the designers of the next generation.

Much the most important and influential of Pakenham's conclusions were those in which he addressed the related issues of the accuracy of long-range gunfire, and the superiority of 12-inch guns over those of a lesser calibre. His views were central to the debate about the design of future battleships, which had begun with the famous article by Colonel Vittorio Cuniberti, the chief constructor of the Italian navy, in the 1903 edition of *Jane's Fighting Ships*. In this he set out the case for a 17,000 ton battleship carrying twelve 12-inch guns, capable of 24 knots, and with 12-inch armour. It was a concept close to that later adopted by Fisher. As commander-in-chief at Portsmouth he developed his thinking about an all big gun battleship, though in 1903 he envisaged such a vessel as carrying sixteen 10-inch guns. This concept came in due course to be known as 'Design A.' On the advice of a number of his trusted subordinates, including in particular Captain Reginald Bacon, he began to come round to the alternative possibility of arming the new vessel with 12-inch guns; this came to be known as 'Design B.'

The arguments in favour of Design A, and the larger number of 10-inch guns, were based on the fact that they fired more quickly than the 12-inch; that their penetrative power was not significantly less; that they were less expensive to mount, and involved the carrying of less and thinner armour; and that, as it was put, 'we get a large proportion of offence to defence on a given displacement.'[18] By October 1904, when Fisher had taken office as First Sea Lord, he and Lord Selborne had now come down more firmly on Design B. In the paper that was produced summarising the opposing

16 Connaughton, pp. 276-277.
17 David K Brown, 'The Russo-Japanese War' in *Warship 1996* (London, 1996), p. 66.
18 Parkes, p. 468.

arguments, it was said that 'the fast ship with the heavier guns and deliberate fire should absolutely knock out a vessel of equal speed with many lighter guns, the very number of which militates against accurate spotting and deliberate hitting.'[19] Fisher wanted an overwhelmingly authoritative opinion to back up the final choice, and in December he caused the Board of Admiralty to establish a Committee on Designs to review the proposals that were up for consideration. Fisher personally chaired the committee; among its members were Captain Bacon, Captain Henry Jackson, shortly to become Controller, Captain John Jellicoe, shortly to become Director of Naval Ordnance, and Captain Charles Madden, naval assistant to the Controller. It also included a number of distinguished civilian experts.

The committee sat between January 3 and February 22 1905, and delivered its report to the Admiralty in March. This was unanimous. The committee had considered, of course, Pakenham's reports from the seat of war. That of August 17, 1904, previously referred to, had examined in particular the question of the accuracy of gunfire at long range. His report had also contained what the committee described as a 'momentous paragraph,' which addressed the relative effect of the fire of guns of the largest calibre, compared with the fire of those of a lesser size. His conclusions had been emphatic:

> The 10-inch guns of the *Peresviet* and *Pobieda* were of 45 calibres, and may also have been of greater range, but the effect of the fire of every gun is so much less than that of the next larger size, that when 12-inch guns are firing, shots from 10-inch pass unnoticed, while, for all the respect they instil, 8-inch or 6-inch guns might then just as well be pea shooters, and the 12-pounder simply does not count. This must be understood to refer entirely to moral effect.[20]

Pakenham's opinion, repeated more than once, was that the outcome of the naval operations during the war was determined by the 12-inch gun, and that 'medium artillery has had its day.' His personal recipe for the design of future battleships was that they should be over 14,500 tons, capable of 21 knots, and should carry six 12-inch guns.[21] Pakenham's report of the battle of Tsushima, which reached the Admiralty just before the *Dreadnought* was laid down, reiterated his opinion as to the effectiveness of the largest guns and of long-range firing, but it was his earlier conclusions about the battle of the Yellow Sea that were of critical importance. In particular, his account of the damage suffered by the *Mikasa* was particularly telling; she had been struck by a 12-inch shell at a range of over 13,000 yards which tore a hole some 3 feet in diameter in her 7 inch armour plate.

On the question of fire control Pakenham had taken the view that even a perfect rangefinder would be of little value, since the performance of individual guns varied

19 Ibid., pp. 468-469.
20 Naval Attaché Reports, p. 166.
21 Marder, *Anatomy*, pp. 531-532.

widely; it would only be of possible value in obtaining an approximation of the opening range – thereafter gun layers would have to spot the fall of shot. As David Brown pointed out, although Pakenham was wrong in this conclusion, his views were probably widely held. Another influential figure who shared his opinion at the time was Commander William Sims, the US naval gunnery expert.

Pakenham had also reported extensively on the performance of the Japanese shells, which caused a number of problems, particularly with premature explosions and an apparent lack of penetrative power. Inspection of the captured *Orel* showed that although hit sixteen times by shells of 8-inch or more, none had penetrated her armour. Brown noted that the poor performance of both Russian and Japanese shells was not recognised in either the British or US navies, and was 'almost certainly the most serious failure to learn from the war.'[22]

Not all Pakenham's recommendations were carried into effect. For instance, the heavily armoured conning towers, the usefulness of which he seriously questioned, continued to be fitted to British battleships, but were in practice little used during the First World War. Nor did his views about high angle fire have any effect on warship design; the Admiralty view appears to have been that the danger from this was not great, because the time length of the shell's flight would make hits unlikely.

Pakenham had in his reports justifiably devoted a lot of space to the question of mine warfare, which had had such a devastating effect. The dramatic losses suffered by both sides due to mines had demonstrated the power of the weapon, and the urgent need to strengthen the underwater protection of new warships. He was particularly concerned to stress the potential value of unpierced transverse bulkheads in enabling a ship to survive when holed beneath the waterline. The only Japanese vessel with such bulkheads was the armoured cruiser *Yakumo*, and it was apparently found that in practice they caused little inconvenience once the crew had become accustomed to them. In Britain, the two *Lord Nelson* battleships were the first to be designed with unpierced main bulkheads, each section having separate drainage, pumping, ventilation systems and lifts, but apparently these were found to cause great inconvenience, especially in reaching the engine and boiler rooms.[23] As for enemy mines, techniques for sweeping them were quickly developed for the Royal Navy, but these were largely kept secret. On the other hand, steps to equip the fleet with a sufficient number of mines to seal off the principal German ports were not energetically pursued, evidently because the offensive use of such weapons was not seen as a high priority.[24] Professor Marder summarised the position: 'British naval officers did not hold mines in high regard; they were the weapons of the weak power on the defensive. There was provision for

22 Brown, p. 69.
23 Parkes, p. 453.
24 Brown, p. 76.

sweeping up enemy mines, but little interest in providing the Navy with effective mines for its own use.[25]

Another issue to which a lot of attention was devoted was the relative ineffectiveness of the Japanese torpedo craft in action, which Pakenham carefully recorded. In his reports he endeavoured to explain how each of the torpedo attacks had fared, and the particular reasons in each case for the lack of success. In two of his reports in particular he went out of his way to urge that the torpedo flotilla should not be regarded as a busted flush. In the first of these, after the battle of the Yellow Sea, he drew attention to the tactics employed by the Japanese. These, he thought, were principally to blame. They derived from the fact that for long periods the principal objective of the torpedo flotillas was seen as being their Russian equivalents. In action, therefore, the Japanese destroyers and torpedo boats tended to concentrate their attention on the Russian destroyers. In his later report of September 28 he explained that the Japanese set all torpedoes to run to their maximum range of 3,000 metres, which reduced their speed to 14 to 15 knots, and thereby reduced the chance of hitting the target. At the same time, the leaders of the torpedo flotillas had been taught to exercise caution, for much the same reason that this had characterised fleet operations.[26]

Internationally there was of course considerable interest in why a weapon which had been seen as potentially decisive had failed to achieve greater results than had proved to be the case. In addition to the effect of firing at long range, other reasons were noted such as poor weapons maintenance, the primitive nature of torpedo technology and design, insufficient training and poor coordination.[27] All these factors were taken carefully into account by the Japanese navy in reviewing the lessons of the war. Another consideration to be borne in mind is the size of the vessels employed; even the largest destroyers were small and inadequately armed and hence extremely vulnerable to the defensive fire of the ships they were attacking. By the start of the First World War, destroyers were more than twice the size of those in the Russo-Japanese war. In spite of Pakenham's careful analysis of the torpedo operations of the Japanese, there was still a tendency in the British navy to believe that the torpedo as a weapon would be of less significance than had been supposed.

In commissioning a specifically naval history of the Russo-Japanese war, the Naval Intelligence Department were looking for a coherent and instructive narrative which would assist the navy in its future planning, and this is what Corbett provided. Summarising his conclusions in their introduction to the 1994 edition of his history, John B Hattendorf and Donald M Schurman noted that he did not approach it as 'a conflict in which its great victories could be utilised to demonstrate lessons contingent upon quick or overwhelming success.'[28] Instead, he pointed out the dangers inherent

25 Arthur J Marder, *From the Dreadnought to Scapa Flow* V (Oxford, 1970), p. 308.
26 Naval Attaché Reports, pp. 210-212.
27 Evans and Peattie, p. 128.
28 Corbett I, pp. xv-xvi.

in the Japanese initial moves, and observed that their success at Port Arthur was not definitive; the Russians still possessed substantial advantages right up to Tsushima. Corbett was clear that fundamentally the reasons why Japan won the war turned on command of the sea, at least temporarily. He saw a parallel with Wellington's campaigns in the Peninsula; the ability to move and supply troops by sea unmolested by the enemy was crucial.

Analysing the key events of the war, Corbett saw the death of Makarov as the turning point:

> Had he lived it would at least have been impossible for the Japanese to conduct it as they did. The strain which their plan of operations put upon the fleet was as great as that which exhausted our own in the Great War after Trafalgar; and had the Port Arthur squadron done anything more enterprising than persist in its passive attitude, the endurance of the Japanese navy might well have proved unequal to the task.[29]

As it was, he concluded that the Japanese approach to the conduct of war deserved to succeed:

> They did display in a conspicuous degree a temper which is perhaps the most creditable that war can show. It was that their long condemnation to a general defensive attitude, the enforced husbanding of their fleet, and shrinking from decisive battle, did not sap their offensive spirit ... It is here, then, if anywhere, in this enduring capacity to withstand the demoralising influences of a prolonged defensive, that the Japanese showed upon the seas, at any rate, a distinctly higher genius for war than their enemy.[30]

Corbett was seeking to enunciate broad general principles. Pakenham's task, on the other hand, had been to identify the practical lessons which might immediately be learned. Overall, Pakenham made a major contribution to the understanding of modern naval warfare and the practical considerations that must be taken into account. Some of his important conclusions, 'ranging from the uselessness of 12-pounders against destroyers to the remarkable freedom from fires caused by wooden decks and fittings' may have been, as Oscar Parkes wrote, largely ignored in Whitehall.[31] But his influence on warship design, as much as his personal courage and inexhaustible devotion to the task in hand, entitles William Pakenham to be regarded as one of the more important figures of the Royal Navy in the twentieth century.

29 Ibid., pp. 396-397.
30 Ibid, p. 398.
31 Parkes, p. 465.

Bibliography

Anon., *Before Port Arthur in a Destroyer*, translated by Captain R. Grant (London, 1907).

Ballard, Vice Admiral G.A., *The Influence of the Sea on the Political History of Japan* (New York, 1921).

Berry, Warren, *The Pre-Dreadnought Revolution* (Stroud, 2013).

Black, Nicholas, *The British Naval Staff during the First World War* (London, 2009).

Blond, Georges, *Admiral Togo* (London, 1961).

Boyce, D. George (ed.), *The Crisis of British Power* (London, 1990).

Brown, David K., 'The Russo-Japanese War' in *Warship 1996* (London, 1996)

Busch, Noel F., *The Emperor's Sword* (New York, 1969).

Chatfield, Admiral of the Fleet Lord, *The Navy and Defence* (London, 1942).

Clements, Jonathan, *Admiral Togo: Nelson of the East* (London, 2010).

Committee of Imperial Defence, *Official History (Naval & Military) of the Russo-Japanese War* (London, 1910).

Connaughton, Richard, *The War of the Rising Sun and Tumbling Bear* (London, 1988).

Corbett, Julian S., *Maritime Operations in the Russo-Japanese War, 1904-1905* (Annapolis, Maryland, 1994).

Crossley, John, *The Hidden Threat* (Barnsley, 2011).

Egerton, Mrs Fred, *Admiral of the Fleet Sir Geoffrey Phipps Hornby* (Edinburgh, 1896).

Evans, David C. and Peattie, Mark R., *Kaigun: Strategy, Tactics and Technology in the Imperial Japanese Navy 1887-1941* (Annapolis, Maryland, 1997).

Falk, Edwin A., *Togo and the Rise of Japanese Sea-Power* (London, 1936).

Freeman, Richard, *The Great Edwardian Naval Feud* (Barnsley, 2009).

Gordon, Andrew, *The Rules of the Game* (London, 2005).

Hargreaves, Reginald, *The Siege of Port Arthur* (London, 1962).

Higginson, Rear Admiral Francis J., *Naval battles in the Century* (London, 1906).

Hohenlohe-Ingelfingen, Prince Kraft zu, *Aus Meinem Leben* (Berlin, 1879).

Hough, Richard, *The Fleet That Had to Die* (London, 1958).

Jane,Fred T.(ed.), *Jane's Fighting Ships 1906-07* (London, 1906).

Jane, Fred T., *The Imperial Japanese Navy* (London 1904)

Jane, Fred T., *The Imperial Russian Navy* (London 1904)

Kelly, Patrick J, *Tirpitz and the Imperial German Navy* (Bloomington, Indiana, 2011)

Kiralfy, Alexander (ed.), 'Japanese Naval Strategy' in *Makers of Modern Strategy* (Princeton, Massachusetts, 1943).
Klado, Nicholas, *The Russian Navy in the Russo-Japanese War and the Battle of the Sea of Japan* (London, 1906).
Langer, William L., *The Diplomacy of Imperialism* (New York, 1935).
Livezey, William E., *Mahan on Sea Power* (Norman, Oklahoma, 1947).
Lowis, Commander G.L., *Fabulous Admirals* (London, 1957).
Macintyre, Captain Donald, *Sea Power in the Pacific* (London, 1972).
Mackay, Ruddock F., *Fisher of Kilverstone* (Oxford, 1973).
Mahan, Capt A T, *Naval Administration and Warfare* (London, 1908).
Makarov, Vice Admiral S.O., *Discussion of Questions in Naval Tactics* (Annapolis, Maryland, 1990).
Marder, Arthur J. (ed.), *Fear God and Dread Nought* (London, 1956).
Marder, Arthur J., *From the Dreadnought to Scapa Flow* (Oxford, 1970).
Marder, Arthur J. (ed.), *Portrait of an Admiral* (London, 1952).
Marder, Arthur J., *The Anatomy of British Sea Power* (London, 1972).
Mariners Mirror, various
McCully, Lieutenant Commander Newton A., *The McCully Report* (Annapolis, Maryland, 1977).
Mitchell, Donald W., *The History of Russian and Soviet Sea Power* (London, 1974).
Nish, Ian, *The Origins of the Russo-Japanese War* (Harlow, 1985).
Ogasawara, Vice Admiral Nagayo, *Life of Admiral Togo*, translated Jukichi Inouye (Tokyo, 1934).
Olender, Piotr, *Russo-Japanese Naval War 1904-1905* (Sandomierz, Poland, 2010).
Padfield, Peter, *Aim Straight* (London, 1966).
Pakenham Archive, Caird Library, National Maritime Museum, Greenwich.
Parkes, Oscar, *British Battleships* (London, 1970).
Pleshakov, Constantine, *The Tsar's Last Armada* (Oxford, 2002).
Politovsky, Eugene S., *From Libau to Tsushima*, trans Major F.R. Godfrey (London, n.d.).
Ranft, B. McL (ed.), *The Beatty Papers* (Aldershot, 1989).
Reports from Naval Attachés, *The Russo-Japanese War 1904-1905* (Nashville, 2003).
Roberts, John, *The Battleship Dreadnought* (London, 2004).
Ropp, Theodore, *The Development of a Modern Navy* (Annapolis, Maryland, 1987).
Sandler, Stanley, *The Emergence of the Modern Capital Ship* (Newark, Delaware, 1979).
Schurman, Donald M, *Julian S. Corbett, 1854-1922* (London, 1981).
Seligman, Matthew S. (ed.), *Naval Intelligence from Germany* (Aldershot, 2007).
Seligman, Matthew S., *The Royal Navy and the German Threat 1901-1914* (Oxford, 2012).
Semenov, Vladimir, *The Russo-Japanese War at Sea* (St Petersburg, 1911).
Seton-Watson, Hugh, *The Russian Empire 1801-1917* (Oxford, 1967).
Spector, Ronald H., *At War at Sea* (New York, 2001).
Vagts, Alfred, *The Military Attaché* (Princeton, 1967).

Warner, Dennis and Peggy, *The Tide at Sunrise* (London, 1974).
Weeks, Charles J. Jr, *An American Naval Diplomat in Revolutionary Russia* (Annapolis, Maryland, 1993).
Westwood, J.N., *Russia Against Japan 1904–05* (New York, 1986).
Westwood, J.N., *Witnesses of Tsushima* (Tokyo, 1970).
Willmott, H.P., *The Last Century of Sea Power, Volume I* (Bloomington, Indiana, 2009).
Wilson, H.W., *Ironclads in Action* (London, 1897).
Wright, Richard N.J., *The Chinese Steam Navy 1862–1945* (London, 2000).

Index

Index of Places

Index of People

Index of Naval Vessels